Tak[illegible]ne
[illegible]ana

7

STORY AND ART BY

Yuki Shiwasu

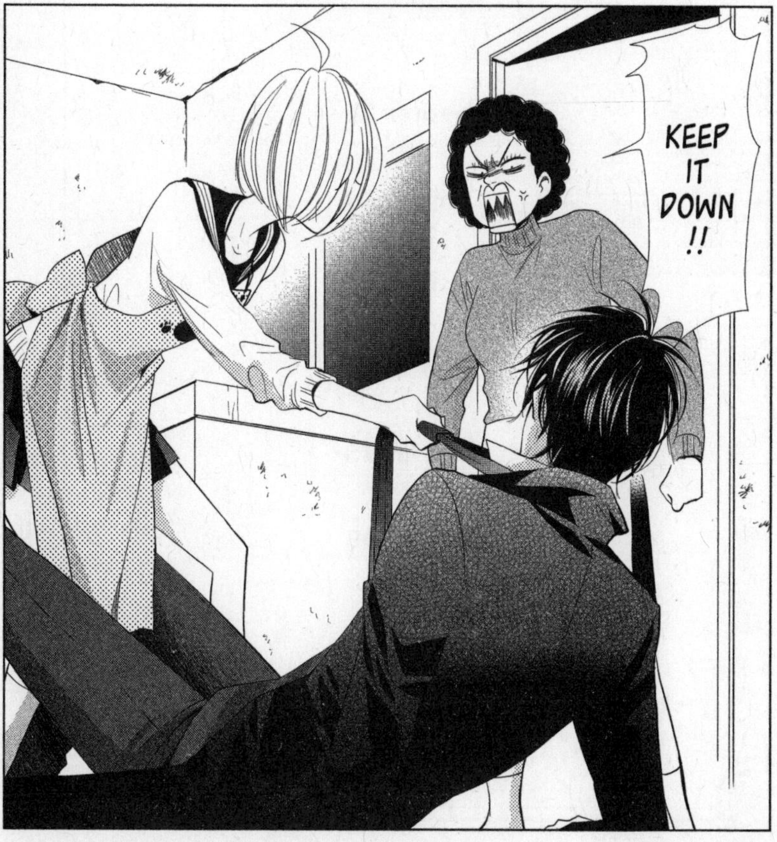
KEEP IT DOWN !!

Takane & Hana

7

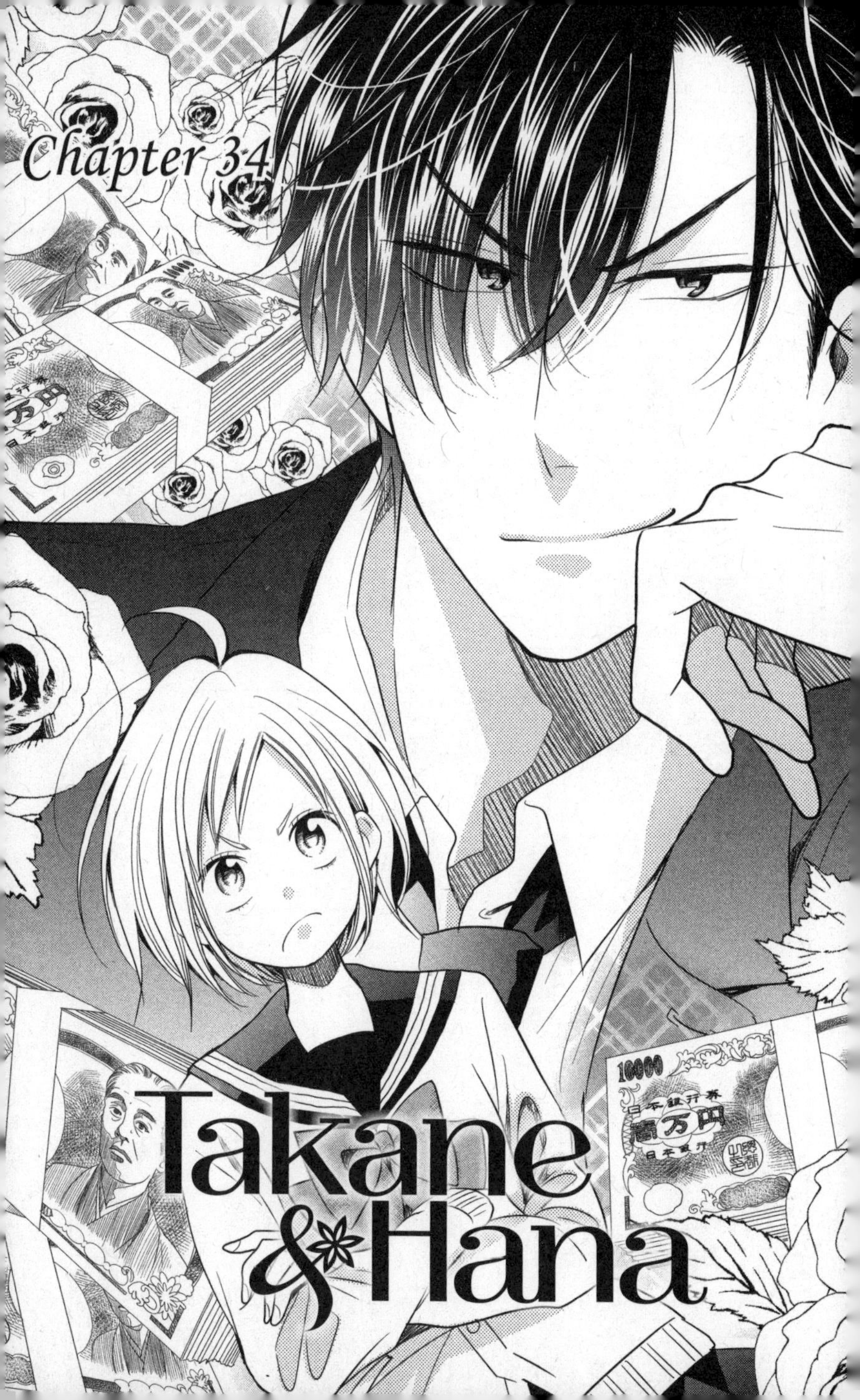
Chapter 34
Takane & Hana

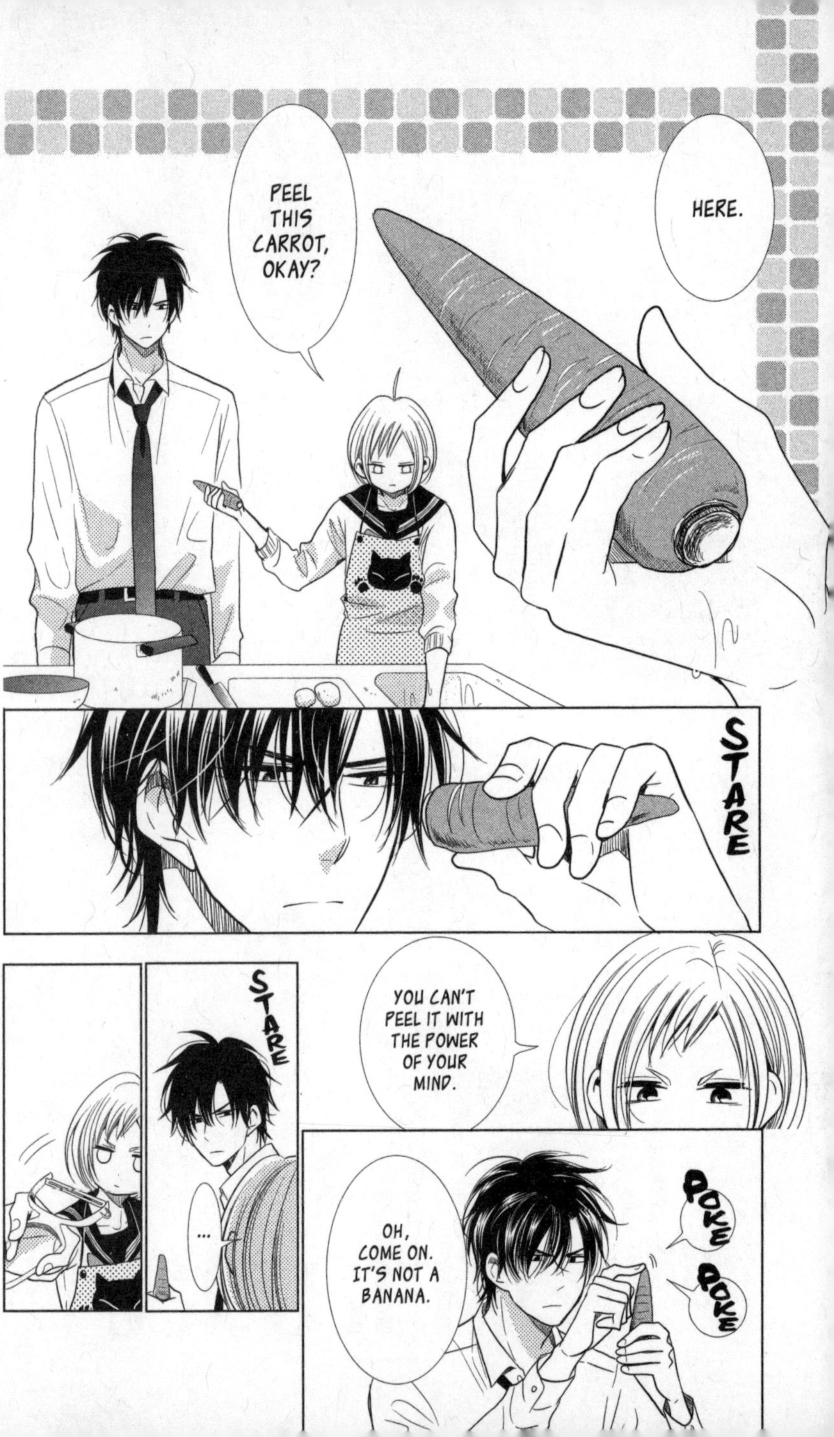
HERE.
PEEL THIS CARROT, OKAY?
STARE
YOU CAN'T PEEL IT WITH THE POWER OF YOUR MIND.
POKE POKE
OH, COME ON. IT'S NOT A BANANA.
STARE
...

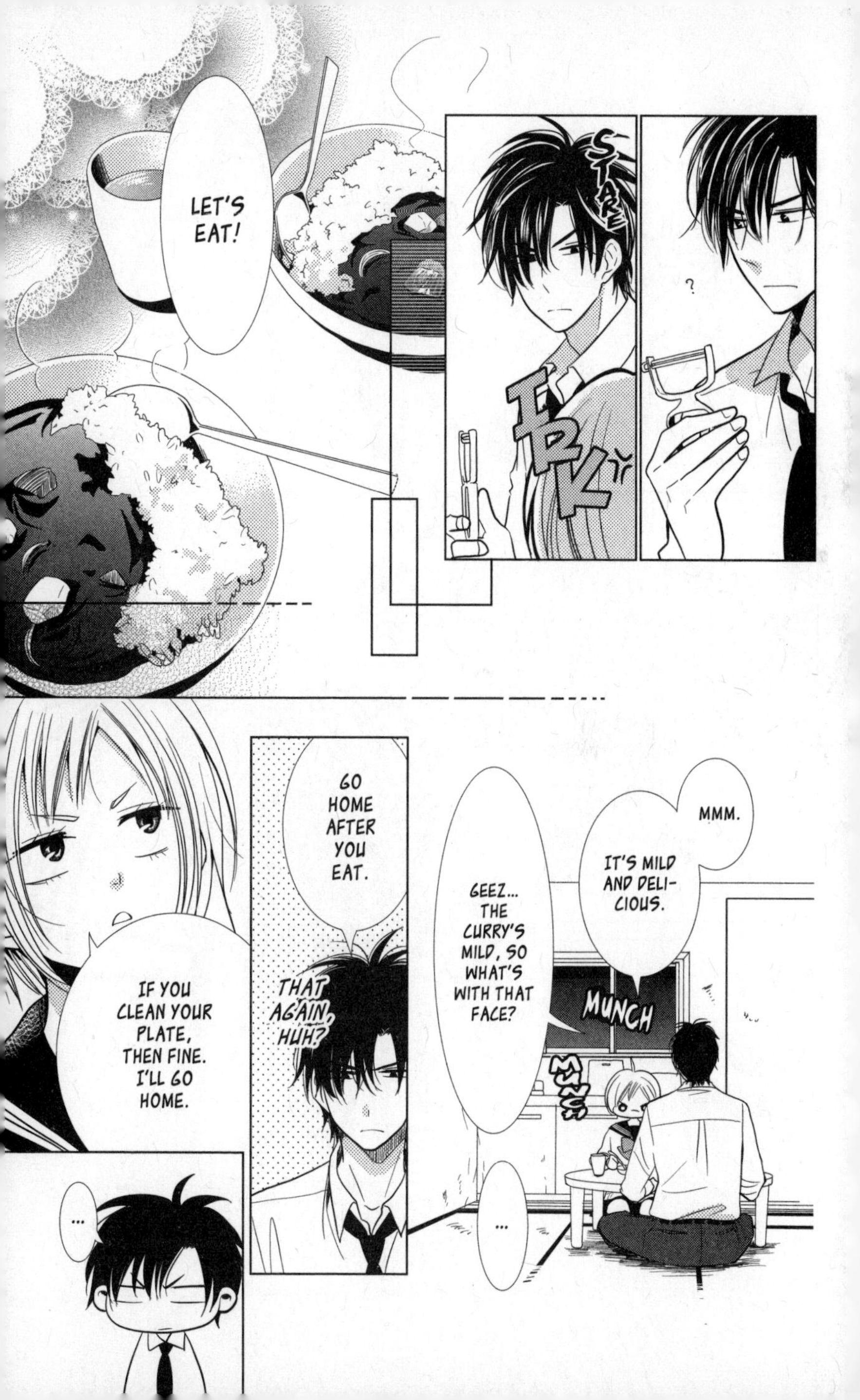
?
STARE
ERK
LET'S EAT!
MMM.
IT'S MILD AND DELICIOUS.
MUNCH
MUNCH
GEEZ... THE CURRY'S MILD, SO WHAT'S WITH THAT FACE?
...
GO HOME AFTER YOU EAT.
THAT AGAIN, HUH?
IF YOU CLEAN YOUR PLATE, THEN FINE. I'LL GO HOME.
...

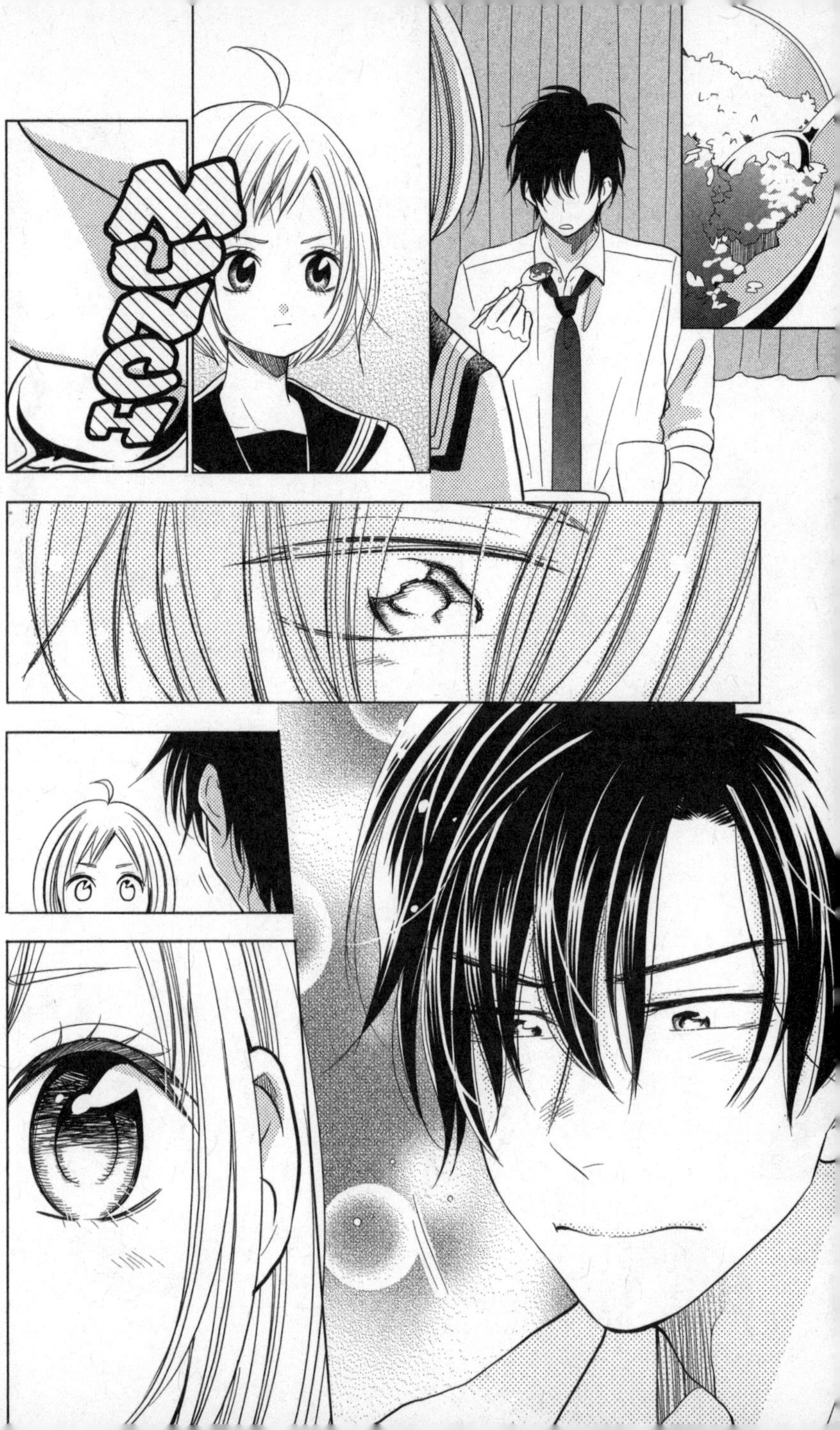

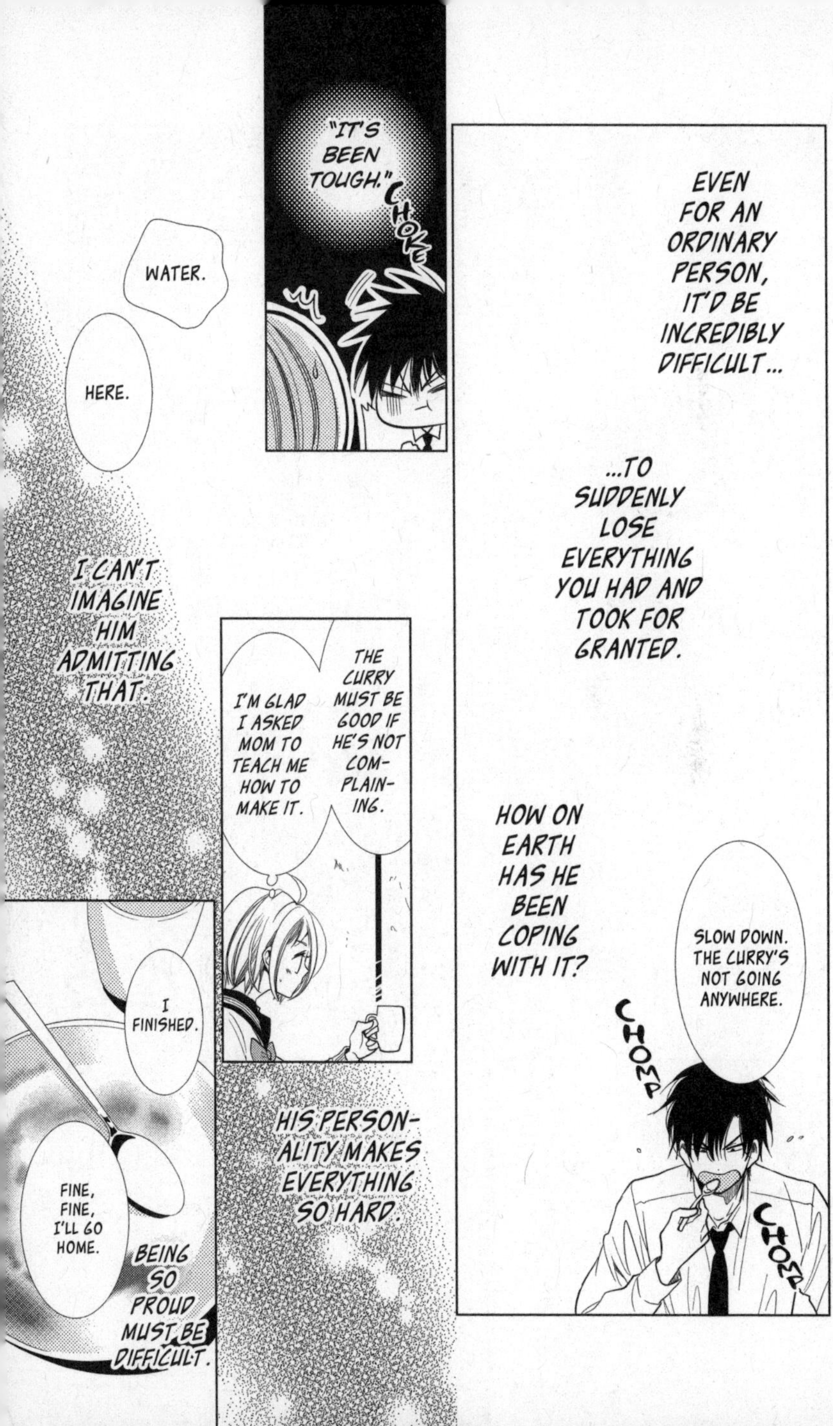
EVEN FOR AN ORDINARY PERSON, IT'D BE INCREDIBLY DIFFICULT...
...TO SUDDENLY LOSE EVERYTHING YOU HAD AND TOOK FOR GRANTED.
HOW ON EARTH HAS HE BEEN COPING WITH IT?
SLOW DOWN. THE CURRY'S NOT GOING ANYWHERE.
CHOMP
CHOMP
"IT'S BEEN TOUGH."
CHOKE
MM
WATER.
HERE.
I CAN'T IMAGINE HIM ADMITTING THAT.
THE CURRY MUST BE GOOD IF HE'S NOT COM-PLAIN-ING.
I'M GLAD I ASKED MOM TO TEACH ME HOW TO MAKE IT.
HIS PERSON-ALITY MAKES EVERYTHING SO HARD.
I FINISHED.
FINE, FINE, I'LL GO HOME.
BEING SO PROUD MUST BE DIFFICULT.

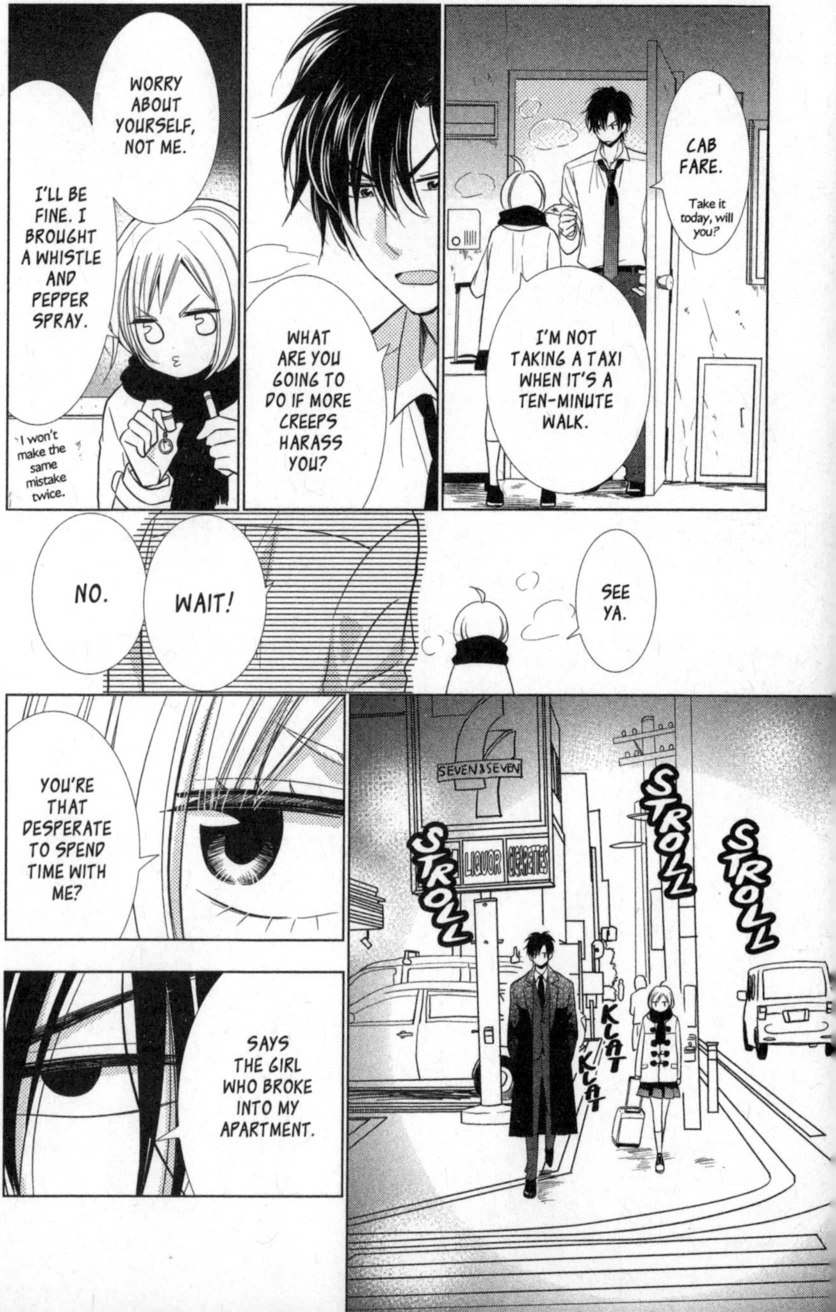
CAB FARE.
Take it today, will you?
I'M NOT TAKING A TAXI WHEN IT'S A TEN-MINUTE WALK.
WHAT ARE YOU GOING TO DO IF MORE CREEPS HARASS YOU?
WORRY ABOUT YOURSELF, NOT ME.
I'LL BE FINE. I BROUGHT A WHISTLE AND PEPPER SPRAY.
I won't make the same mistake twice.
SEE YA.
WAIT!
NO.
SEVEN & SEVEN
LIQUOR
CIGARETTES
STROLL
STROLL
STROLL
KLAT
KLAT
YOU'RE THAT DESPERATE TO SPEND TIME WITH ME?
SAYS THE GIRL WHO BROKE INTO MY APARTMENT.

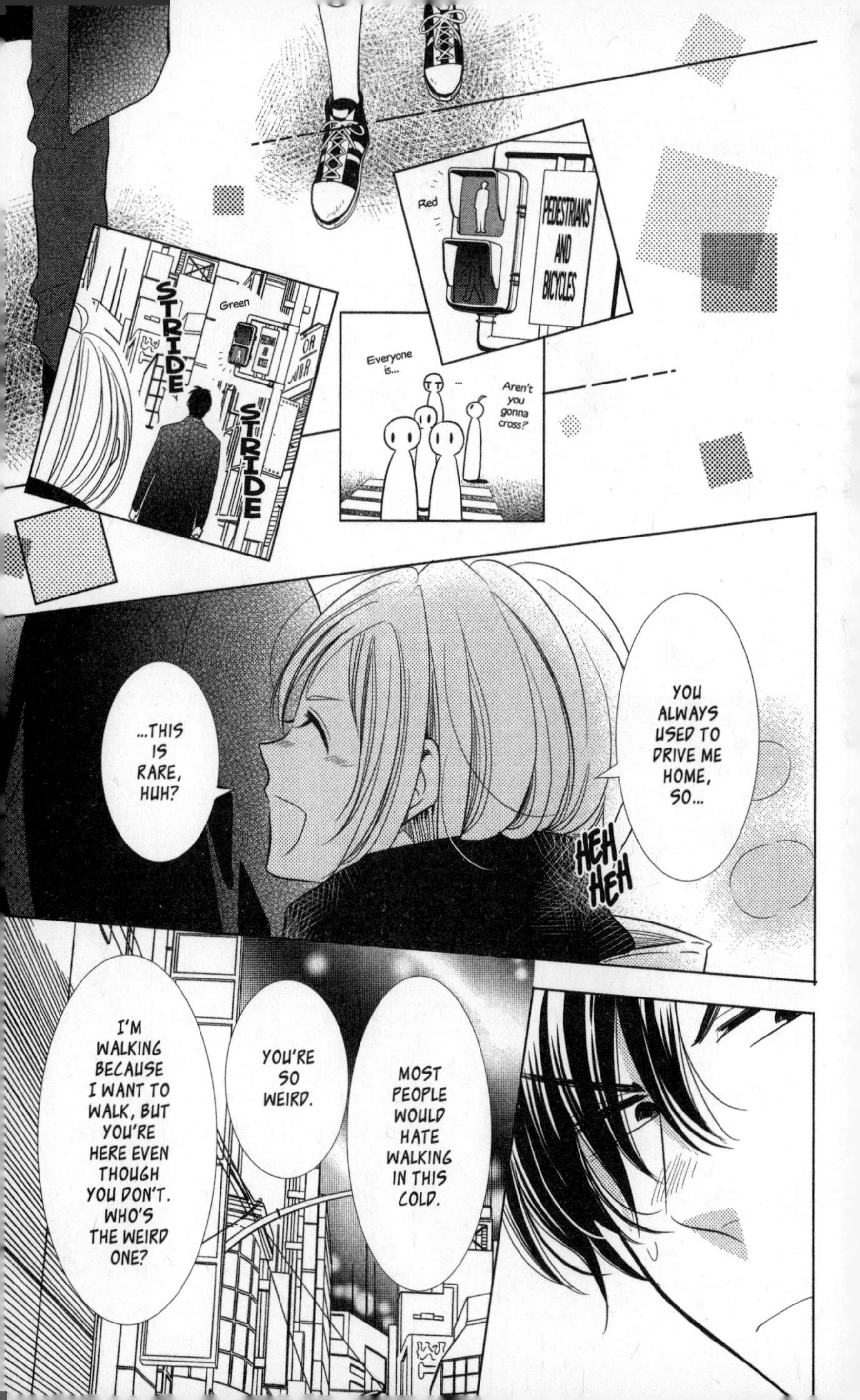

Red
PEDESTRIANS AND BICYCLES
Everyone is...
...
Aren't you gonna cross?
STRIDE
Green
STRIDE
YOU ALWAYS USED TO DRIVE ME HOME, SO...
HEH HEH
...THIS IS RARE, HUH?
MOST PEOPLE WOULD HATE WALKING IN THIS COLD.
YOU'RE SO WEIRD.
I'M WALKING BECAUSE I WANT TO WALK, BUT YOU'RE HERE EVEN THOUGH YOU DON'T. WHO'S THE WEIRD ONE?

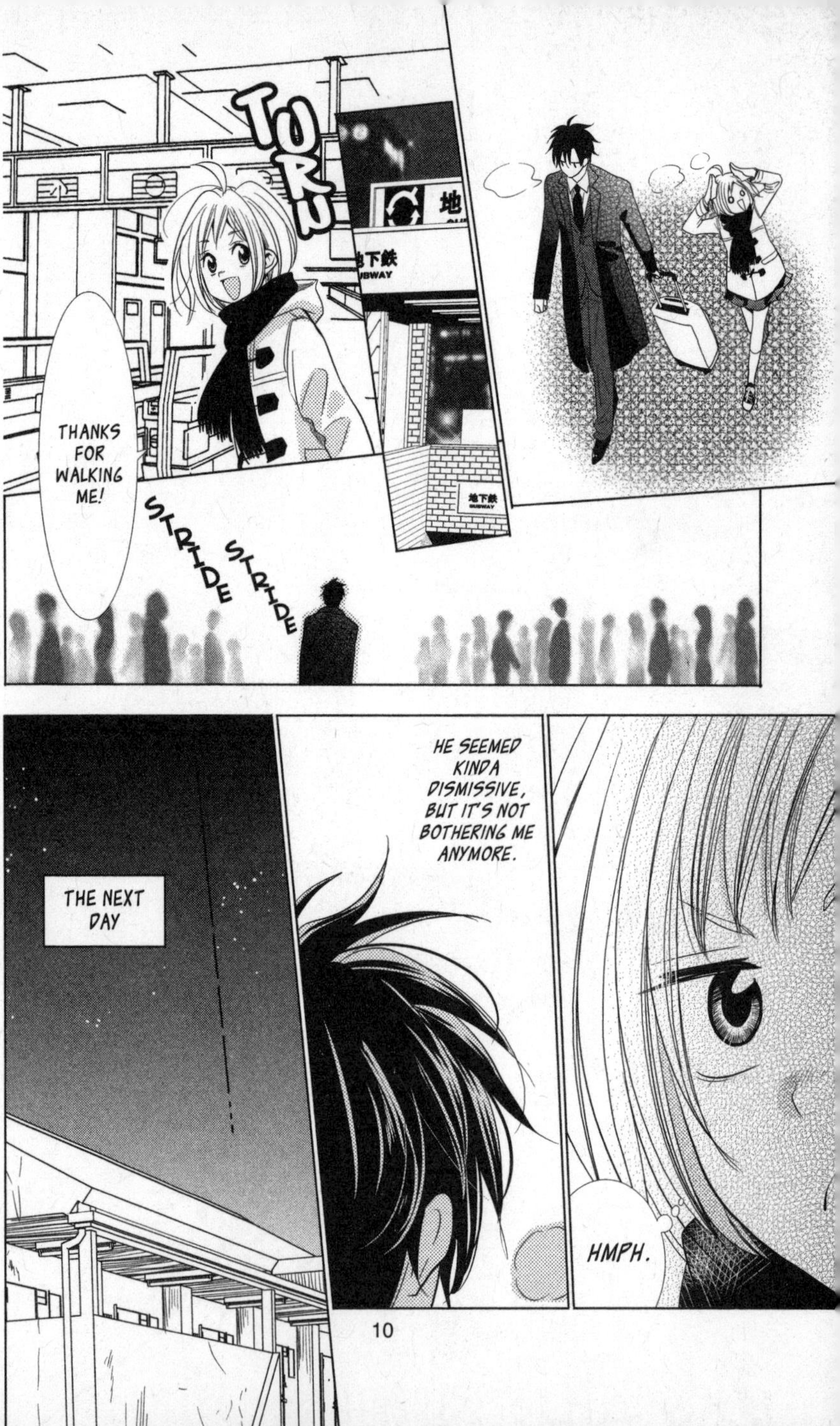
TORU
THANKS FOR WALKING ME!
地下鉄
SUBWAY
STRIDE STRIDE
HMPH.
HE SEEMED KINDA DISMISSIVE, BUT IT'S NOT BOTHERING ME ANYMORE.
THE NEXT DAY

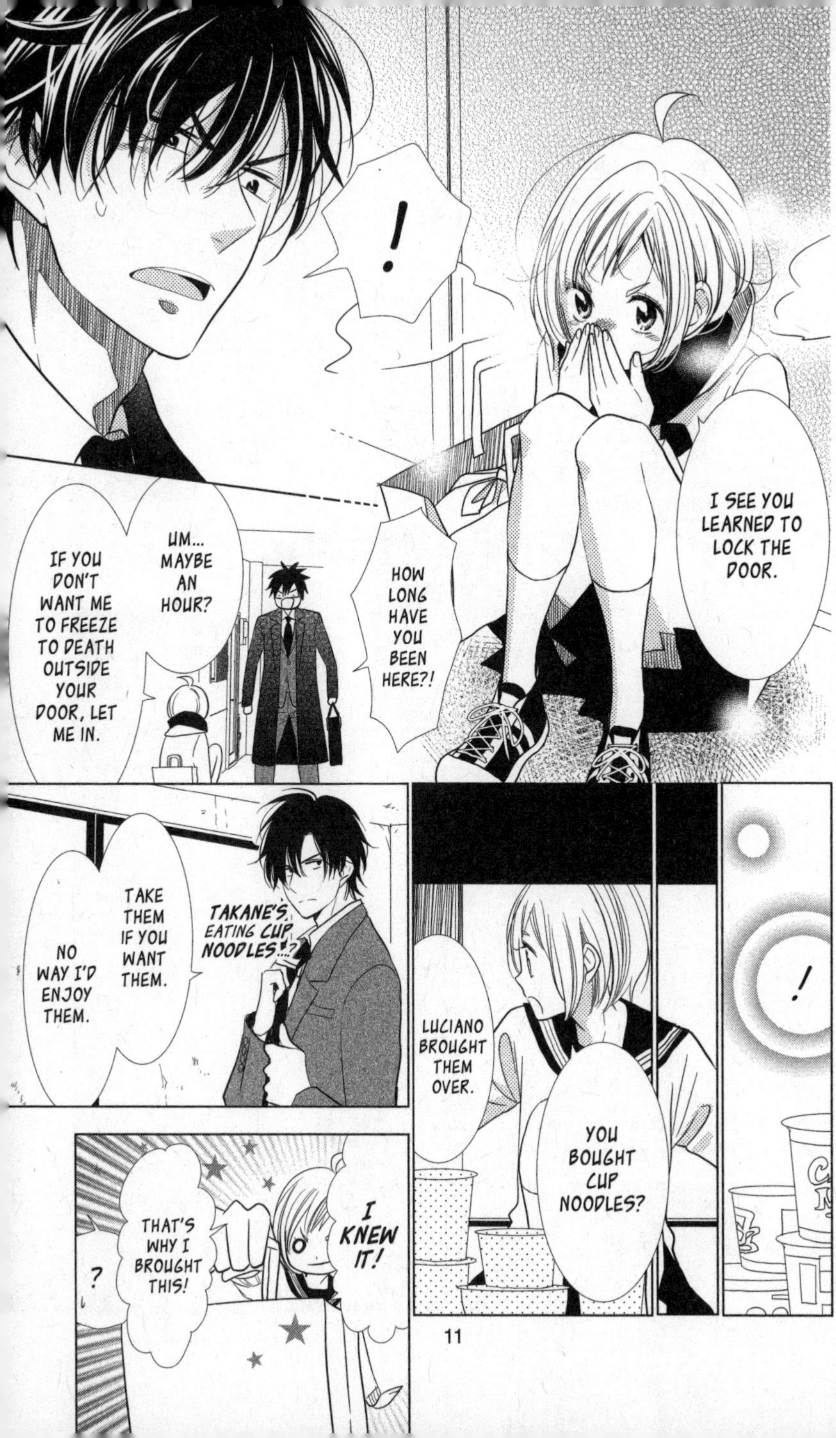
!
I SEE YOU LEARNED TO LOCK THE DOOR.
HOW LONG HAVE YOU BEEN HERE?!
UM... MAYBE AN HOUR?
IF YOU DON'T WANT ME TO FREEZE TO DEATH OUTSIDE YOUR DOOR, LET ME IN.
!
YOU BOUGHT CUP NOODLES?
LUCIANO BROUGHT THEM OVER.
TAKANE'S EATING CUP NOODLES...?
TAKE THEM IF YOU WANT THEM.
NO WAY I'D ENJOY THEM.
I KNEW IT!
THAT'S WHY I BROUGHT THIS!
?

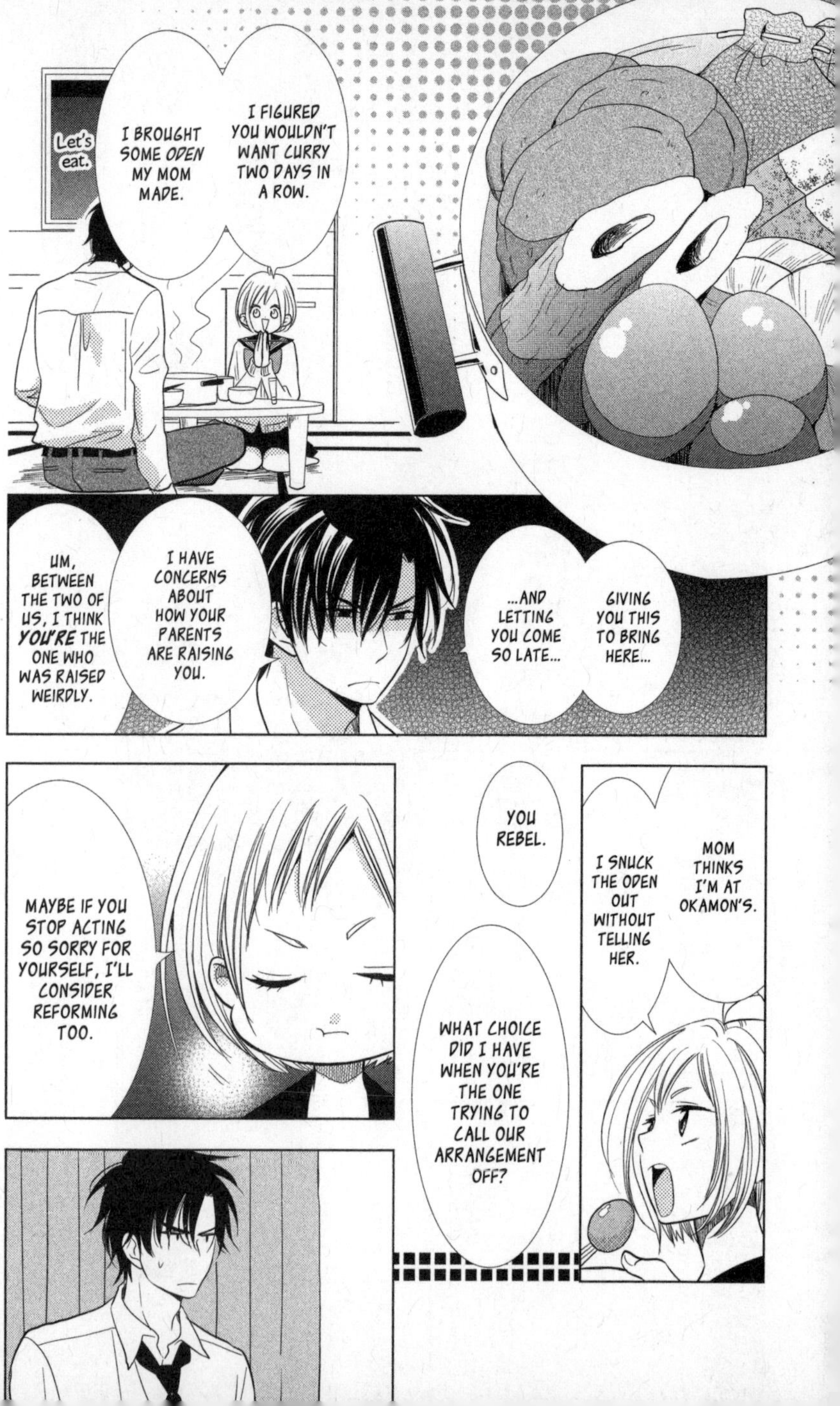
I FIGURED YOU WOULDN'T WANT CURRY TWO DAYS IN A ROW.
I BROUGHT SOME *ODEN* MY MOM MADE.
Let's eat.
GIVING YOU THIS TO BRING HERE...
...AND LETTING YOU COME SO LATE...
I HAVE CONCERNS ABOUT HOW YOUR PARENTS ARE RAISING YOU.
UM, BETWEEN THE TWO OF US, I THINK ***YOU'RE*** THE ONE WHO WAS RAISED WEIRDLY.
MOM THINKS I'M AT OKAMON'S.
I SNUCK THE ODEN OUT WITHOUT TELLING HER.
YOU REBEL.
WHAT CHOICE DID I HAVE WHEN YOU'RE THE ONE TRYING TO CALL OUR ARRANGEMENT OFF?
MAYBE IF YOU STOP ACTING SO SORRY FOR YOURSELF, I'LL CONSIDER REFORMING TOO.

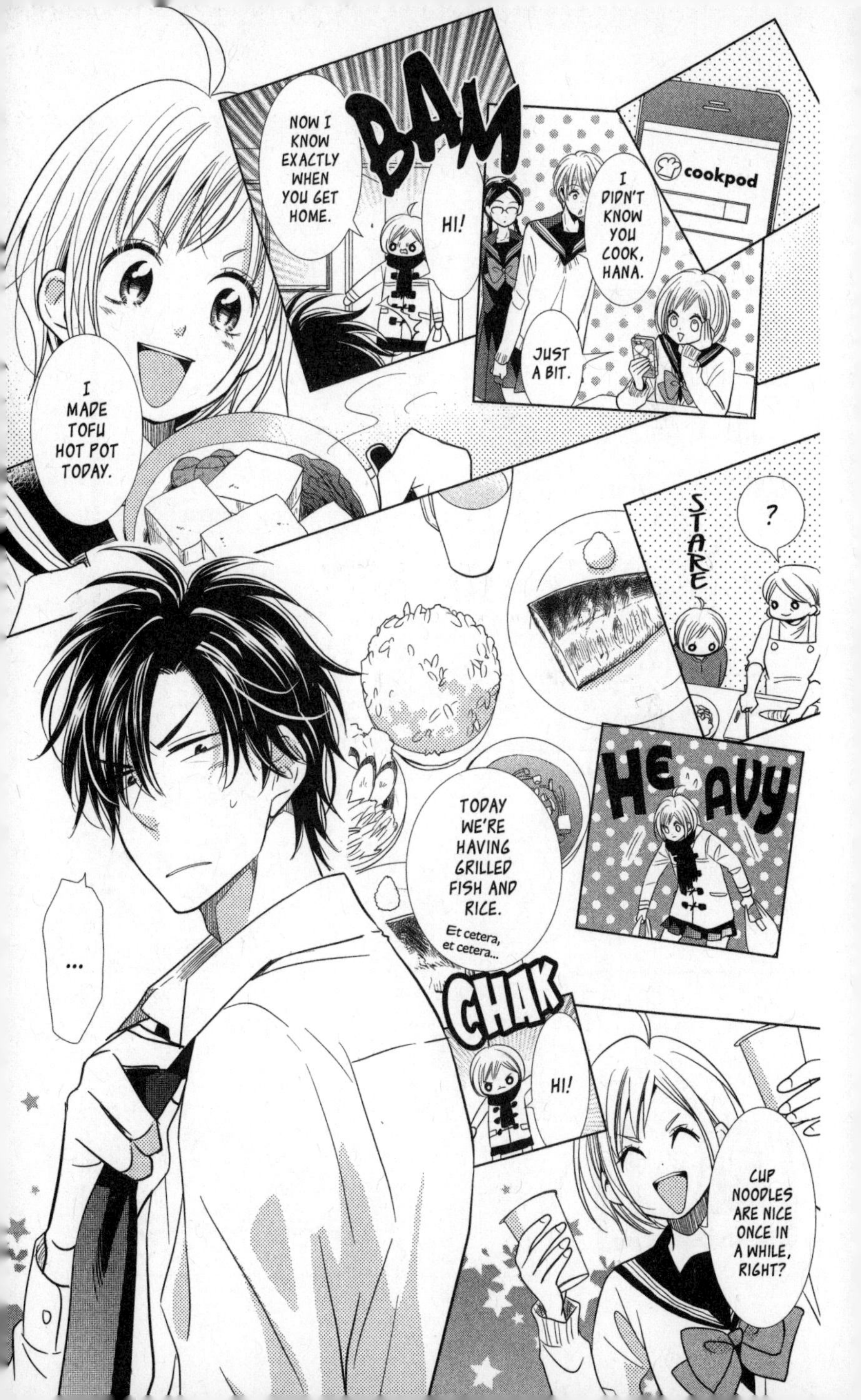
cookpod
I DIDN'T KNOW YOU COOK, HANA.
JUST A BIT.
BAM
NOW I KNOW EXACTLY WHEN YOU GET HOME.
HI!
I MADE TOFU HOT POT TODAY.
?
STARE
HEAVY
TODAY WE'RE HAVING GRILLED FISH AND RICE.
Et cetera, et cetera...
...
CHAK
HI!
CUP NOODLES ARE NICE ONCE IN A WHILE, RIGHT?

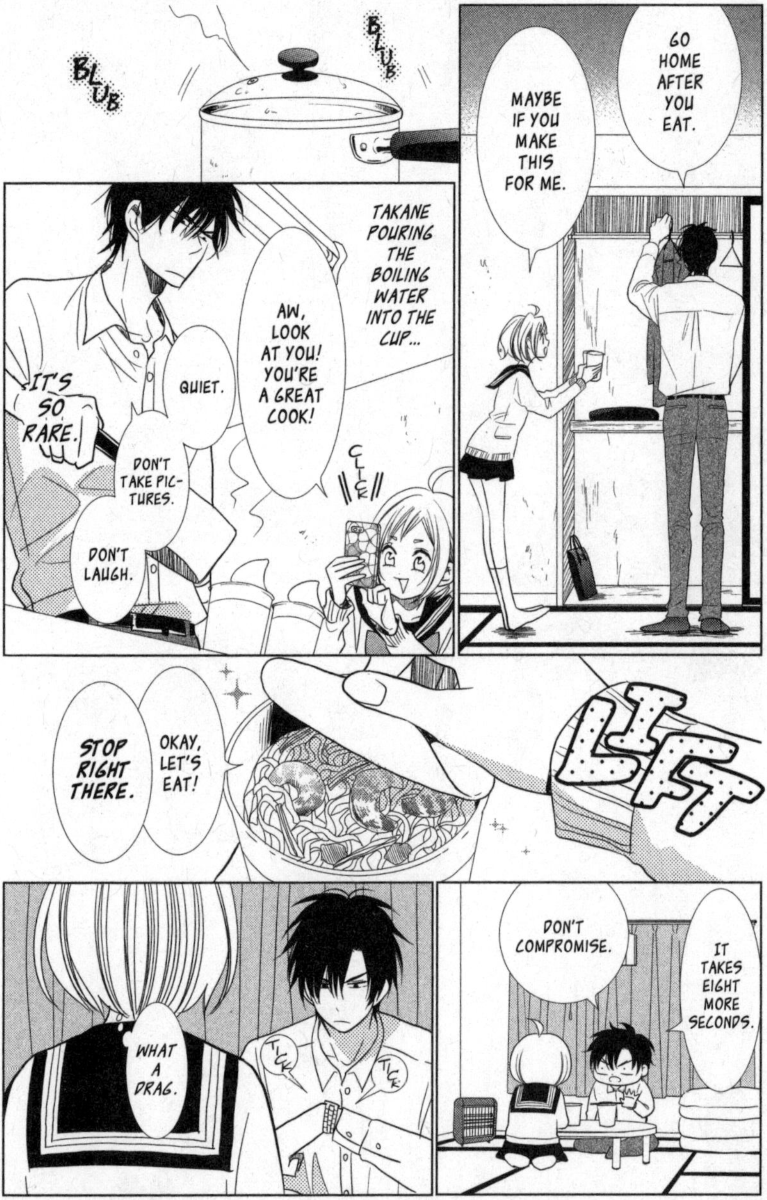
GO HOME AFTER YOU EAT.
MAYBE IF YOU MAKE THIS FOR ME.
BLUB
BLUB
TAKANE POURING THE BOILING WATER INTO THE CUP...
AW, LOOK AT YOU! YOU'RE A GREAT COOK!
CLICK
QUIET.
DON'T TAKE PIC-TURES.
IT'S SO RARE.
DON'T LAUGH.
LIFT
OKAY, LET'S EAT!
STOP RIGHT THERE.
IT TAKES EIGHT MORE SECONDS.
DON'T COMPROMISE.
TICK
TICK
WHAT A DRAG.

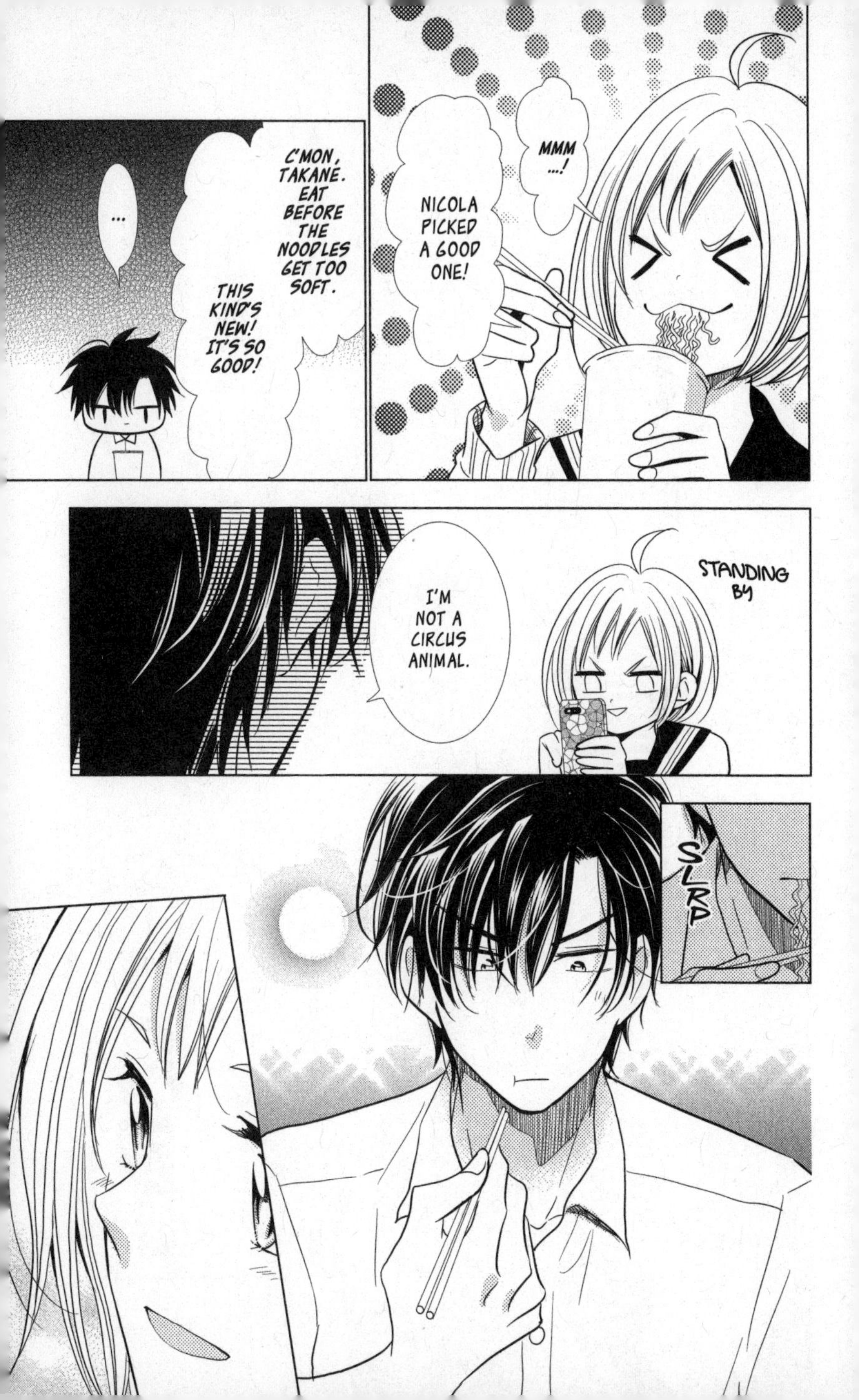
MMM...!
NICOLA PICKED A GOOD ONE!
C'MON, TAKANE. EAT BEFORE THE NOODLES GET TOO SOFT.
THIS KIND'S NEW! IT'S SO GOOD!
...
STANDING BY
I'M NOT A CIRCUS ANIMAL.
SLRP

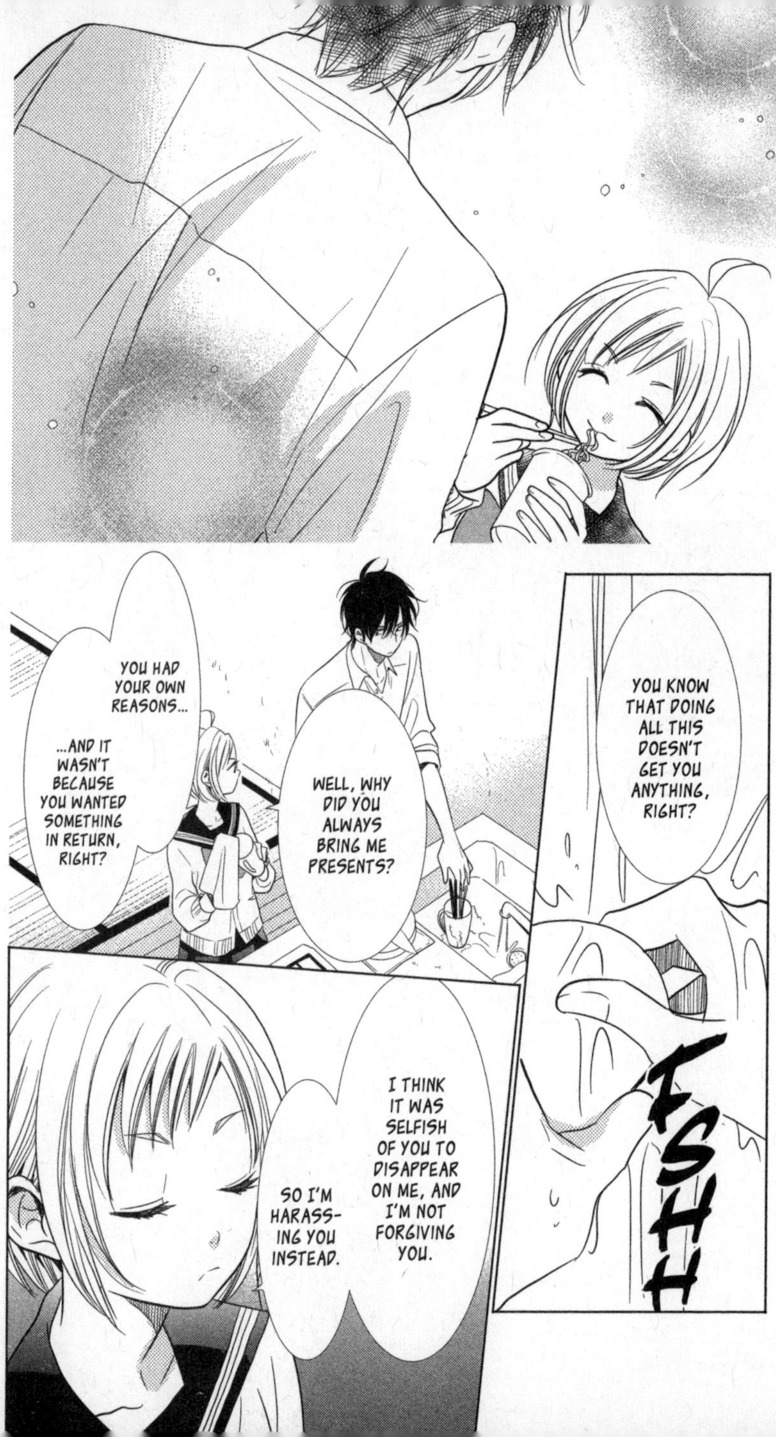
YOU KNOW THAT DOING ALL THIS DOESN'T GET YOU ANYTHING, RIGHT?
FSHH
WELL, WHY DID YOU ALWAYS BRING ME PRESENTS?
YOU HAD YOUR OWN REASONS...
...AND IT WASN'T BECAUSE YOU WANTED SOMETHING IN RETURN, RIGHT?
I THINK IT WAS SELFISH OF YOU TO DISAPPEAR ON ME, AND I'M NOT FORGIVING YOU.
SO I'M HARASS-ING YOU INSTEAD.

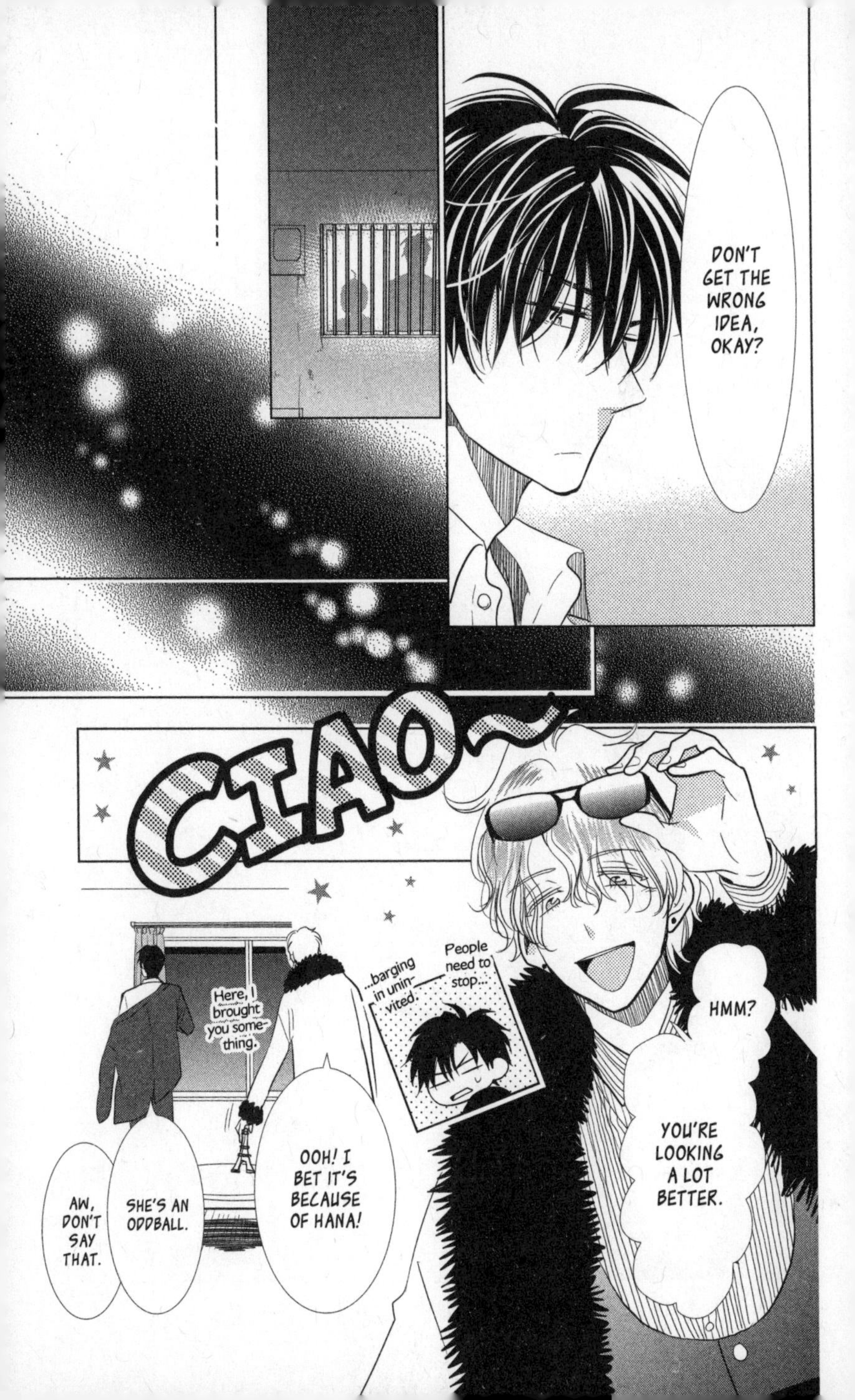
DON'T GET THE WRONG IDEA, OKAY?
CIAO~
HMM?
YOU'RE LOOKING A LOT BETTER.
People need to stop...
...barging in uninvited.
Here, I brought you something.
OOH! I BET IT'S BECAUSE OF HANA!
SHE'S AN ODDBALL.
AW, DON'T SAY THAT.

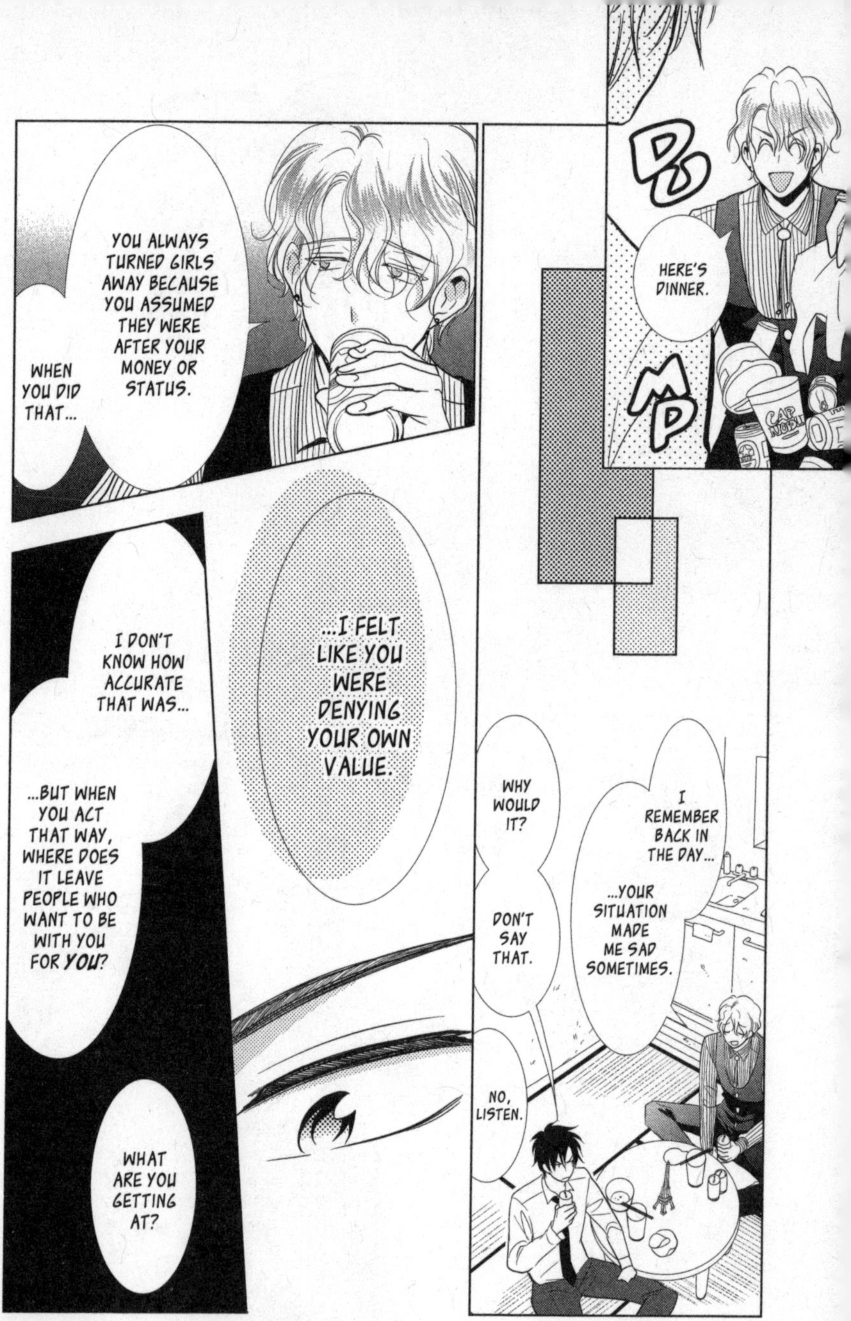
DOMP
HERE'S DINNER.
CAP NOODL
I REMEMBER BACK IN THE DAY...
...YOUR SITUATION MADE ME SAD SOMETIMES.
WHY WOULD IT?
DON'T SAY THAT.
NO, LISTEN.
YOU ALWAYS TURNED GIRLS AWAY BECAUSE YOU ASSUMED THEY WERE AFTER YOUR MONEY OR STATUS.
WHEN YOU DID THAT...
...I FELT LIKE YOU WERE DENYING YOUR OWN VALUE.
I DON'T KNOW HOW ACCURATE THAT WAS...
...BUT WHEN YOU ACT THAT WAY, WHERE DOES IT LEAVE PEOPLE WHO WANT TO BE WITH YOU FOR *YOU*?
WHAT ARE YOU GETTING AT?

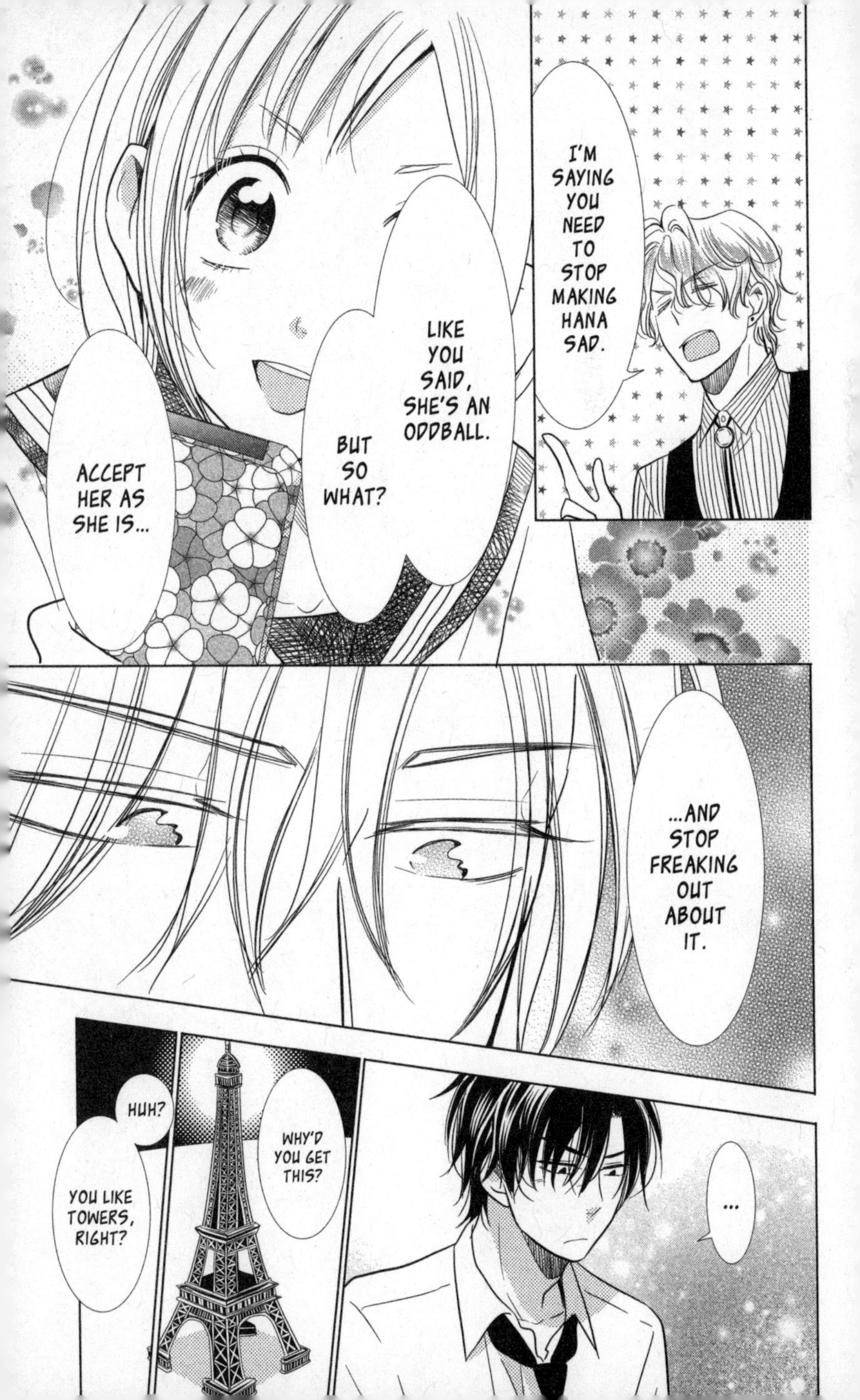
I'M SAYING YOU NEED TO STOP MAKING HANA SAD.
LIKE YOU SAID, SHE'S AN ODDBALL.
BUT SO WHAT?
ACCEPT HER AS SHE IS...
...AND STOP FREAKING OUT ABOUT IT.
...
WHY'D YOU GET THIS?
HUH?
YOU LIKE TOWERS, RIGHT?

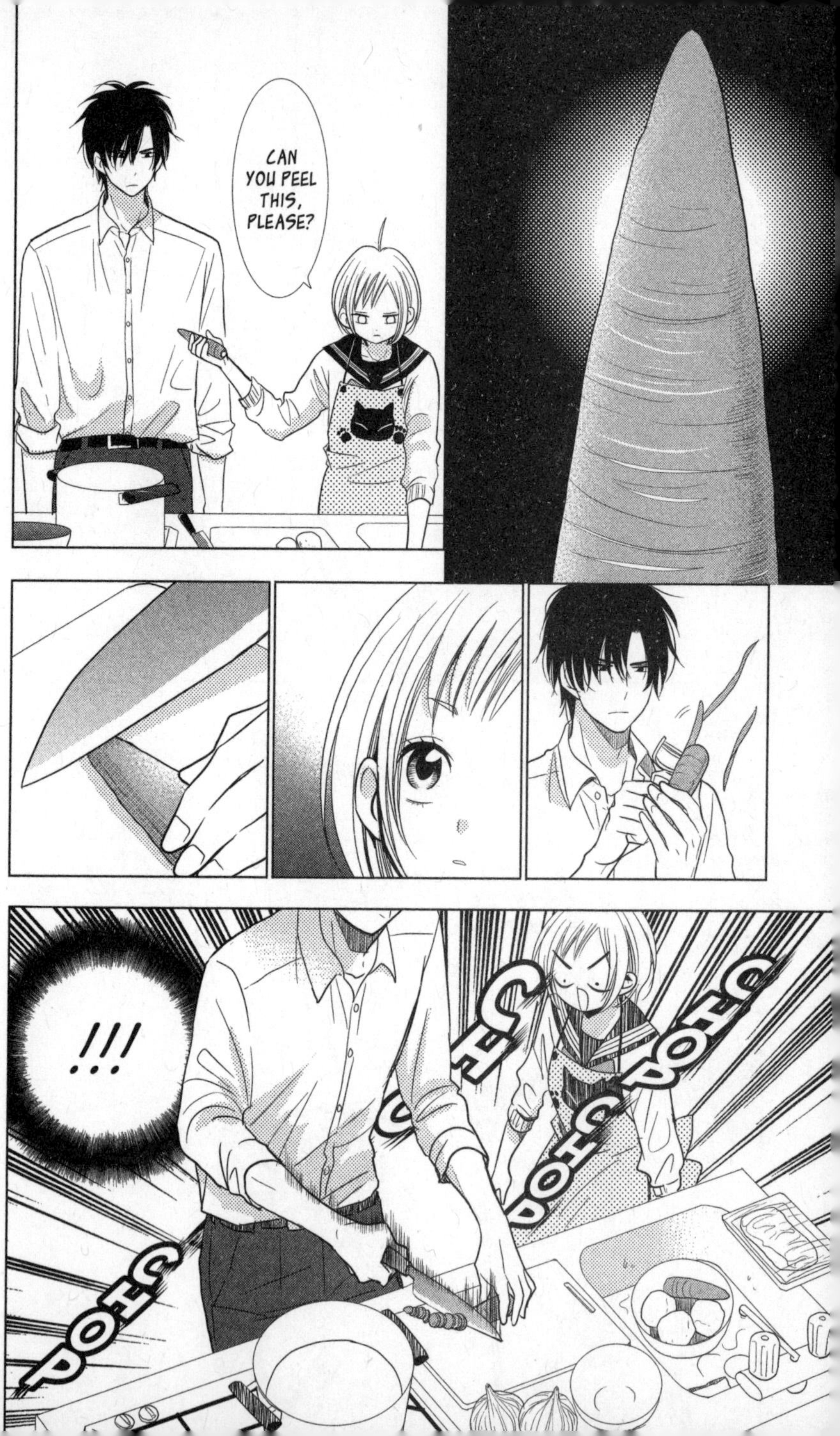
CAN YOU PEEL THIS, PLEASE?
!!!
CHOP CHOP
CHOP CHOP
CHOP

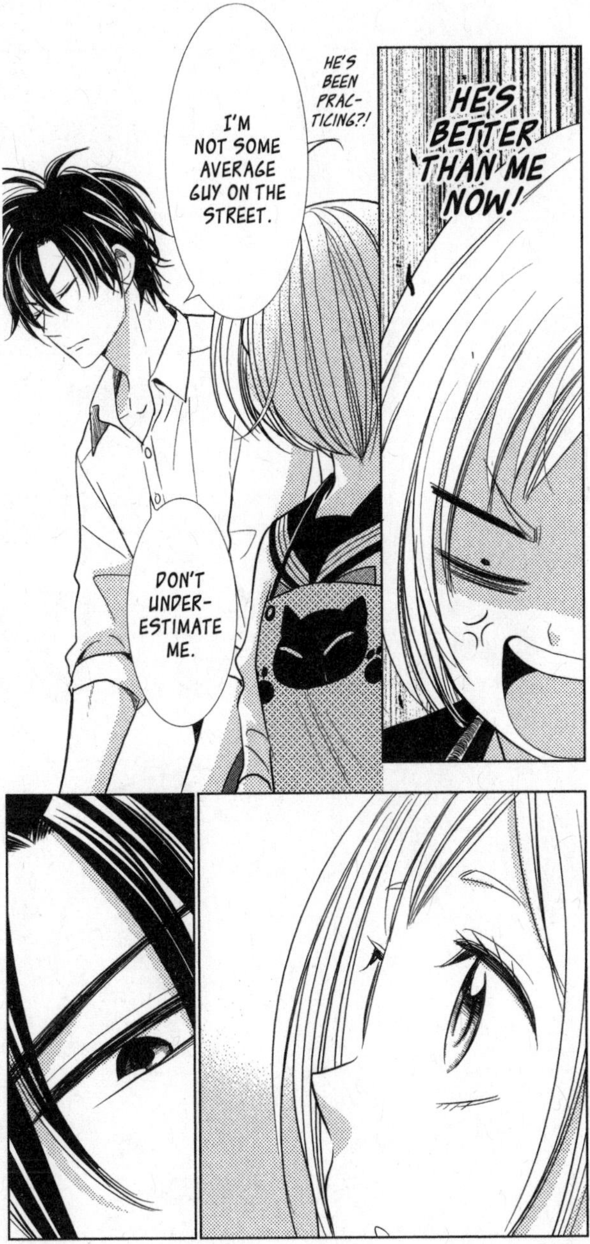
HE'S BEEN PRAC-TICING?!
HE'S BETTER THAN ME NOW!
I'M NOT SOME AVERAGE GUY ON THE STREET.
DON'T UNDER-ESTIMATE ME.

• Height Chart •

I've included the height chart at the end of this book. I hope you'll take a close look so you can see how tall everyone is. As I mentioned in volume 6, I'd already decided Takane was six feet tall, so I chose the other characters' heights based on that.

For some reason, the younger the character, the more squat and cute they look, so Hana and the kids look even smaller than I'd thought. At first I thought I'd draw them according to the heights I'd imagined for them, but when I did, their heads seemed unnaturally large compared to the adult characters, so I opted against that.

My first thought after putting the chart together was "Rino has a great figure!" When drawing her on her own I didn't notice it as much, but she's definitely built like a model.

I don't usually have a clear image in my head when I draw, so any given character can be proportionally different from panel to panel. But when they're all together like this, Mizuki looks pretty tall. Grandpa Chairman is hunched, but if he straightens up, he's a little taller.

The kids and Okamon are still growing, so they might look different when I draw them around when Hana's finishing up high school. I hope I'll be able to draw that for you someday!

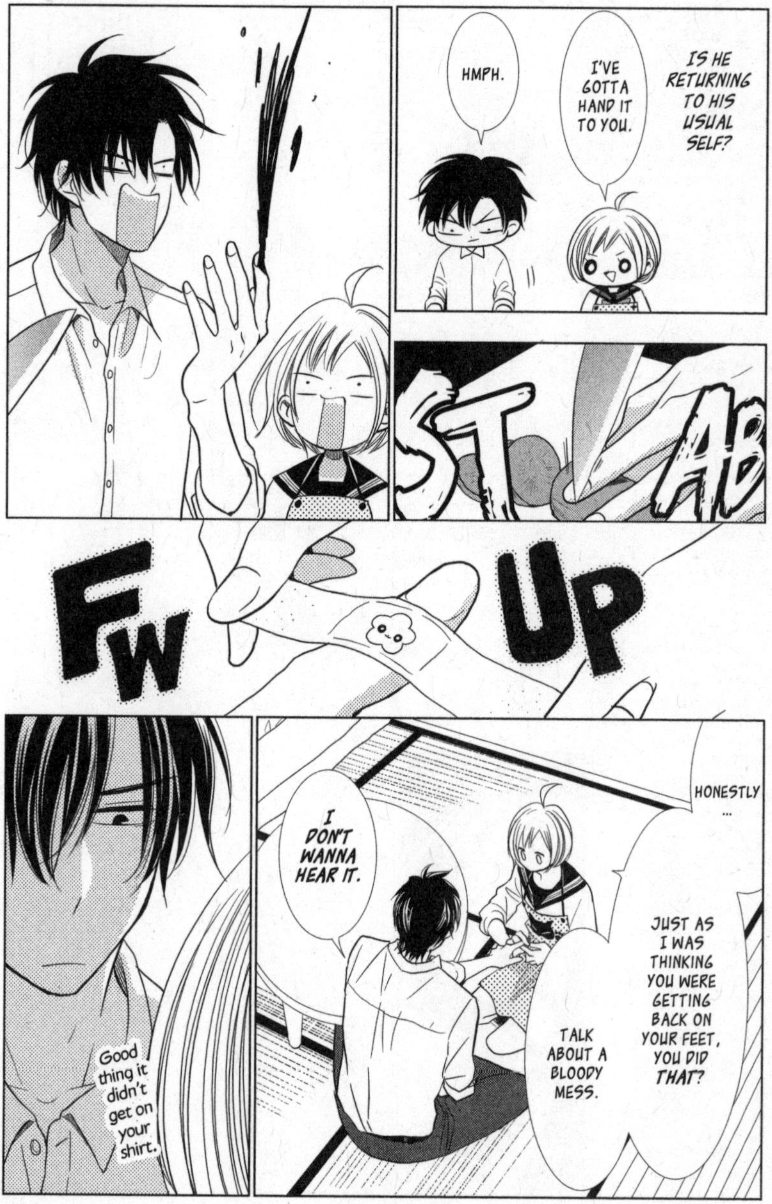
IS HE RETURNING TO HIS USUAL SELF?
I'VE GOTTA HAND IT TO YOU.
HMPH.
STAB
FWUP
HONESTLY...
JUST AS I WAS THINKING YOU WERE GETTING BACK ON YOUR FEET, YOU DID *THAT*?
TALK ABOUT A BLOODY MESS.
I DON'T WANNA HEAR IT.
Good thing it didn't get on your shirt.

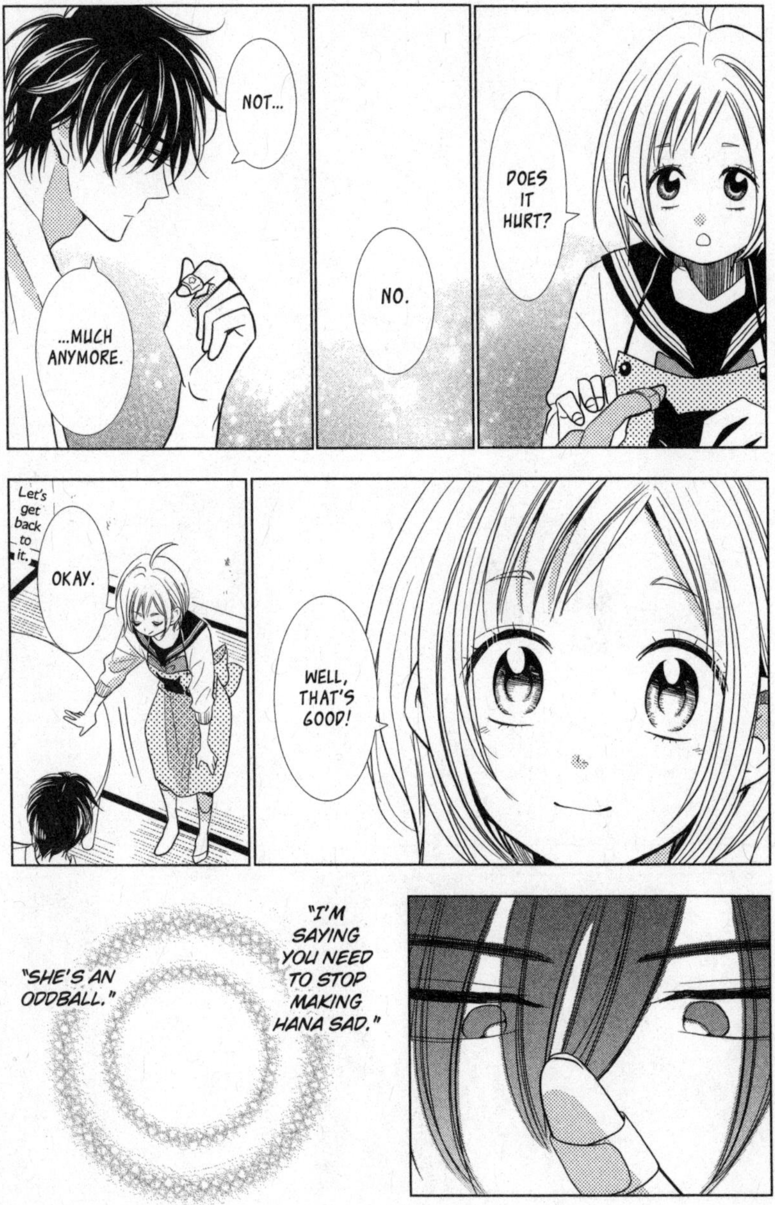
DOES IT HURT?
NO.
NOT...
...MUCH ANYMORE.
WELL, THAT'S GOOD!
OKAY.
Let's get back to it.
"I'M SAYING YOU NEED TO STOP MAKING HANA SAD."
"SHE'S AN ODDBALL."

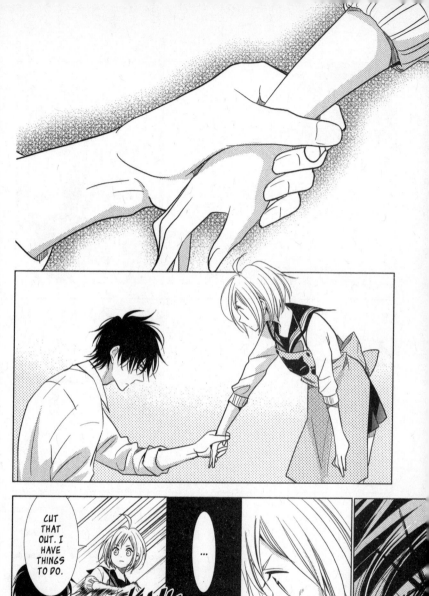

CUT THAT OUT. I HAVE THINGS TO DO.

...

YANK

?

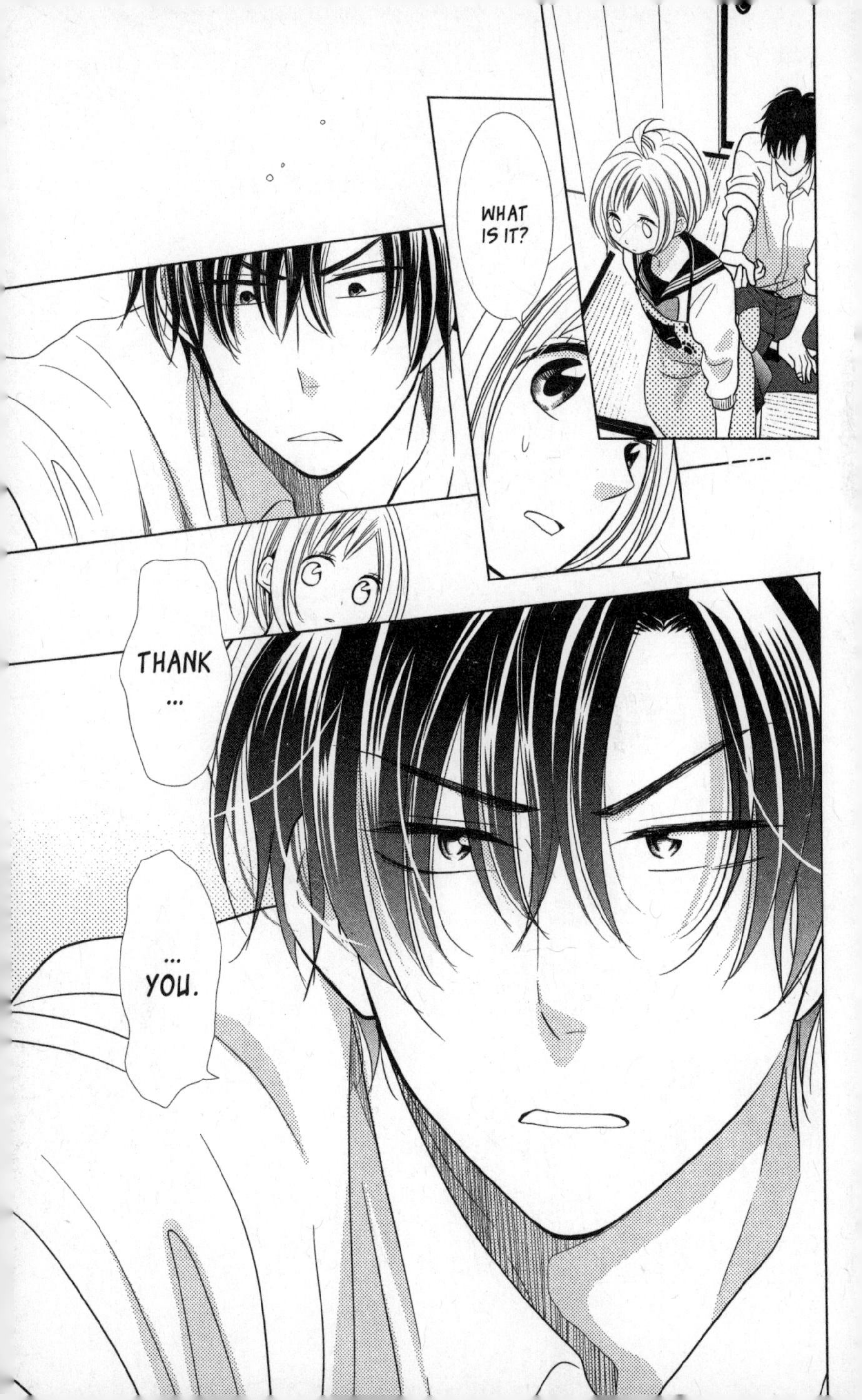
WHAT IS IT?
THANK...
...YOU.

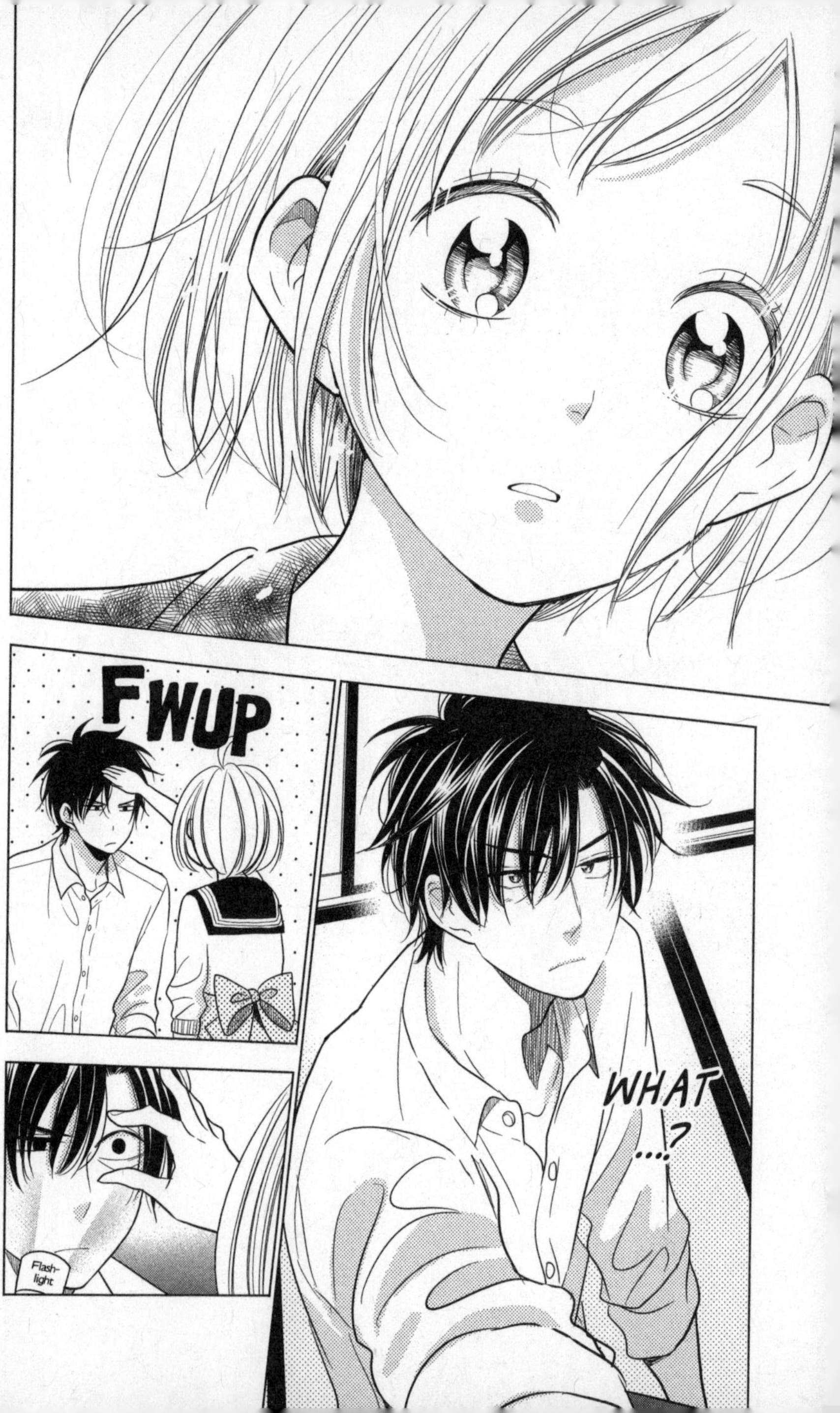
WHAT ...?
FWUP
Flash-light

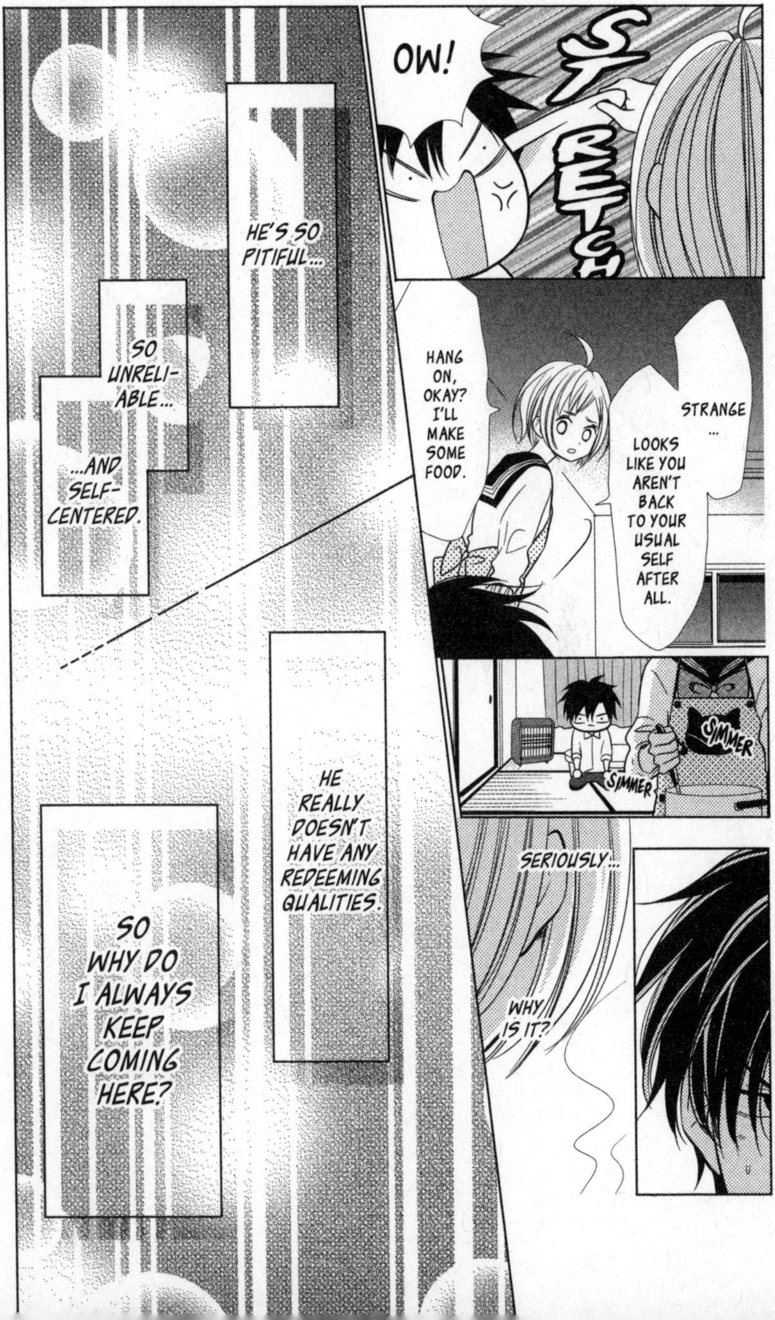
STRETCH
OW!
STRANGE... LOOKS LIKE YOU AREN'T BACK TO YOUR USUAL SELF AFTER ALL.
HANG ON, OKAY? I'LL MAKE SOME FOOD.
SIMMER
SIMMER
SERIOUSLY...
WHY IS IT?
HE'S SO PITIFUL...
SO UNRELI-ABLE...
...AND SELF-CENTERED.
HE REALLY DOESN'T HAVE ANY REDEEMING QUALITIES.
SO WHY DO I ALWAYS KEEP COMING HERE?

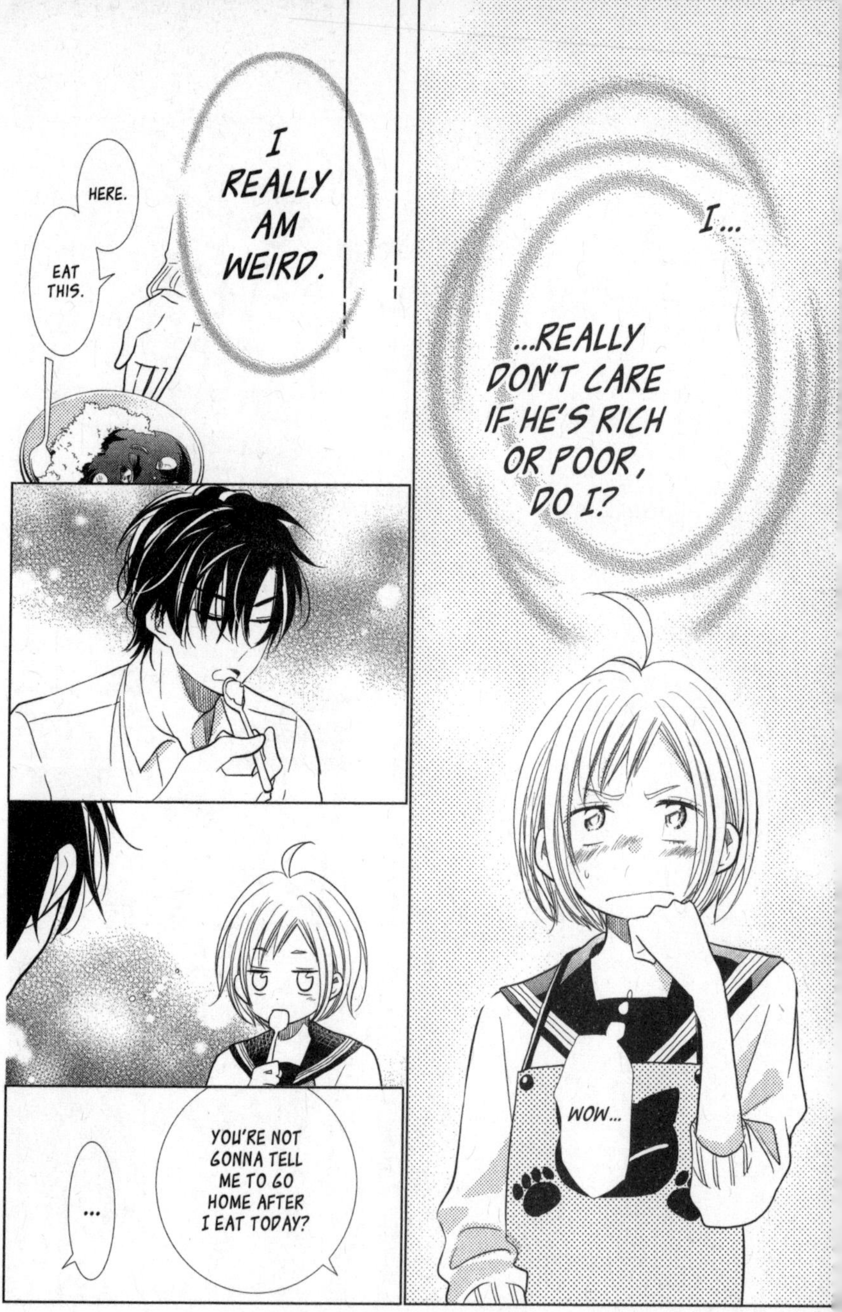
I...
...REALLY DON'T CARE IF HE'S RICH OR POOR, DO I?
WOW...
I REALLY AM WEIRD.
HERE.
EAT THIS.
YOU'RE NOT GONNA TELL ME TO GO HOME AFTER I EAT TODAY?
...

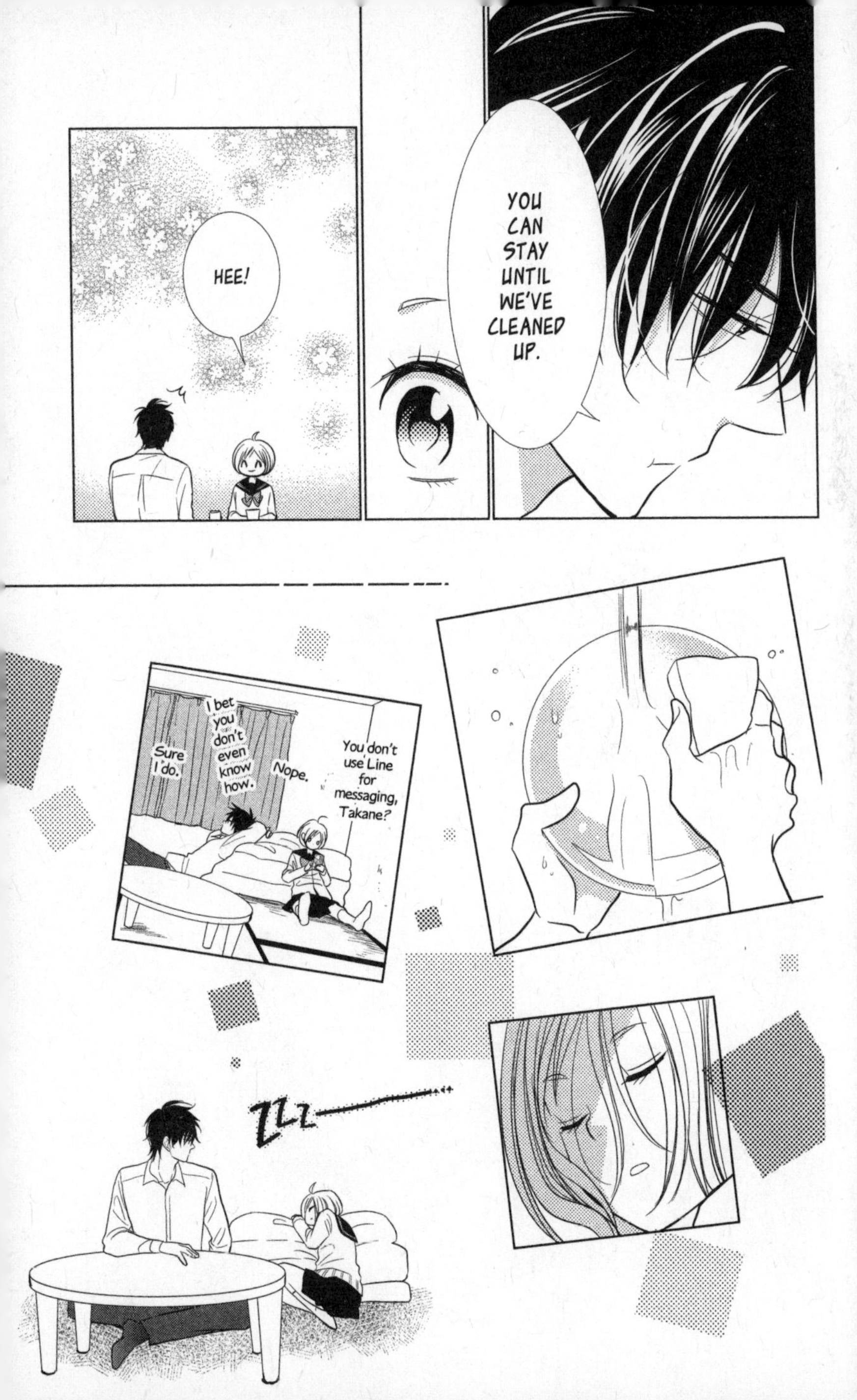
YOU CAN STAY UNTIL WE'VE CLEANED UP.
HEE!
You don't use Line for messaging, Takane?
Nope.
I bet you don't even know how.
Sure I do.
ZZZ

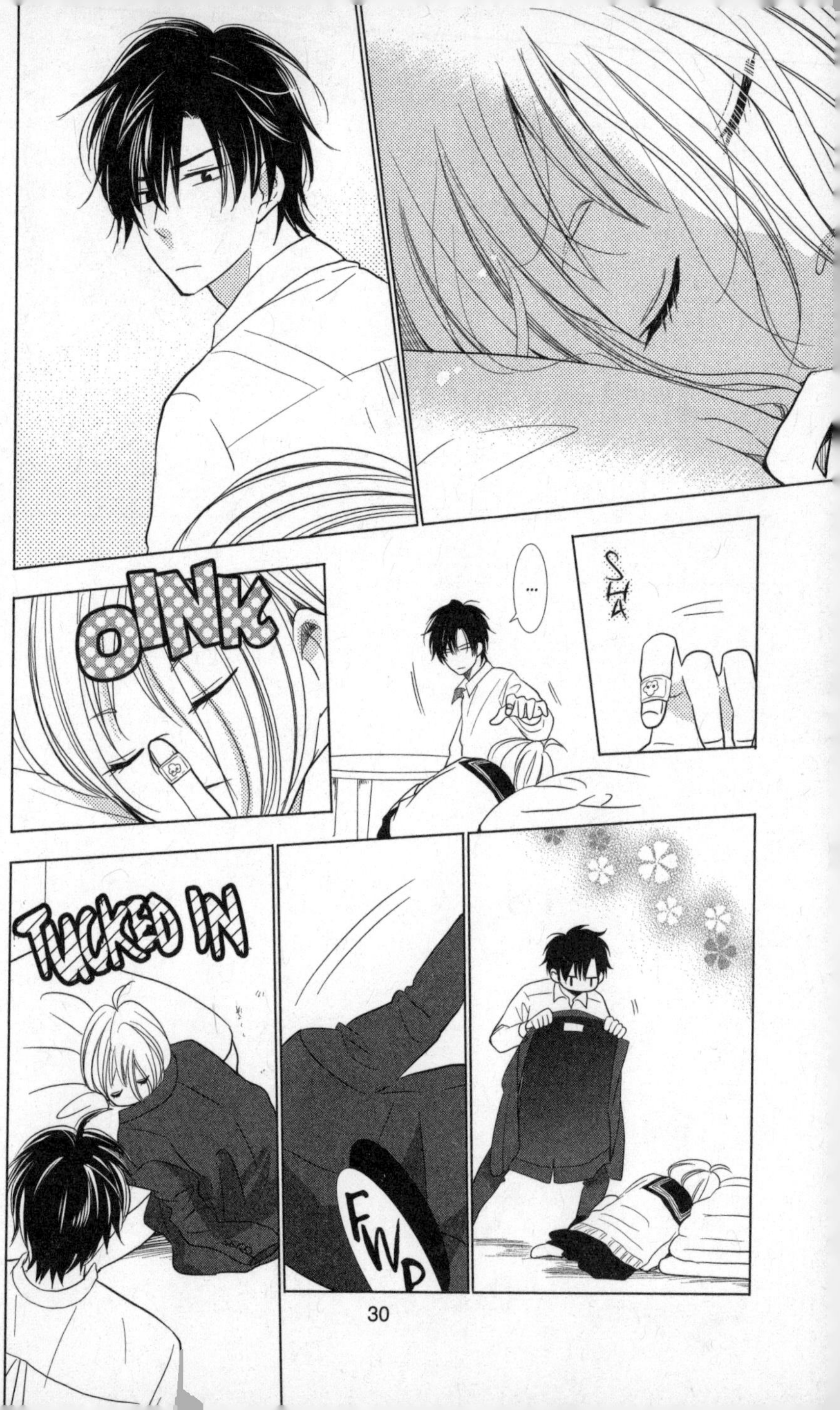
SHA
...
OINK
FWP
TUCKED IN

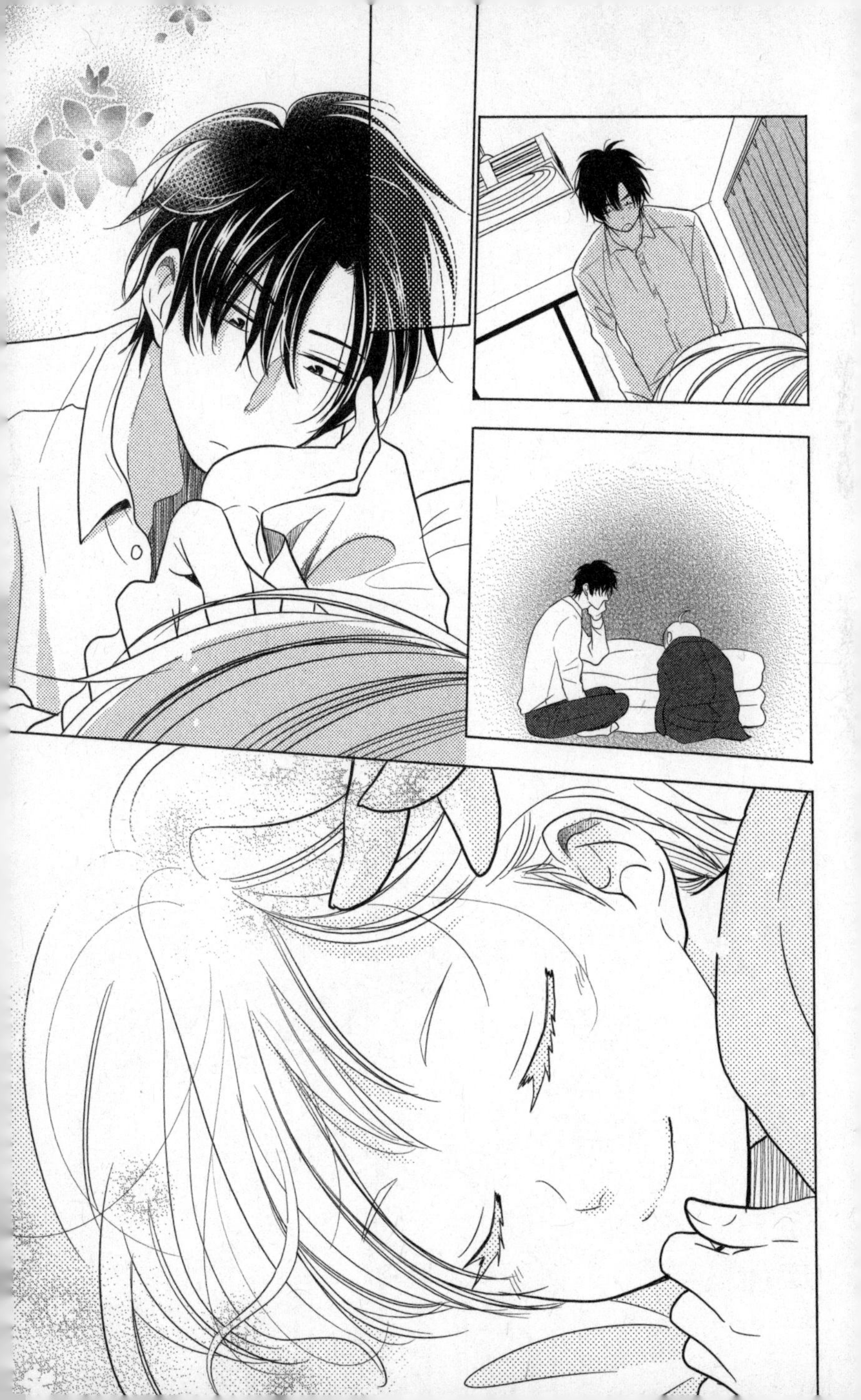

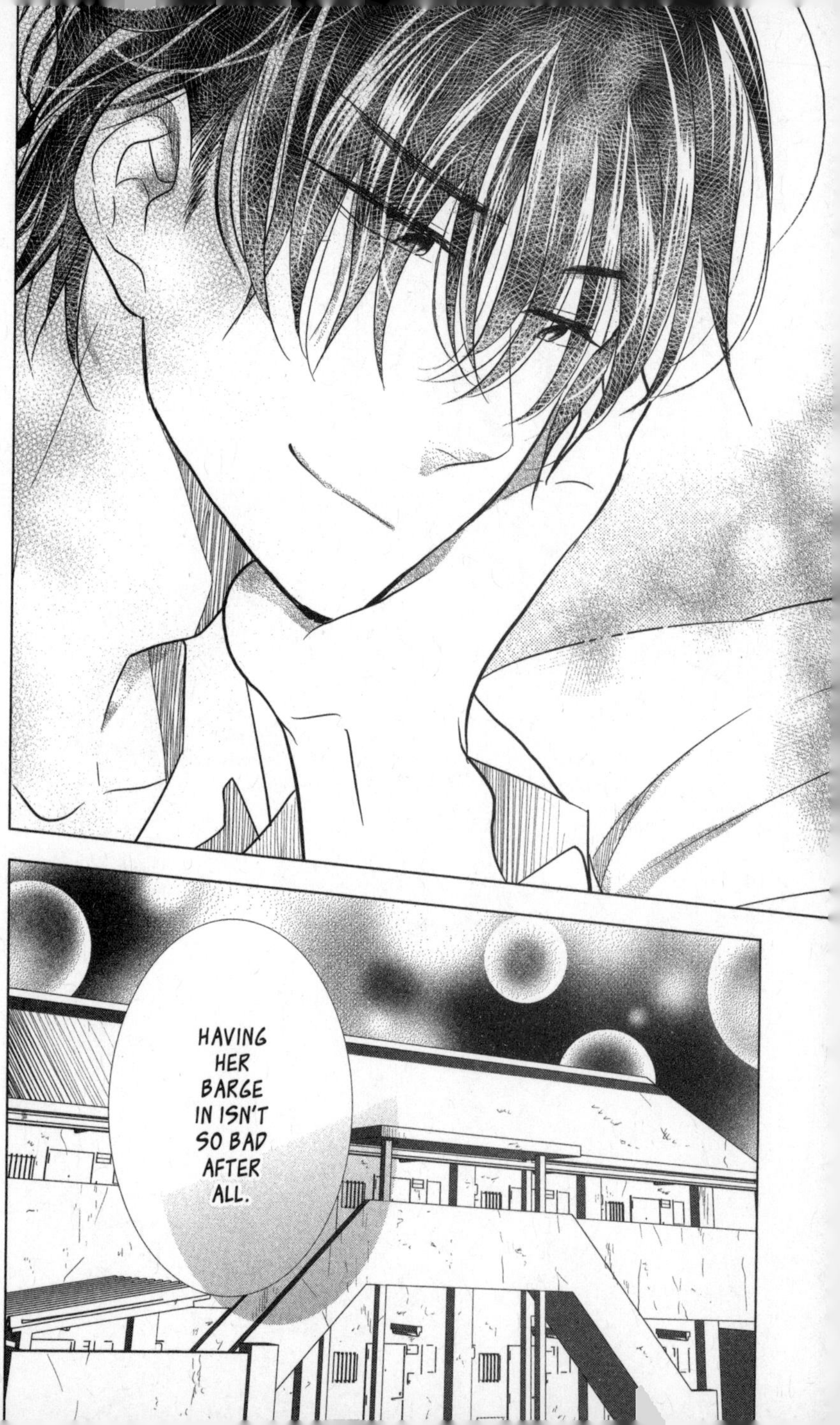
HAVING HER BARGE IN ISN'T SO BAD AFTER ALL.

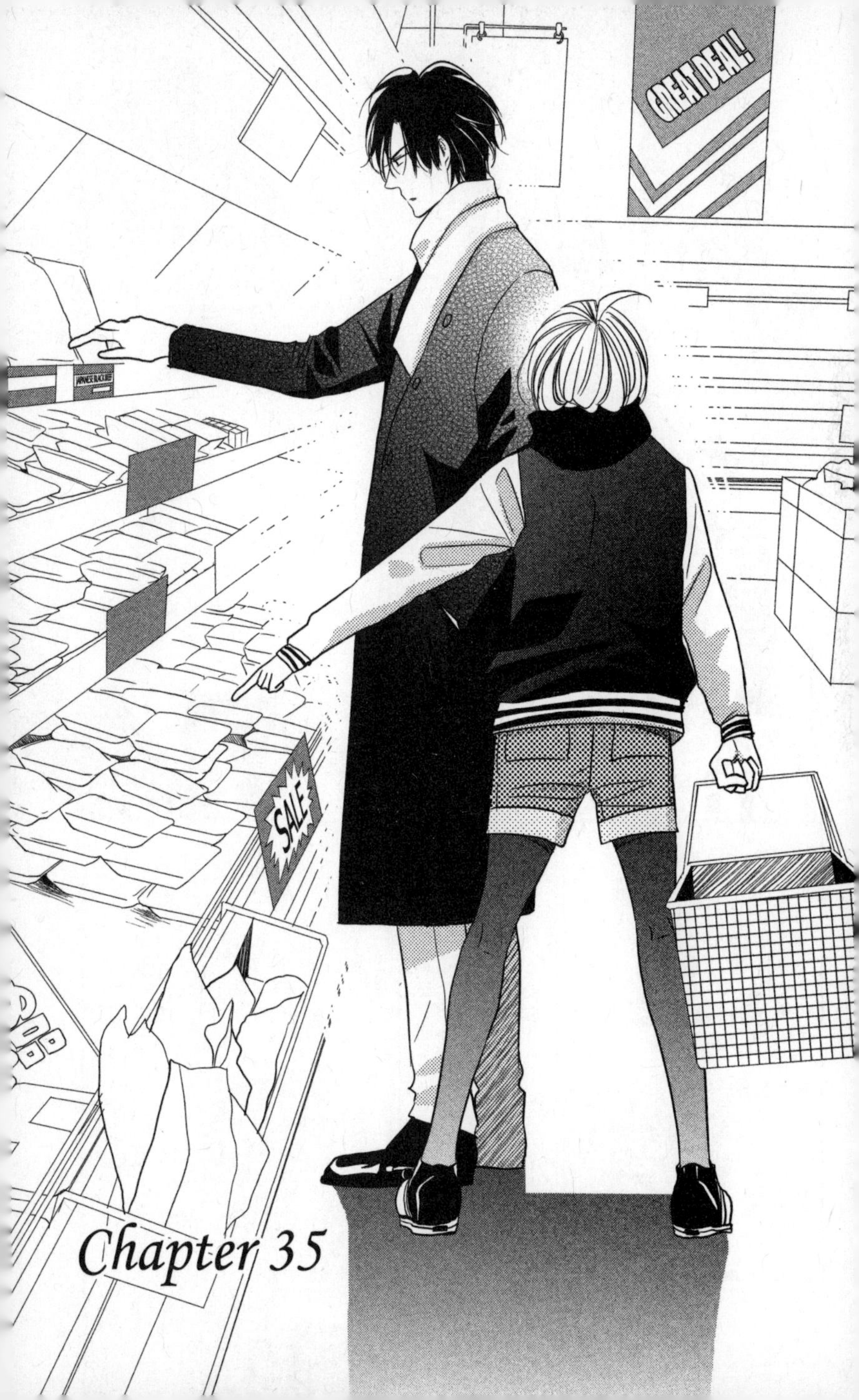
GREAT DEAL!
SALE
Chapter 35

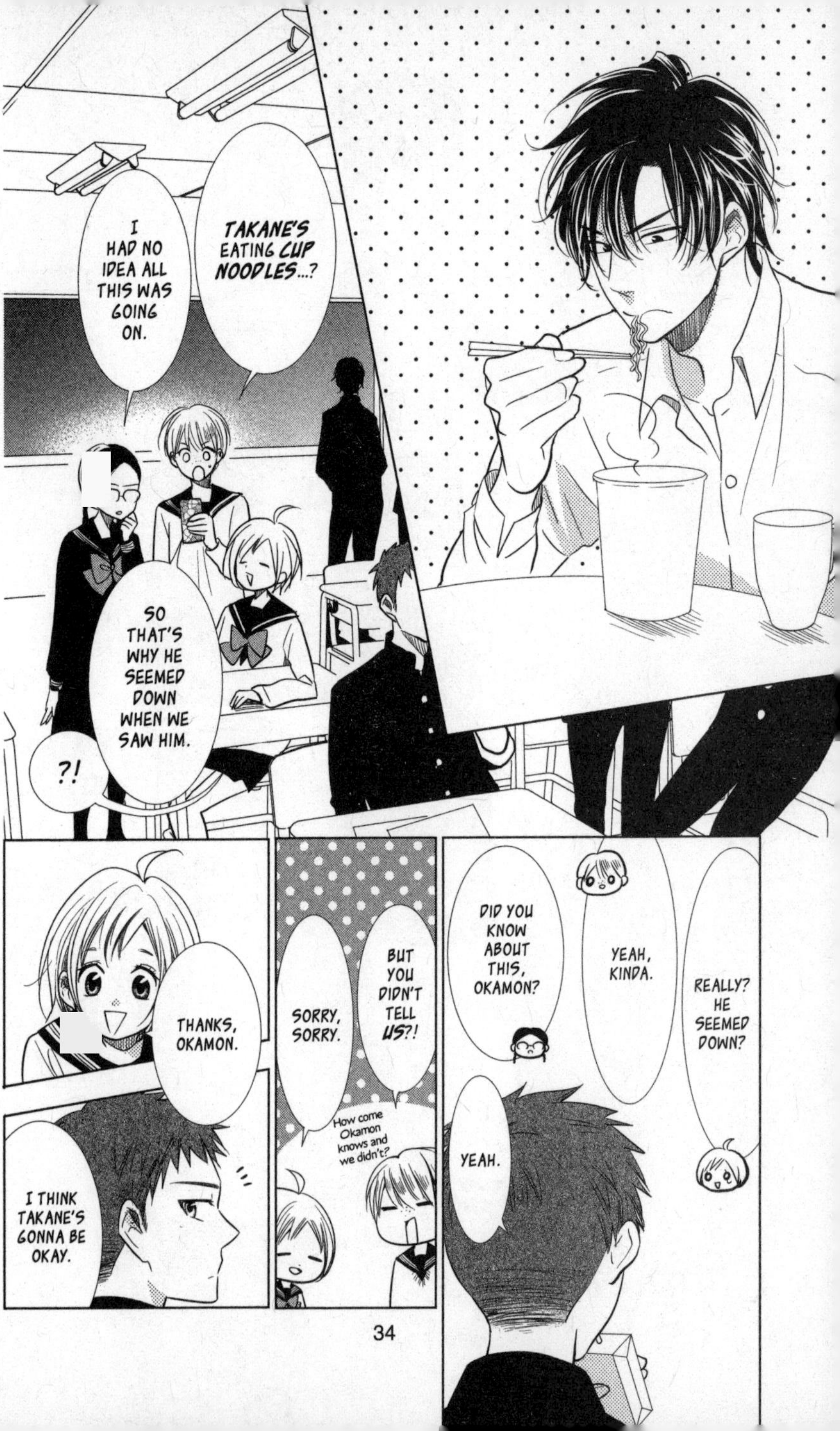
TAKANE'S EATING CUP NOODLES...?
I HAD NO IDEA ALL THIS WAS GOING ON.
SO THAT'S WHY HE SEEMED DOWN WHEN WE SAW HIM.
?!
DID YOU KNOW ABOUT THIS, OKAMON?
YEAH, KINDA.
REALLY? HE SEEMED DOWN?
YEAH.
BUT YOU DIDN'T TELL US?!
SORRY, SORRY.
How come Okamon knows and we didn't?
THANKS, OKAMON.
I THINK TAKANE'S GONNA BE OKAY.

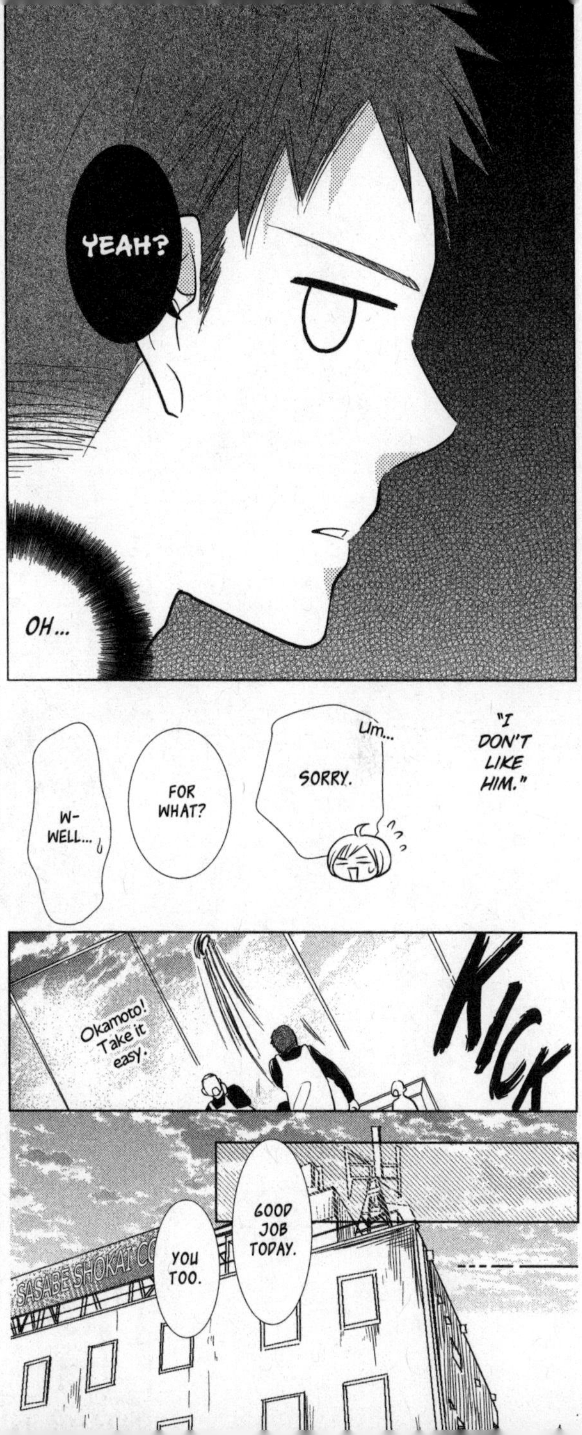
YEAH?
OH...
"I DON'T LIKE HIM."
Um...
SORRY.
FOR WHAT?
W-WELL...
KICK
Okamoto! Take it easy.
GOOD JOB TODAY.
YOU TOO.
SASABE SHOKAI CO

• Hikune •

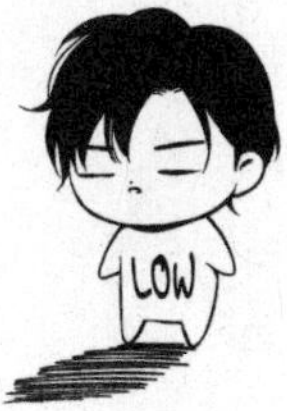
LOW

〈Characteristics〉

- He feels cool to the touch, but you can still tell he's alive. A warmth-seeking creature.
- He's extremely pale.
- When Hana treats Takane coldly, he turns into Hikune. He returns to his usual self when Hana is nice to him or praises him.
- At this point, we've never seen him say anything during his appearances. He probably has no desire to speak.
- If he's feeling good, he walks.
- He's about half a foot tall. He could get smaller depending on the severity of the shock that transforms him.
- Takane's memories of his times as Hikune are inconsistent. Sometimes he remembers, but at other times he has no recollection at all.
- He may look as if he's naked, but in some scenes his clothes shrank along with him, so we're reasonably sure he's wearing something.

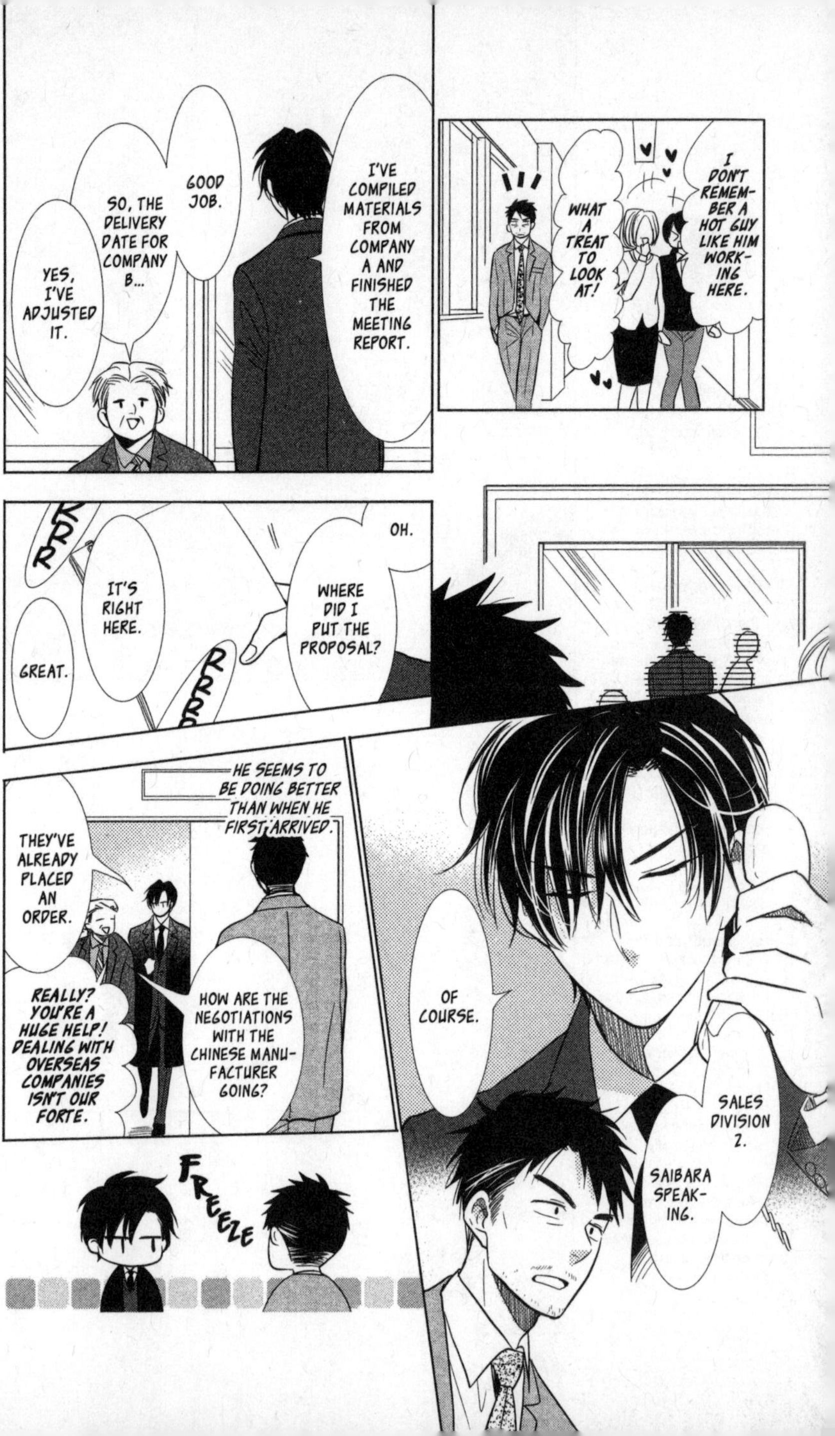
I DON'T REMEMBER A HOT GUY LIKE HIM WORKING HERE.
WHAT A TREAT TO LOOK AT!
I'VE COMPILED MATERIALS FROM COMPANY A AND FINISHED THE MEETING REPORT.
GOOD JOB.
SO, THE DELIVERY DATE FOR COMPANY B...
YES, I'VE ADJUSTED IT.
RRR
OH.
WHERE DID I PUT THE PROPOSAL?
RRRR
IT'S RIGHT HERE.
GREAT.
SALES DIVISION 2.
SAIBARA SPEAKING.
OF COURSE.
HE SEEMS TO BE DOING BETTER THAN WHEN HE FIRST ARRIVED.
HOW ARE THE NEGOTIATIONS WITH THE CHINESE MANUFACTURER GOING?
THEY'VE ALREADY PLACED AN ORDER.
REALLY? YOU'RE A HUGE HELP! DEALING WITH OVERSEAS COMPANIES ISN'T OUR FORTE.
FREEZE

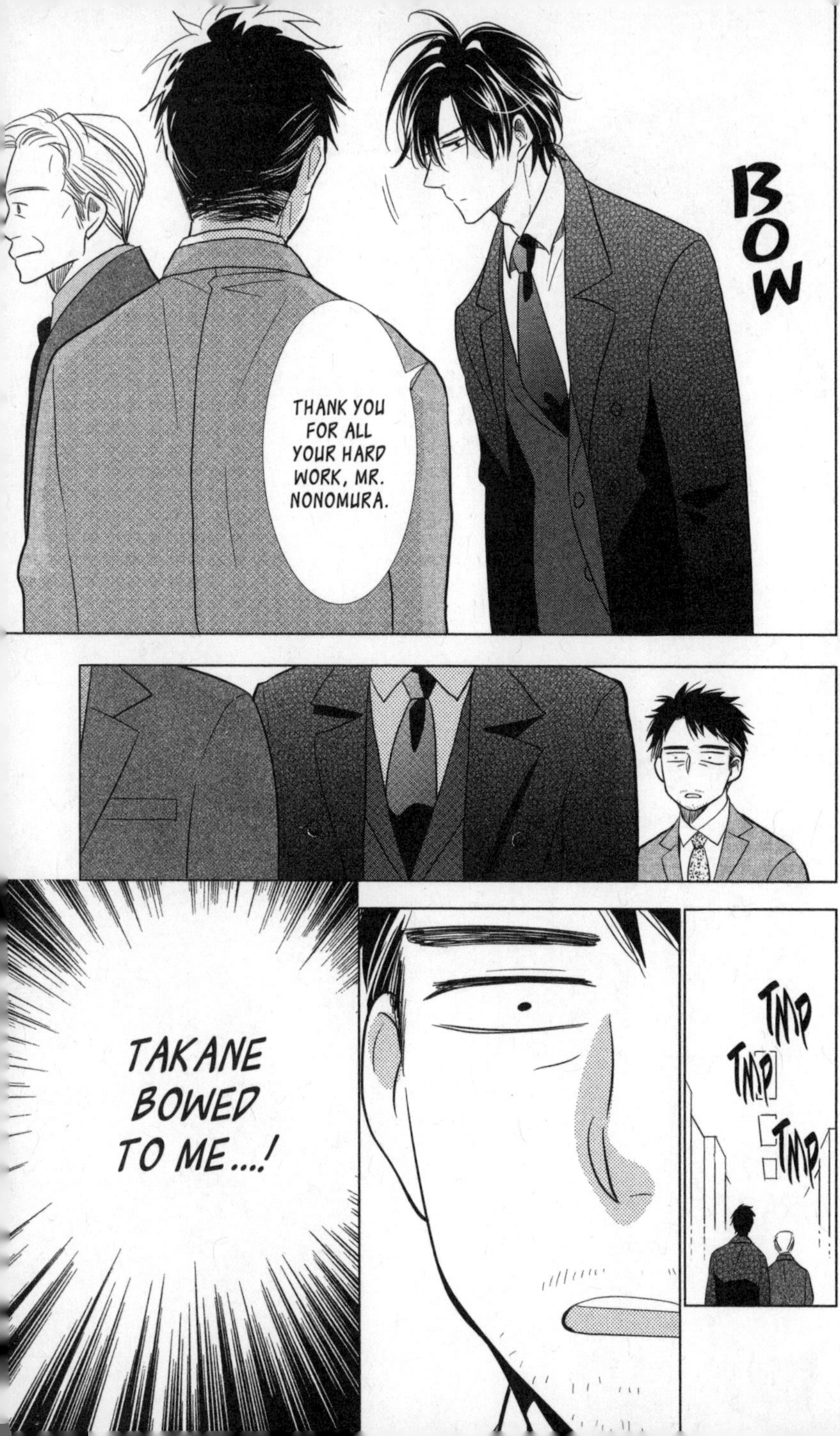
BOW
THANK YOU FOR ALL YOUR HARD WORK, MR. NONOMURA.
TMP
TMP
TMP
TAKANE BOWED TO ME...!

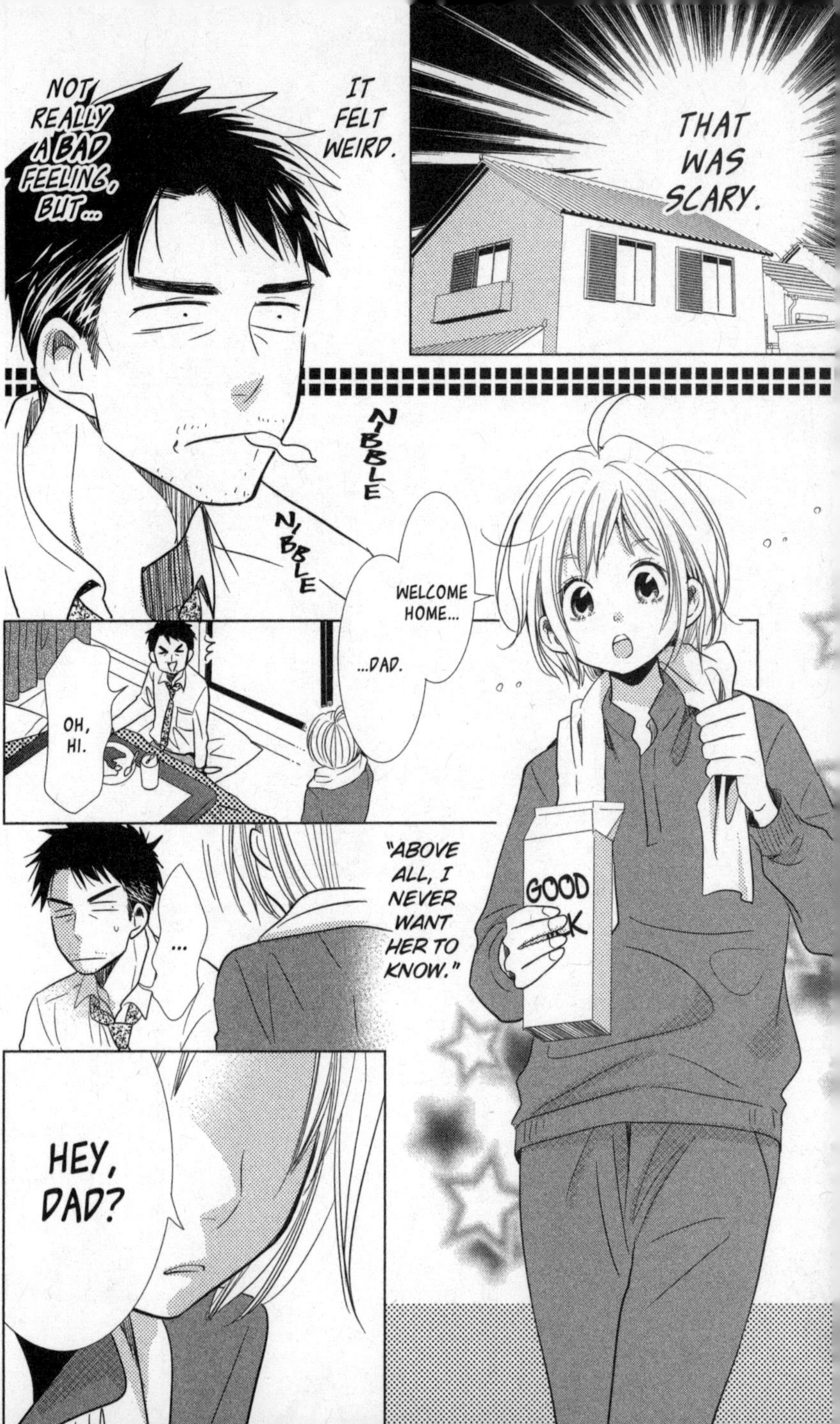
THAT WAS SCARY.
IT FELT WEIRD.
NOT REALLY A BAD FEELING, BUT...
NIBBLE
NIBBLE
WELCOME HOME...
...DAD.
GOOD
OH, HI.
"ABOVE ALL, I NEVER WANT HER TO KNOW."
...
HEY, DAD?

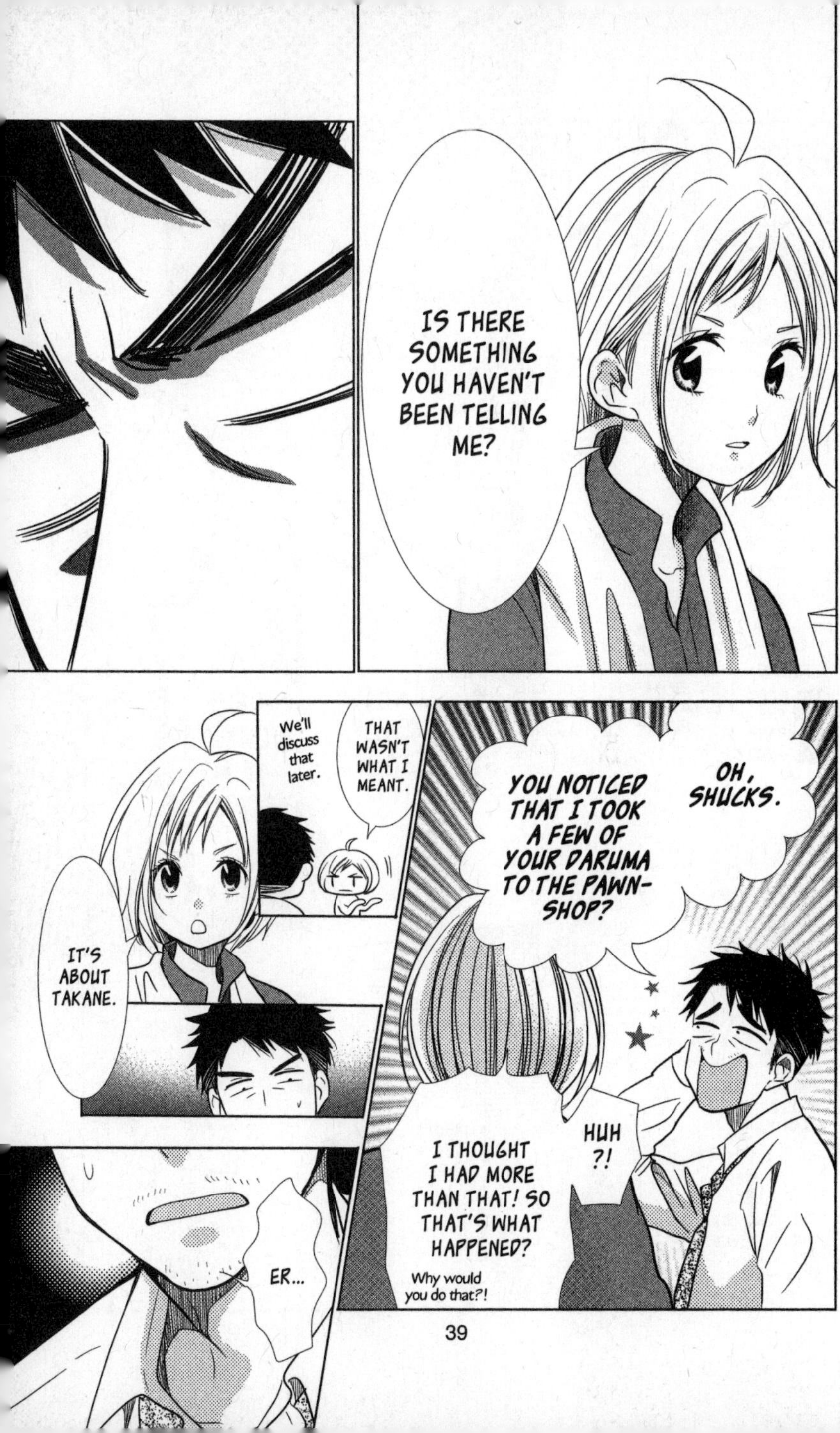
IS THERE SOMETHING YOU HAVEN'T BEEN TELLING ME?
OH, SHUCKS.
YOU NOTICED THAT I TOOK A FEW OF YOUR DARUMA TO THE PAWN-SHOP?
HUH?!
I THOUGHT I HAD MORE THAN THAT! SO THAT'S WHAT HAPPENED?
Why would you do that?!
THAT WASN'T WHAT I MEANT.
We'll discuss that later.
IT'S ABOUT TAKANE.
ER...

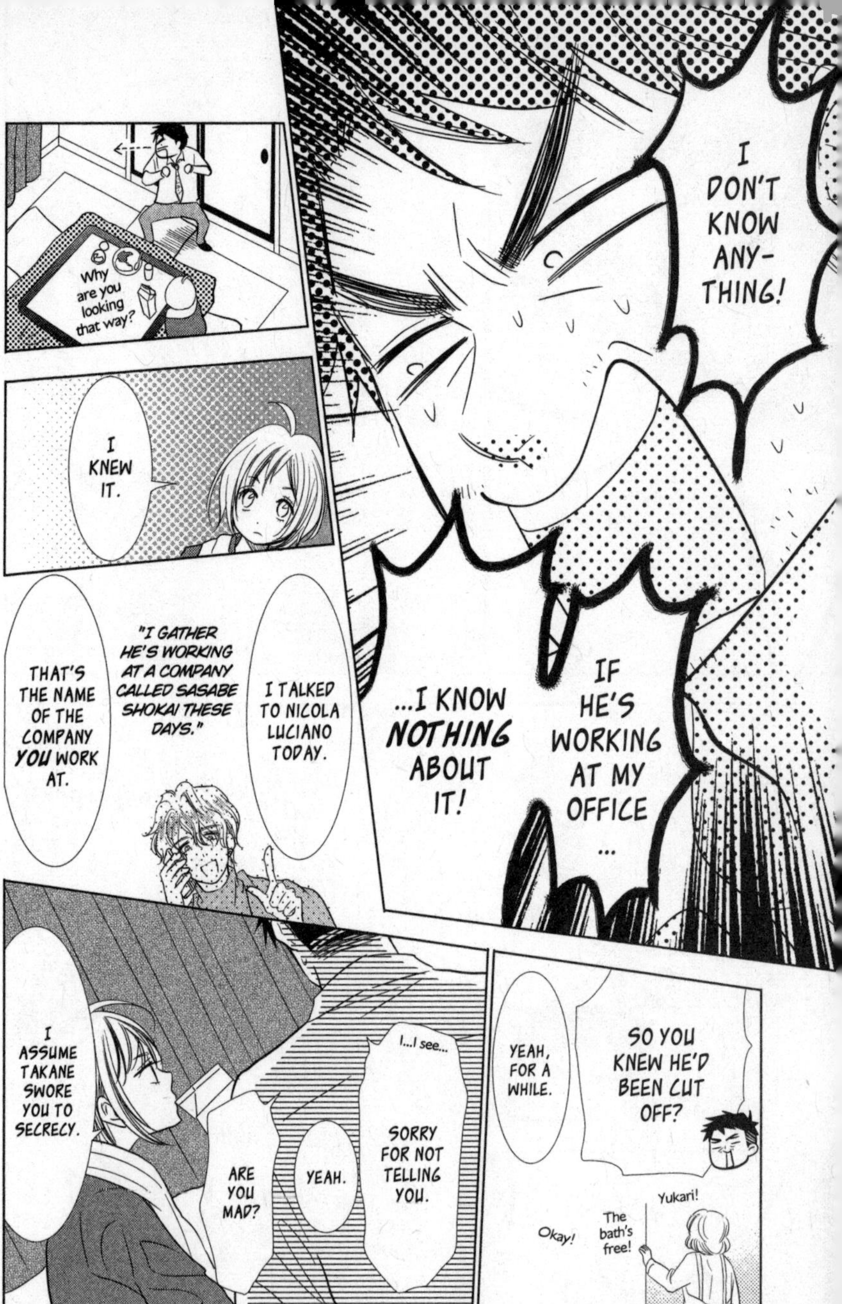

I DON'T KNOW ANYTHING!
IF HE'S WORKING AT MY OFFICE...
...I KNOW **NOTHING** ABOUT IT!
Why are you looking that way?
I KNEW IT.
I TALKED TO NICOLA LUCIANO TODAY.
"I GATHER HE'S WORKING AT A COMPANY CALLED SASABE SHOKAI THESE DAYS."
THAT'S THE NAME OF THE COMPANY **YOU** WORK AT.
SO YOU KNEW HE'D BEEN CUT OFF?
YEAH, FOR A WHILE.
Yukari!
The bath's free!
Okay!
I...I see...
SORRY FOR NOT TELLING YOU.
YEAH.
ARE YOU MAD?
I ASSUME TAKANE SWORE YOU TO SECRECY.

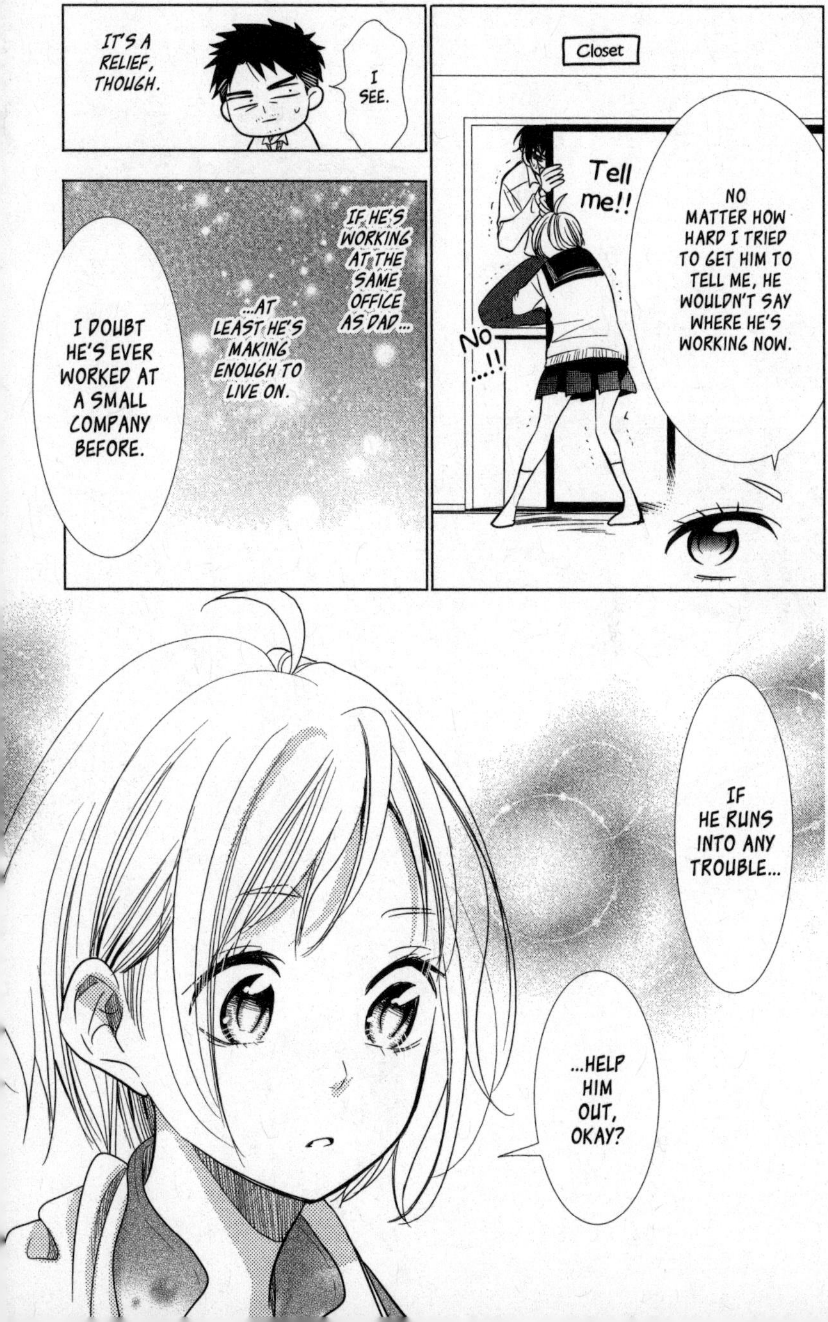
Closet
NO MATTER HOW HARD I TRIED TO GET HIM TO TELL ME, HE WOULDN'T SAY WHERE HE'S WORKING NOW.
Tell me!!
No ...!!
I SEE.
IT'S A RELIEF, THOUGH.
IF HE'S WORKING AT THE SAME OFFICE AS DAD...
...AT LEAST HE'S MAKING ENOUGH TO LIVE ON.
I DOUBT HE'S EVER WORKED AT A SMALL COMPANY BEFORE.
IF HE RUNS INTO ANY TROUBLE...
...HELP HIM OUT, OKAY?

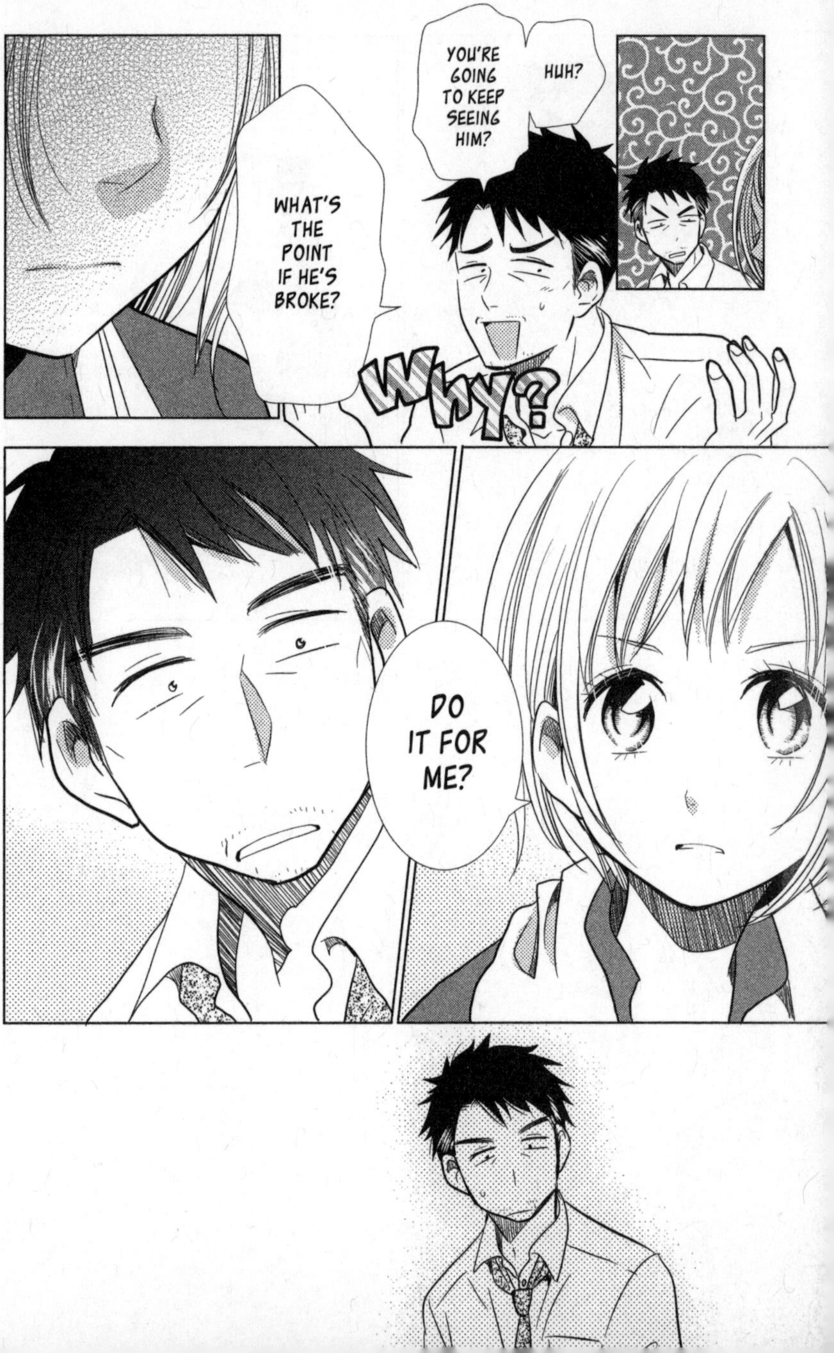
HUH?
YOU'RE GOING TO KEEP SEEING HIM?
WHY?
WHAT'S THE POINT IF HE'S BROKE?
DO IT FOR ME?

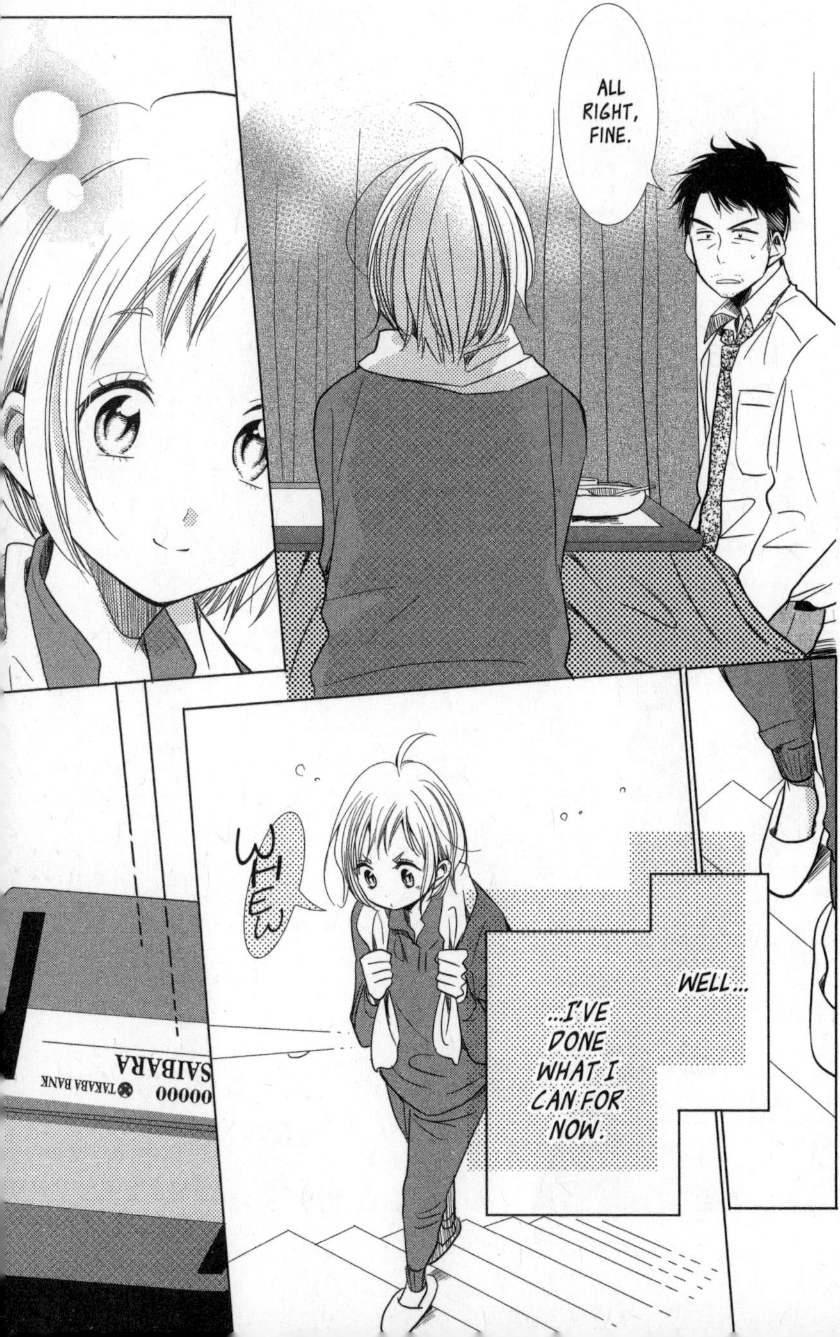
ALL RIGHT, FINE.
WELL...
...I'VE DONE WHAT I CAN FOR NOW.
WHEW
SAIBARA
TAKABA BANK
00000

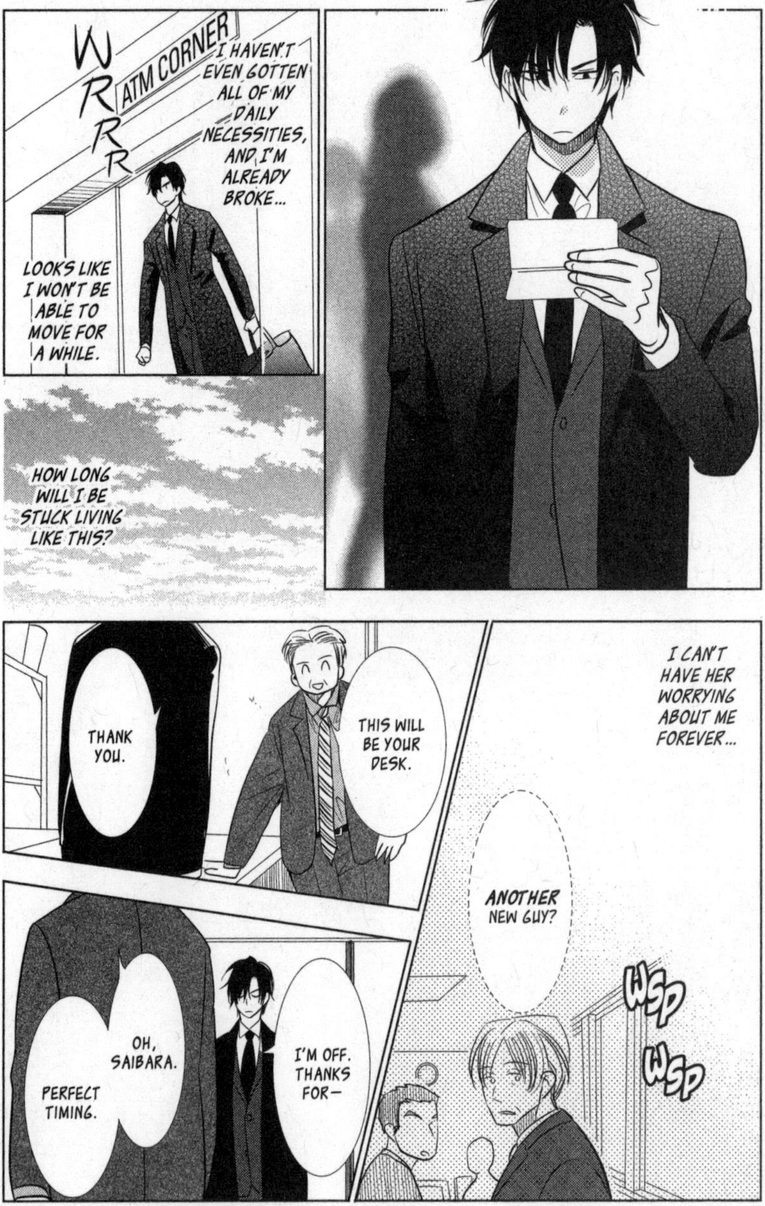
WRRR
ATM CORNER
I HAVEN'T EVEN GOTTEN ALL OF MY DAILY NECESSITIES, AND I'M ALREADY BROKE...
LOOKS LIKE I WON'T BE ABLE TO MOVE FOR A WHILE.
HOW LONG WILL I BE STUCK LIVING LIKE THIS?
I CAN'T HAVE HER WORRYING ABOUT ME FOREVER...
ANOTHER NEW GUY?
WSP
WSP
THIS WILL BE YOUR DESK.
THANK YOU.
I'M OFF. THANKS FOR—
OH, SAIBARA.
PERFECT TIMING.

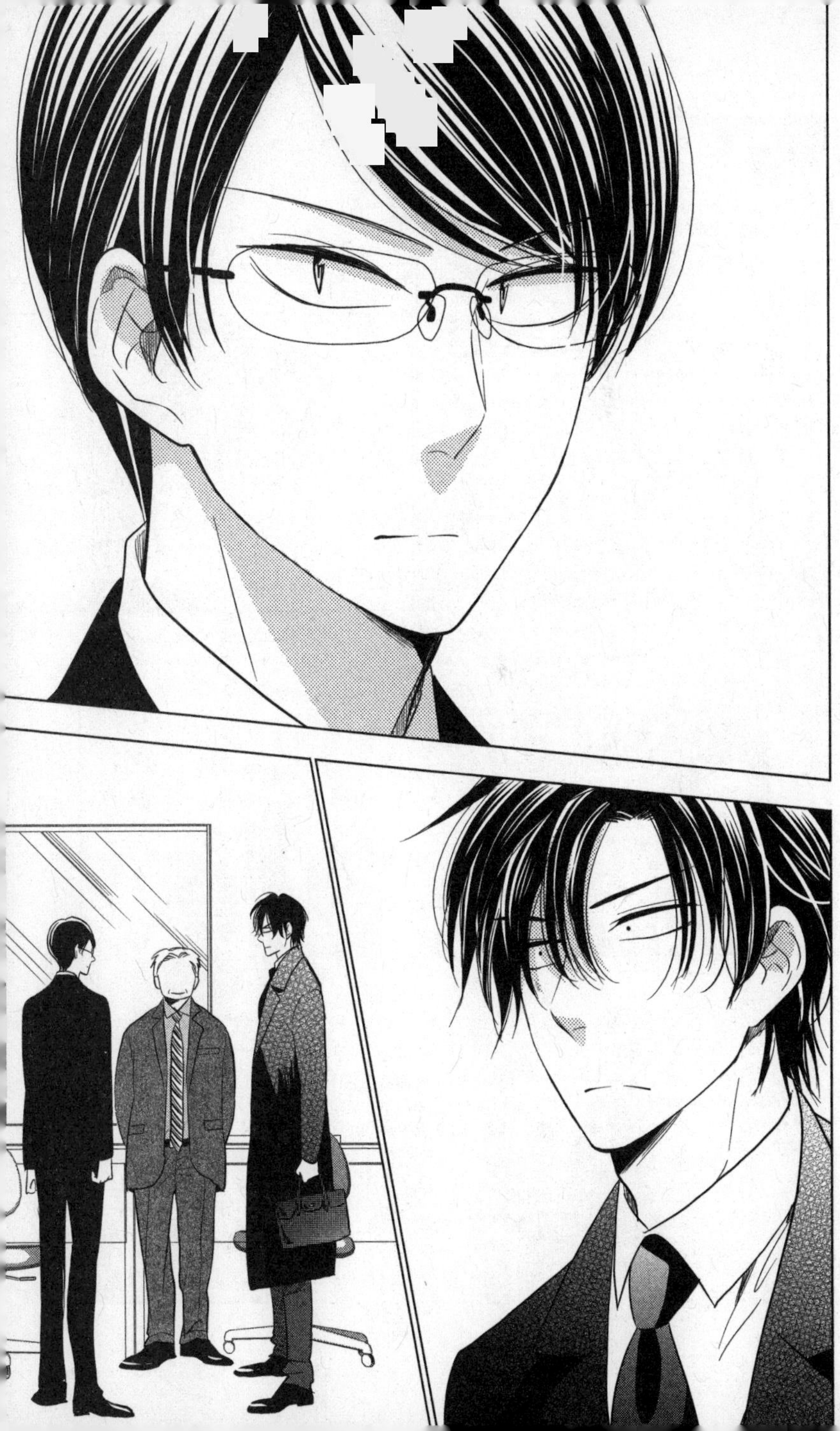

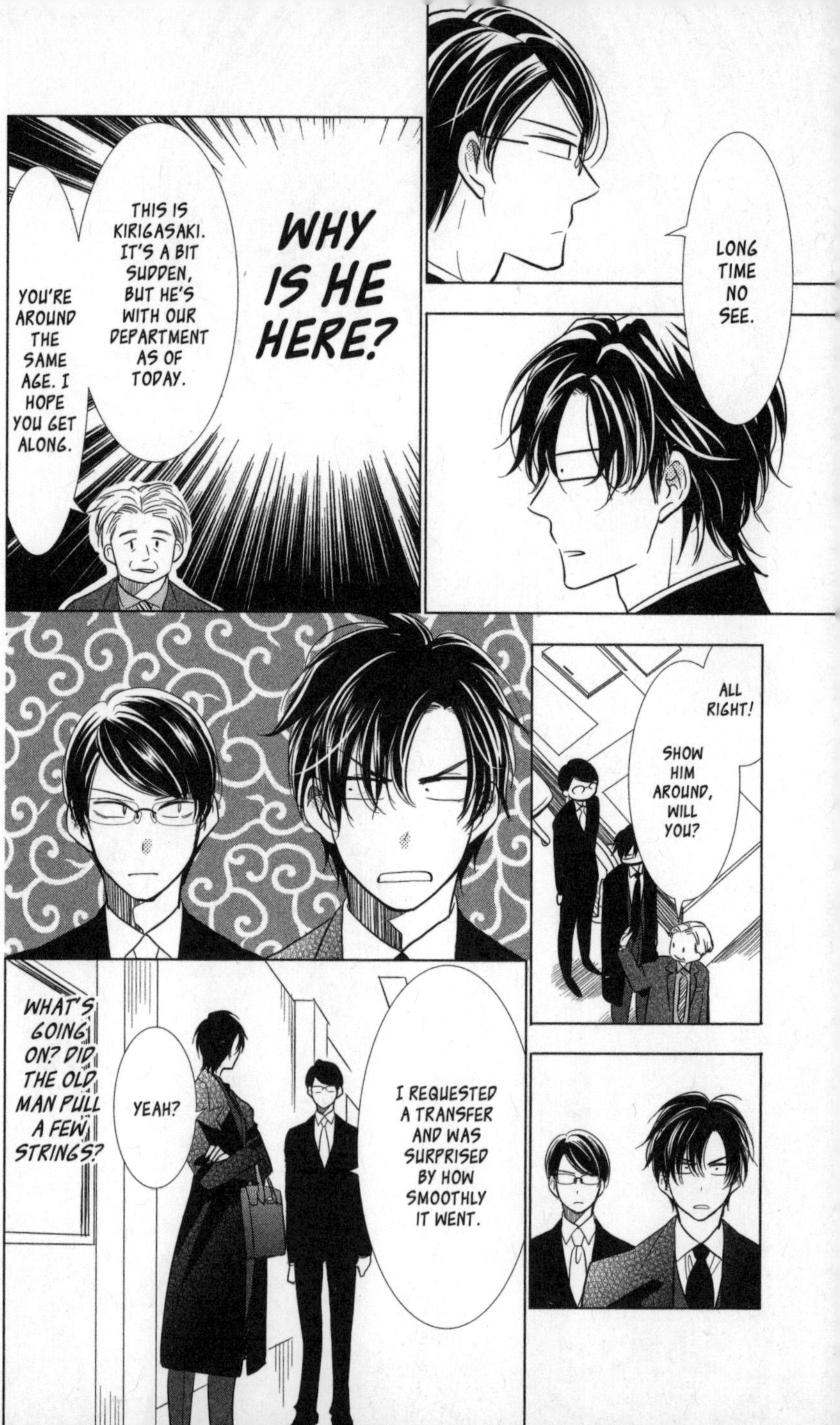
LONG TIME NO SEE.
WHY IS HE HERE?
THIS IS KIRIGASAKI. IT'S A BIT SUDDEN, BUT HE'S WITH OUR DEPARTMENT AS OF TODAY.
YOU'RE AROUND THE SAME AGE. I HOPE YOU GET ALONG.
ALL RIGHT!
SHOW HIM AROUND, WILL YOU?
I REQUESTED A TRANSFER AND WAS SURPRISED BY HOW SMOOTHLY IT WENT.
YEAH?
WHAT'S GOING ON? DID THE OLD MAN PULL A FEW STRINGS?

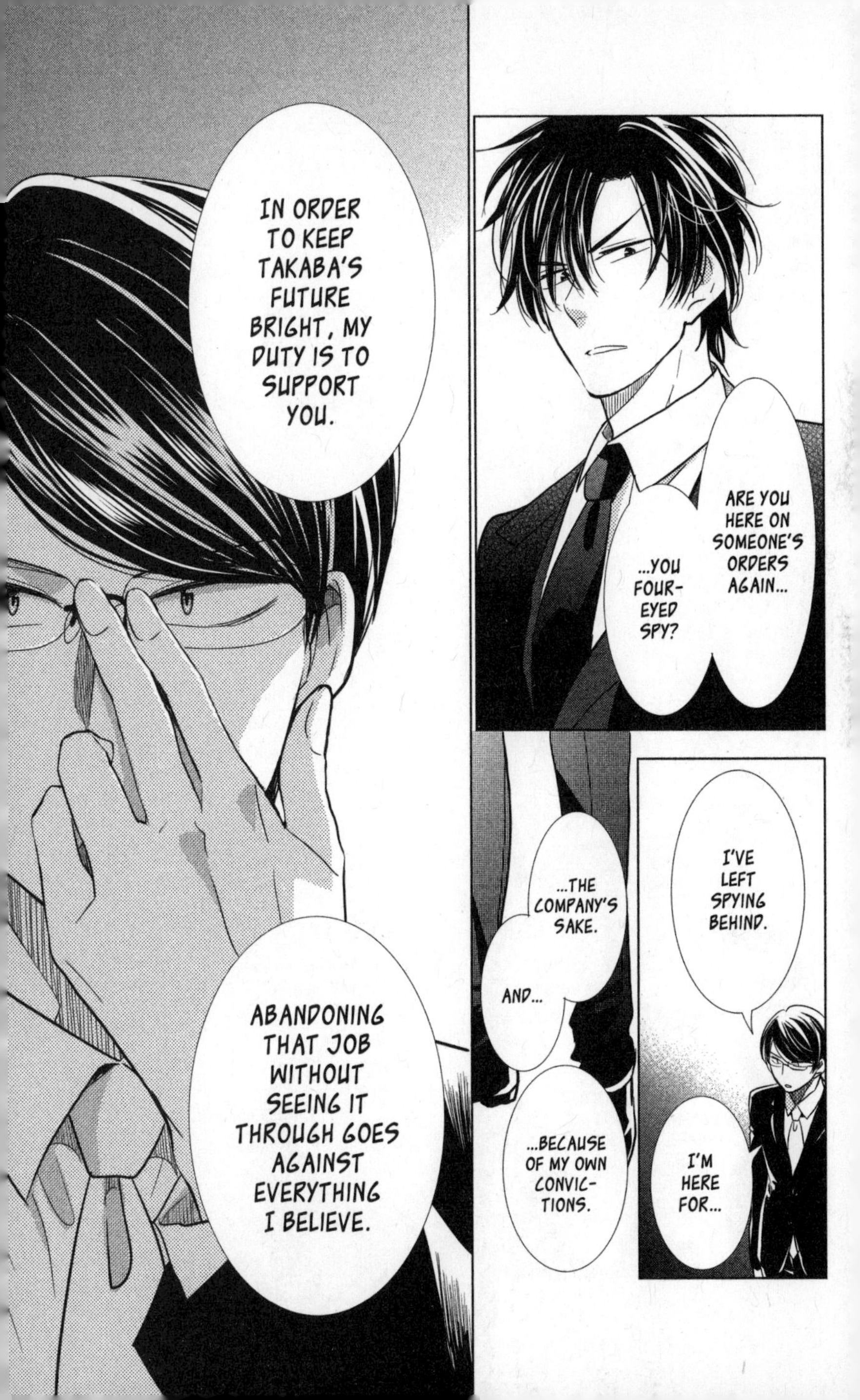

ARE YOU HERE ON SOMEONE'S ORDERS AGAIN...
...YOU FOUR-EYED SPY?
I'VE LEFT SPYING BEHIND.
I'M HERE FOR...
...THE COMPANY'S SAKE.
AND...
...BECAUSE OF MY OWN CONVIC-TIONS.
IN ORDER TO KEEP TAKABA'S FUTURE BRIGHT, MY DUTY IS TO SUPPORT YOU.
ABANDONING THAT JOB WITHOUT SEEING IT THROUGH GOES AGAINST EVERYTHING I BELIEVE.

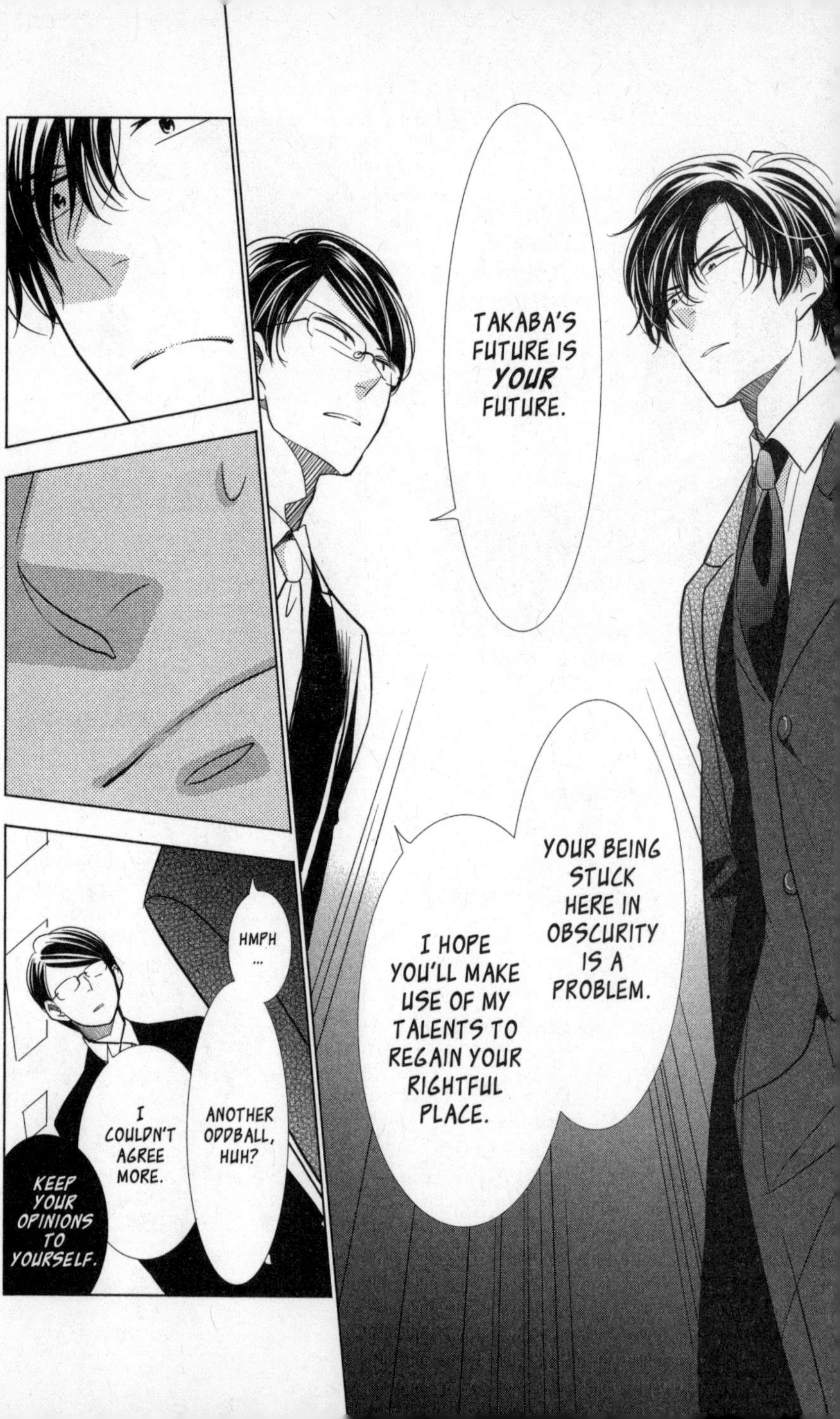
TAKABA'S FUTURE IS YOUR FUTURE.
YOUR BEING STUCK HERE IN OBSCURITY IS A PROBLEM.
I HOPE YOU'LL MAKE USE OF MY TALENTS TO REGAIN YOUR RIGHTFUL PLACE.
HMPH ...
ANOTHER ODDBALL, HUH?
I COULDN'T AGREE MORE.
KEEP YOUR OPINIONS TO YOURSELF.

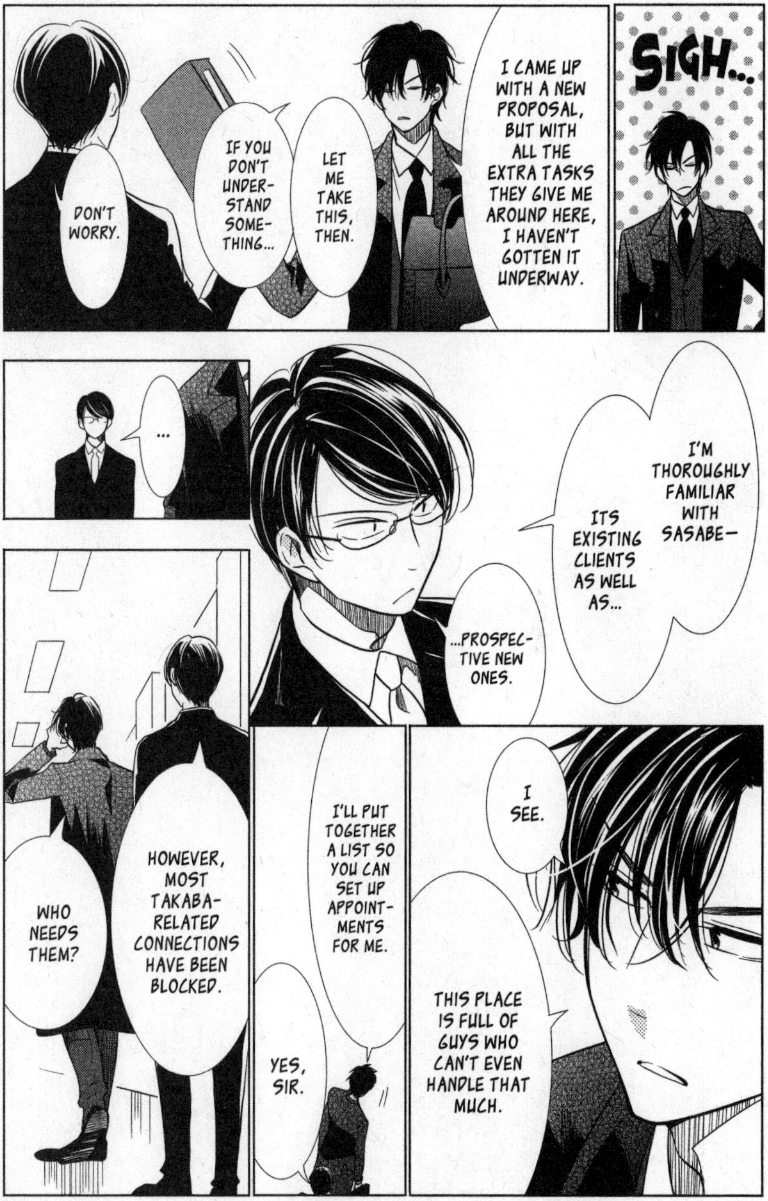
SIGH...
I CAME UP WITH A NEW PROPOSAL, BUT WITH ALL THE EXTRA TASKS THEY GIVE ME AROUND HERE, I HAVEN'T GOTTEN IT UNDERWAY.
LET ME TAKE THIS, THEN.
IF YOU DON'T UNDER-STAND SOME-THING...
DON'T WORRY.
I'M THOROUGHLY FAMILIAR WITH SASABE—
ITS EXISTING CLIENTS AS WELL AS...
...PROSPEC-TIVE NEW ONES.
...
I SEE.
THIS PLACE IS FULL OF GUYS WHO CAN'T EVEN HANDLE THAT MUCH.
I'LL PUT TOGETHER A LIST SO YOU CAN SET UP APPOINT-MENTS FOR ME.
YES, SIR.
HOWEVER, MOST TAKABA-RELATED CONNECTIONS HAVE BEEN BLOCKED.
WHO NEEDS THEM?

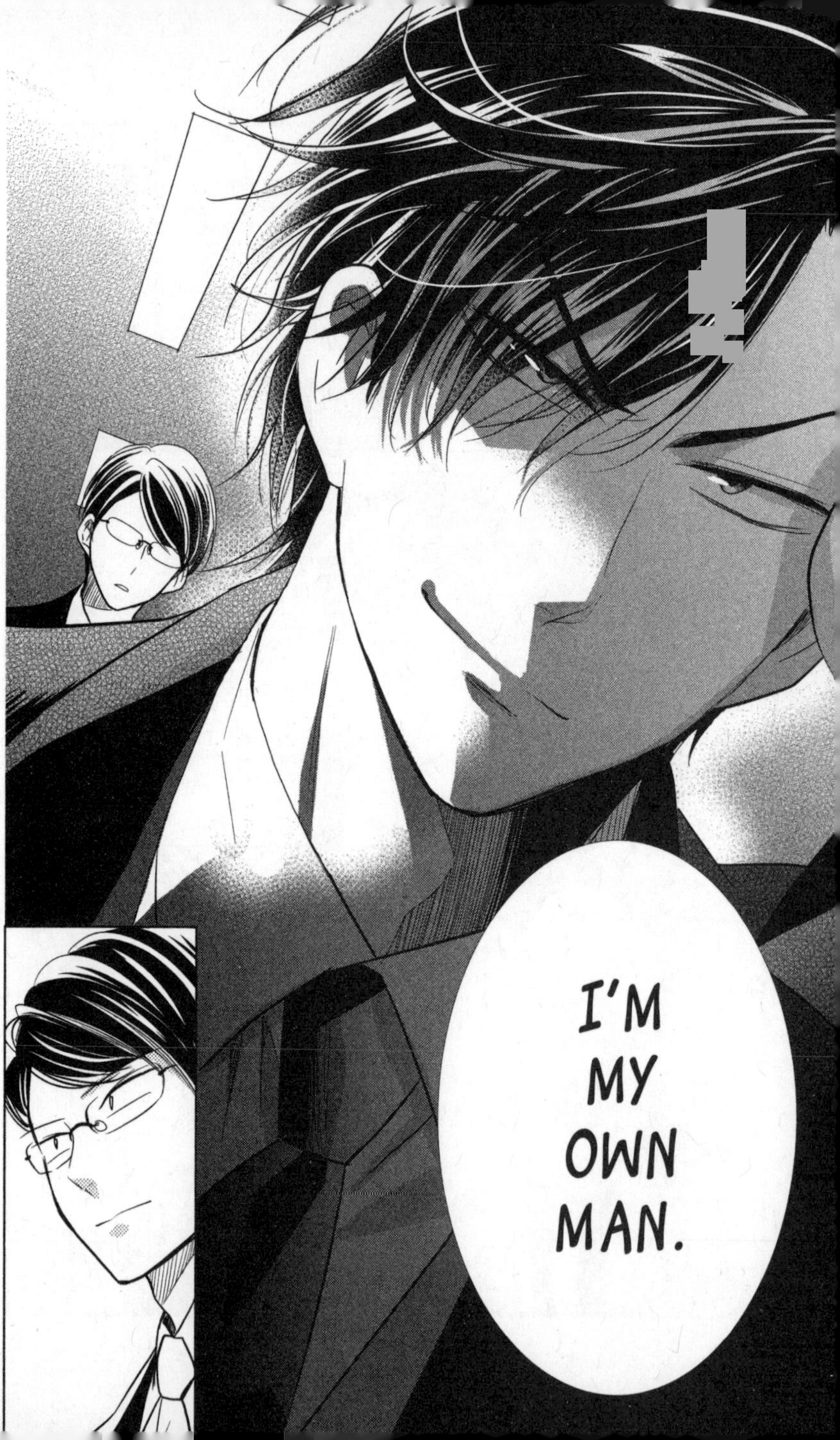
I'M MY OWN MAN.

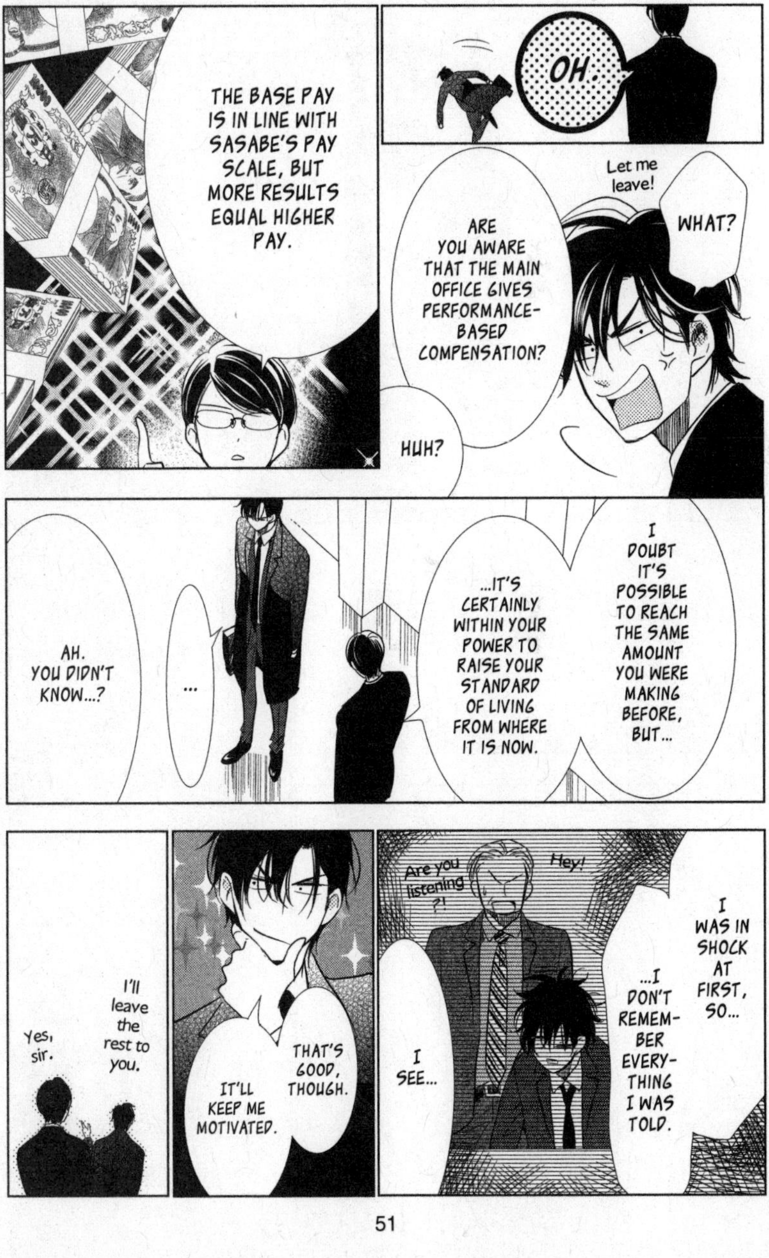
OH.
Let me leave!
WHAT?
ARE YOU AWARE THAT THE MAIN OFFICE GIVES PERFORMANCE-BASED COMPENSATION?
HUH?
THE BASE PAY IS IN LINE WITH SASABE'S PAY SCALE, BUT MORE RESULTS EQUAL HIGHER PAY.
I DOUBT IT'S POSSIBLE TO REACH THE SAME AMOUNT YOU WERE MAKING BEFORE, BUT...
...IT'S CERTAINLY WITHIN YOUR POWER TO RAISE YOUR STANDARD OF LIVING FROM WHERE IT IS NOW.
...
AH. YOU DIDN'T KNOW...?
I WAS IN SHOCK AT FIRST, SO...
Hey!
...I DON'T REMEM-BER EVERY-THING I WAS TOLD.
Are you listening?!
I SEE...
THAT'S GOOD, THOUGH.
IT'LL KEEP ME MOTIVATED.
I'll leave the rest to you.
Yes, sir.

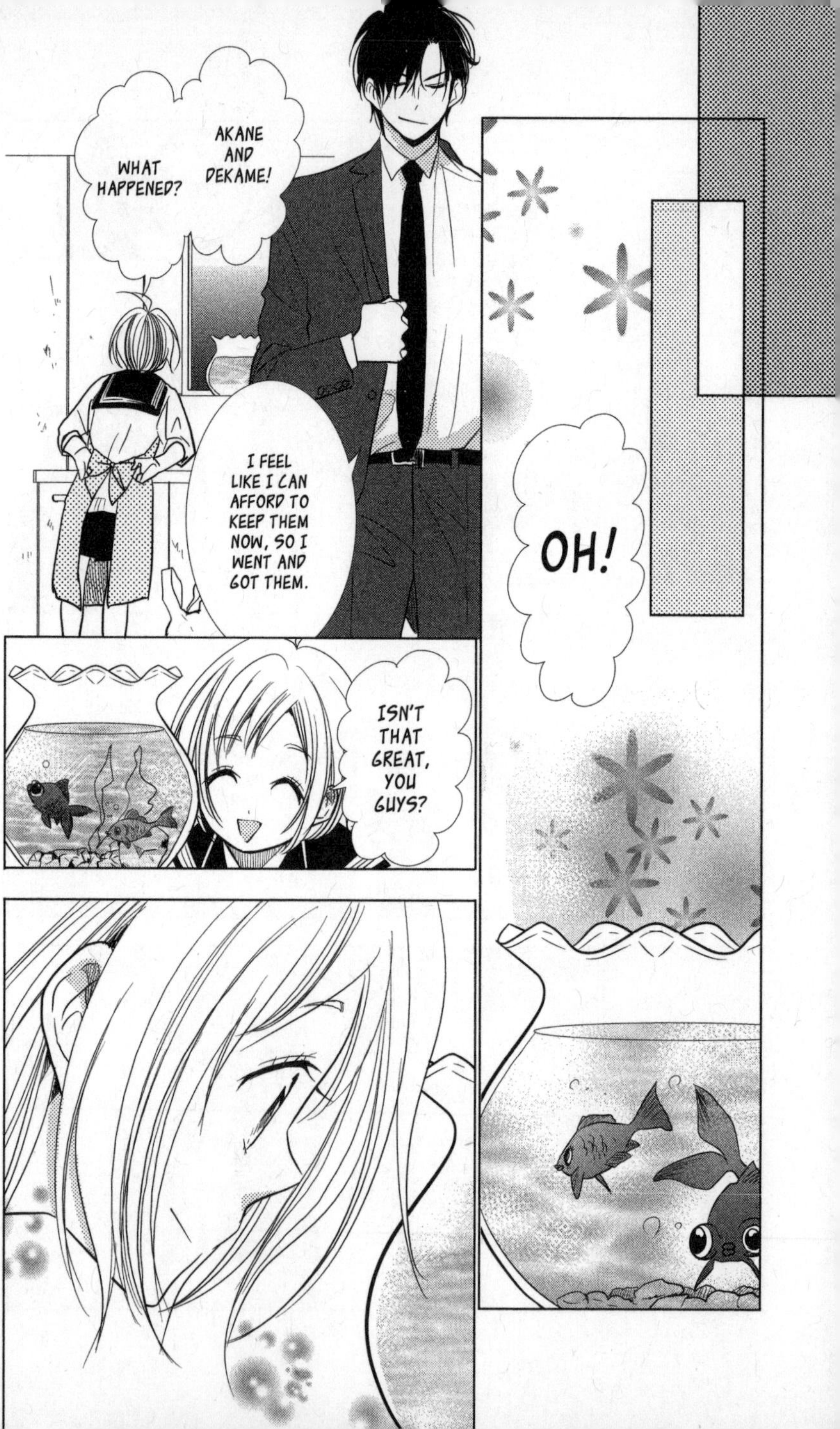
OH!
AKANE AND DEKAME!
WHAT HAPPENED?
I FEEL LIKE I CAN AFFORD TO KEEP THEM NOW, SO I WENT AND GOT THEM.
ISN'T THAT GREAT, YOU GUYS?

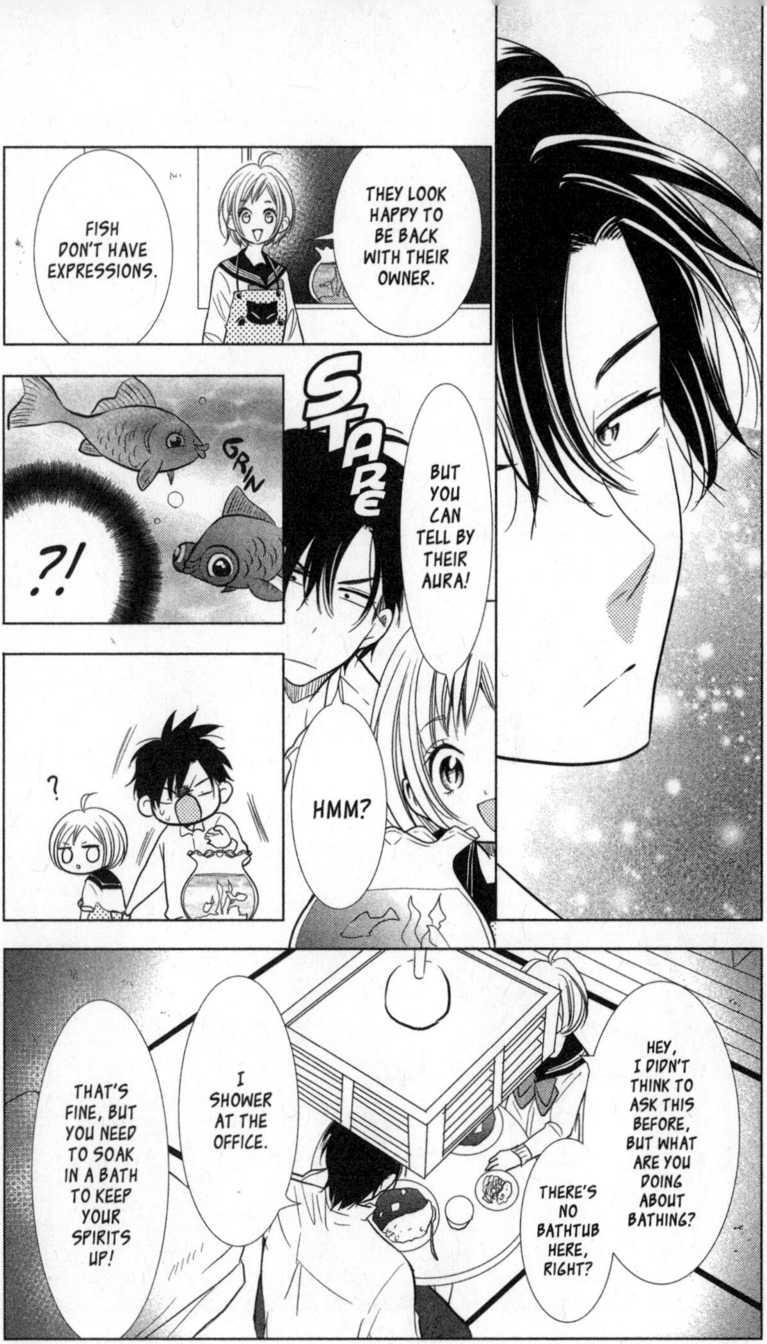

THEY LOOK HAPPY TO BE BACK WITH THEIR OWNER.
FISH DON'T HAVE EXPRESSIONS.
STARE
BUT YOU CAN TELL BY THEIR AURA!
GRIN
?!
HMM?
?
HEY, I DIDN'T THINK TO ASK THIS BEFORE, BUT WHAT ARE YOU DOING ABOUT BATHING?
THERE'S NO BATHTUB HERE, RIGHT?
I SHOWER AT THE OFFICE.
THAT'S FINE, BUT YOU NEED TO SOAK IN A BATH TO KEEP YOUR SPIRITS UP!

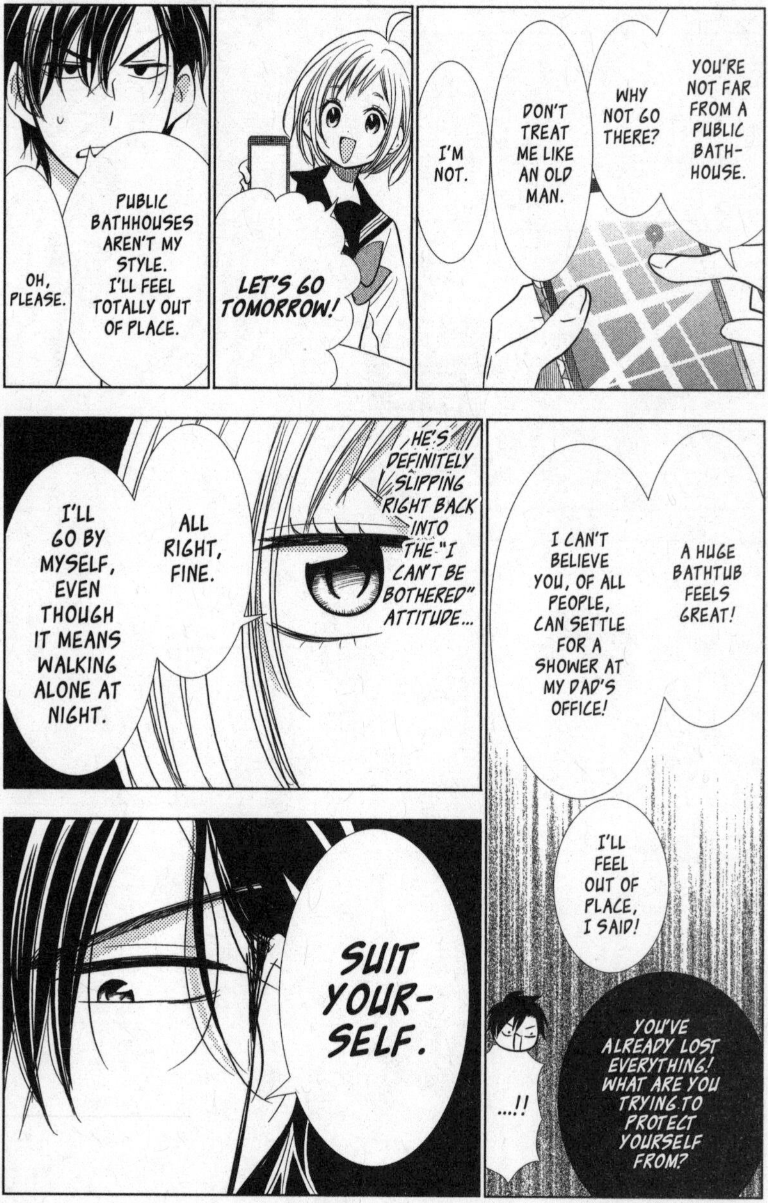
YOU'RE NOT FAR FROM A PUBLIC BATH-HOUSE.
WHY NOT GO THERE?
DON'T TREAT ME LIKE AN OLD MAN.
I'M NOT.
LET'S GO TOMORROW!
PUBLIC BATHHOUSES AREN'T MY STYLE. I'LL FEEL TOTALLY OUT OF PLACE.
OH, PLEASE.
A HUGE BATHTUB FEELS GREAT!
I CAN'T BELIEVE YOU, OF ALL PEOPLE, CAN SETTLE FOR A SHOWER AT MY DAD'S OFFICE!
I'LL FEEL OUT OF PLACE, I SAID!
YOU'VE ALREADY LOST EVERYTHING! WHAT ARE YOU TRYING TO PROTECT YOURSELF FROM?
...!!
HE'S DEFINITELY SLIPPING RIGHT BACK INTO THE "I CAN'T BE BOTHERED" ATTITUDE...
ALL RIGHT, FINE.
I'LL GO BY MYSELF, EVEN THOUGH IT MEANS WALKING ALONE AT NIGHT.
SUIT YOURSELF.

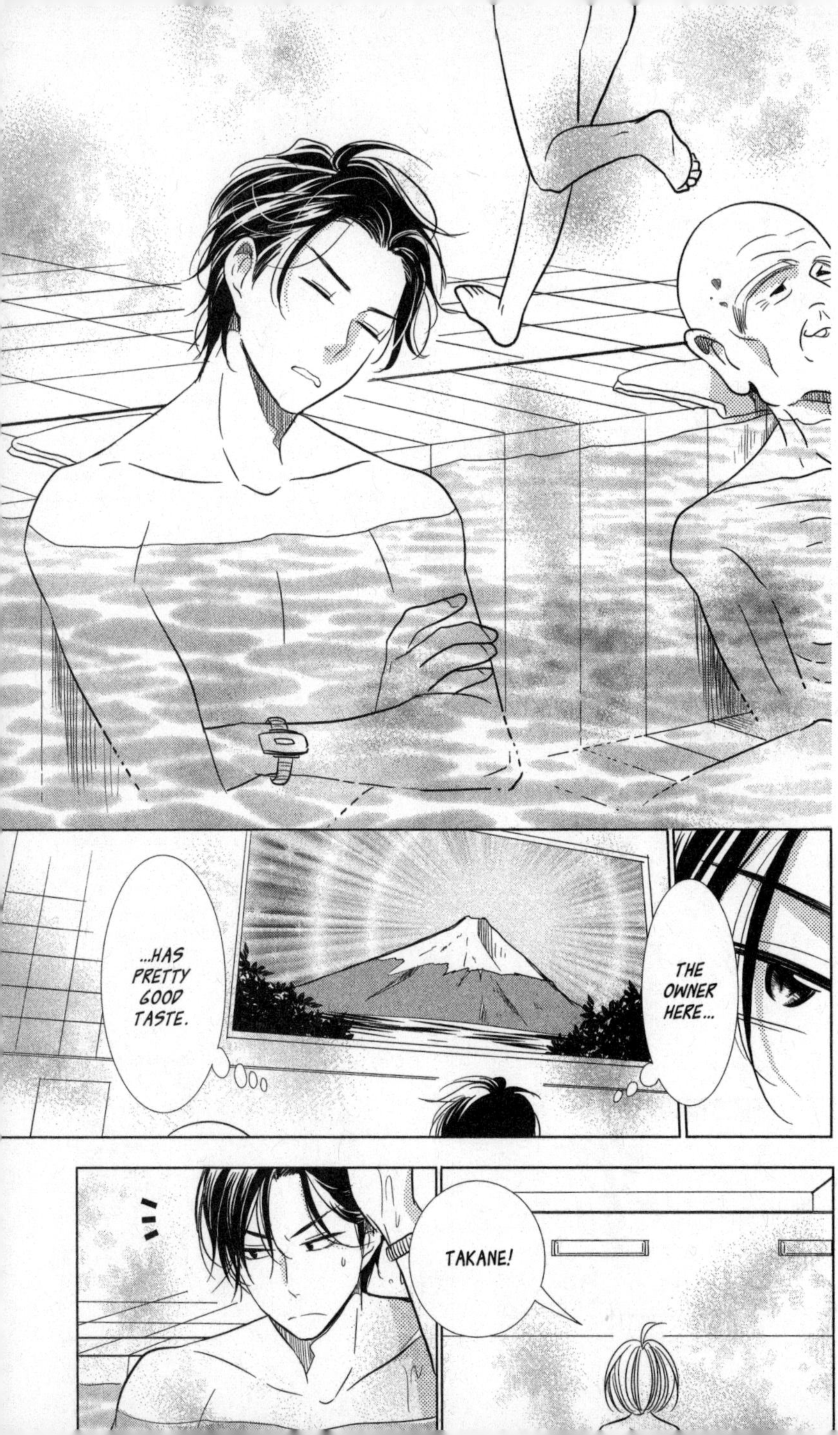
THE OWNER HERE...
...HAS PRETTY GOOD TASTE.
TAKANE!

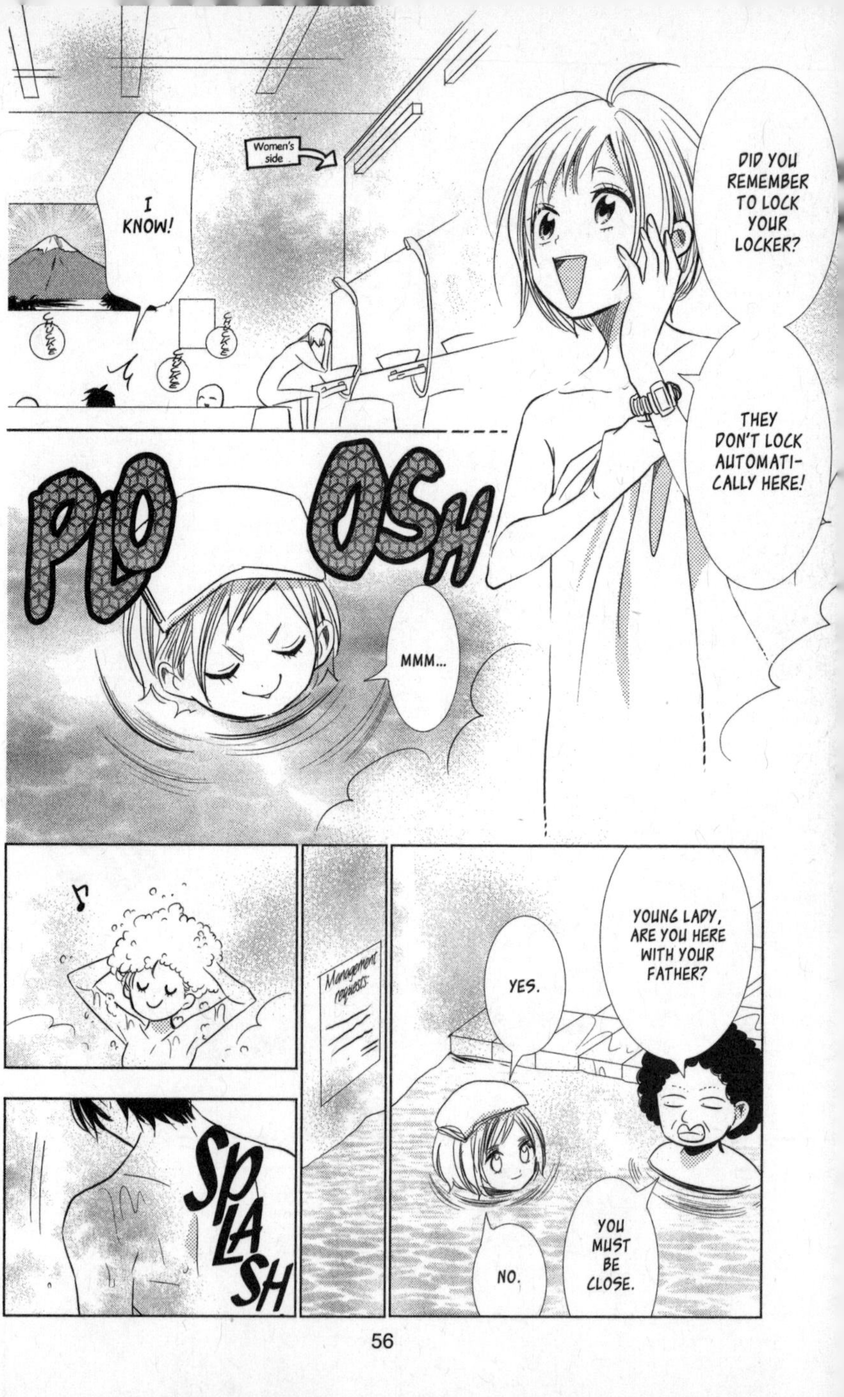
DID YOU REMEMBER TO LOCK YOUR LOCKER?
THEY DON'T LOCK AUTOMATI-CALLY HERE!
Women's side
I KNOW!
CHUCKLE
CHUCKLE
CHUCKLE
PLOOSH
MMM...
YOUNG LADY, ARE YOU HERE WITH YOUR FATHER?
YES.
YOU MUST BE CLOSE.
NO.
Management requests:
SPLASH

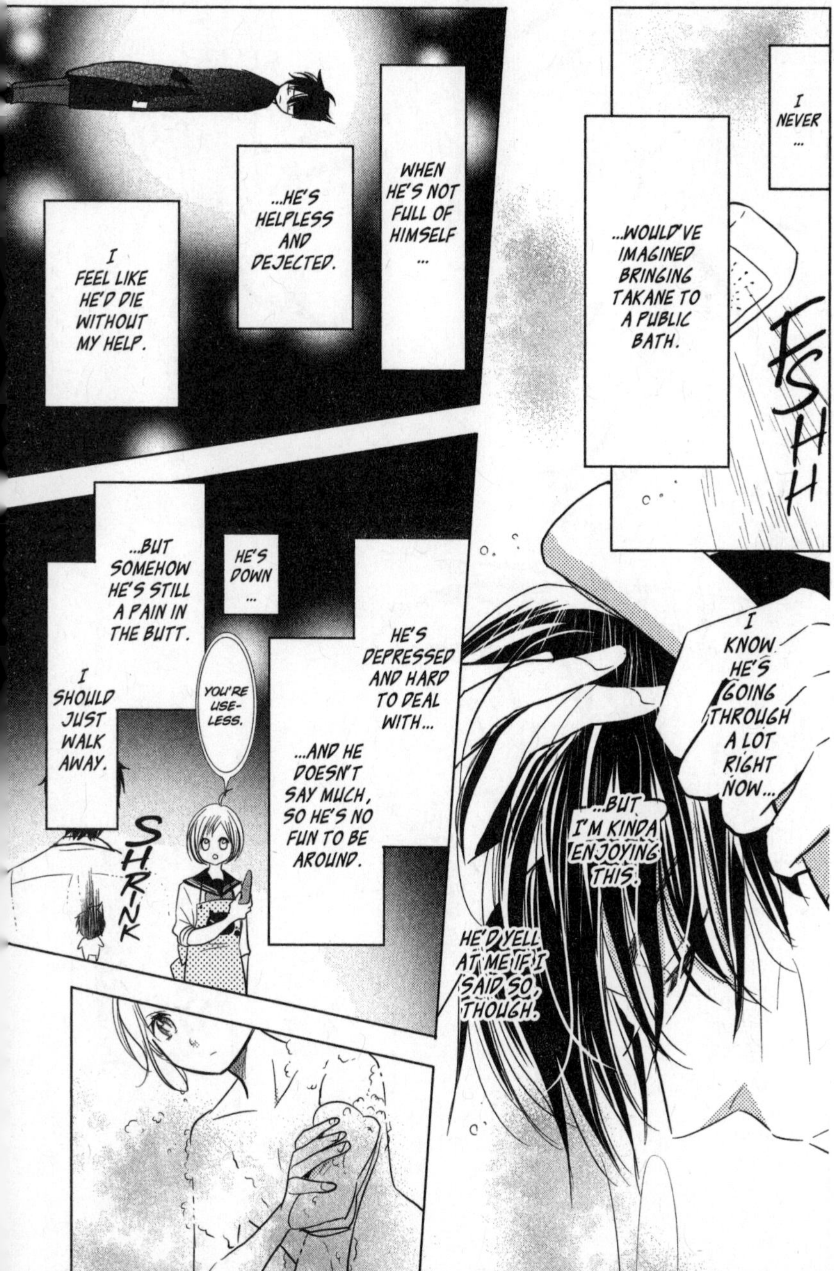
I NEVER ...
...WOULD'VE IMAGINED BRINGING TAKANE TO A PUBLIC BATH.
FSHH
I KNOW HE'S GOING THROUGH A LOT RIGHT NOW...
...BUT I'M KINDA ENJOYING THIS.
HE'D YELL AT ME IF I SAID SO, THOUGH.
WHEN HE'S NOT FULL OF HIMSELF ...
...HE'S HELPLESS AND DEJECTED.
I FEEL LIKE HE'D DIE WITHOUT MY HELP.
HE'S DOWN ...
...BUT SOMEHOW HE'S STILL A PAIN IN THE BUTT.
HE'S DEPRESSED AND HARD TO DEAL WITH...
...AND HE DOESN'T SAY MUCH, SO HE'S NO FUN TO BE AROUND.
I SHOULD JUST WALK AWAY.
YOU'RE USELESS.
SHRINK

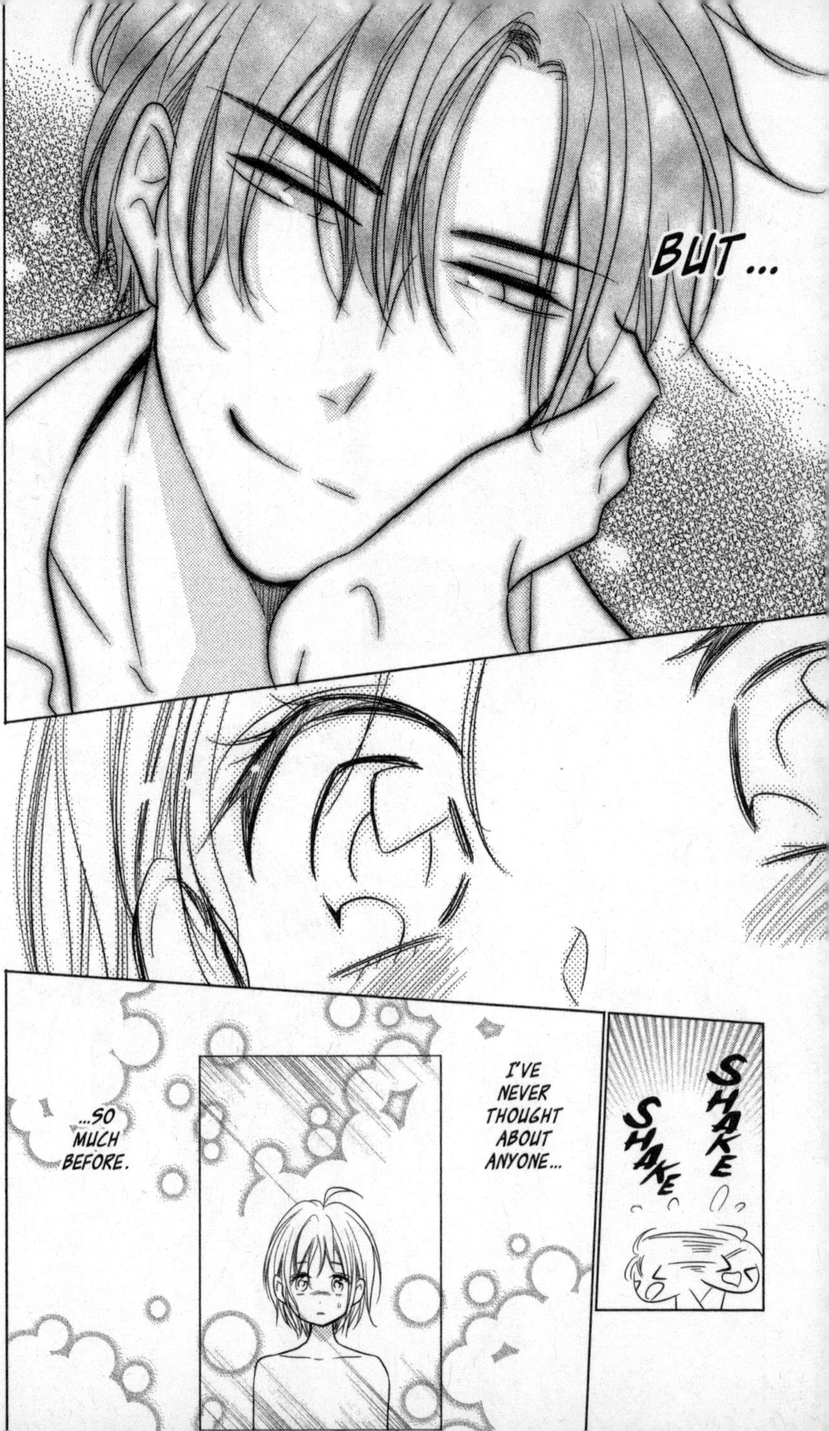
BUT...
SHAKE
SHAKE
I'VE NEVER THOUGHT ABOUT ANYONE...
...SO MUCH BEFORE.

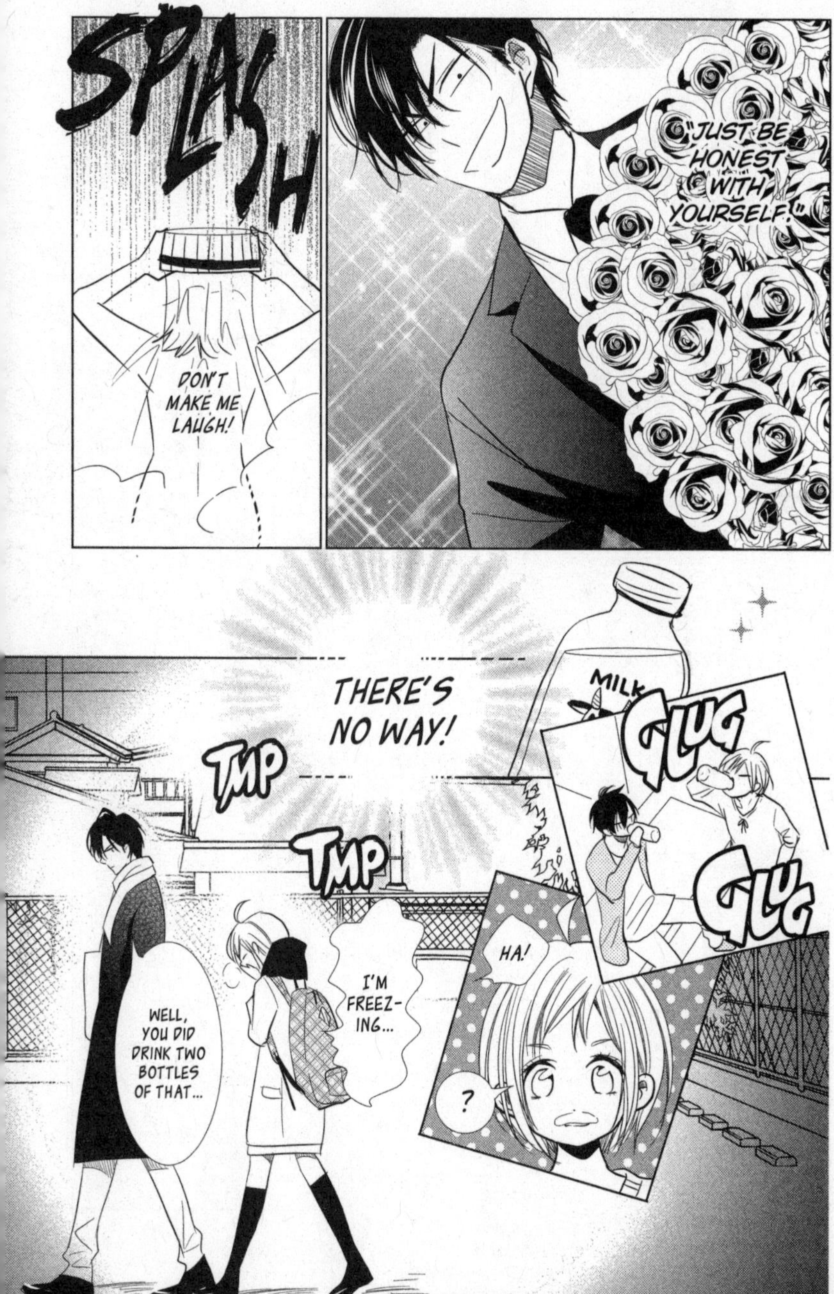
"JUST BE HONEST WITH YOURSELF!"
SPLASH
DON'T MAKE ME LAUGH!
THERE'S NO WAY!
MILK
GLUG
GLUG
HA!
?
TMP
TMP
I'M FREEZ-ING...
WELL, YOU DID DRINK TWO BOTTLES OF THAT...

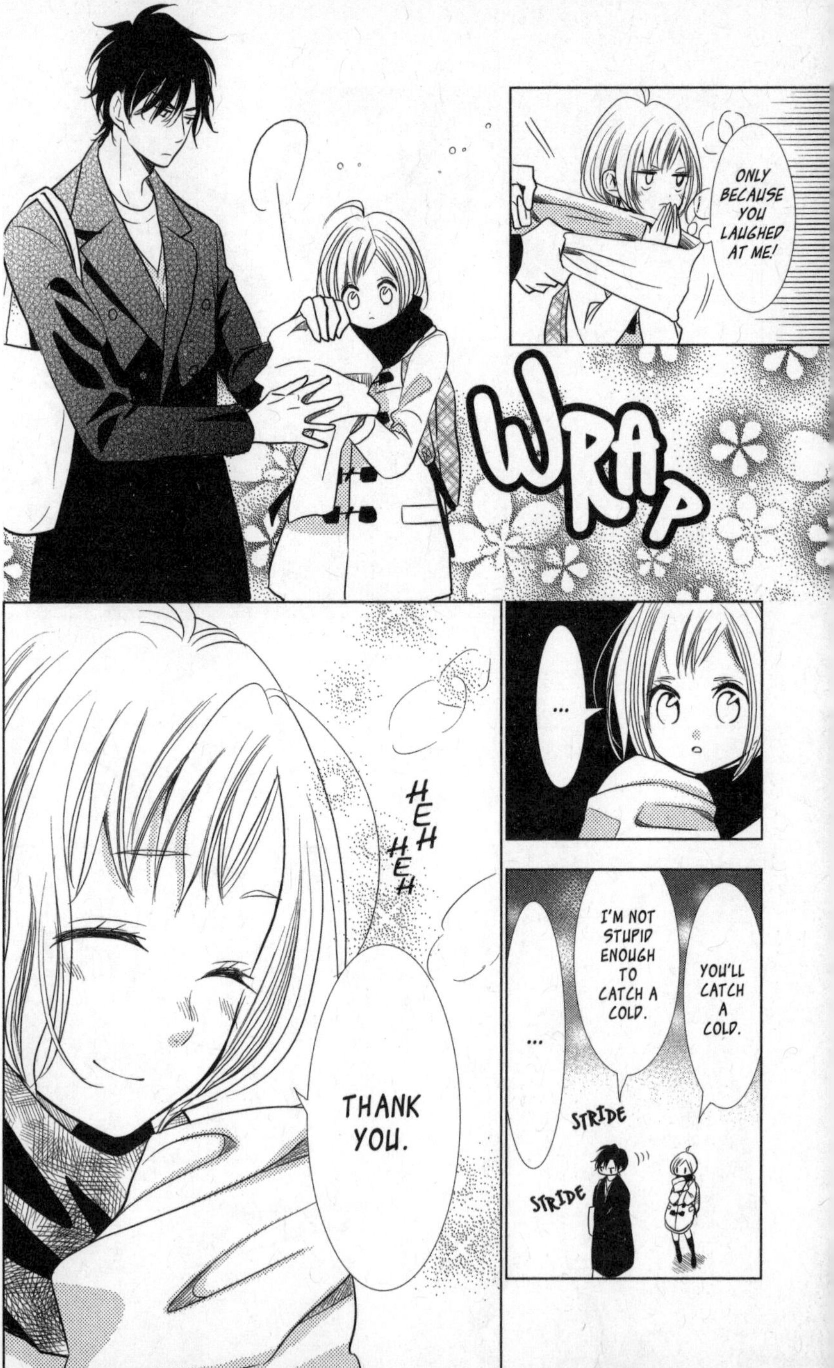
ONLY BECAUSE YOU LAUGHED AT ME!
WRAP
...
YOU'LL CATCH A COLD.
I'M NOT STUPID ENOUGH TO CATCH A COLD.
...
STRIDE
STRIDE
HEH HEH
THANK YOU.

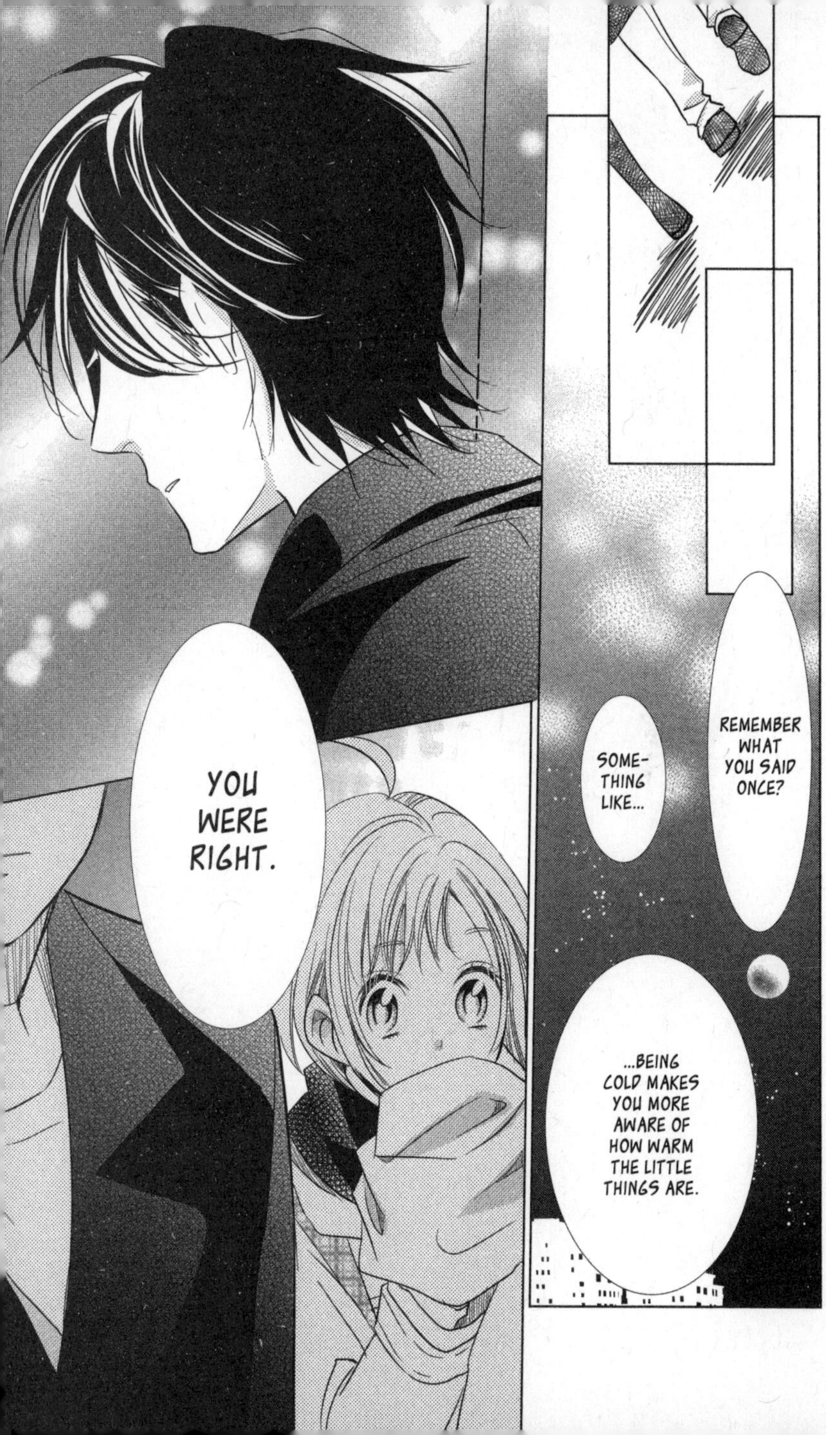
REMEMBER WHAT YOU SAID ONCE?
SOME-THING LIKE...
...BEING COLD MAKES YOU MORE AWARE OF HOW WARM THE LITTLE THINGS ARE.
YOU WERE RIGHT.

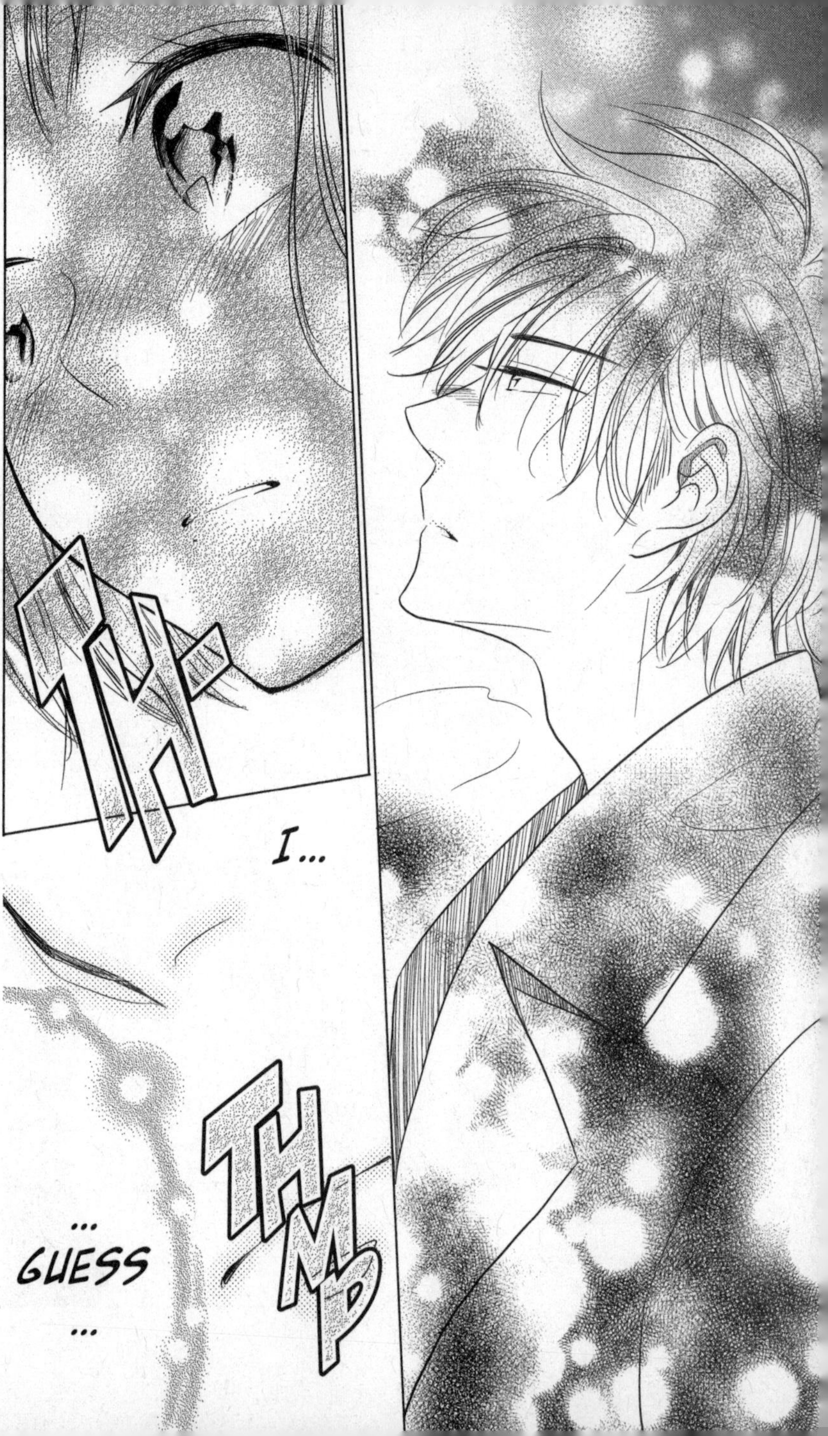
THMP
I...
THMP
... GUESS ...

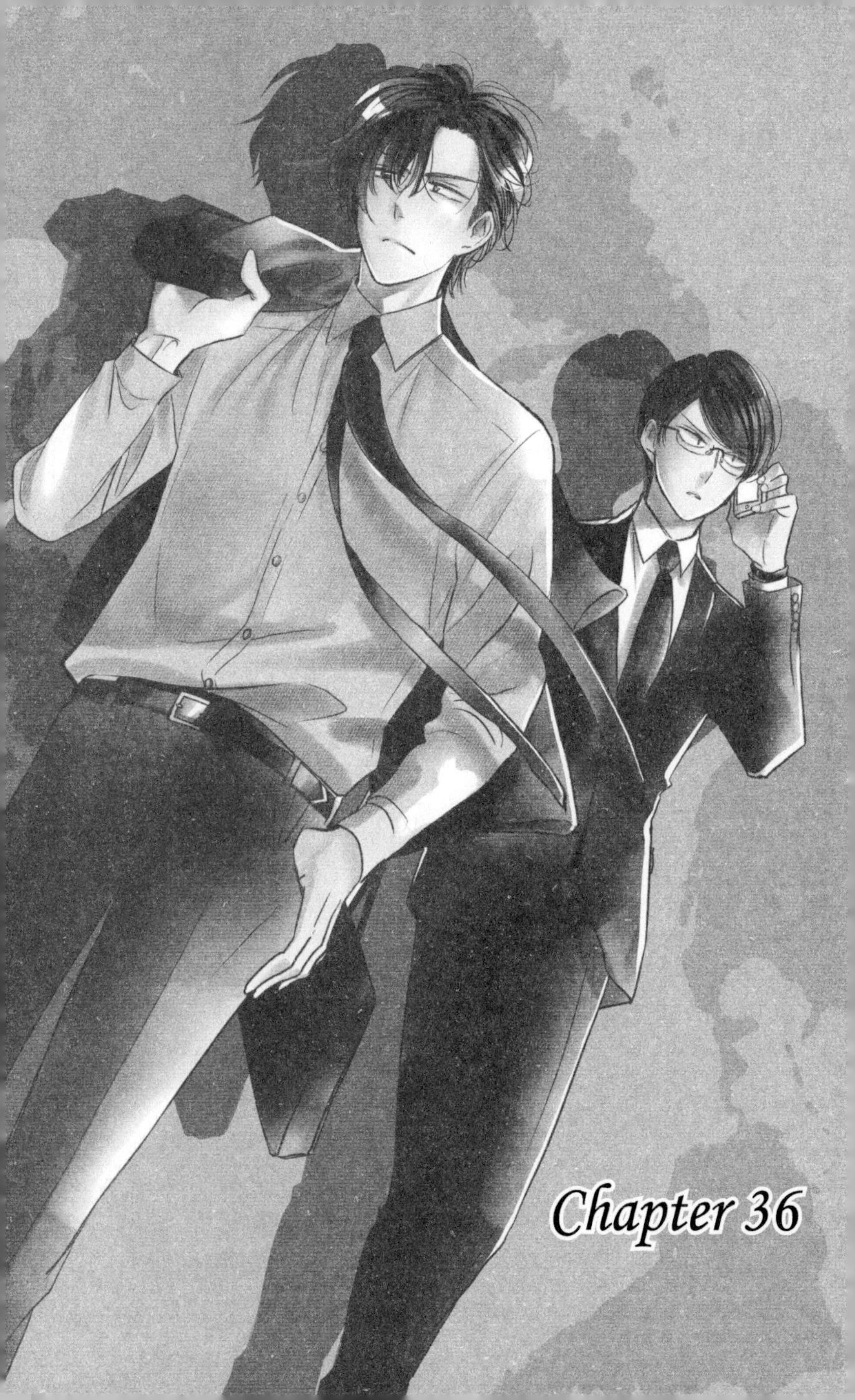
Chapter 36

Reading Each Other's Minds

HEY ...
TENMA KEEPS CRYING. I WONDER WHAT'S WRONG?
WAAH!
HMM?
AH HA HA HA HA!
TEN STARTS CRYING WHEN KAZU CRIES.
THAT DOESN'T SEEM TO BE WHAT'S GOING ON.
ARE YOU HURT SOME-WHERE, TEN?
There, there.
SOUMA ...
...HAS ANYTHING PAINFUL HAPPENED TO *YOU*?
IF HE CRIES WHEN ONE BROTHER DOES...
HUH?
...MAYBE TENMA CAN ALSO TELL IF *YOU'RE* HURTING.
?!
WAAH!

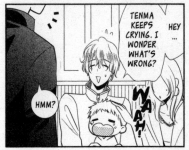

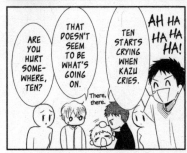

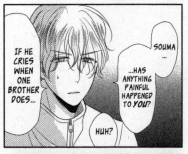

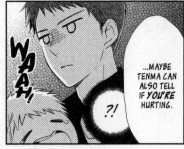

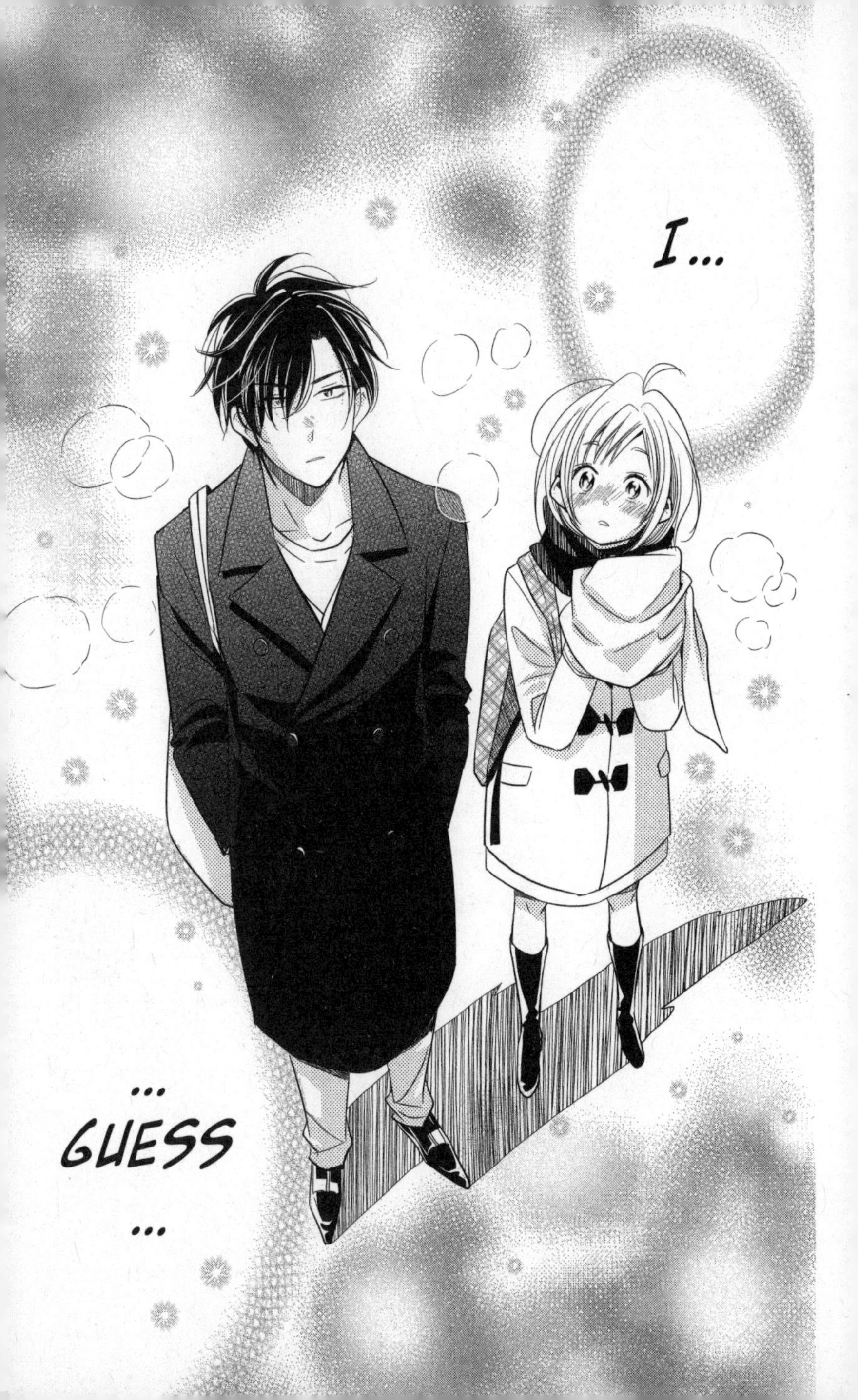
I...
...GUESS...

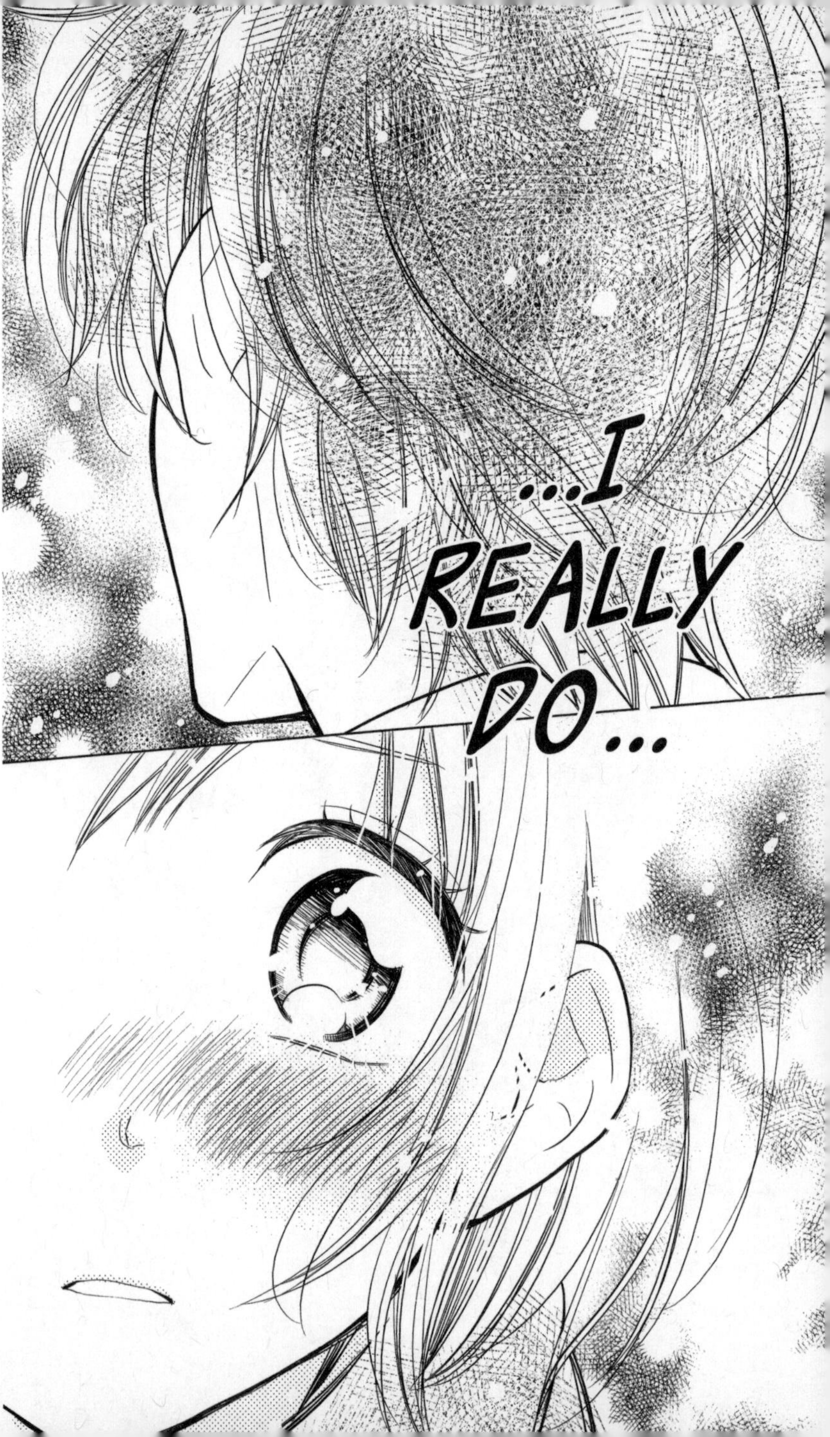
...I REALLY DO...

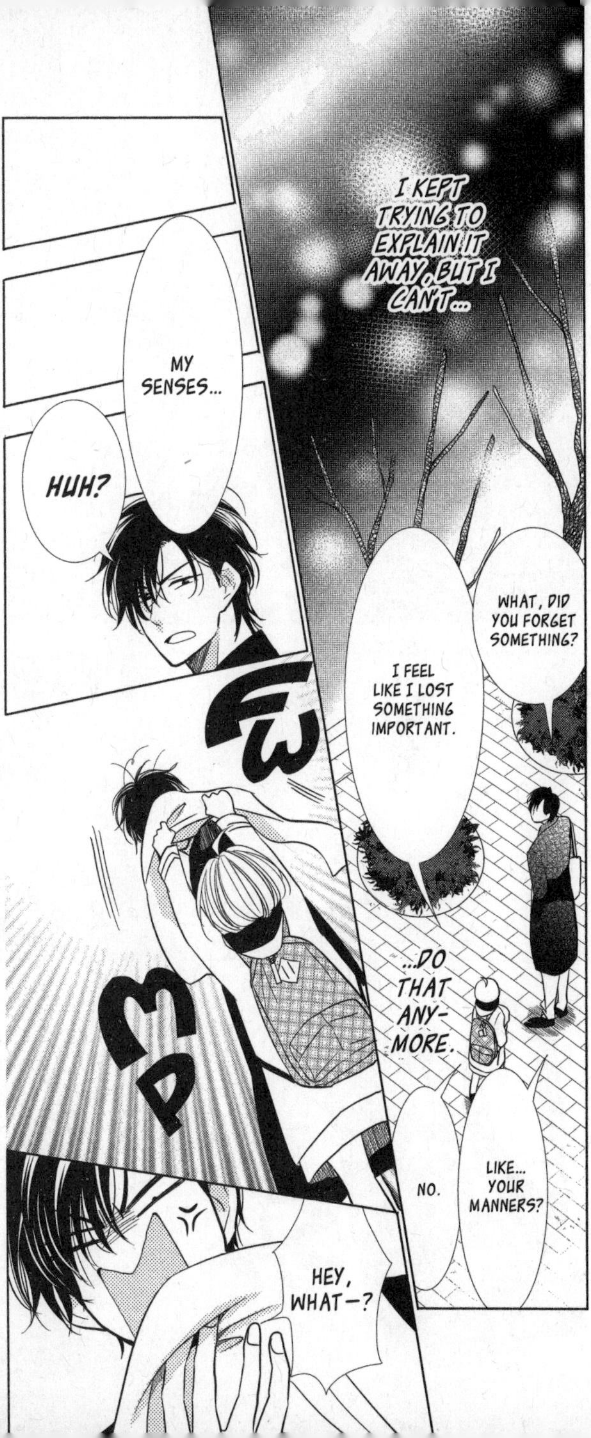
I KEPT TRYING TO EXPLAIN IT AWAY, BUT I CAN'T...
WHAT, DID YOU FORGET SOMETHING?
I FEEL LIKE I LOST SOMETHING IMPORTANT.
...DO THAT ANY-MORE.
LIKE... YOUR MANNERS?
NO.
MY SENSES...
HUH?
FWP
HEY, WHAT—?

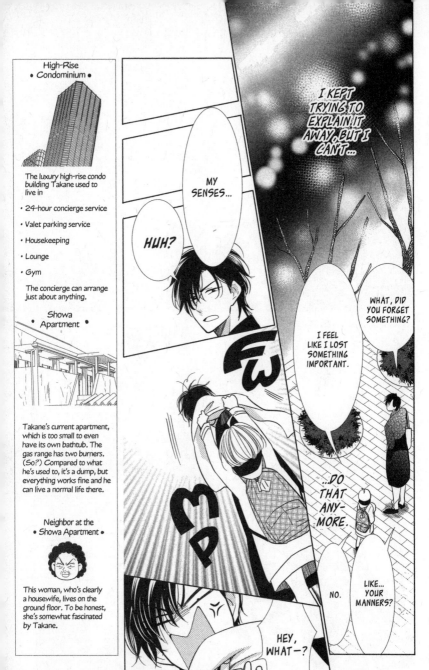

High-Rise
• Condominium •

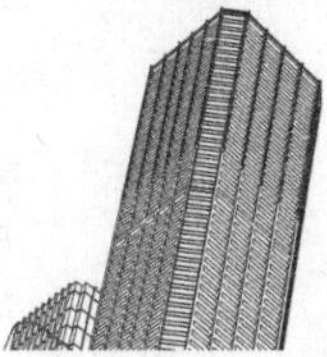

The luxury high-rise condo building Takane used to live in

- 24-hour concierge service
- Valet parking service
- Housekeeping
- Lounge
- Gym

The concierge can arrange just about anything.

Showa
• Apartment •

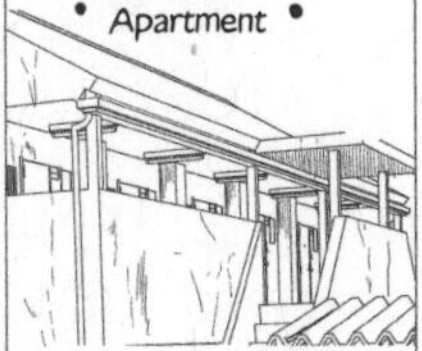

Takane's current apartment, which is too small to even have its own bathtub. The gas range has two burners. (So?) Compared to what he's used to, it's a dump, but everything works fine and he can live a normal life there.

Neighbor at the
• Showa Apartment •

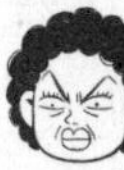

This woman, who's clearly a housewife, lives on the ground floor. To be honest, she's somewhat fascinated by Takane.

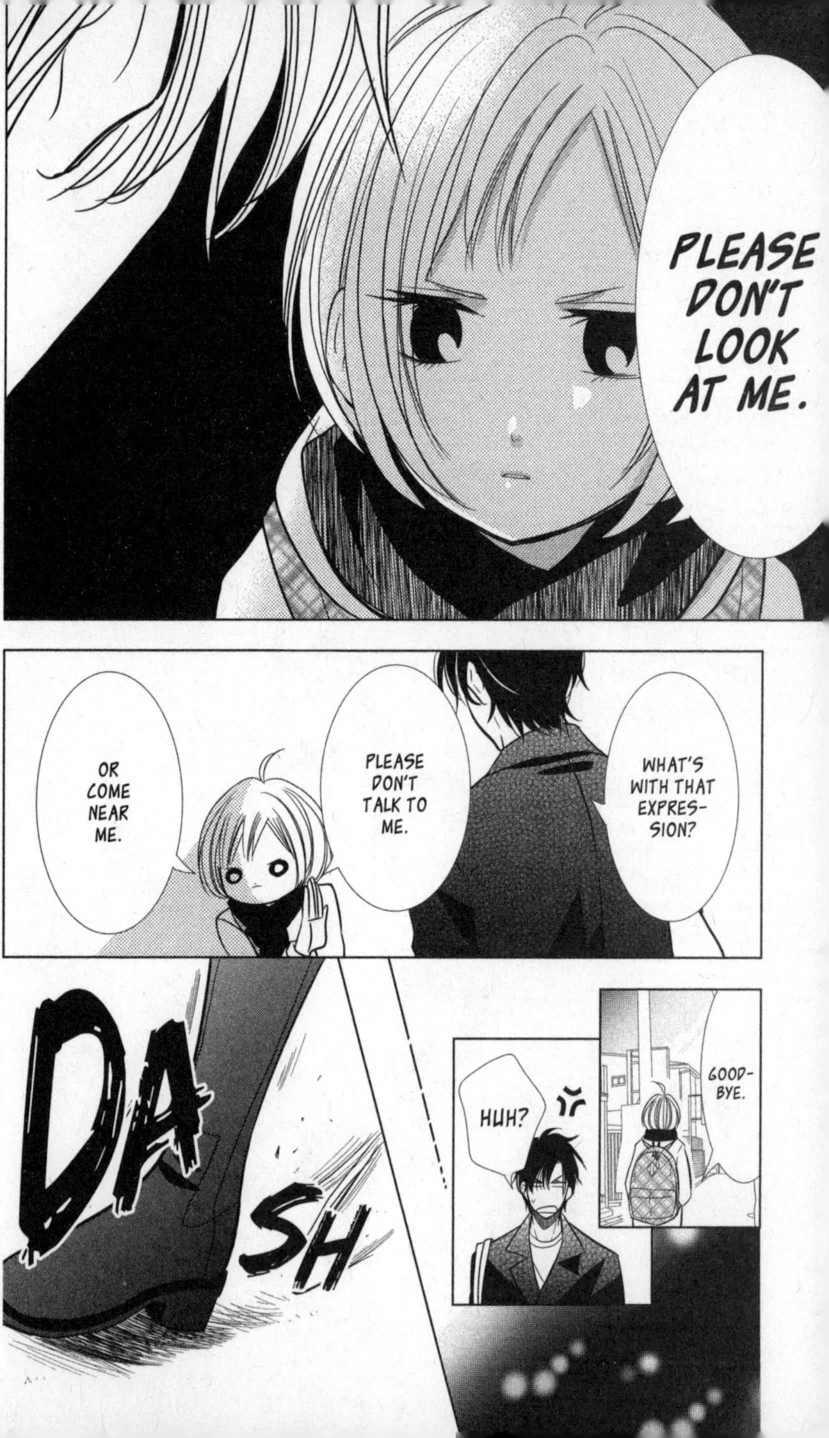
PLEASE DON'T LOOK AT ME.
WHAT'S WITH THAT EXPRES-SION?
PLEASE DON'T TALK TO ME.
OR COME NEAR ME.
GOOD-BYE.
HUH?
DASH

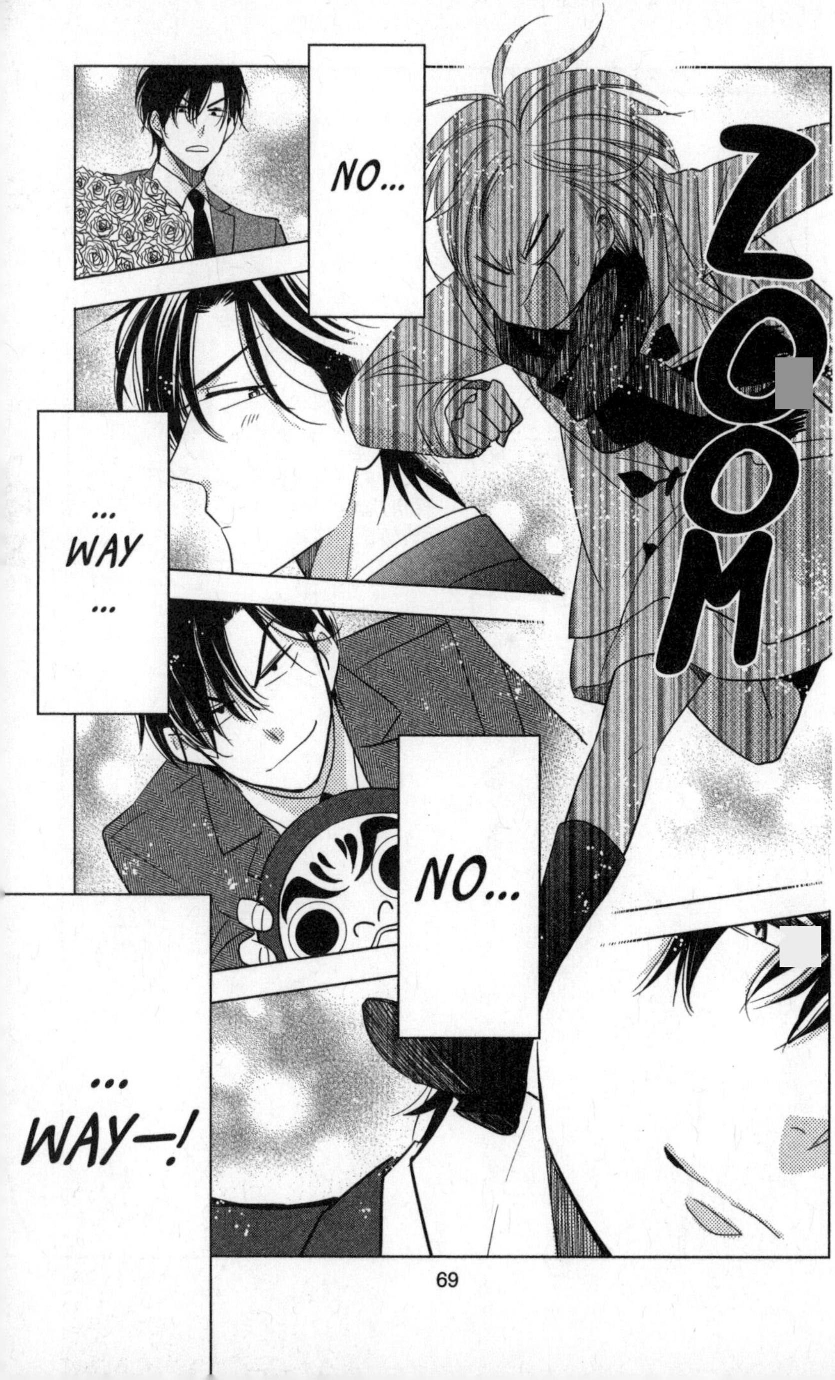
ZOOM
NO...
... WAY ...
NO...
... WAY—!

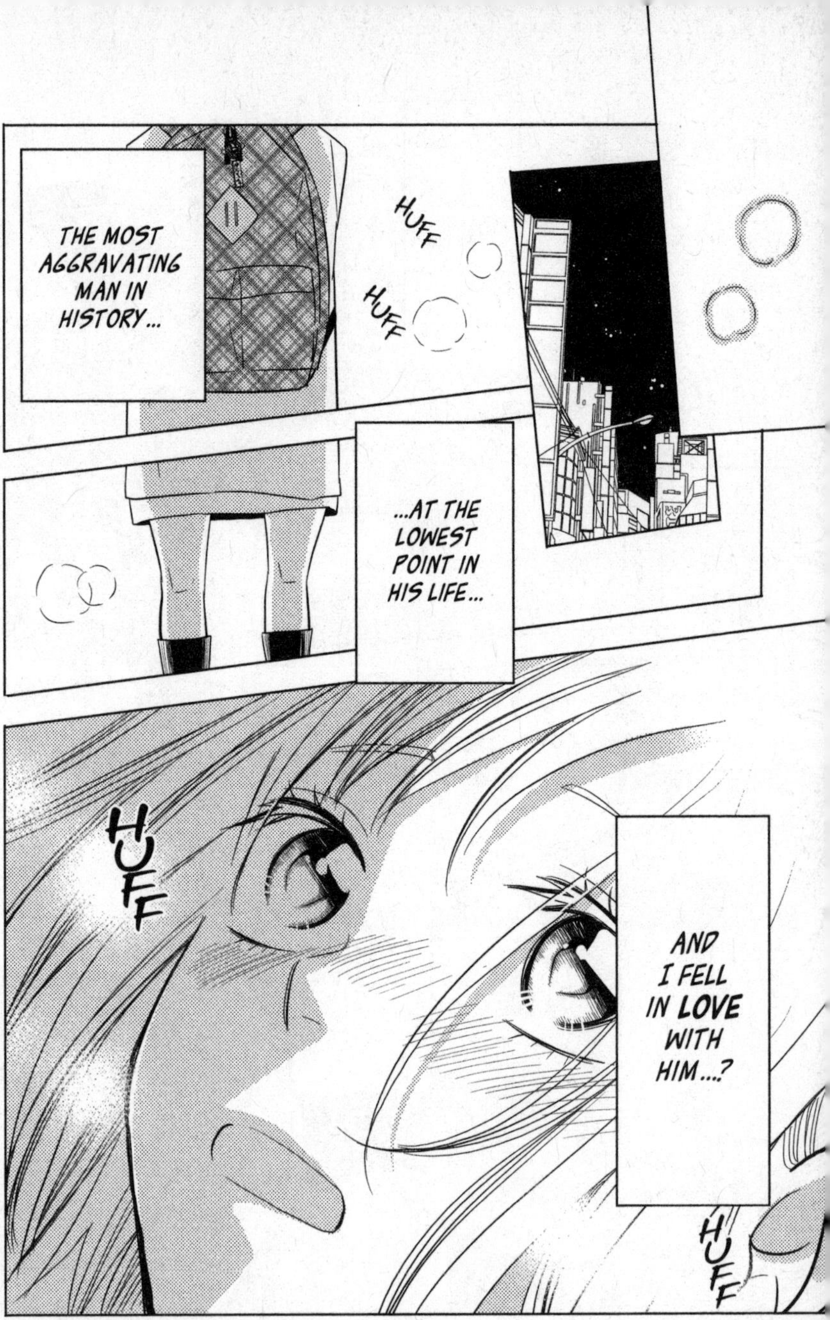
HUFF
HUFF
THE MOST AGGRAVATING MAN IN HISTORY...
...AT THE LOWEST POINT IN HIS LIFE...
AND I FELL IN **LOVE** WITH HIM...?
HUFF
HUFF

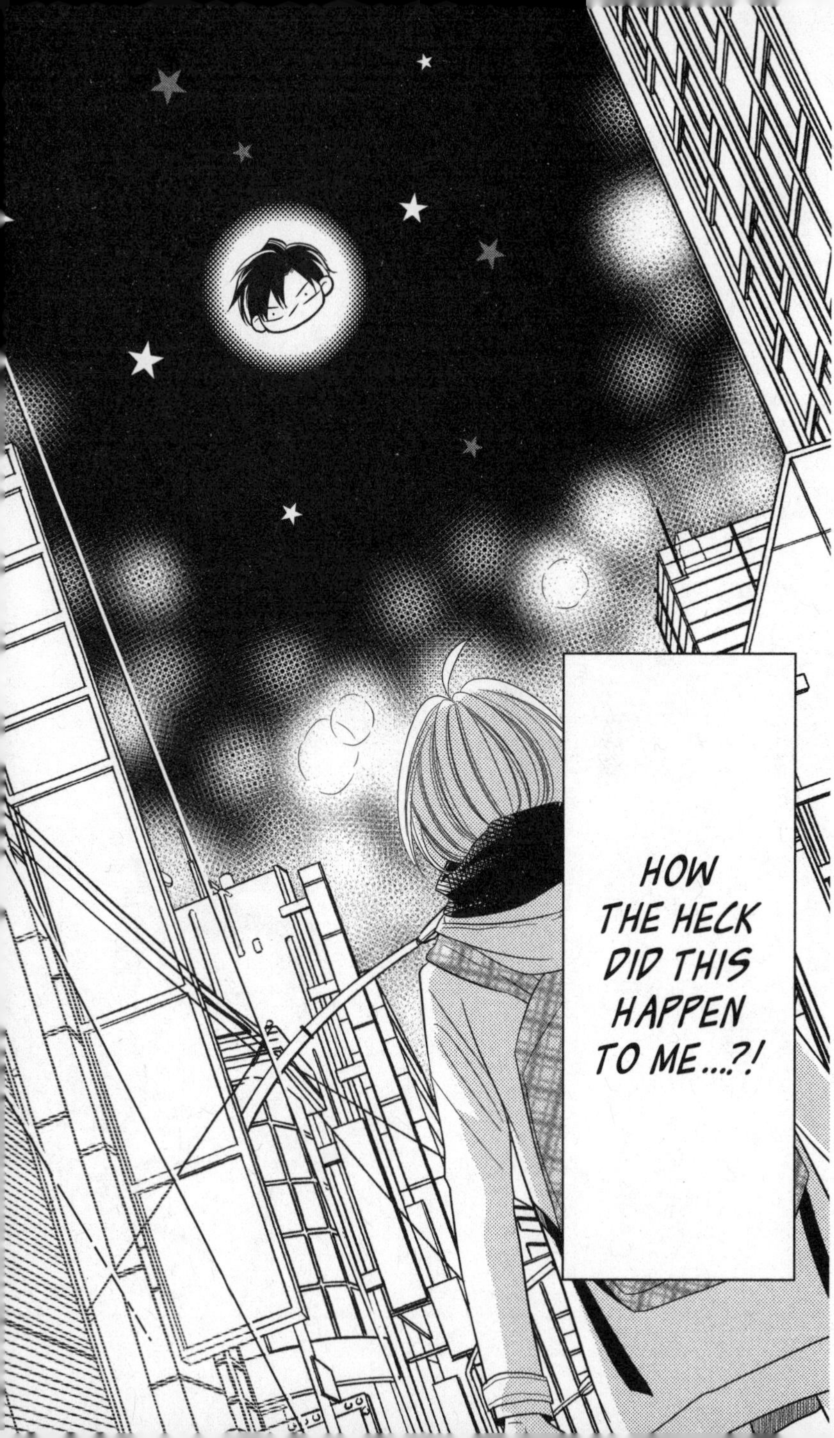
HOW THE HECK DID THIS HAPPEN TO ME...?!

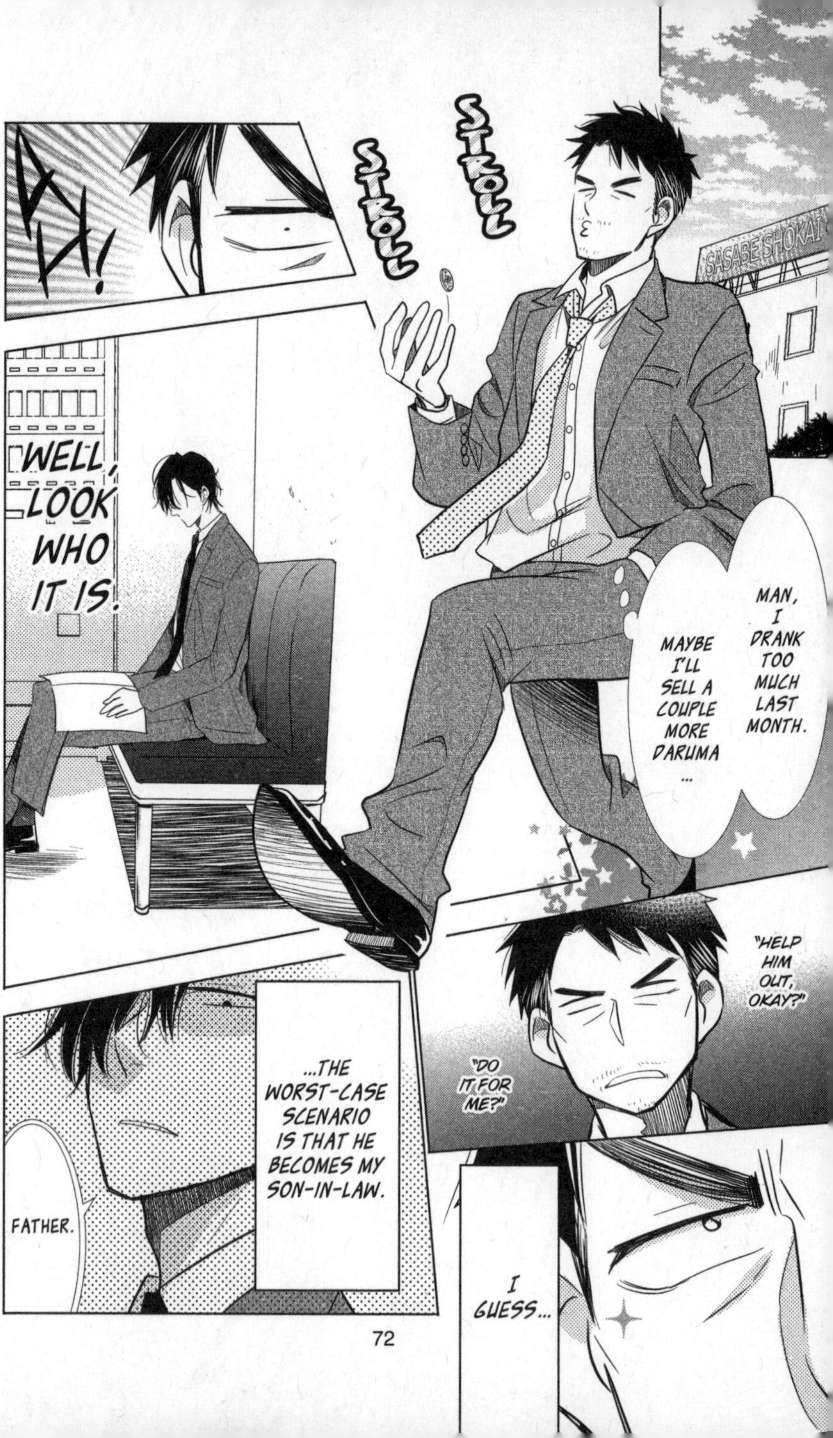
SASABE SHOKAI
STROLL
STROLL
MAN, I DRANK TOO MUCH LAST MONTH.
MAYBE I'LL SELL A COUPLE MORE DARUMA...
AH!
WELL, LOOK WHO IT IS.
"HELP HIM OUT, OKAY?"
"DO IT FOR ME?"
I GUESS...
...THE WORST-CASE SCENARIO IS THAT HE BECOMES MY SON-IN-LAW.
FATHER.

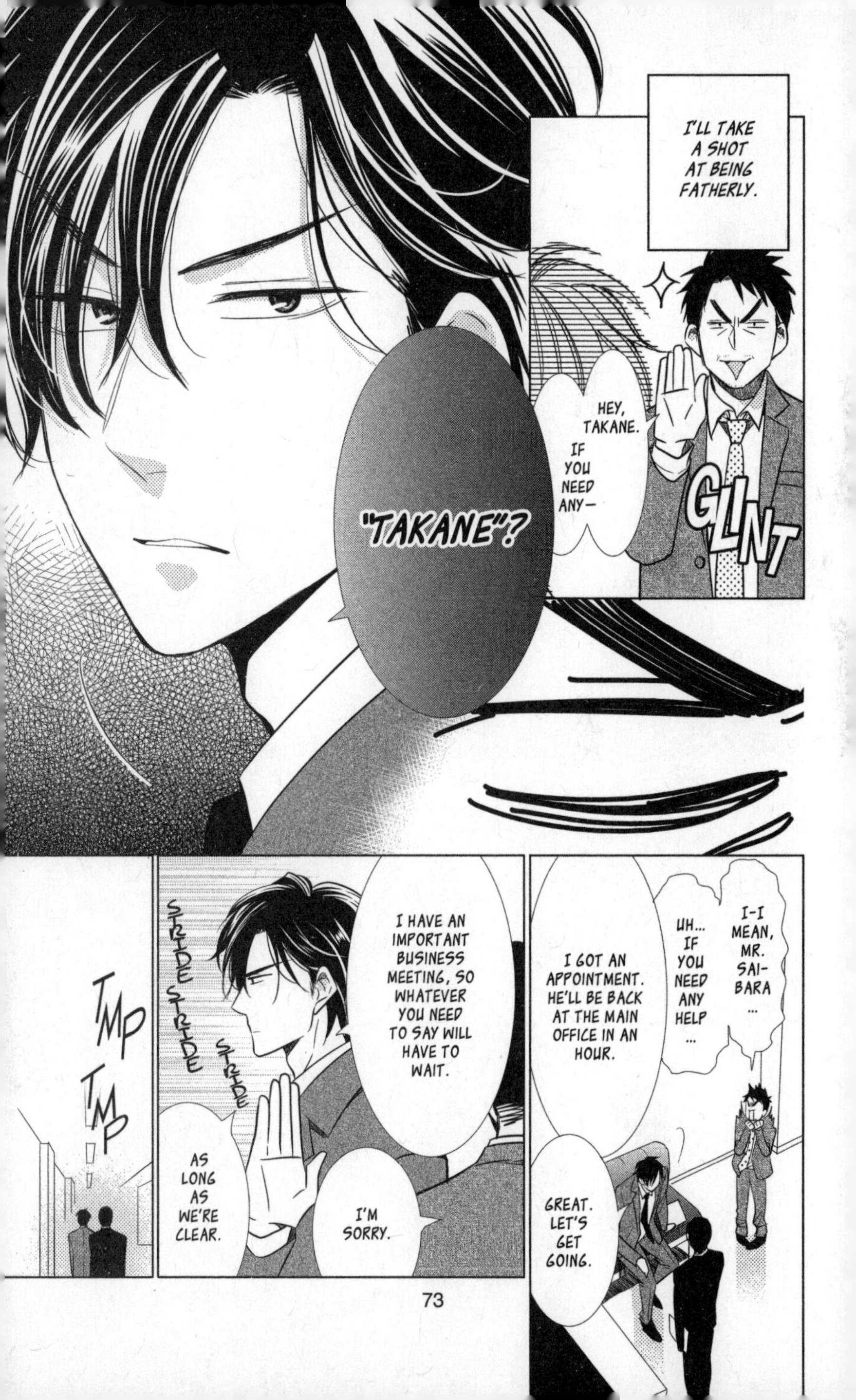
I'LL TAKE A SHOT AT BEING FATHERLY.
HEY, TAKANE. IF YOU NEED ANY—
GLINT
"TAKANE"?
I-I MEAN, MR. SAI-BARA ...
UH... IF YOU NEED ANY HELP ...
I GOT AN APPOINTMENT. HE'LL BE BACK AT THE MAIN OFFICE IN AN HOUR.
GREAT. LET'S GET GOING.
I HAVE AN IMPORTANT BUSINESS MEETING, SO WHATEVER YOU NEED TO SAY WILL HAVE TO WAIT.
I'M SORRY.
AS LONG AS WE'RE CLEAR.
STRIDE STRIDE STRIDE
TMP TMP

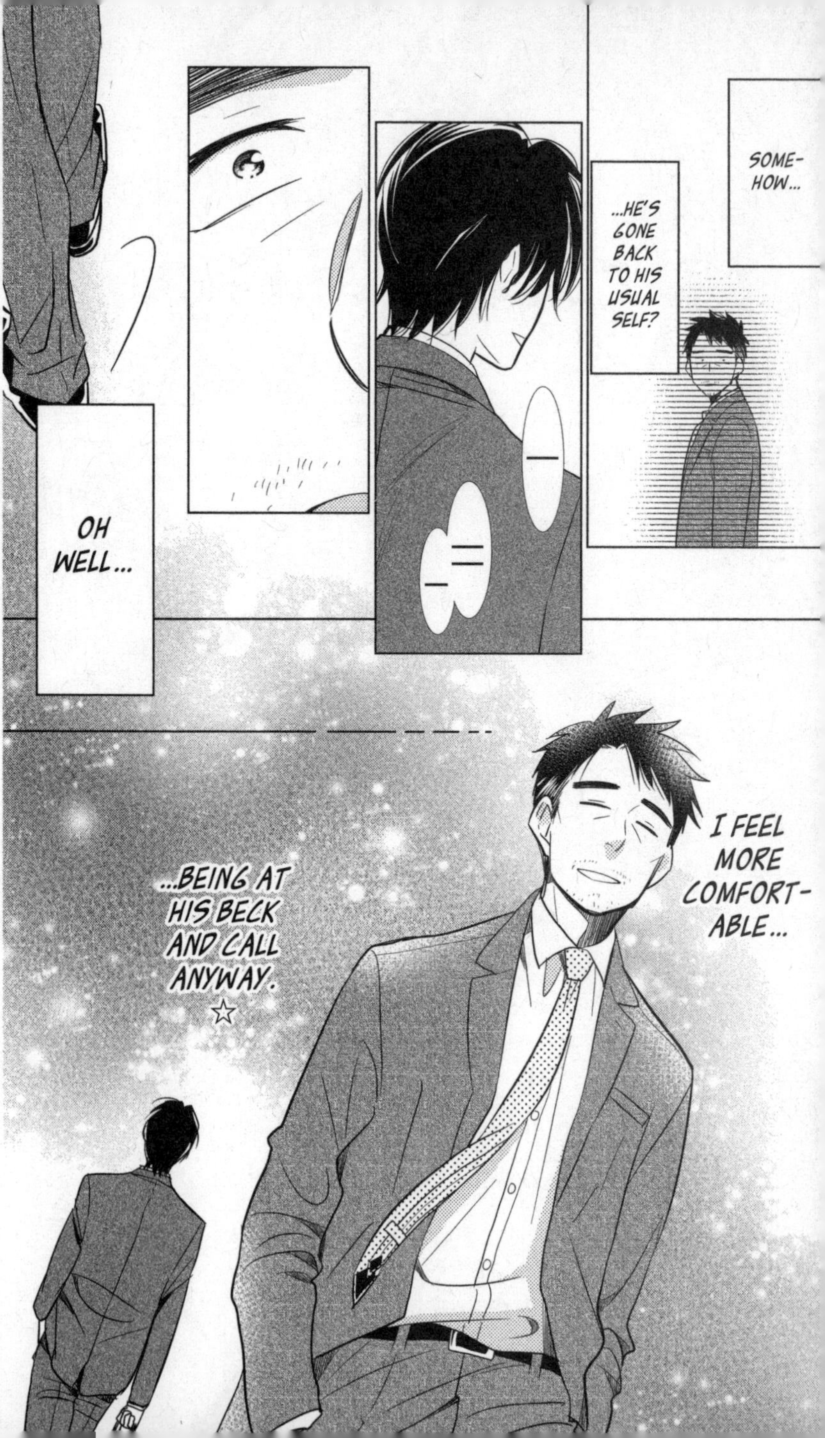
SOME-HOW...
...HE'S GONE BACK TO HIS USUAL SELF?
—
—
—
OH WELL...
I FEEL MORE COMFORT-ABLE...
...BEING AT HIS BECK AND CALL ANYWAY. ☆

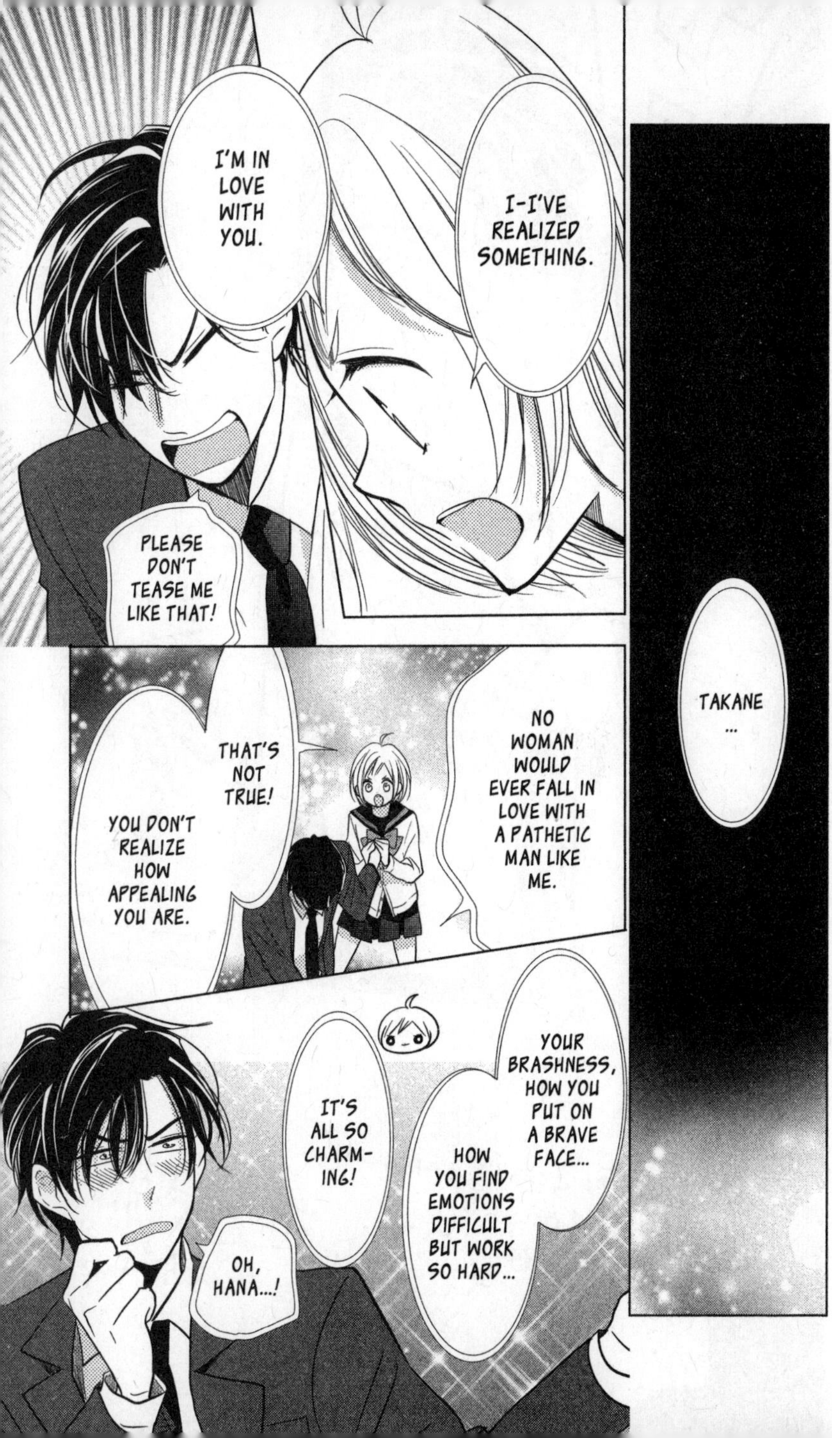
TAKANE ...
I-I'VE REALIZED SOMETHING.
I'M IN LOVE WITH YOU.
PLEASE DON'T TEASE ME LIKE THAT!
NO WOMAN WOULD EVER FALL IN LOVE WITH A PATHETIC MAN LIKE ME.
THAT'S NOT TRUE!
YOU DON'T REALIZE HOW APPEALING YOU ARE.
YOUR BRASHNESS, HOW YOU PUT ON A BRAVE FACE...
HOW YOU FIND EMOTIONS DIFFICULT BUT WORK SO HARD...
IT'S ALL SO CHARM-ING!
OH, HANA...!

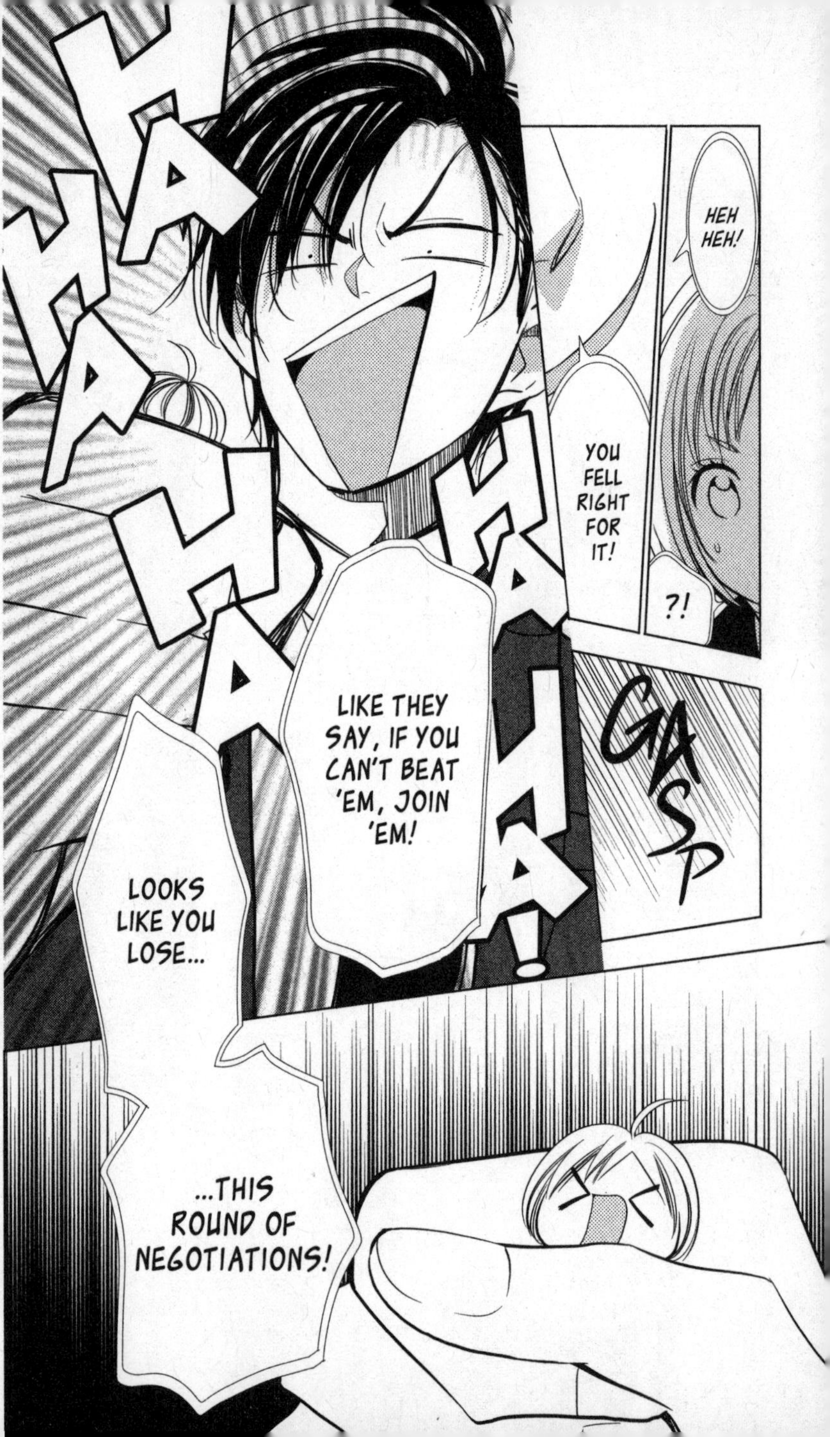

HEH HEH!
YOU FELL RIGHT FOR IT!
?!
GASP
HAHAHAHAHA!
LIKE THEY SAY, IF YOU CAN'T BEAT 'EM, JOIN 'EM!
LOOKS LIKE YOU LOSE...
...THIS ROUND OF NEGOTIATIONS!

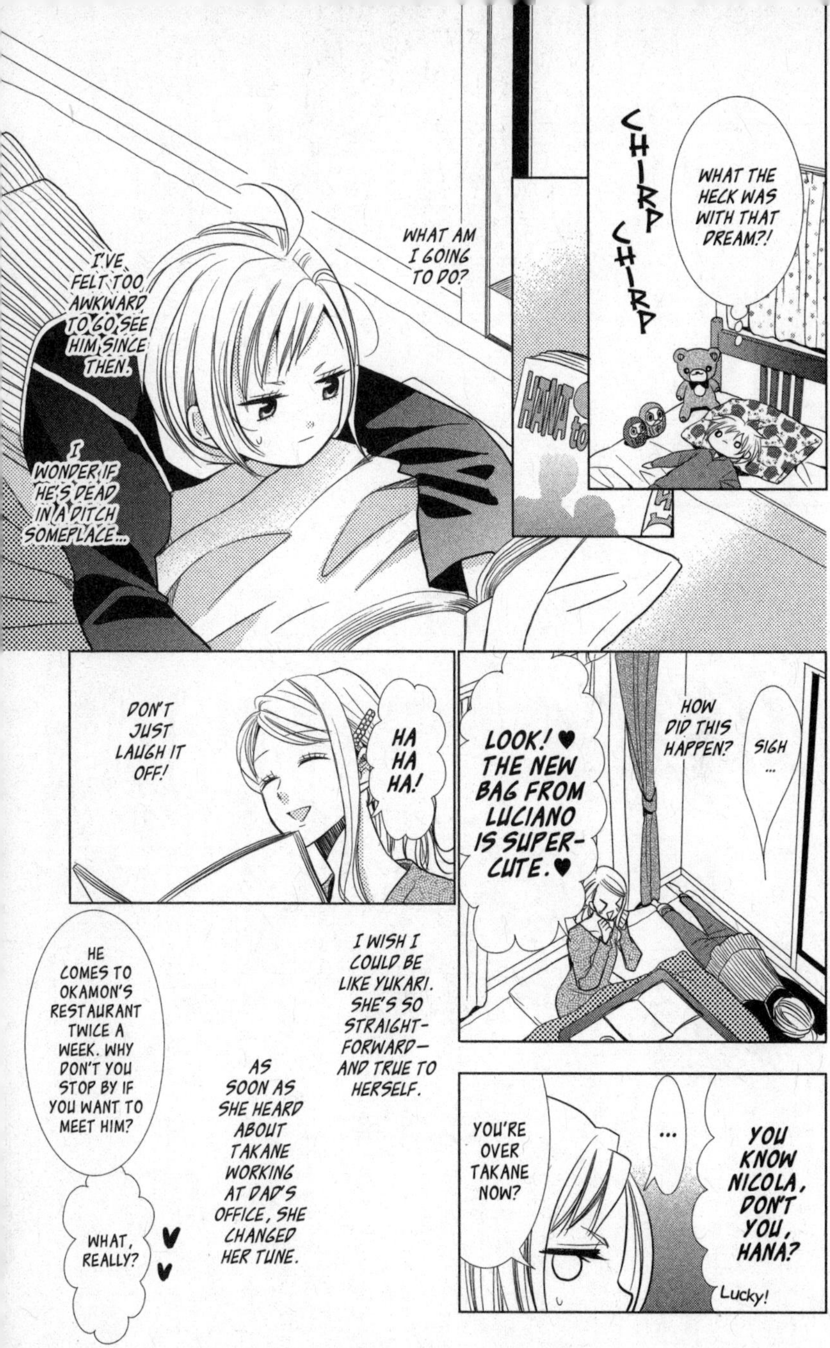
CHIRP CHIRP
WHAT THE HECK WAS WITH THAT DREAM?!
WHAT AM I GOING TO DO?
I'VE FELT TOO AWKWARD TO GO SEE HIM SINCE THEN.
I WONDER IF HE'S DEAD IN A DITCH SOMEPLACE...
SIGH...
HOW DID THIS HAPPEN?
LOOK! ♥ THE NEW BAG FROM LUCIANO IS SUPER-CUTE. ♥
HA HA HA!
DON'T JUST LAUGH IT OFF!
YOU KNOW NICOLA, DON'T YOU, HANA?
Lucky!
...
YOU'RE OVER TAKANE NOW?
I WISH I COULD BE LIKE YUKARI. SHE'S SO STRAIGHT-FORWARD—AND TRUE TO HERSELF.
AS SOON AS SHE HEARD ABOUT TAKANE WORKING AT DAD'S OFFICE, SHE CHANGED HER TUNE.
HE COMES TO OKAMON'S RESTAURANT TWICE A WEEK. WHY DON'T YOU STOP BY IF YOU WANT TO MEET HIM?
WHAT, REALLY? ♥ ♥

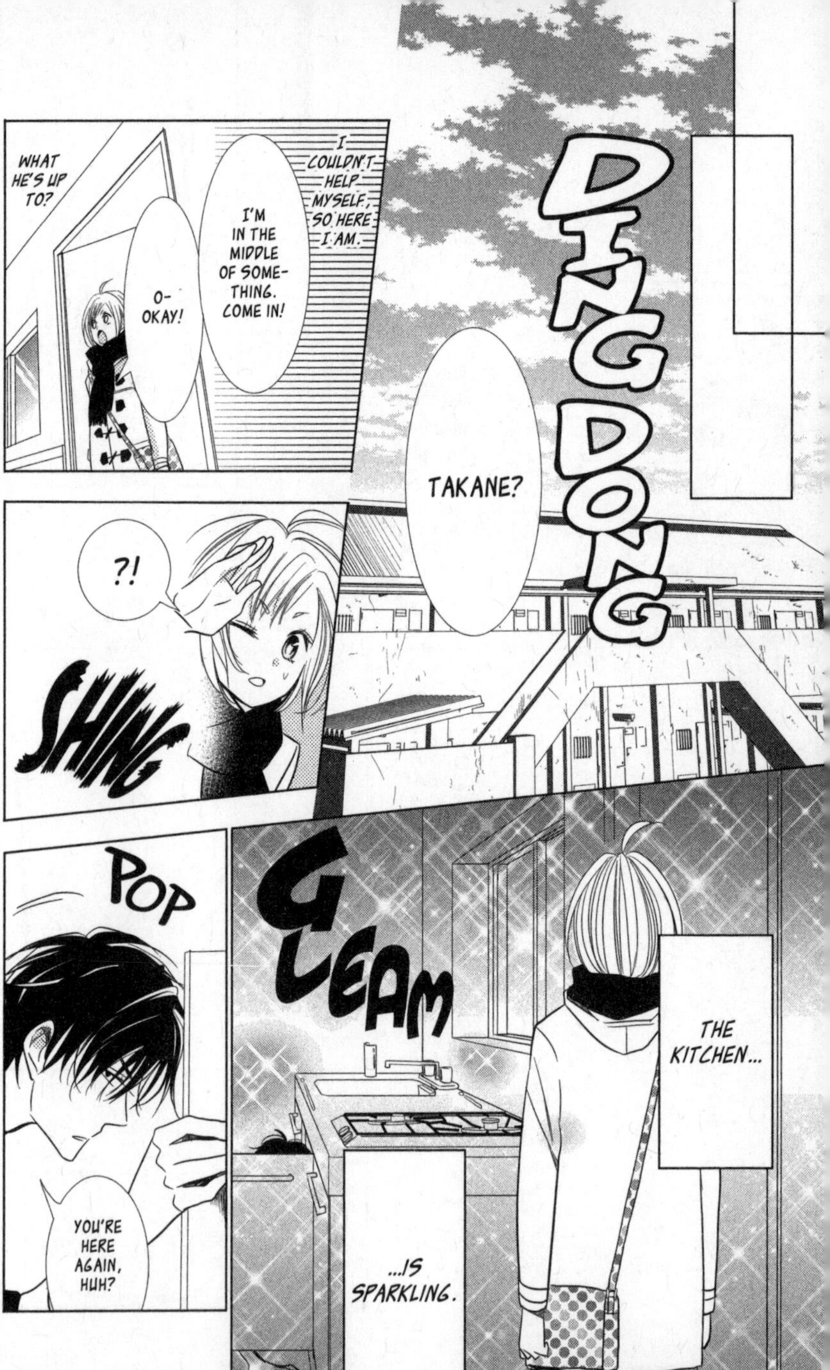
DING DONG
TAKANE?
I COULDN'T HELP MYSELF, SO HERE I AM.
I'M IN THE MIDDLE OF SOMETHING. COME IN!
O-OKAY!
WHAT HE'S UP TO?
?!
SHING
GLEAM
THE KITCHEN...
...IS SPARKLING.
POP
YOU'RE HERE AGAIN, HUH?

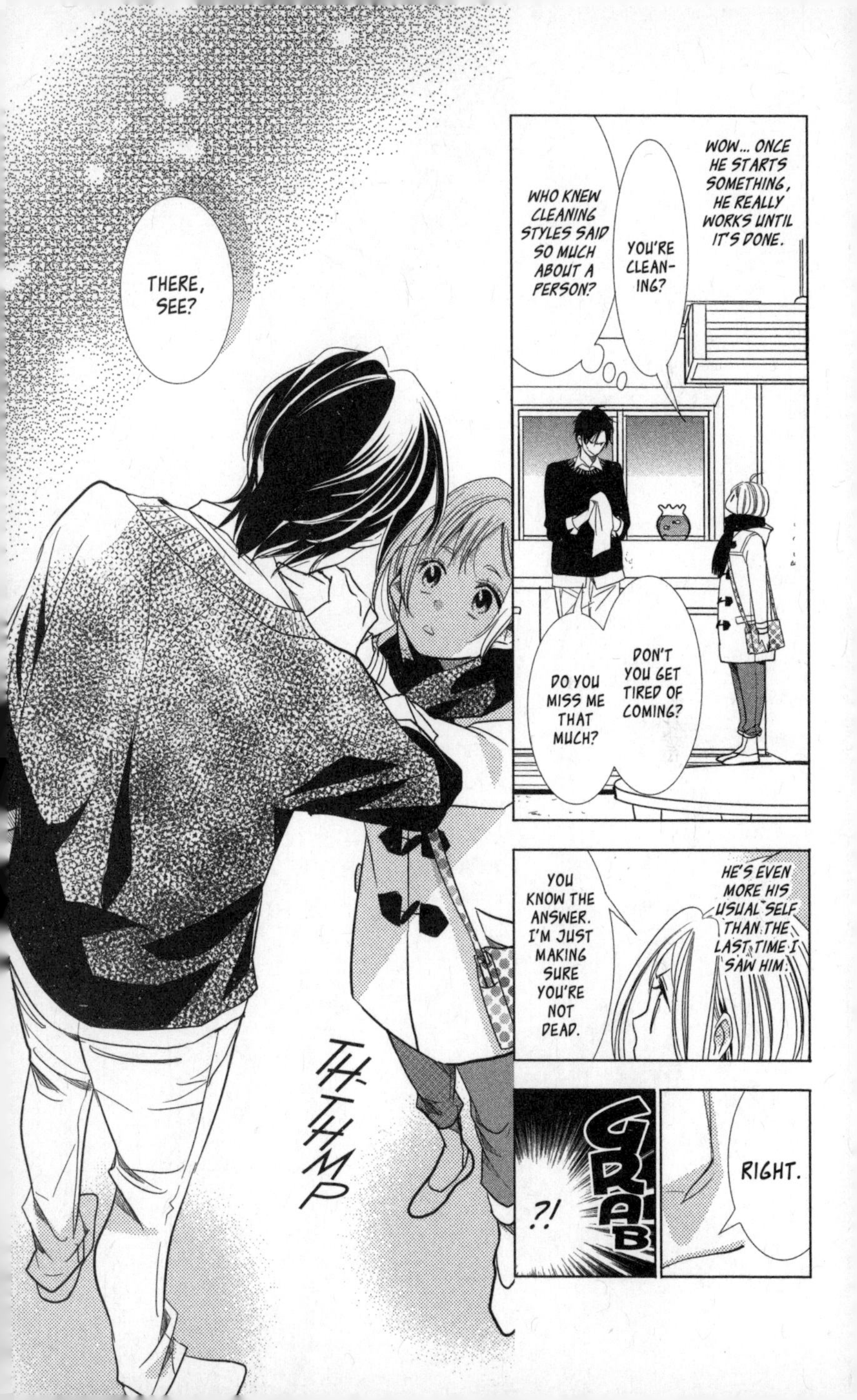
WOW... ONCE HE STARTS SOMETHING, HE REALLY WORKS UNTIL IT'S DONE.
YOU'RE CLEAN-ING?
WHO KNEW CLEANING STYLES SAID SO MUCH ABOUT A PERSON?
DON'T YOU GET TIRED OF COMING?
DO YOU MISS ME THAT MUCH?
HE'S EVEN MORE HIS USUAL SELF THAN THE LAST TIME I SAW HIM.
YOU KNOW THE ANSWER. I'M JUST MAKING SURE YOU'RE NOT DEAD.
RIGHT.
GRAB
?!
THERE, SEE?
TH-THMP

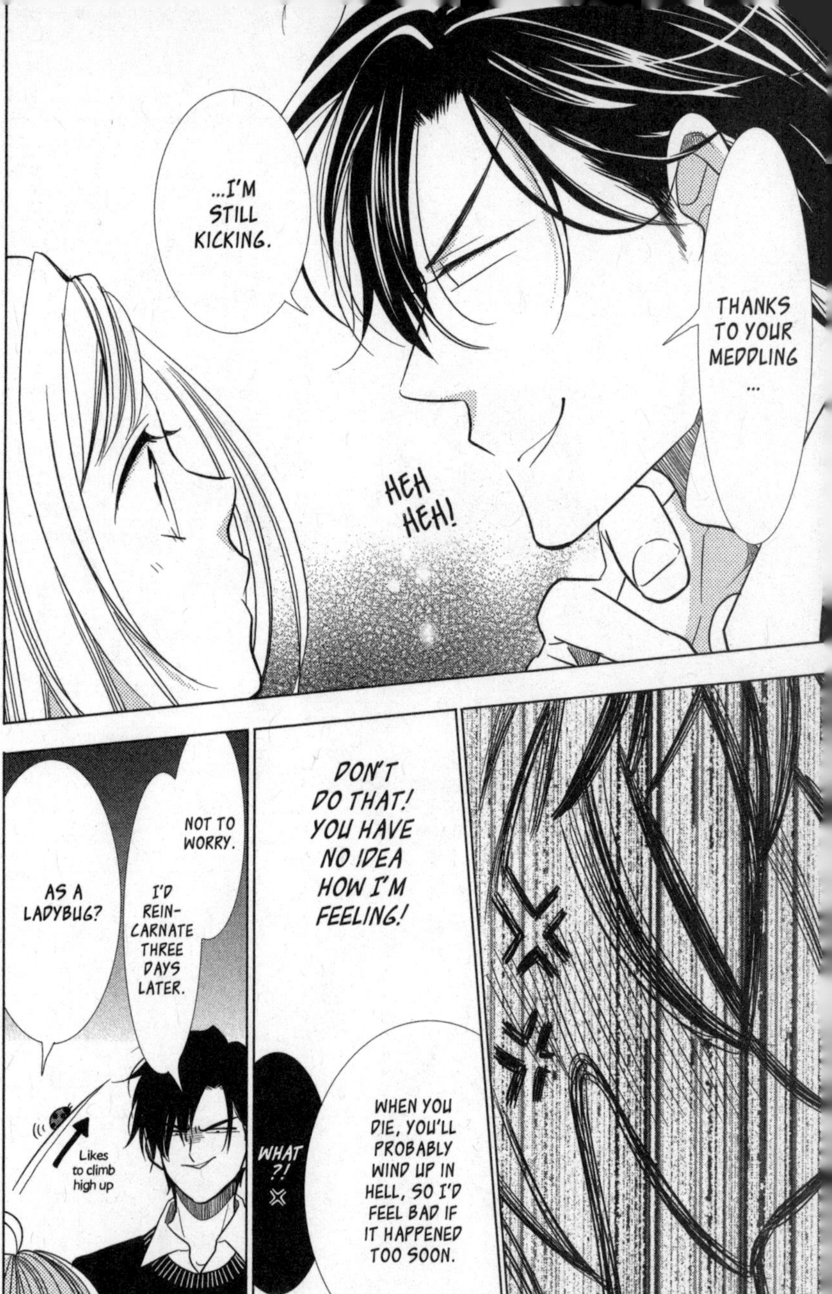
THANKS TO YOUR MEDDLING ...
...I'M STILL KICKING.
HEH HEH!
DON'T DO THAT! YOU HAVE NO IDEA HOW I'M FEELING!
WHEN YOU DIE, YOU'LL PROBABLY WIND UP IN HELL, SO I'D FEEL BAD IF IT HAPPENED TOO SOON.
WHAT?!
NOT TO WORRY.
I'D REIN-CARNATE THREE DAYS LATER.
AS A LADYBUG?
Likes to climb high up

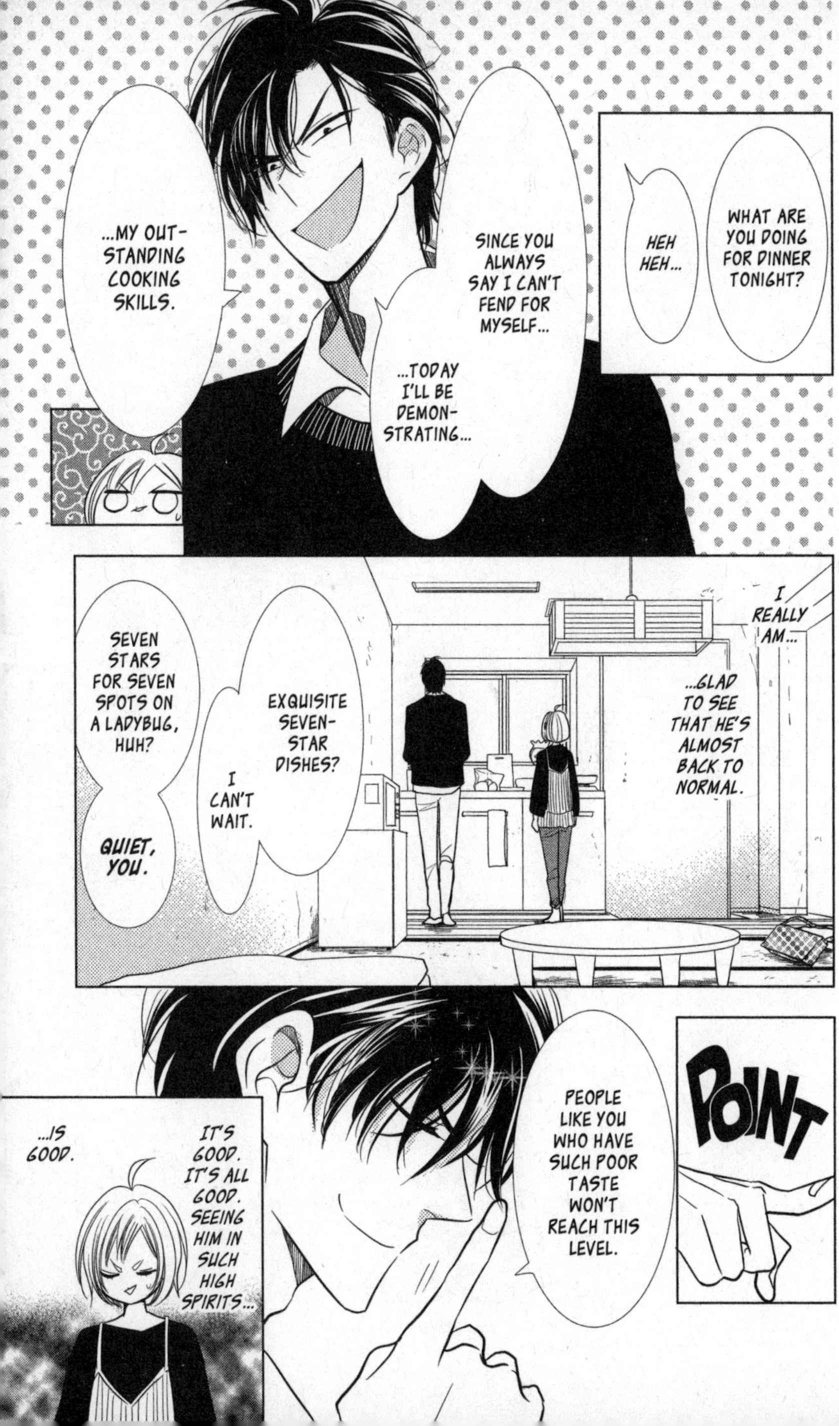
WHAT ARE YOU DOING FOR DINNER TONIGHT?
HEH HEH...
SINCE YOU ALWAYS SAY I CAN'T FEND FOR MYSELF...
...TODAY I'LL BE DEMON-STRATING...
...MY OUT-STANDING COOKING SKILLS.
I REALLY AM...
...GLAD TO SEE THAT HE'S ALMOST BACK TO NORMAL.
EXQUISITE SEVEN-STAR DISHES?
I CAN'T WAIT.
SEVEN STARS FOR SEVEN SPOTS ON A LADYBUG, HUH?
QUIET, YOU.
POINT
PEOPLE LIKE YOU WHO HAVE SUCH POOR TASTE WON'T REACH THIS LEVEL.
IT'S GOOD. IT'S ALL GOOD. SEEING HIM IN SUCH HIGH SPIRITS...
...IS GOOD.

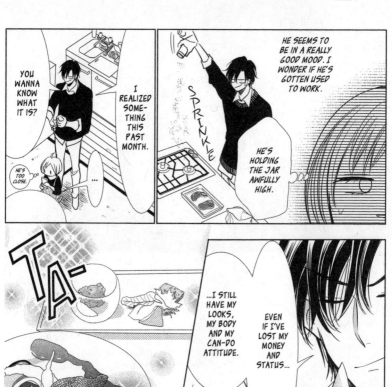

HE SEEMS TO BE IN A REALLY GOOD MOOD. I WONDER IF HE'S GOTTEN USED TO WORK.
SPRINKLE
HE'S HOLDING THE JAR AWFULLY HIGH.
I REALIZED SOMETHING THIS PAST MONTH.
YOU WANNA KNOW WHAT IT IS?
HE'S TOO CLOSE.
...
EVEN IF I'VE LOST MY MONEY AND STATUS...
...I STILL HAVE MY LOOKS, MY BODY AND MY CAN-DO ATTITUDE.
YEAH, YEAH.
IT'S GOOD. IT'S ALL GOOD...
FOOM
TA-DA

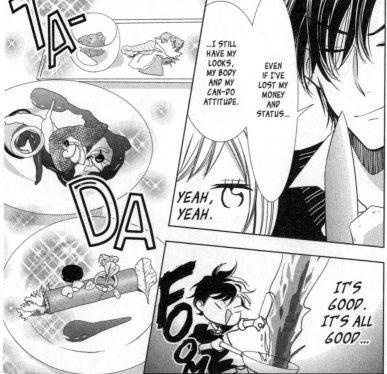

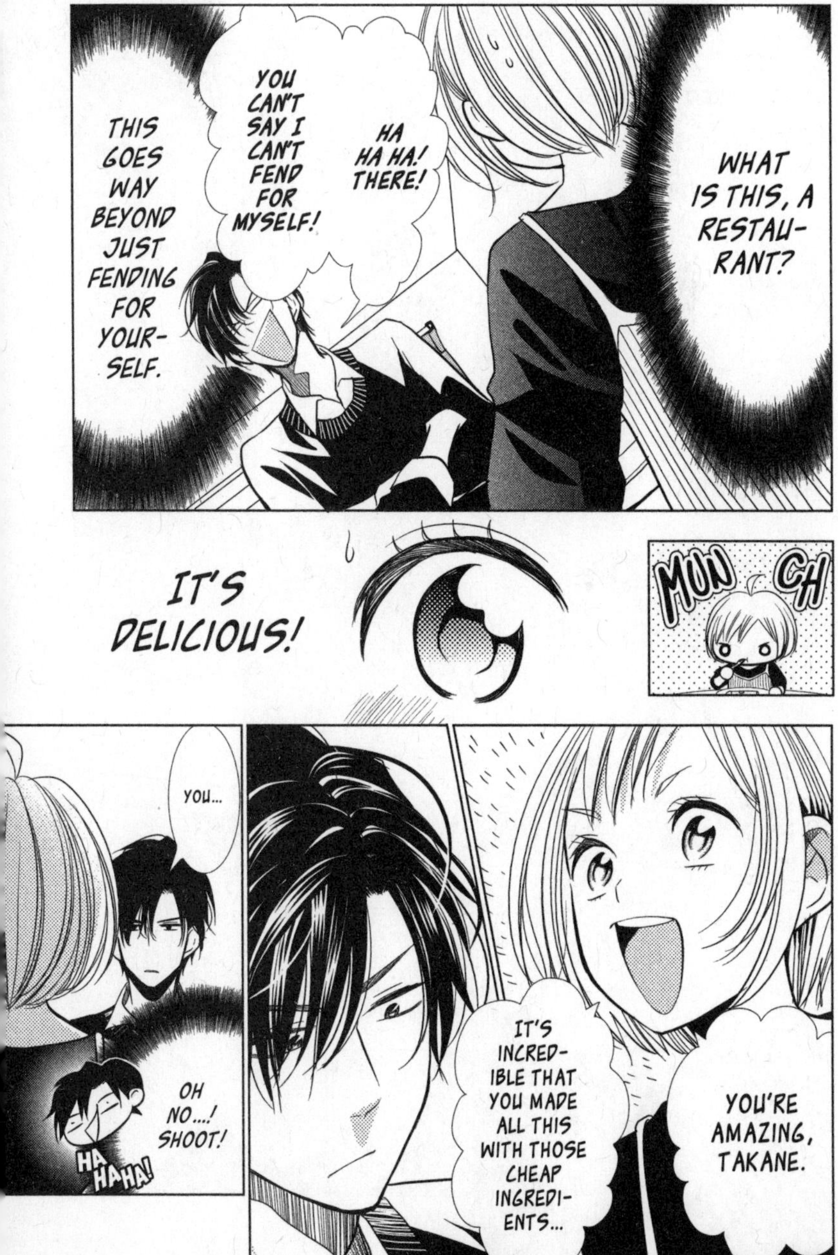
WHAT IS THIS, A RESTAURANT?
HA HA HA! THERE!
YOU CAN'T SAY I CAN'T FEND FOR MYSELF!
THIS GOES WAY BEYOND JUST FENDING FOR YOURSELF.
MUNCH
IT'S DELICIOUS!
YOU'RE AMAZING, TAKANE.
IT'S INCREDIBLE THAT YOU MADE ALL THIS WITH THOSE CHEAP INGREDIENTS...
YOU...
OH NO...! SHOOT!
HA HA HA!

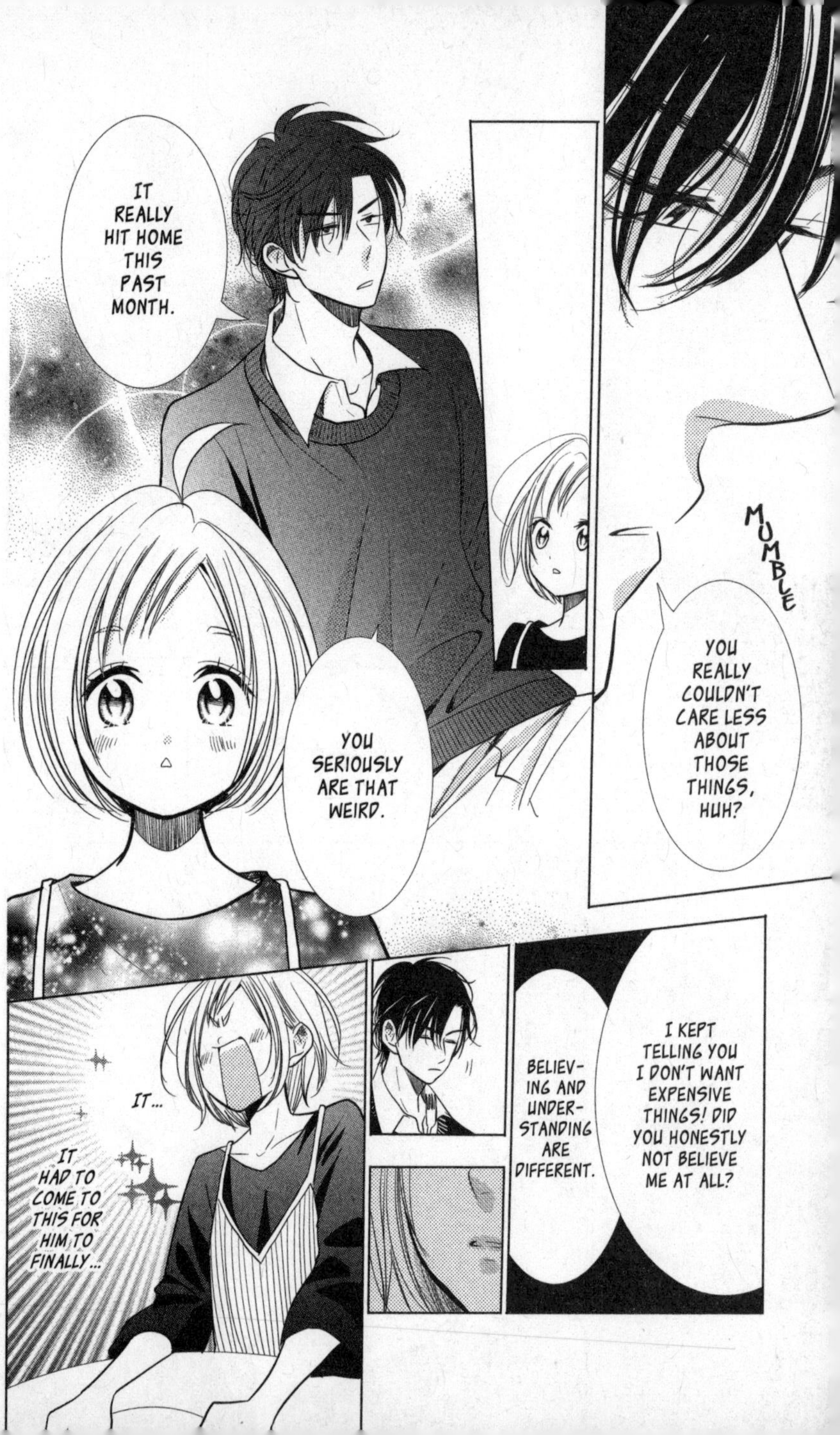
MUMBLE
YOU REALLY COULDN'T CARE LESS ABOUT THOSE THINGS, HUH?
IT REALLY HIT HOME THIS PAST MONTH.
YOU SERIOUSLY ARE THAT WEIRD.
I KEPT TELLING YOU I DON'T WANT EXPENSIVE THINGS! DID YOU HONESTLY NOT BELIEVE ME AT ALL?
BELIEV-ING AND UNDER-STANDING ARE DIFFERENT.
IT...
IT HAD TO COME TO THIS FOR HIM TO FINALLY...

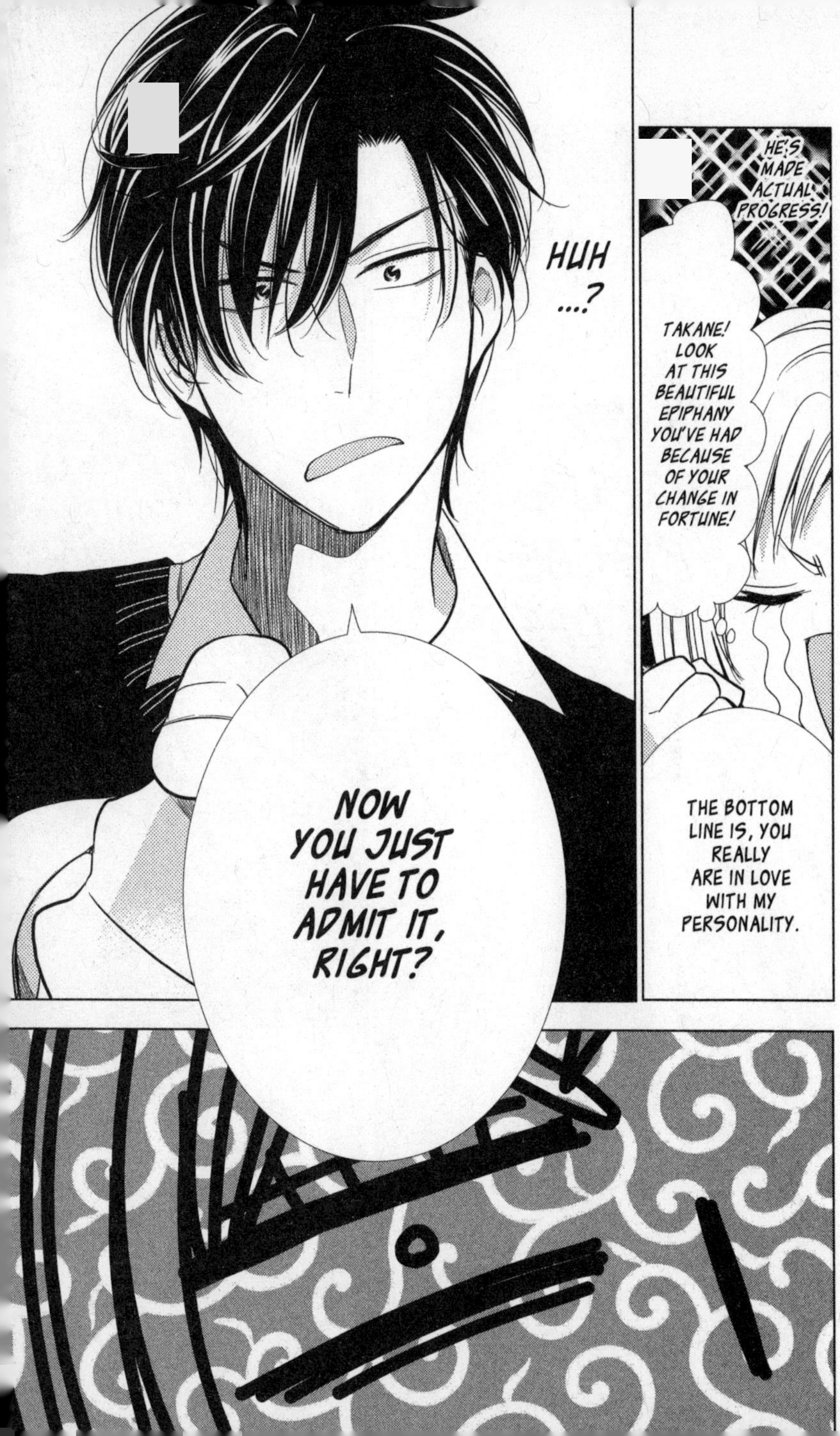

HE'S MADE ACTUAL PROGRESS!
TAKANE! LOOK AT THIS BEAUTIFUL EPIPHANY YOU'VE HAD BECAUSE OF YOUR CHANGE IN FORTUNE!
THE BOTTOM LINE IS, YOU REALLY ARE IN LOVE WITH MY PERSONALITY.
HUH ...?
NOW YOU JUST HAVE TO ADMIT IT, RIGHT?

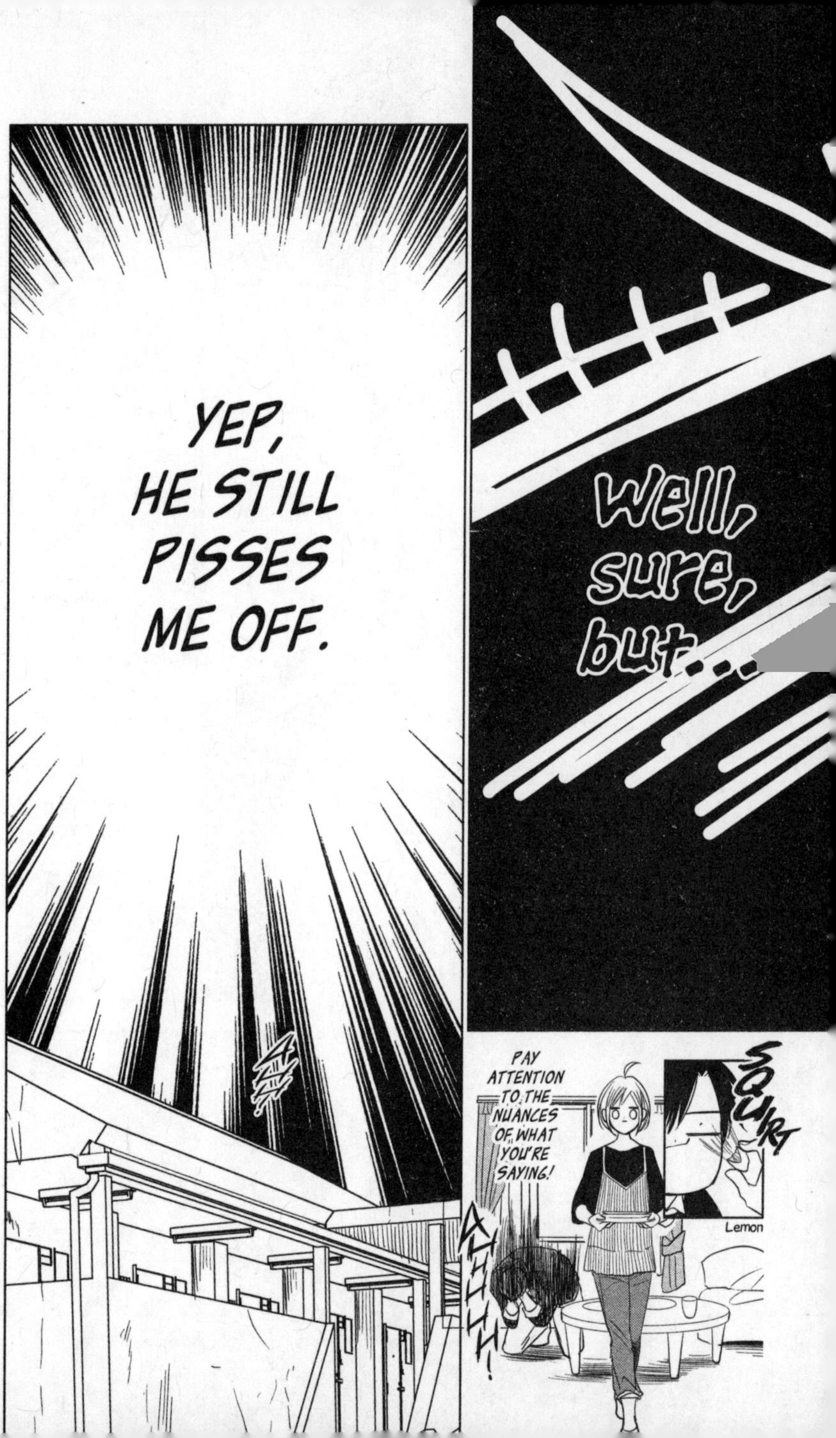
Well, sure, but...
PAY ATTENTION TO THE NUANCES OF WHAT YOU'RE SAYING!
SQUIRT
Lemon
AHHHHH!
YEP, HE STILL PISSES ME OFF.

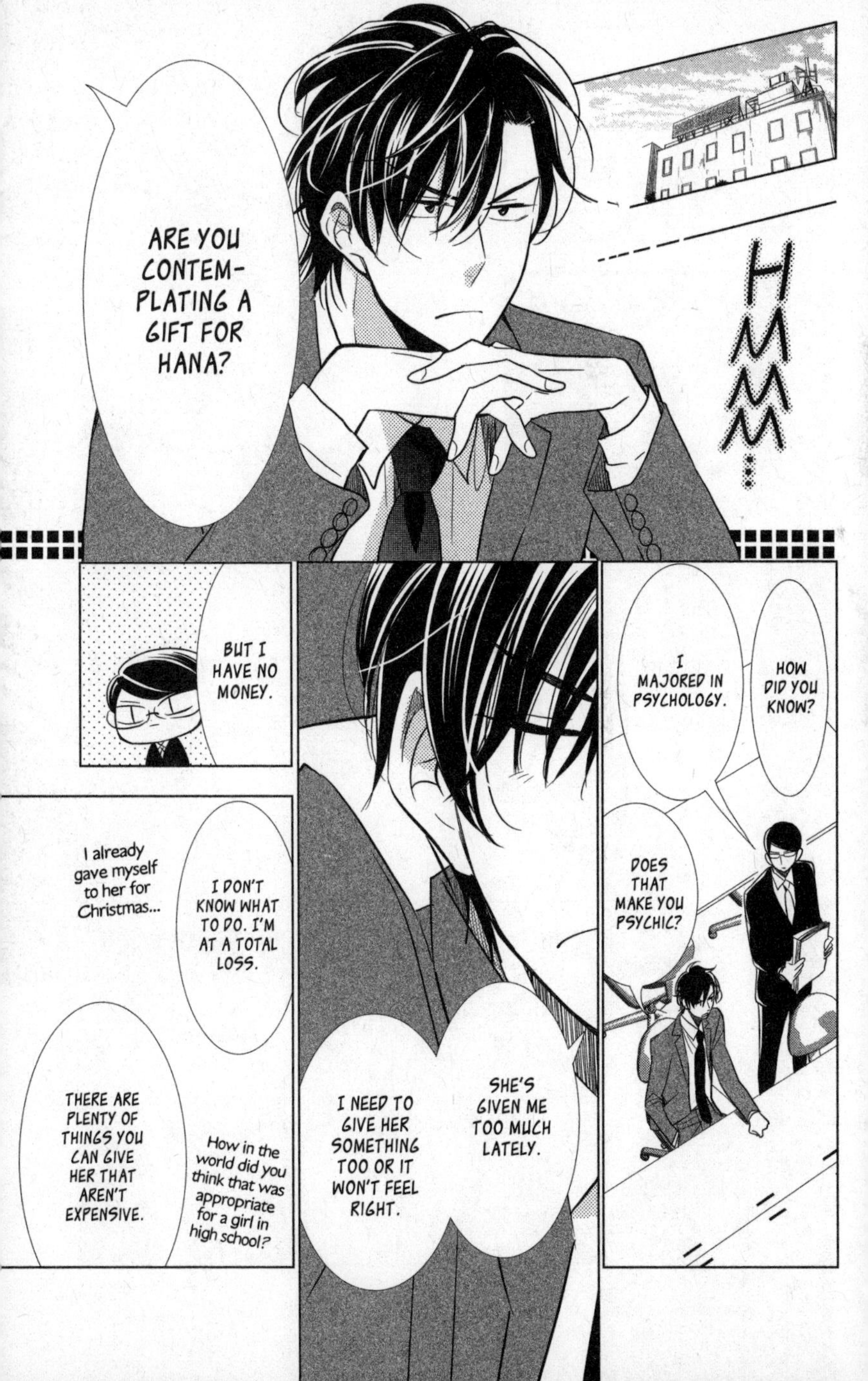
HMMM...
ARE YOU CONTEM-PLATING A GIFT FOR HANA?
HOW DID YOU KNOW?
I MAJORED IN PSYCHOLOGY.
DOES THAT MAKE YOU PSYCHIC?
SHE'S GIVEN ME TOO MUCH LATELY.
I NEED TO GIVE HER SOMETHING TOO OR IT WON'T FEEL RIGHT.
BUT I HAVE NO MONEY.
I DON'T KNOW WHAT TO DO. I'M AT A TOTAL LOSS.
I already gave myself to her for Christmas...
How in the world did you think that was appropriate for a girl in high school?
THERE ARE PLENTY OF THINGS YOU CAN GIVE HER THAT AREN'T EXPENSIVE.

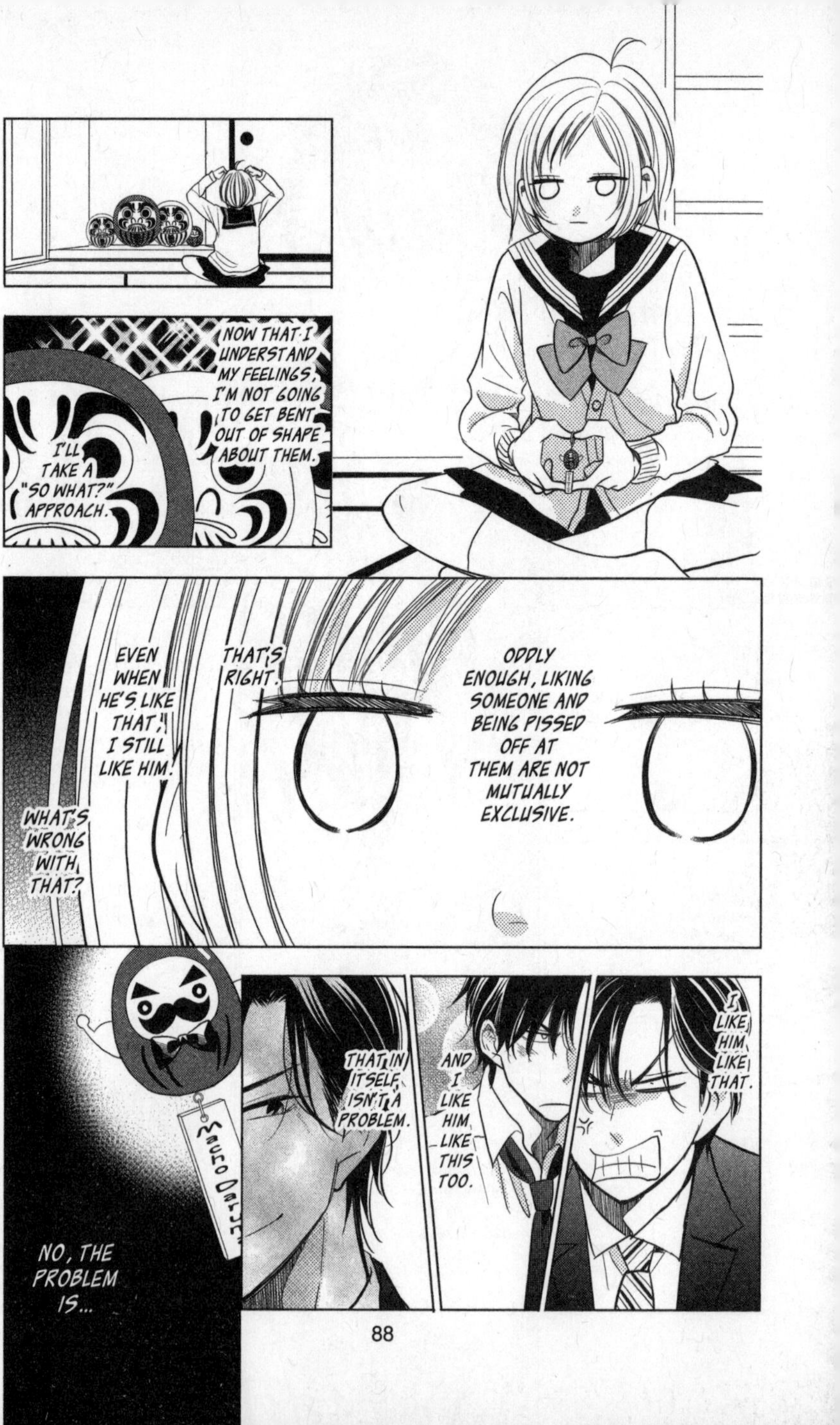
NOW THAT I UNDERSTAND MY FEELINGS, I'M NOT GOING TO GET BENT OUT OF SHAPE ABOUT THEM.
I'LL TAKE A "SO WHAT?" APPROACH.
ODDLY ENOUGH, LIKING SOMEONE AND BEING PISSED OFF AT THEM ARE NOT MUTUALLY EXCLUSIVE.
THAT'S RIGHT.
EVEN WHEN HE'S LIKE THAT, I STILL LIKE HIM.
WHAT'S WRONG WITH THAT?
I LIKE HIM LIKE THAT.
AND I LIKE HIM LIKE THIS TOO.
THAT IN ITSELF ISN'T A PROBLEM.
NO, THE PROBLEM IS...

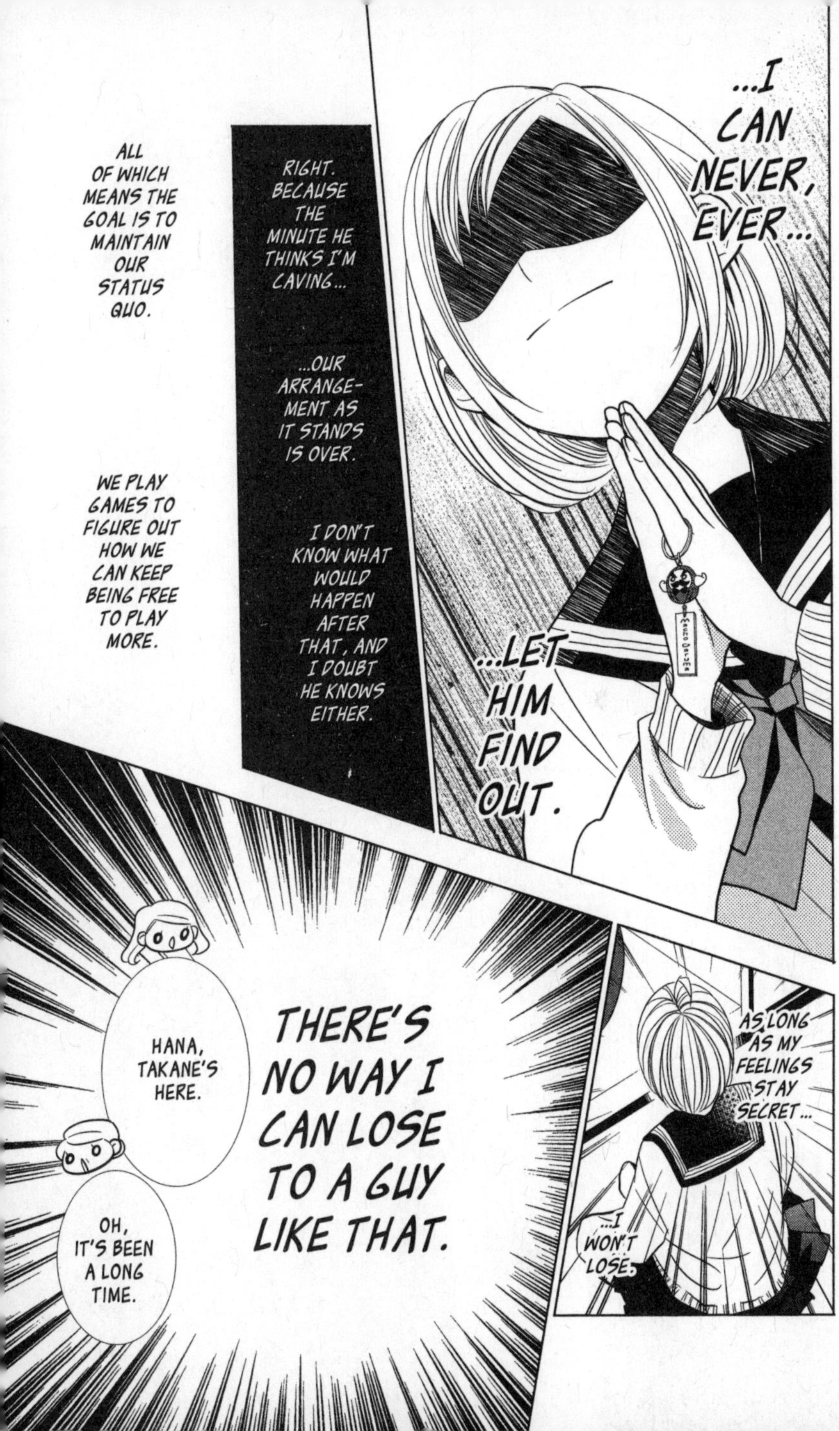
...I CAN NEVER, EVER...
...LET HIM FIND OUT.
RIGHT. BECAUSE THE MINUTE HE THINKS I'M CAVING...
...OUR ARRANGE-MENT AS IT STANDS IS OVER.
I DON'T KNOW WHAT WOULD HAPPEN AFTER THAT, AND I DOUBT HE KNOWS EITHER.
ALL OF WHICH MEANS THE GOAL IS TO MAINTAIN OUR STATUS QUO.
WE PLAY GAMES TO FIGURE OUT HOW WE CAN KEEP BEING FREE TO PLAY MORE.
AS LONG AS MY FEELINGS STAY SECRET...
...I WON'T LOSE.
THERE'S NO WAY I CAN LOSE TO A GUY LIKE THAT.
HANA, TAKANE'S HERE.
OH, IT'S BEEN A LONG TIME.

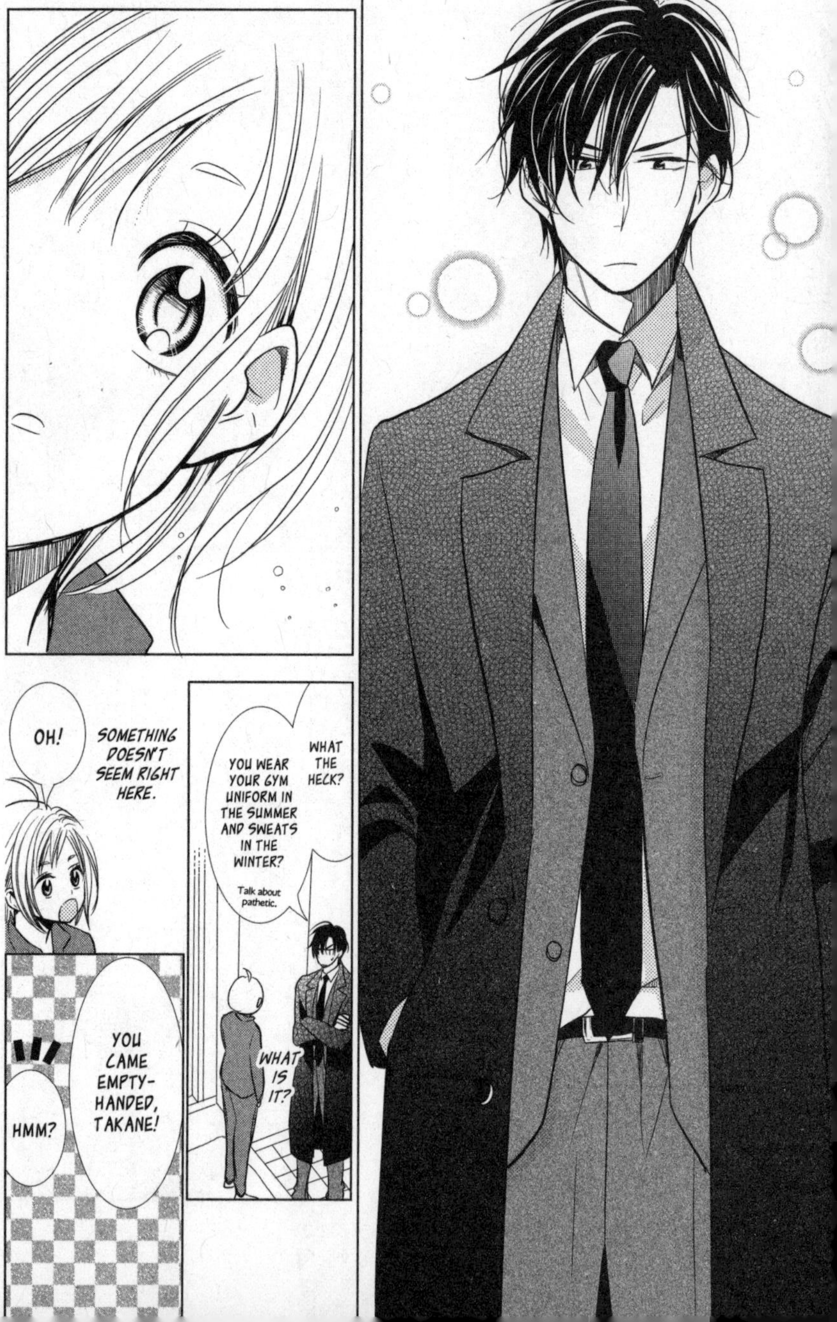
WHAT THE HECK?
YOU WEAR YOUR GYM UNIFORM IN THE SUMMER AND SWEATS IN THE WINTER?
Talk about pathetic.
WHAT IS IT?
SOMETHING DOESN'T SEEM RIGHT HERE.
OH!
YOU CAME EMPTY-HANDED, TAKANE!
HMM?

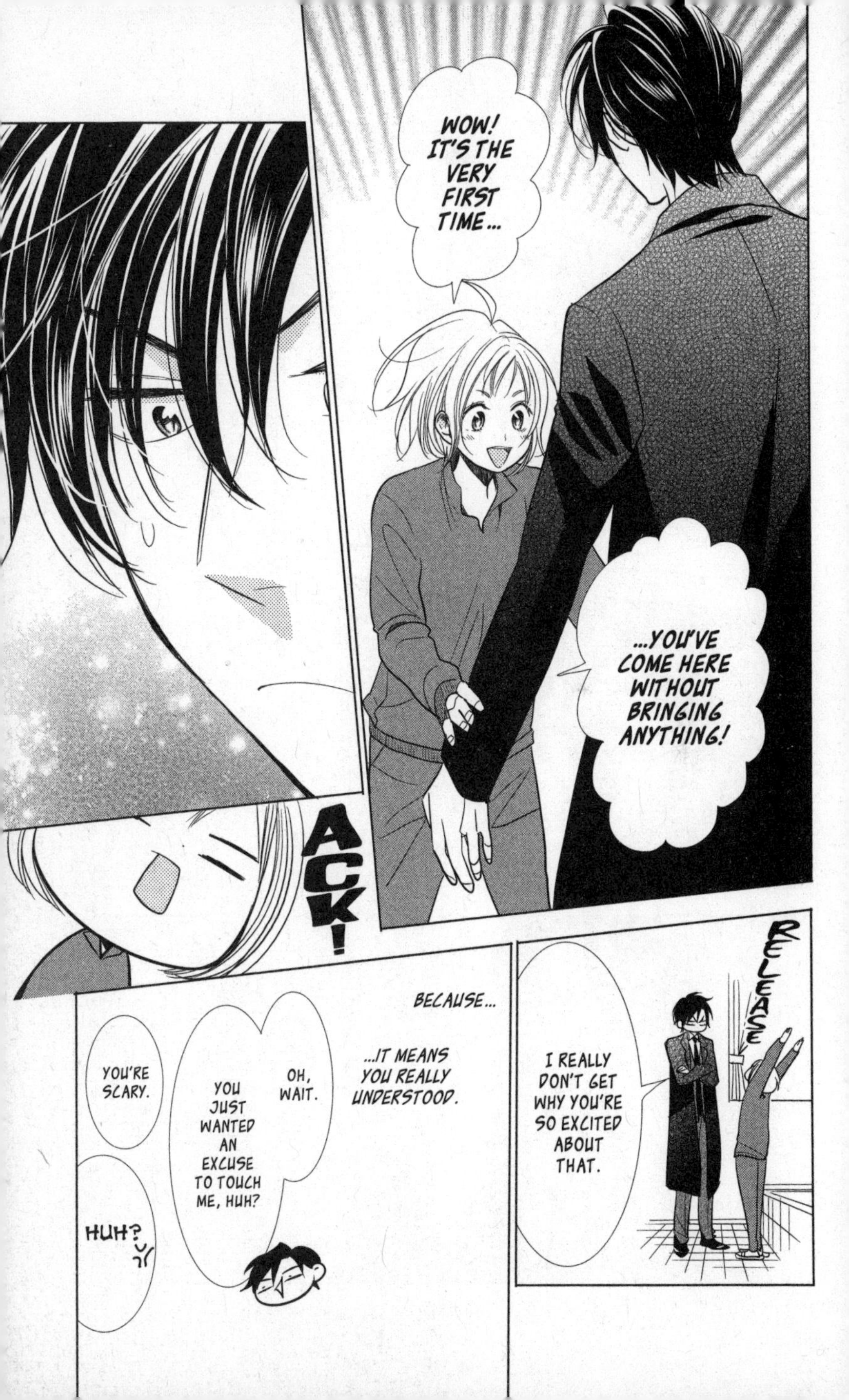
WOW! IT'S THE VERY FIRST TIME...
...YOU'VE COME HERE WITHOUT BRINGING ANYTHING!
ACK!
RELEASE
I REALLY DON'T GET WHY YOU'RE SO EXCITED ABOUT THAT.
BECAUSE...
...IT MEANS YOU REALLY UNDERSTOOD.
OH, WAIT.
YOU JUST WANTED AN EXCUSE TO TOUCH ME, HUH?
YOU'RE SCARY.
HUH?

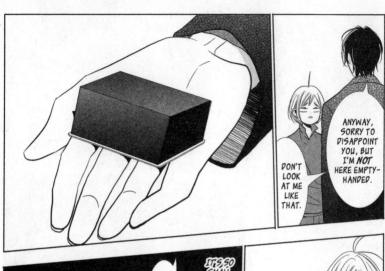

ANYWAY, SORRY TO DISAPPOINT YOU, BUT I'M **NOT** HERE EMPTY-HANDED.
DON'T LOOK AT ME LIKE THAT.
IT'S SO SMALL. WHAT COULD IT BE?
OPEN IT.
WHAT IS IT?
IT LOOKS... KINDA EXPENSIVE...?
AFTER EVERYTHING I DID FOR HIM...
...DOES HE **STILL** NOT GET IT...?
I GUESS...
...YOU CAN CALL THE GIFT "THE RIGHT TO SEE ME."

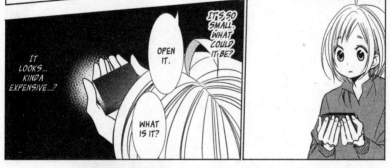

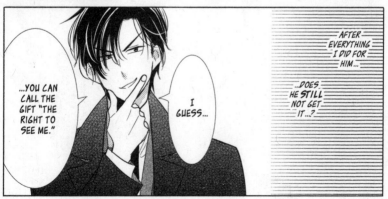

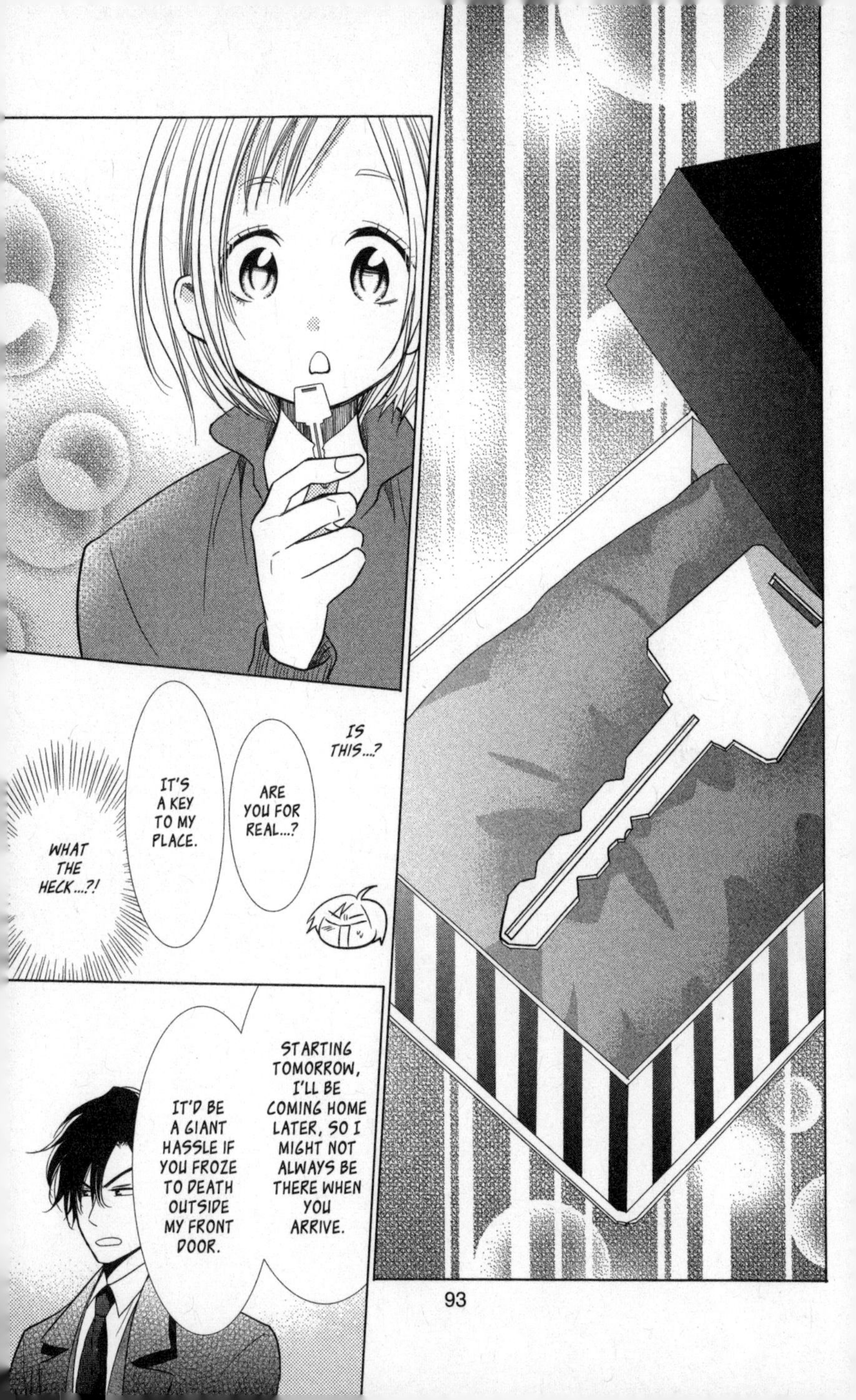
IS THIS...?
ARE YOU FOR REAL...?
IT'S A KEY TO MY PLACE.
WHAT THE HECK...?!
STARTING TOMORROW, I'LL BE COMING HOME LATER, SO I MIGHT NOT ALWAYS BE THERE WHEN YOU ARRIVE.
IT'D BE A GIANT HASSLE IF YOU FROZE TO DEATH OUTSIDE MY FRONT DOOR.

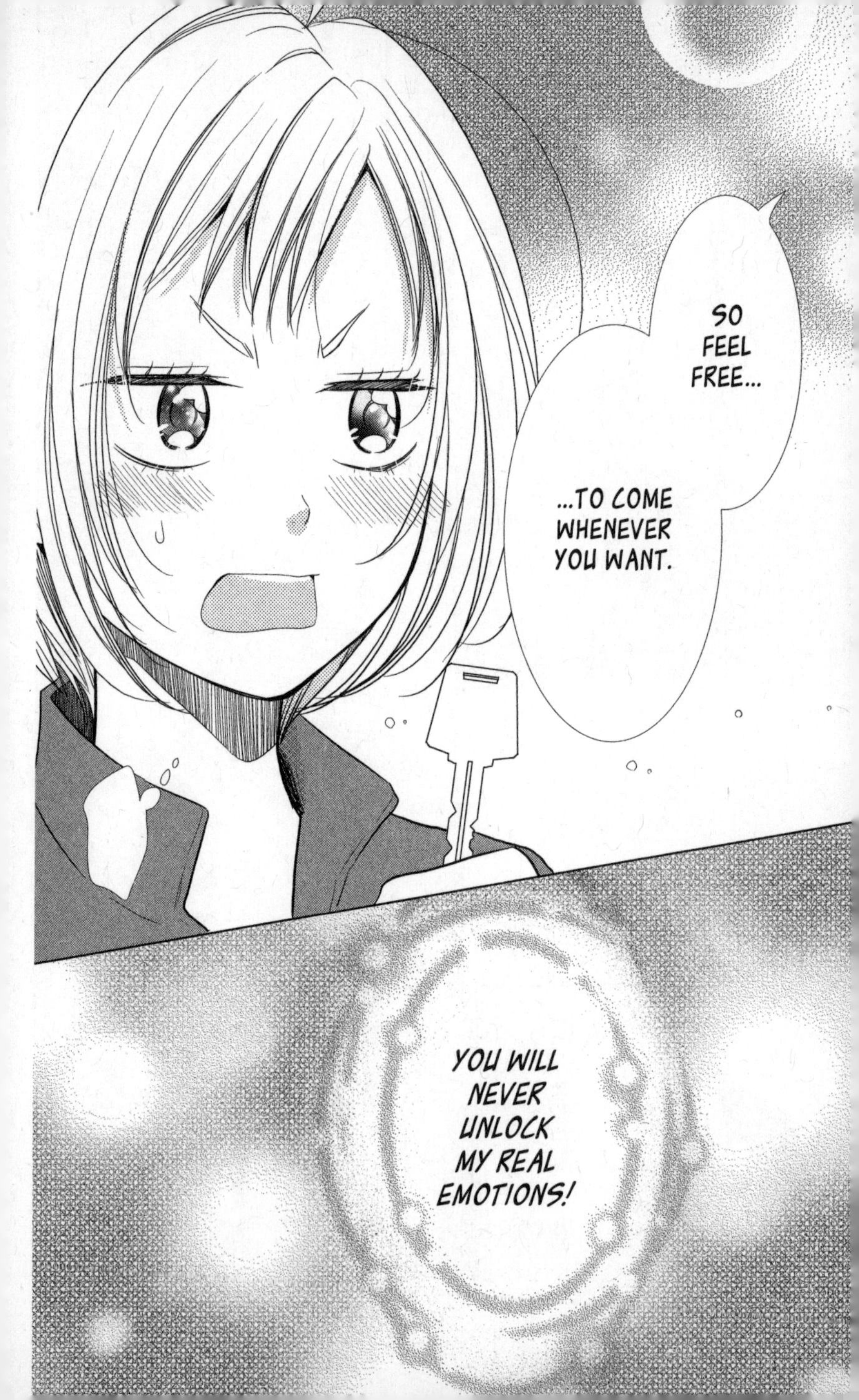
SO FEEL FREE...
...TO COME WHENEVER YOU WANT.
YOU WILL NEVER UNLOCK MY REAL EMOTIONS!

Reading Each Other's Minds ②

OKAY!
LET'S ALL CHEER SOUMA UP!
I don't know what happened, but cheer up!
Souma, Souma!
You're perfect!
DON'T WORRY, SOUMA.
YOU'RE YOUNG AND CUTE. ♡
IN FIVE YEARS I'LL TOTALLY DATE YOU. ♡
YAY, SOUMA!
SLAM
NICOLA... ...DOESN'T UNDERSTAND GUYS.

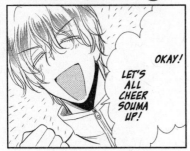

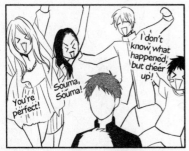

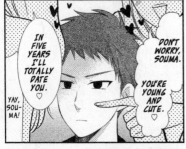

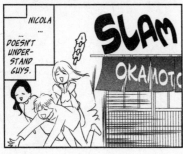

Reading Each Other's Minds ③

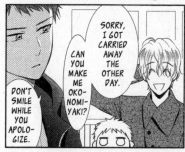

SORRY, I GOT CARRIED AWAY THE OTHER DAY.
CAN YOU MAKE ME OKONOMIYAKI?
DON'T SMILE WHILE YOU APOLOGIZE.
TO MAKE IT UP TO YOU, I'VE ARRANGED FOR ONE BLACK SANDARA, YOUR FAVORITE, TO BE DELIVERED PERIODICALLY.
BLACK SANDARA
WHAT DOES "PERIODICALLY" MEAN?!
AND I GOT AUTOGRAPHS FROM THE ITALIAN NATIONAL SOCCER TEAM.
YOU MADE THEM SIGN A NAPKIN?!
OH, TENMA!
I SEE YOU SENSE SOUMA'S INNER JOY!
?!

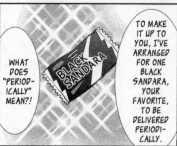

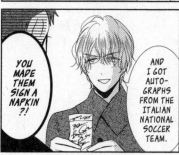

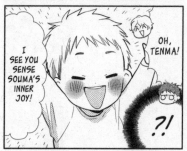

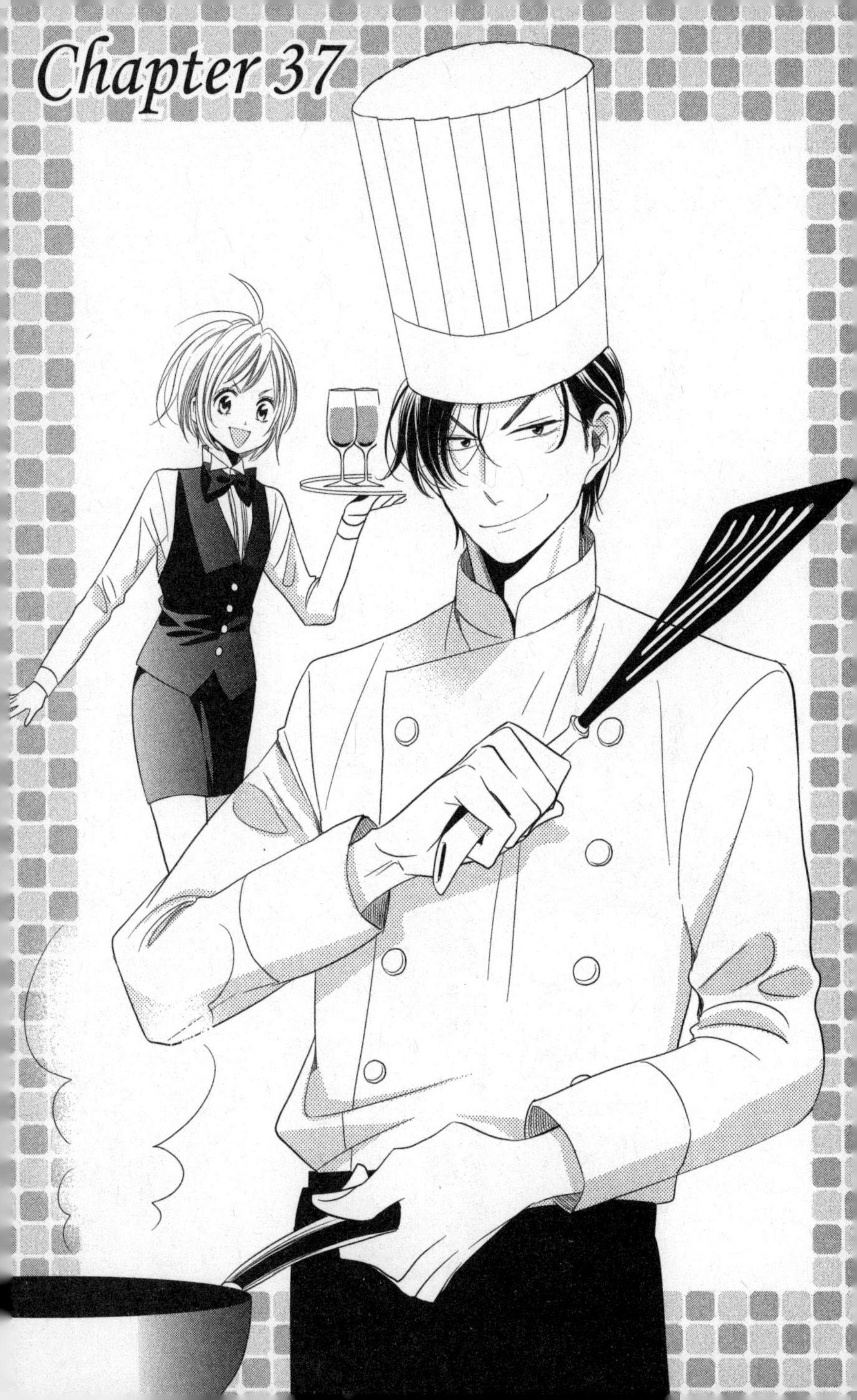
Chapter 37

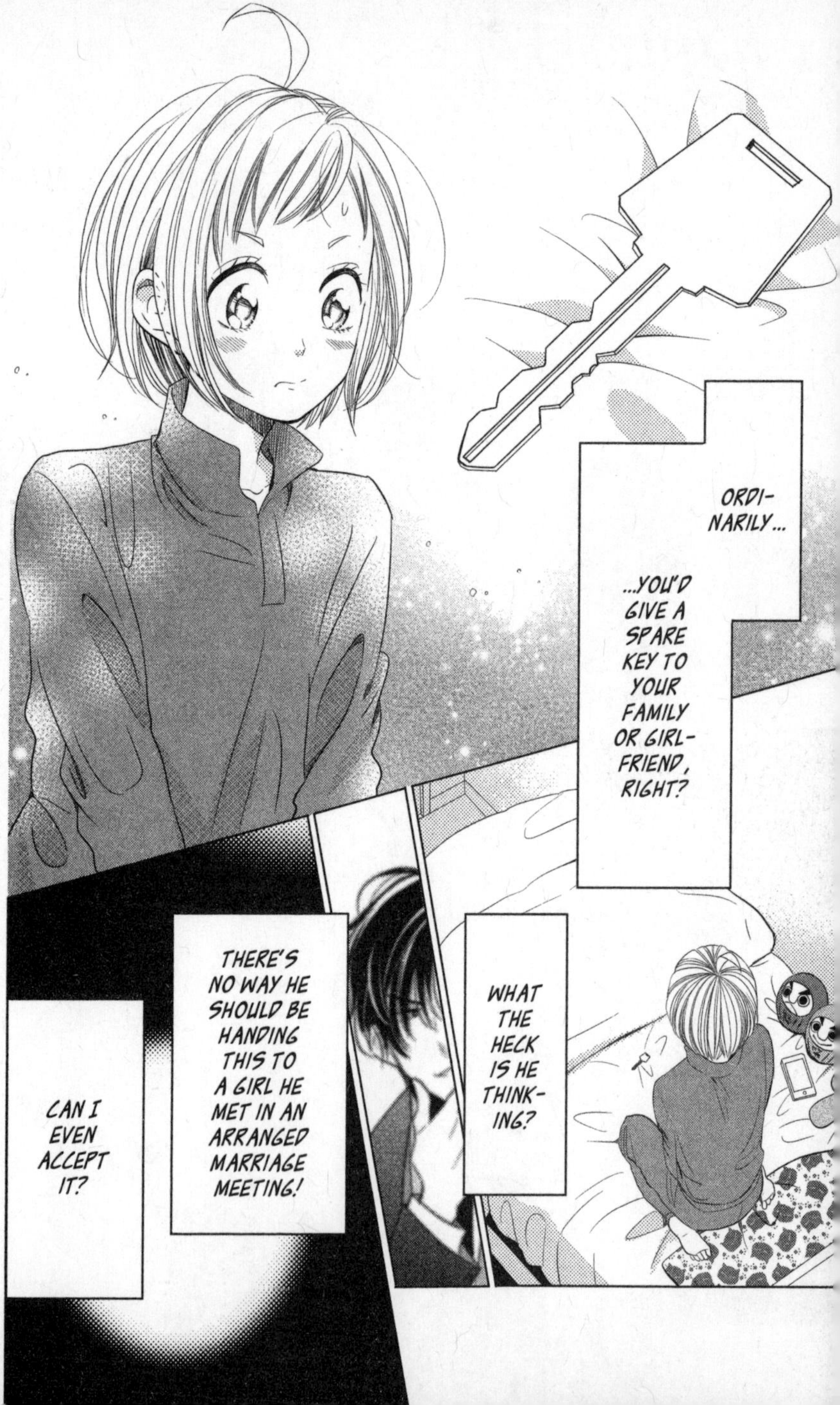
ORDI-NARILY...
...YOU'D GIVE A SPARE KEY TO YOUR FAMILY OR GIRL-FRIEND, RIGHT?
WHAT THE HECK IS HE THINK-ING?
THERE'S NO WAY HE SHOULD BE HANDING THIS TO A GIRL HE MET IN AN ARRANGED MARRIAGE MEETING!
CAN I EVEN ACCEPT IT?

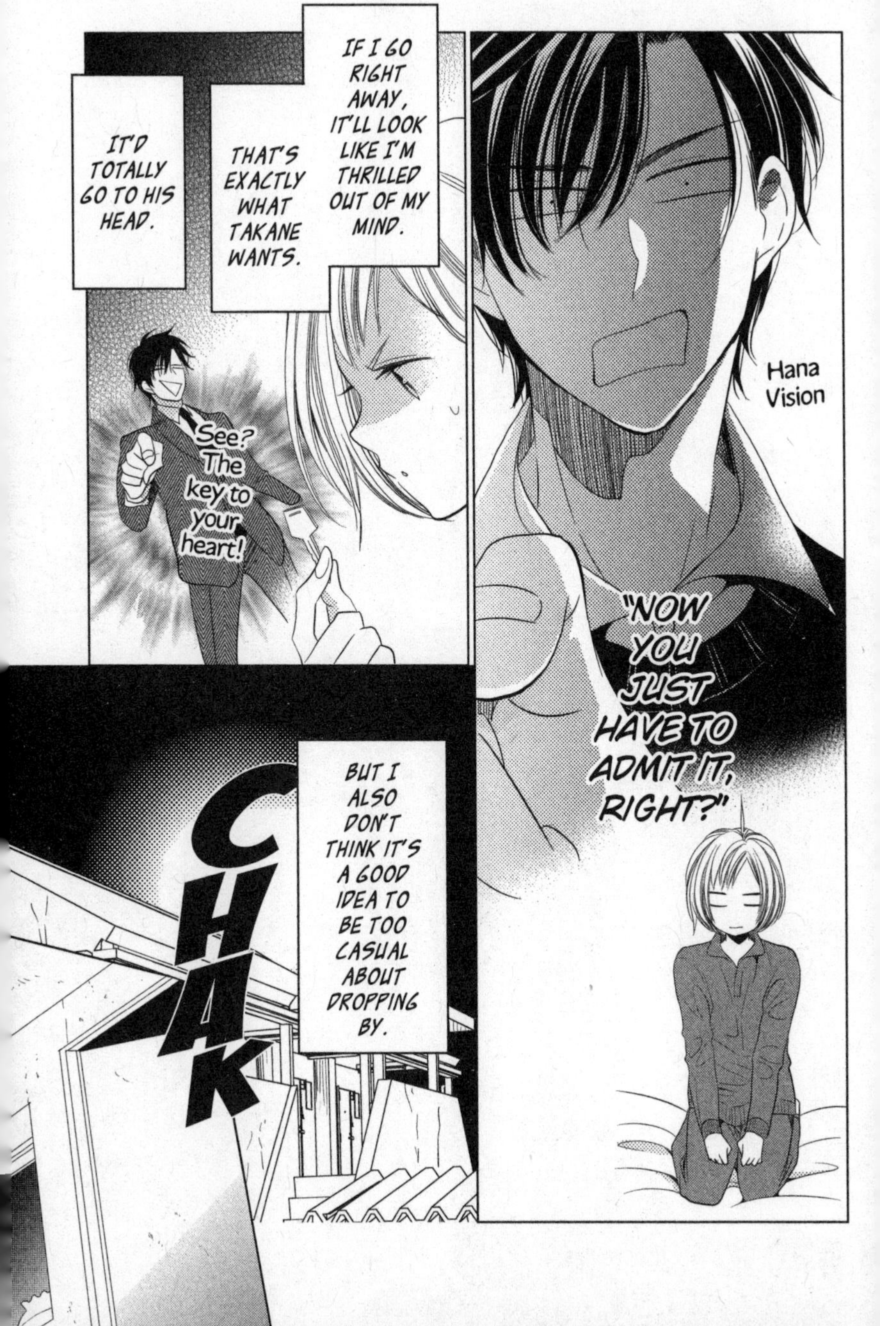
Hana Vision
"NOW YOU JUST HAVE TO ADMIT IT, RIGHT?"
IF I GO RIGHT AWAY, IT'LL LOOK LIKE I'M THRILLED OUT OF MY MIND.
THAT'S EXACTLY WHAT TAKANE WANTS.
IT'D TOTALLY GO TO HIS HEAD.
See? The key to your heart!
BUT I ALSO DON'T THINK IT'S A GOOD IDEA TO BE TOO CASUAL ABOUT DROPPING BY.
CHAK

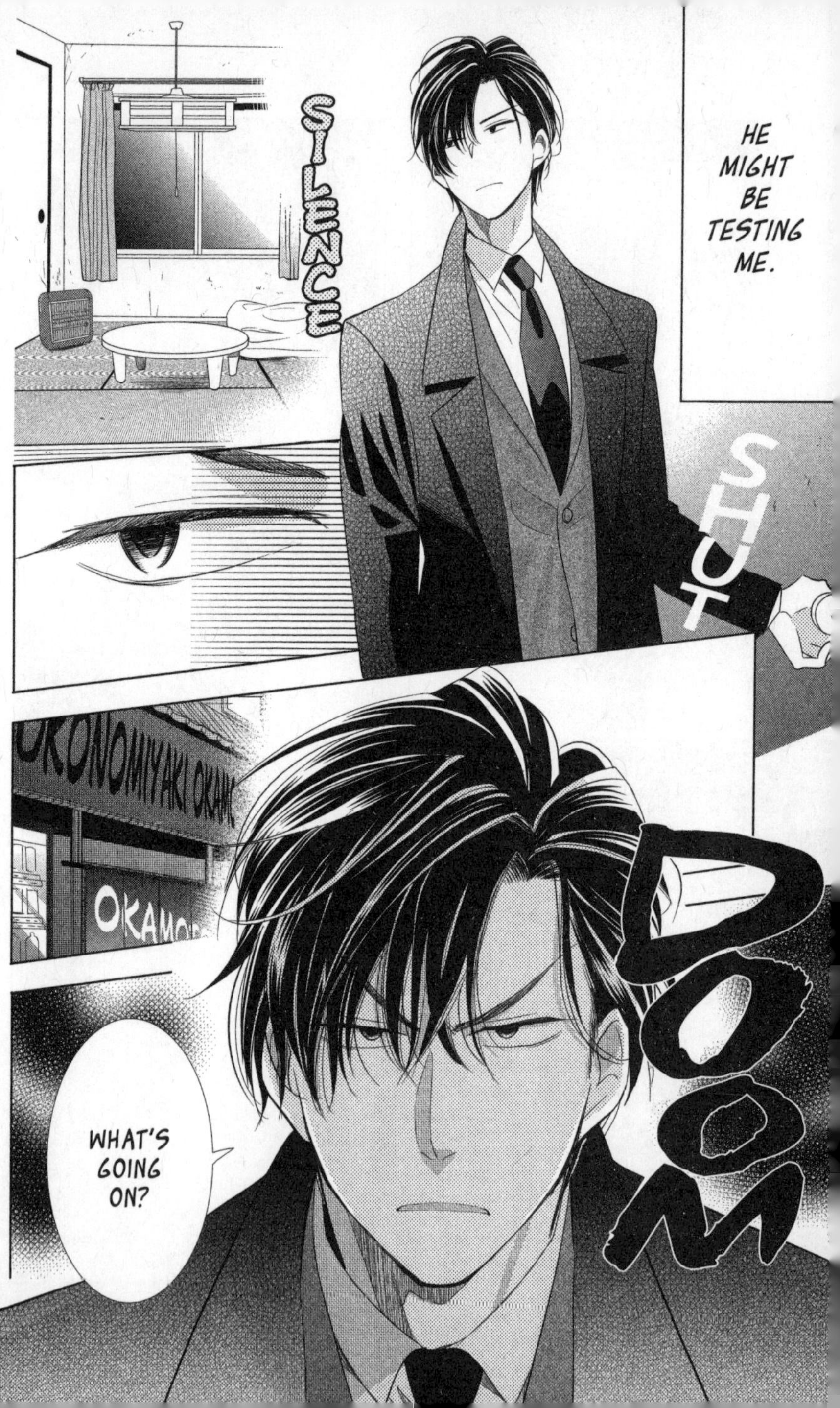
HE MIGHT BE TESTING ME.
SHUT
SILENCE
DOOM
WHAT'S GOING ON?

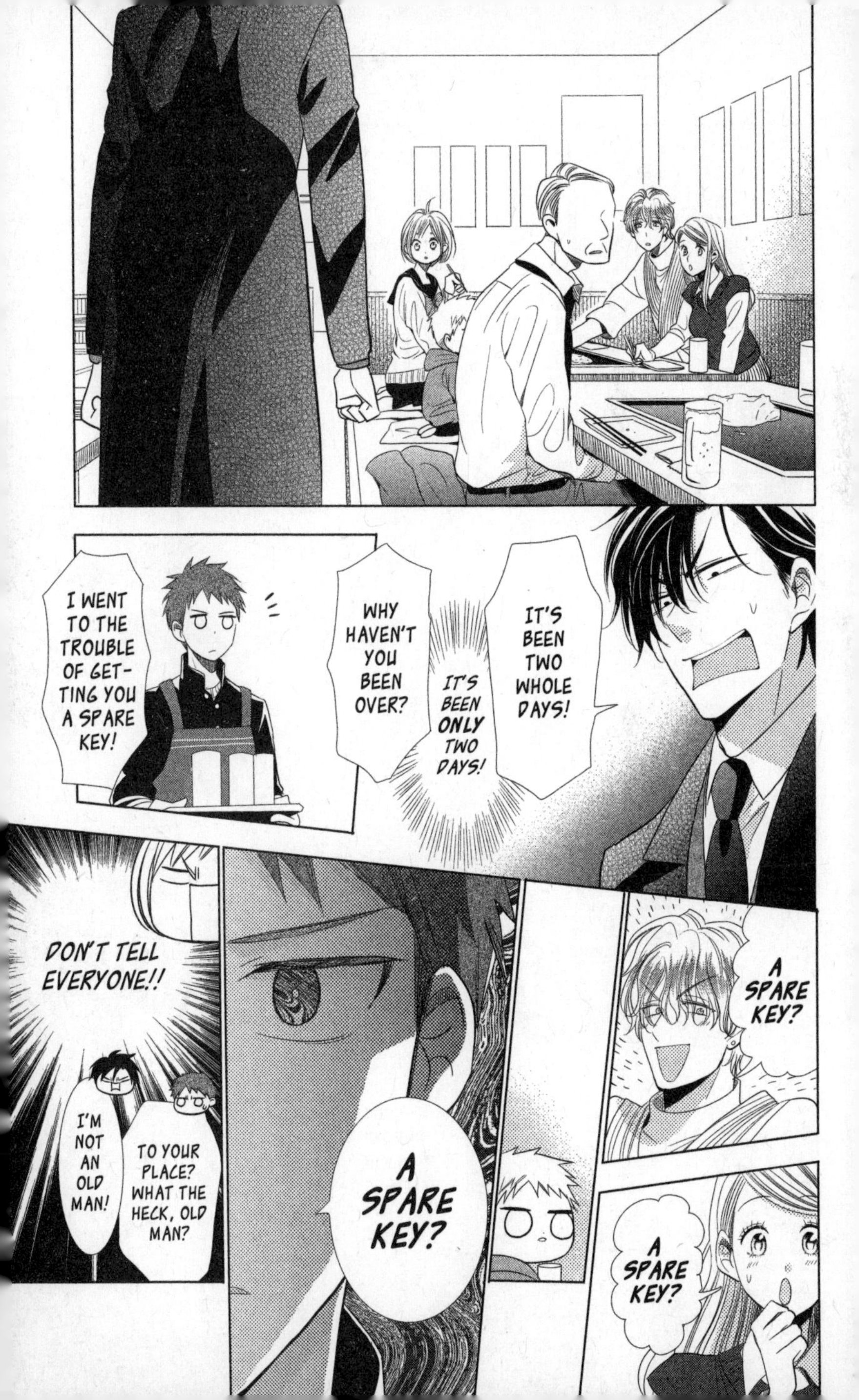
IT'S BEEN TWO WHOLE DAYS!
IT'S BEEN ONLY TWO DAYS!
WHY HAVEN'T YOU BEEN OVER?
I WENT TO THE TROUBLE OF GET-TING YOU A SPARE KEY!
A SPARE KEY?
A SPARE KEY?
A SPARE KEY?
DON'T TELL EVERYONE!!
TO YOUR PLACE? WHAT THE HECK, OLD MAN?
I'M NOT AN OLD MAN!

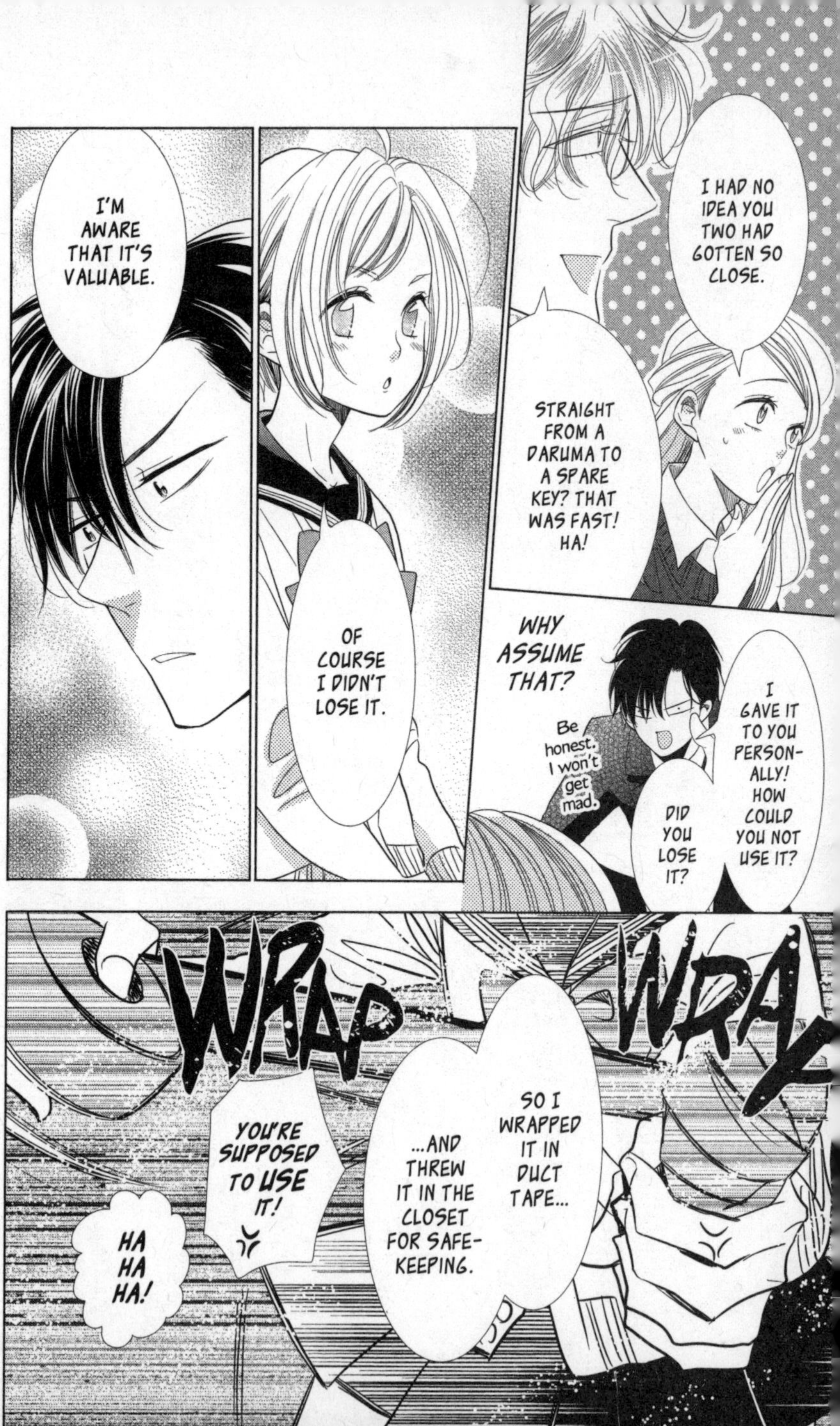
I HAD NO IDEA YOU TWO HAD GOTTEN SO CLOSE.
STRAIGHT FROM A DARUMA TO A SPARE KEY? THAT WAS FAST! HA!
I GAVE IT TO YOU PERSONALLY! HOW COULD YOU NOT USE IT?
WHY ASSUME THAT?
DID YOU LOSE IT?
Be honest. I won't get mad.
OF COURSE I DIDN'T LOSE IT.
I'M AWARE THAT IT'S VALUABLE.
WRAP
WRAP
SO I WRAPPED IT IN DUCT TAPE...
...AND THREW IT IN THE CLOSET FOR SAFE-KEEPING.
YOU'RE SUPPOSED TO USE IT!
HA HA HA!

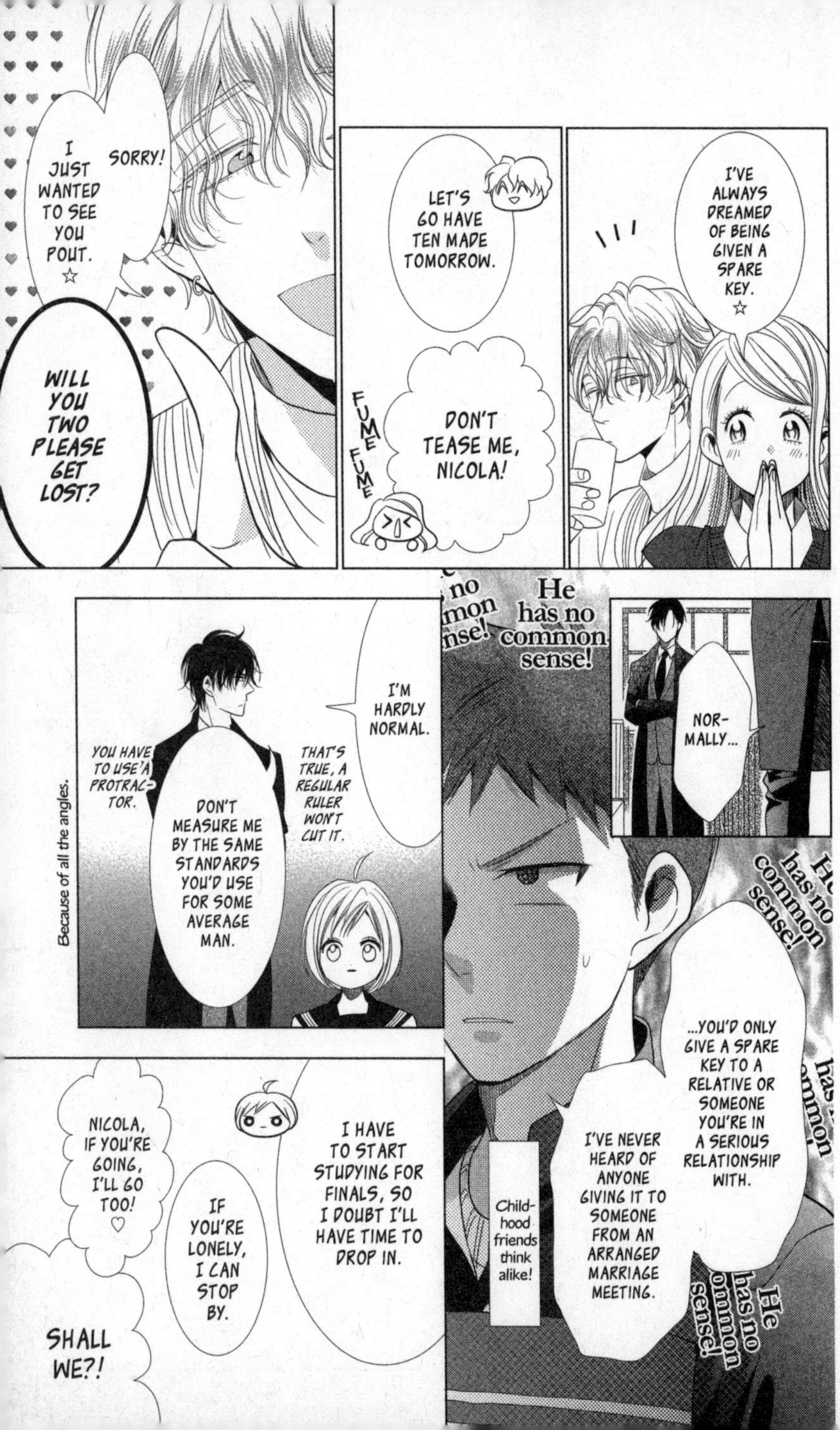
I'VE ALWAYS DREAMED OF BEING GIVEN A SPARE KEY. ☆
LET'S GO HAVE TEN MADE TOMORROW.
FUME FUME
DON'T TEASE ME, NICOLA!
SORRY!
I JUST WANTED TO SEE YOU POUT. ☆
WILL YOU TWO PLEASE GET LOST?
NOR-MALLY...
He has no common sense!
He has no common sense!
...YOU'D ONLY GIVE A SPARE KEY TO A RELATIVE OR SOMEONE YOU'RE IN A SERIOUS RELATIONSHIP WITH.
I'VE NEVER HEARD OF ANYONE GIVING IT TO SOMEONE FROM AN ARRANGED MARRIAGE MEETING.
Child-hood friends think alike!
He has no common sense!
I'M HARDLY NORMAL.
DON'T MEASURE ME BY THE SAME STANDARDS YOU'D USE FOR SOME AVERAGE MAN.
THAT'S TRUE, A REGULAR RULER WON'T CUT IT.
YOU HAVE TO USE A PROTRAC-TOR.
Because of all the angles.
I HAVE TO START STUDYING FOR FINALS, SO I DOUBT I'LL HAVE TIME TO DROP IN.
IF YOU'RE LONELY, I CAN STOP BY.
NICOLA, IF YOU'RE GOING, I'LL GO TOO! ♡
SHALL WE?!

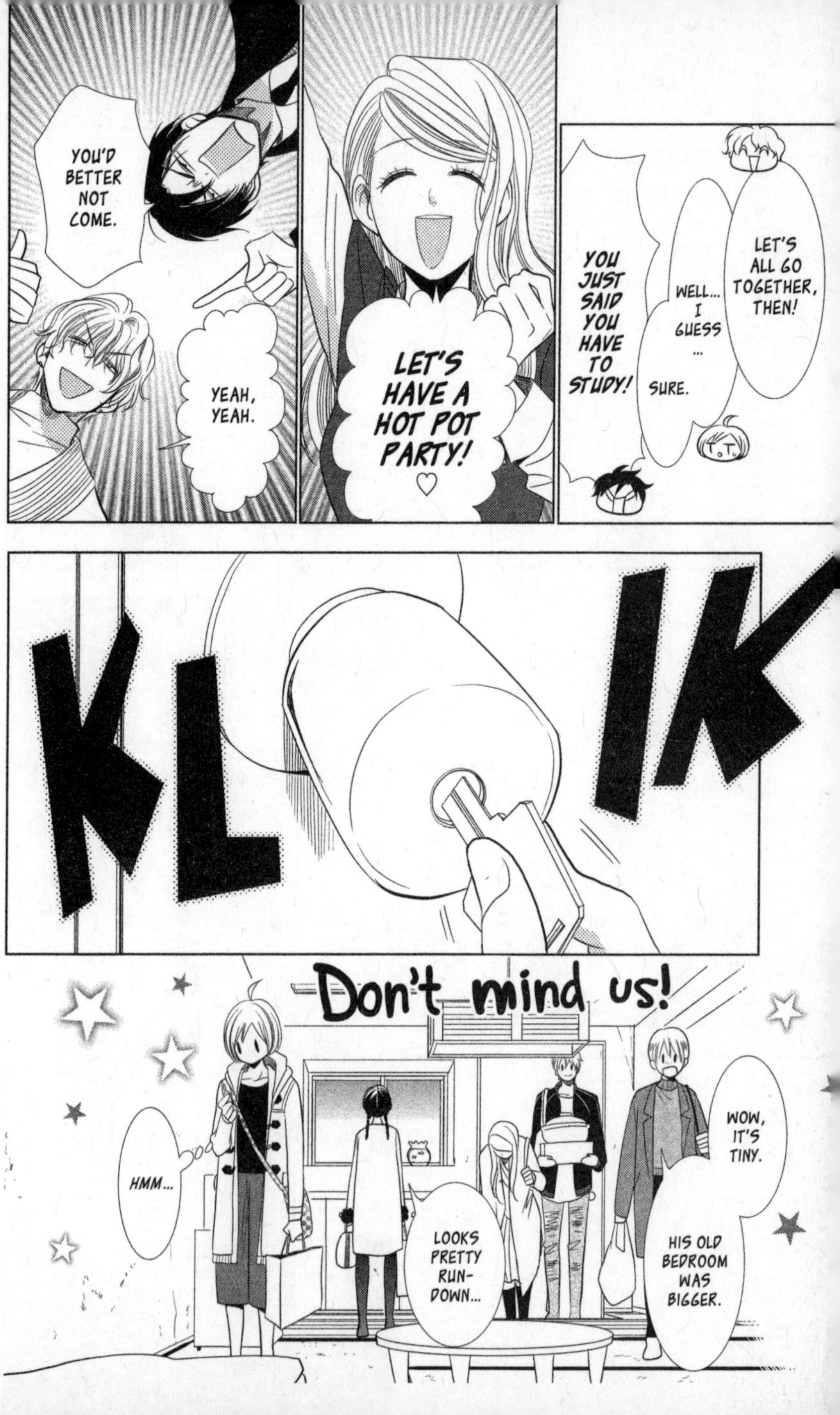
LET'S ALL GO TOGETHER, THEN!
WELL... I GUESS... SURE.
YOU JUST SAID YOU HAVE TO STUDY!
LET'S HAVE A HOT POT PARTY! ♡
YOU'D BETTER NOT COME.
YEAH, YEAH.
KLIK
Don't mind us!
WOW, IT'S TINY.
HIS OLD BEDROOM WAS BIGGER.
LOOKS PRETTY RUN-DOWN...
HMM...

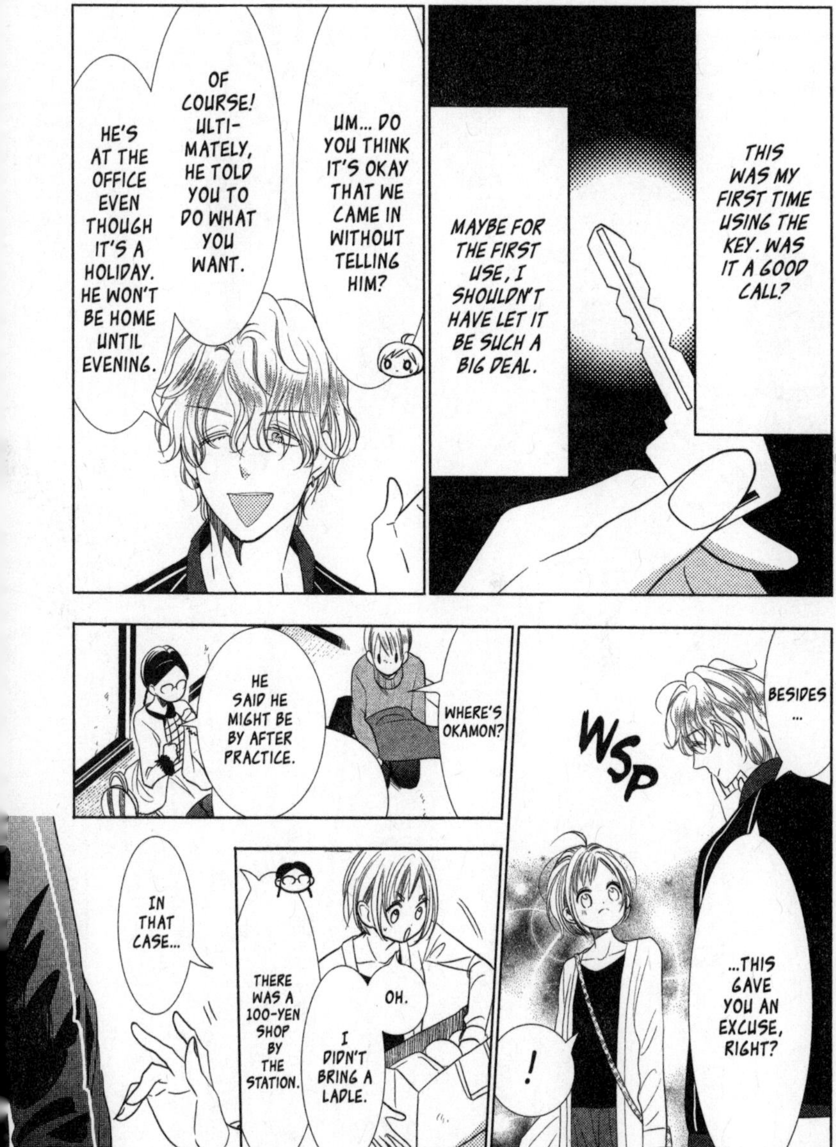
THIS WAS MY FIRST TIME USING THE KEY. WAS IT A GOOD CALL?
MAYBE FOR THE FIRST USE, I SHOULDN'T HAVE LET IT BE SUCH A BIG DEAL.
UM... DO YOU THINK IT'S OKAY THAT WE CAME IN WITHOUT TELLING HIM?
OF COURSE! ULTI-MATELY, HE TOLD YOU TO DO WHAT YOU WANT.
HE'S AT THE OFFICE EVEN THOUGH IT'S A HOLIDAY. HE WON'T BE HOME UNTIL EVENING.
BESIDES...
WSP
...THIS GAVE YOU AN EXCUSE, RIGHT?
!
WHERE'S OKAMON?
HE SAID HE MIGHT BE BY AFTER PRACTICE.
OH.
I DIDN'T BRING A LADLE.
THERE WAS A 100-YEN SHOP BY THE STATION.
IN THAT CASE...

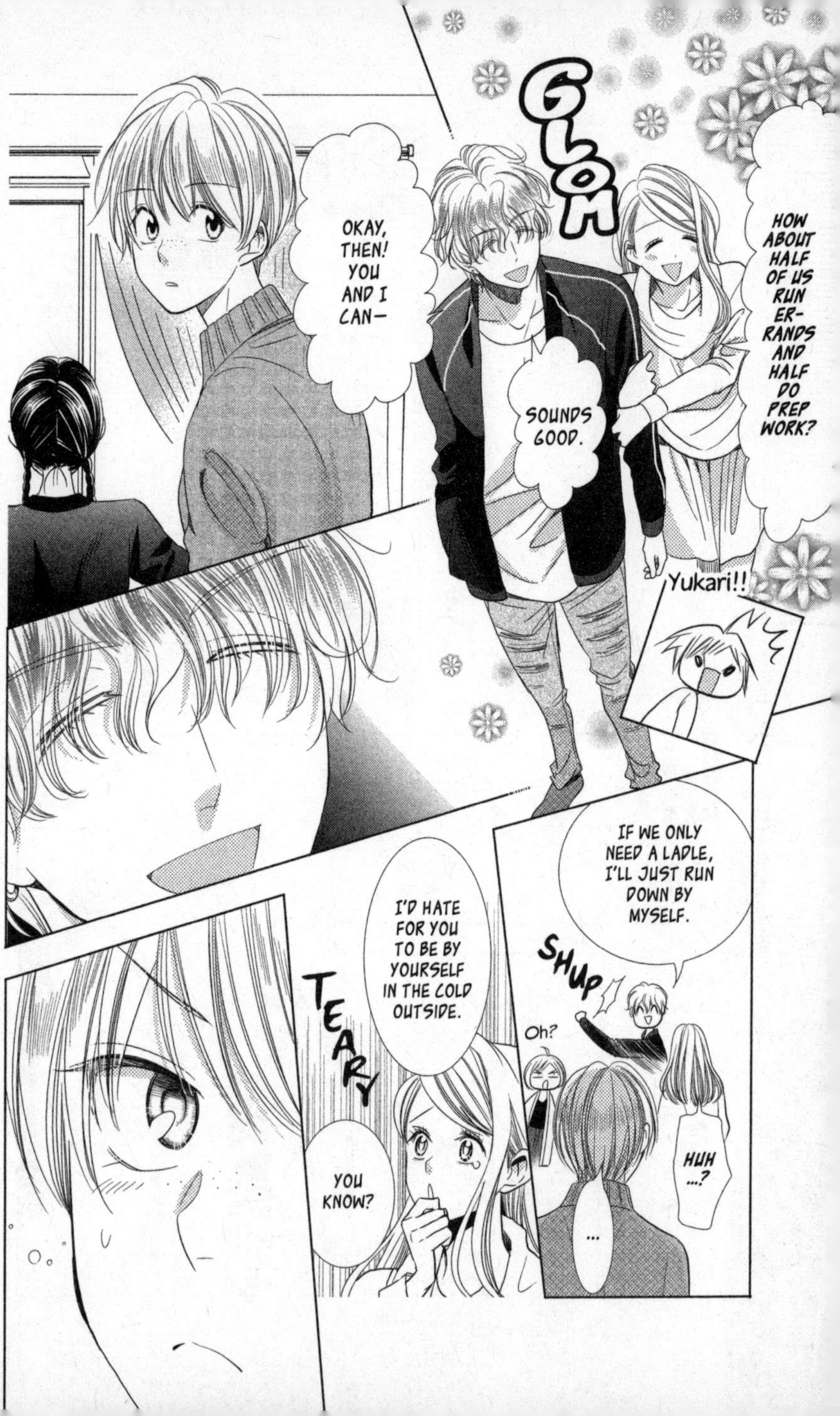
HOW ABOUT HALF OF US RUN ER-RANDS AND HALF DO PREP WORK?
SOUNDS GOOD.
GLOM
OKAY, THEN! YOU AND I CAN—
Yukari!!
IF WE ONLY NEED A LADLE, I'LL JUST RUN DOWN BY MYSELF.
SHUP
Oh?
HUH ...?
...
I'D HATE FOR YOU TO BE BY YOURSELF IN THE COLD OUTSIDE.
TEARY
YOU KNOW?

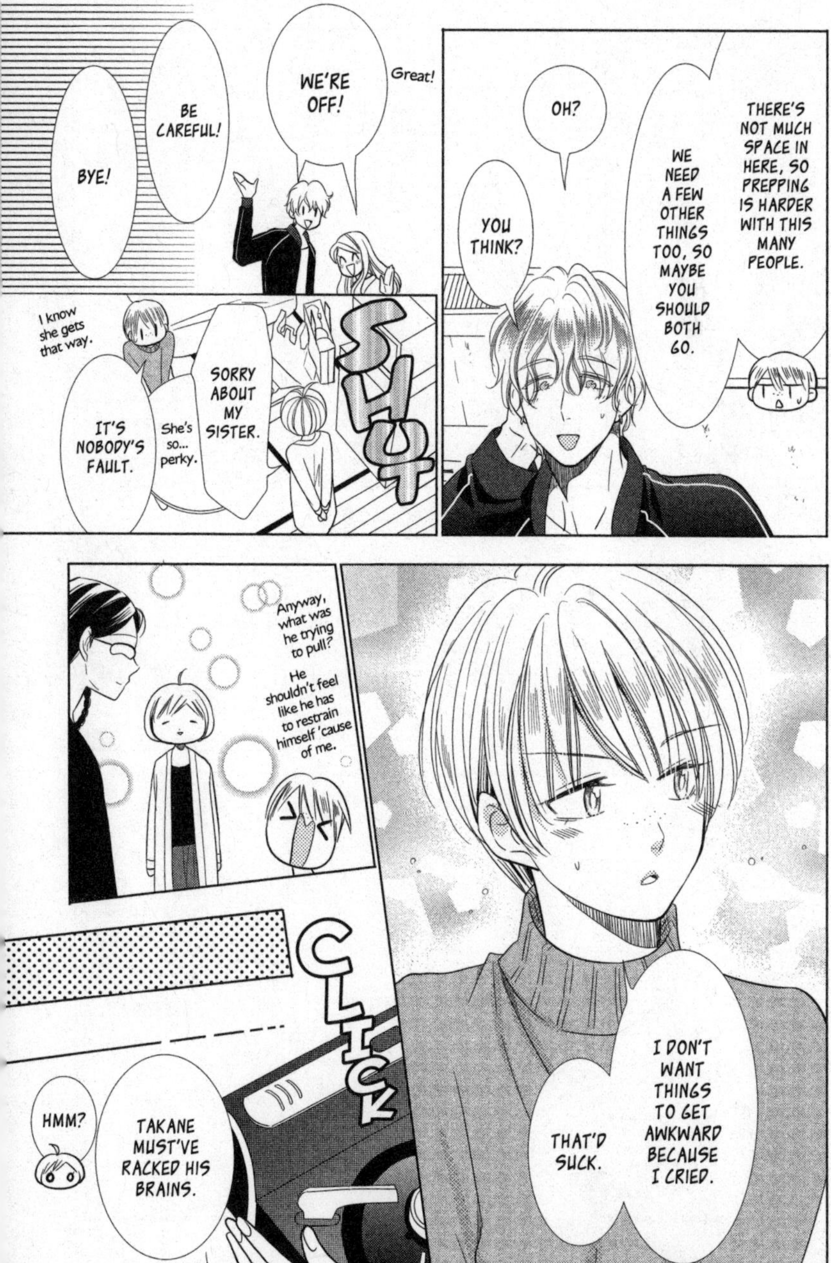

THERE'S NOT MUCH SPACE IN HERE, SO PREPPING IS HARDER WITH THIS MANY PEOPLE.
WE NEED A FEW OTHER THINGS TOO, SO MAYBE YOU SHOULD BOTH GO.
OH?
YOU THINK?
Great!
WE'RE OFF!
BE CAREFUL!
BYE!
SHUT
SORRY ABOUT MY SISTER.
She's so... perky.
IT'S NOBODY'S FAULT.
I know she gets that way.
I DON'T WANT THINGS TO GET AWKWARD BECAUSE I CRIED.
THAT'D SUCK.
Anyway, what was he trying to pull?
He shouldn't feel like he has to restrain himself 'cause of me.
CLICK
TAKANE MUST'VE RACKED HIS BRAINS.
HMM?

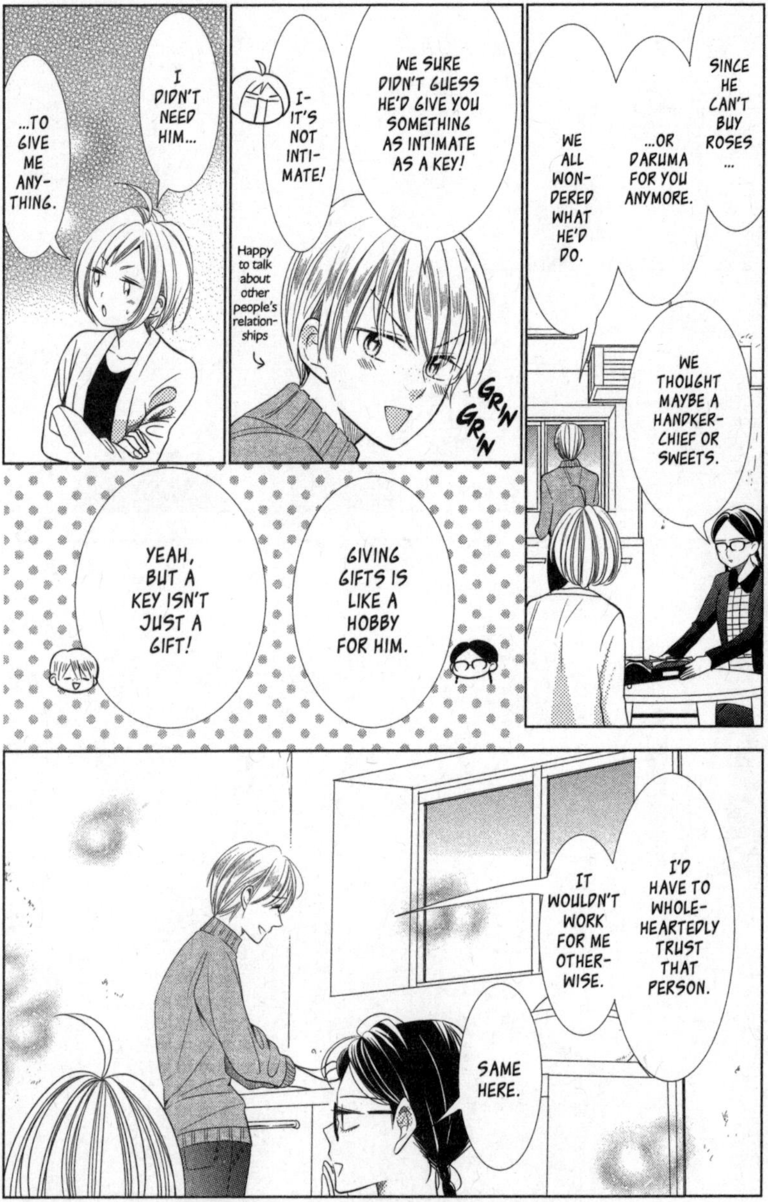
SINCE HE CAN'T BUY ROSES ...
...OR DARUMA FOR YOU ANYMORE.
WE ALL WONDERED WHAT HE'D DO.
WE THOUGHT MAYBE A HANDKERCHIEF OR SWEETS.
WE SURE DIDN'T GUESS HE'D GIVE YOU SOMETHING AS INTIMATE AS A KEY!
GRIN GRIN
I-IT'S NOT INTIMATE!
Happy to talk about other people's relationships
I DIDN'T NEED HIM...
...TO GIVE ME ANYTHING.
GIVING GIFTS IS LIKE A HOBBY FOR HIM.
YEAH, BUT A KEY ISN'T JUST A GIFT!
I'D HAVE TO WHOLEHEARTEDLY TRUST THAT PERSON.
IT WOULDN'T WORK FOR ME OTHERWISE.
SAME HERE.

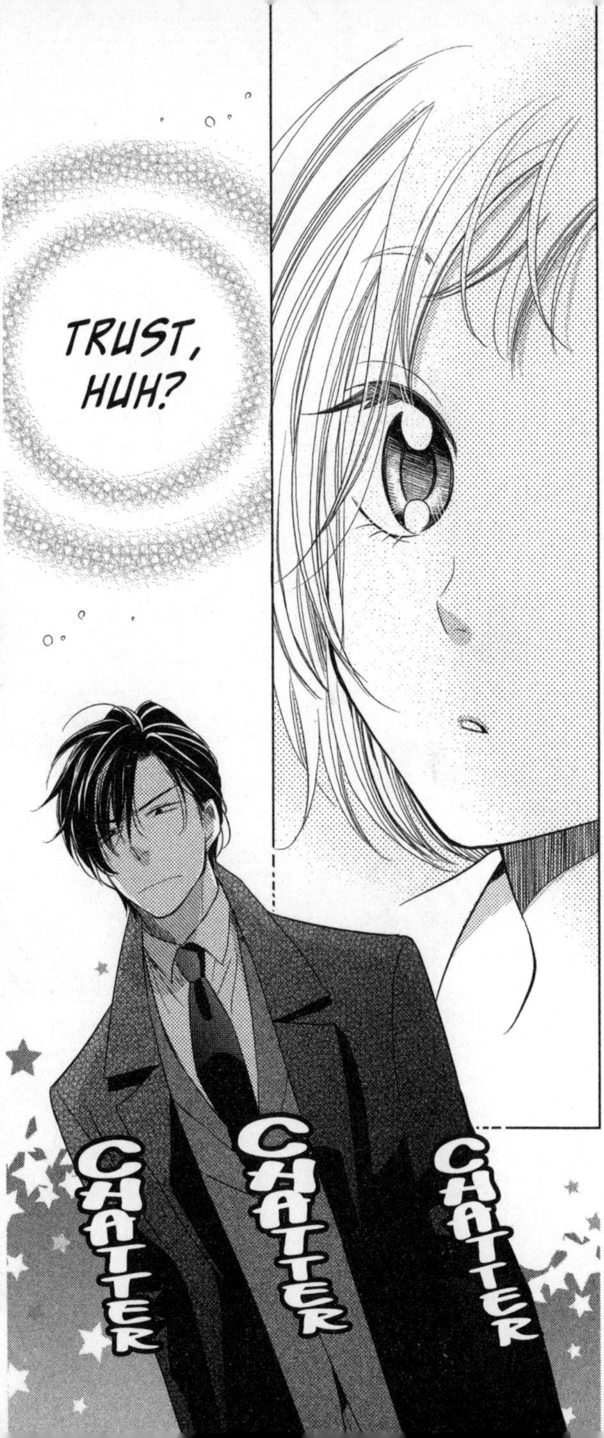
TRUST, HUH?
CHATTER
CHATTER
CHATTER

A
• Request •

Someone wrote to me and said, "I want to see Takane in drag!" Now, that's something I can always get behind, so I was excited. But of all my male characters, Takane's the one who dresses in the most masculine clothing, so putting him in women's clothes is pretty intimidating.

I'm not positive there's enough demand for it at the moment, so for now, I'll stick with this picture.

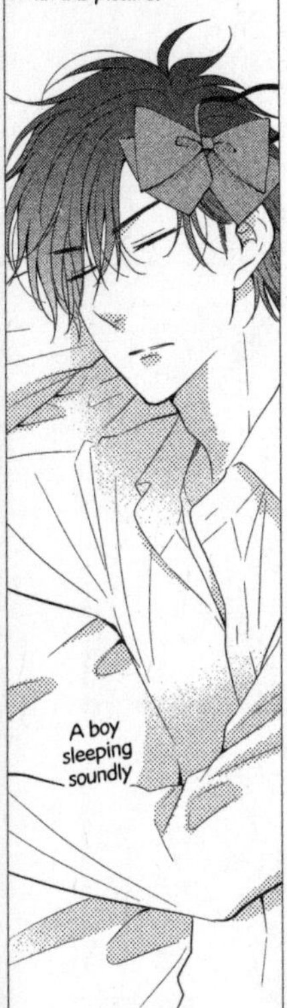
A boy sleeping soundly

Takane dozed off and someone stuck a bow in his hair.

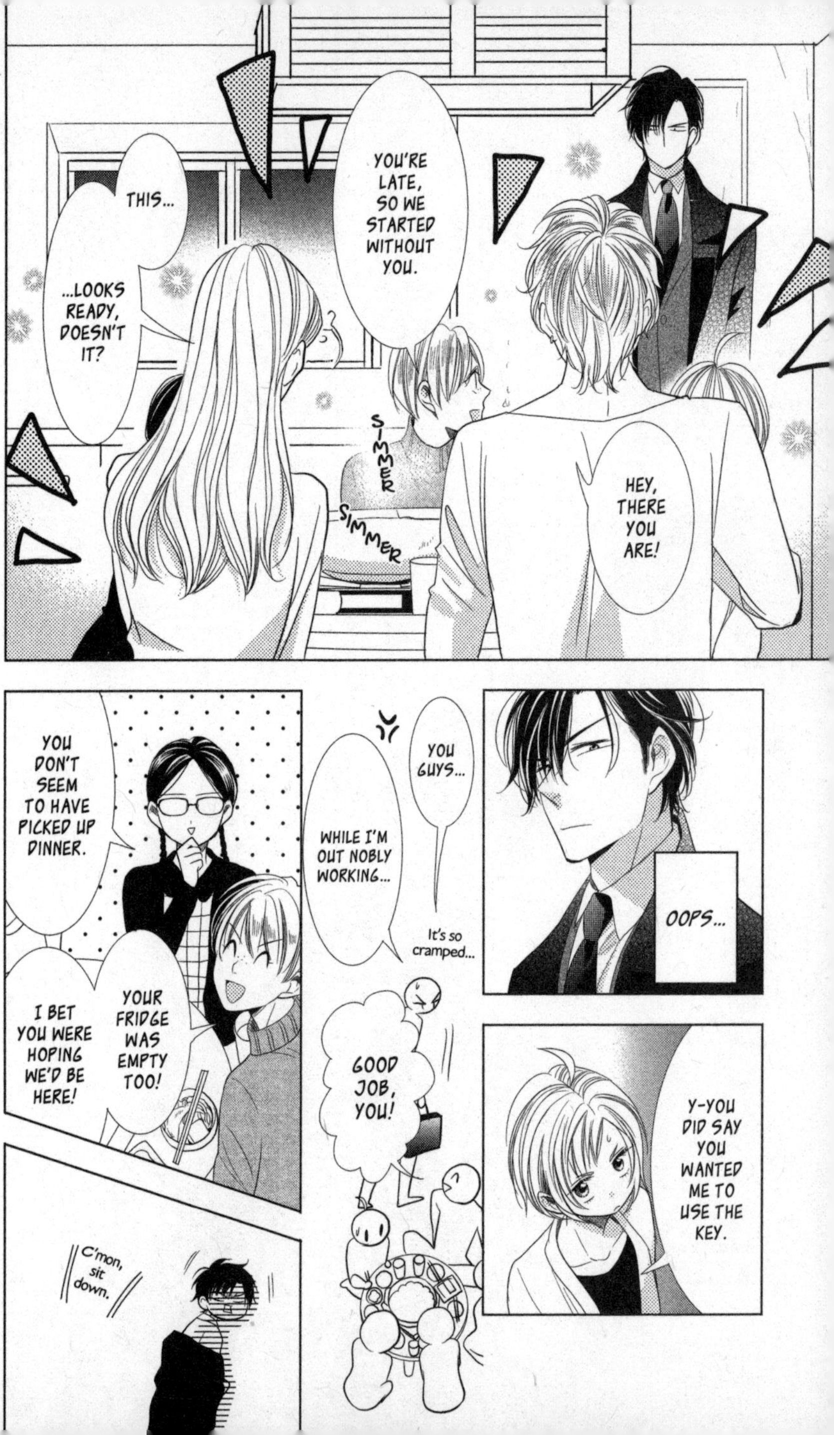
HEY, THERE YOU ARE!
YOU'RE LATE, SO WE STARTED WITHOUT YOU.
THIS...
...LOOKS READY, DOESN'T IT?
SIMMER SIMMER
OOPS...
Y-YOU DID SAY YOU WANTED ME TO USE THE KEY.
YOU GUYS...
WHILE I'M OUT NOBLY WORKING...
It's so cramped...
GOOD JOB, YOU!
YOU DON'T SEEM TO HAVE PICKED UP DINNER.
YOUR FRIDGE WAS EMPTY TOO!
I BET YOU WERE HOPING WE'D BE HERE!
C'mon, sit down.

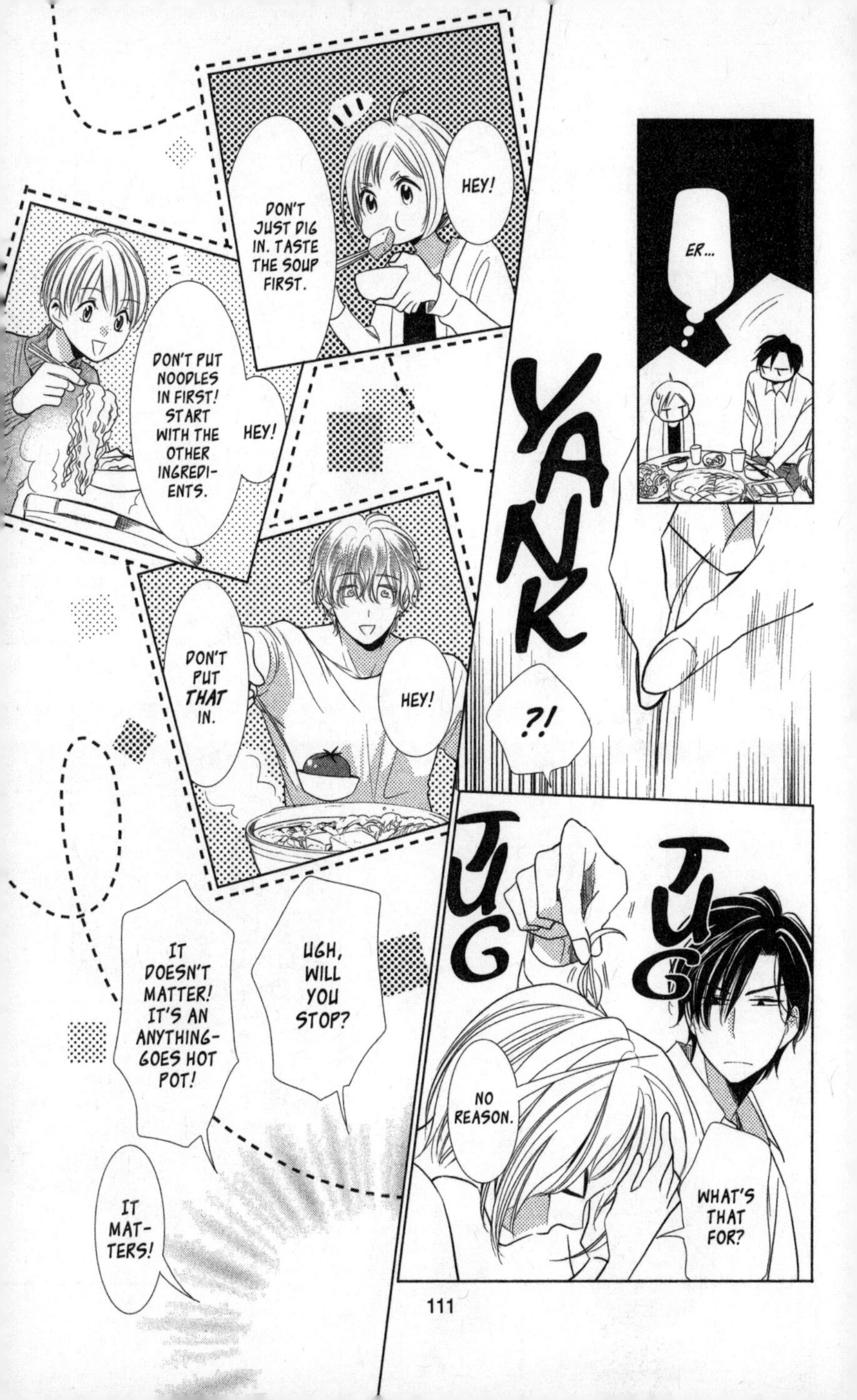

ER...
YANK
?!
TUG
TUG
WHAT'S THAT FOR?
NO REASON.
HEY!
DON'T JUST DIG IN. TASTE THE SOUP FIRST.
HEY!
DON'T PUT NOODLES IN FIRST! START WITH THE OTHER INGREDI-ENTS.
HEY!
DON'T PUT *THAT* IN.
UGH, WILL YOU STOP?
IT DOESN'T MATTER! IT'S AN ANYTHING-GOES HOT POT!
IT MAT-TERS!

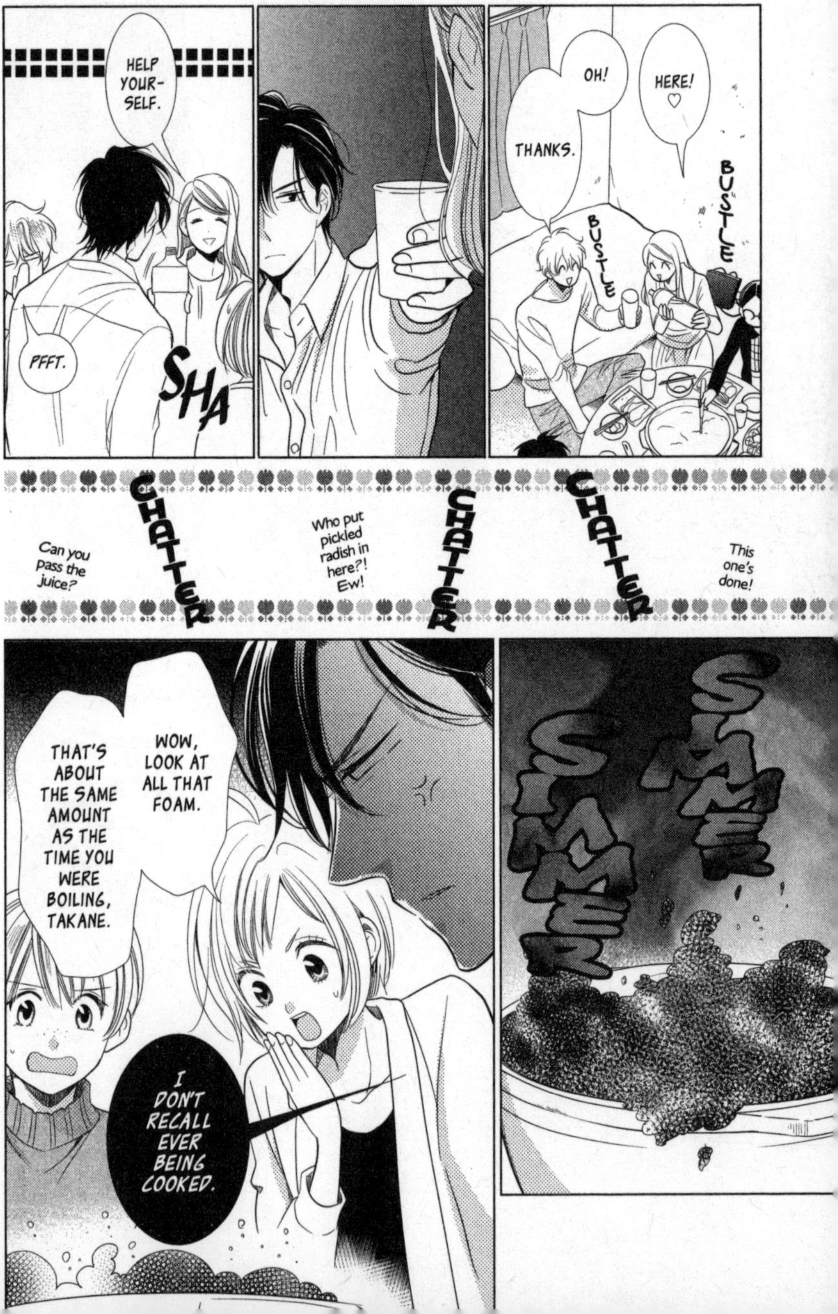
HERE! ♡
OH!
THANKS.
BUSTLE
BUSTLE
HELP YOURSELF.
PFFT.
SHA
This one's done!
CHATTER
Who put pickled radish in here?! Ew!
CHATTER
CHATTER
Can you pass the juice?
SIMMER
SIMMER
WOW, LOOK AT ALL THAT FOAM.
THAT'S ABOUT THE SAME AMOUNT AS THE TIME YOU WERE BOILING, TAKANE.
I DON'T RECALL EVER BEING COOKED.

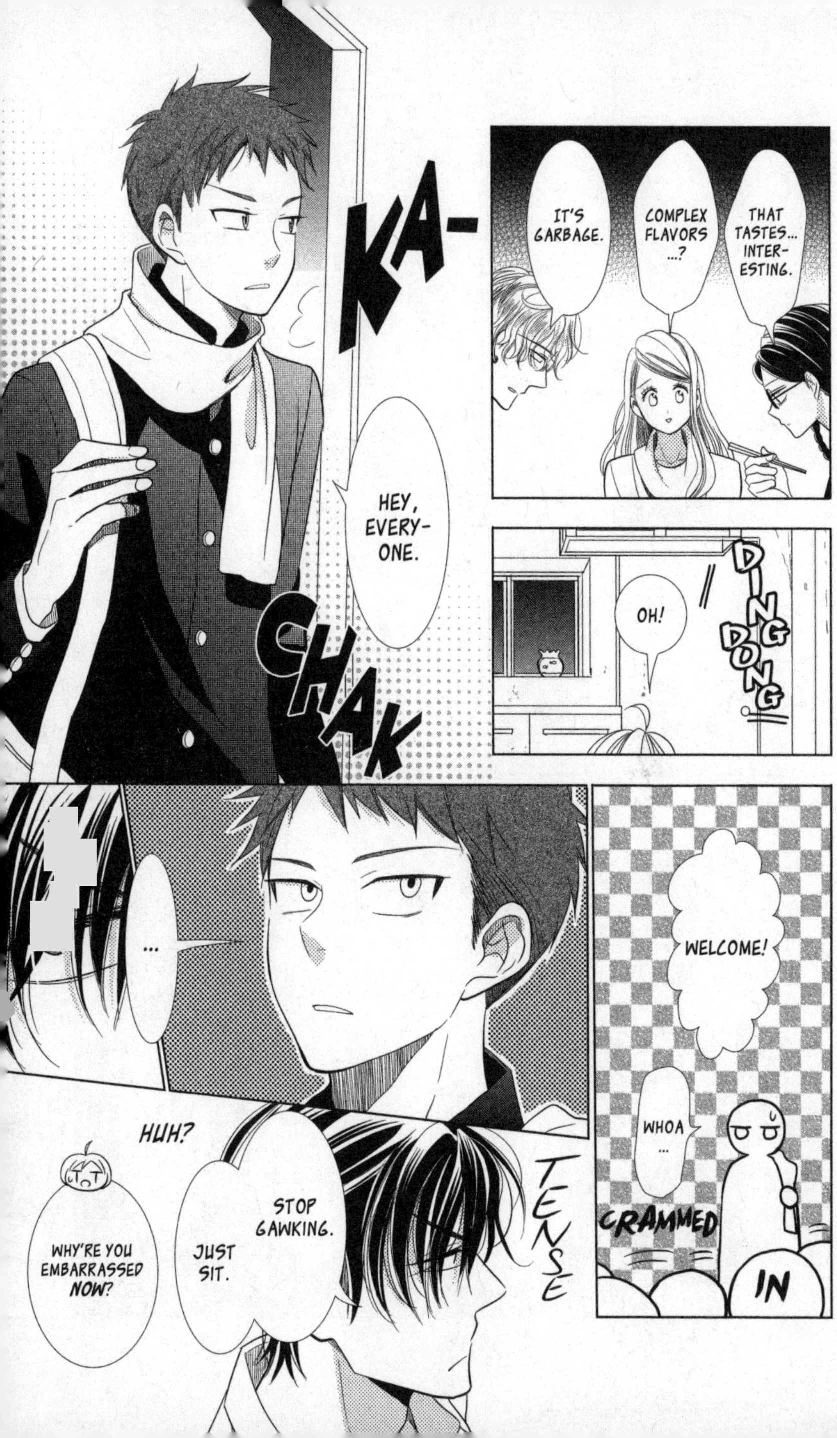
THAT TASTES... INTERESTING.
COMPLEX FLAVORS ...?
IT'S GARBAGE.
DING DONG
OH!
KA-CHAK
HEY, EVERYONE.
WELCOME!
WHOA ...
CRAMMED IN
...
TENSE
STOP GAWKING.
JUST SIT.
HUH?
WHY'RE YOU EMBARRASSED NOW?

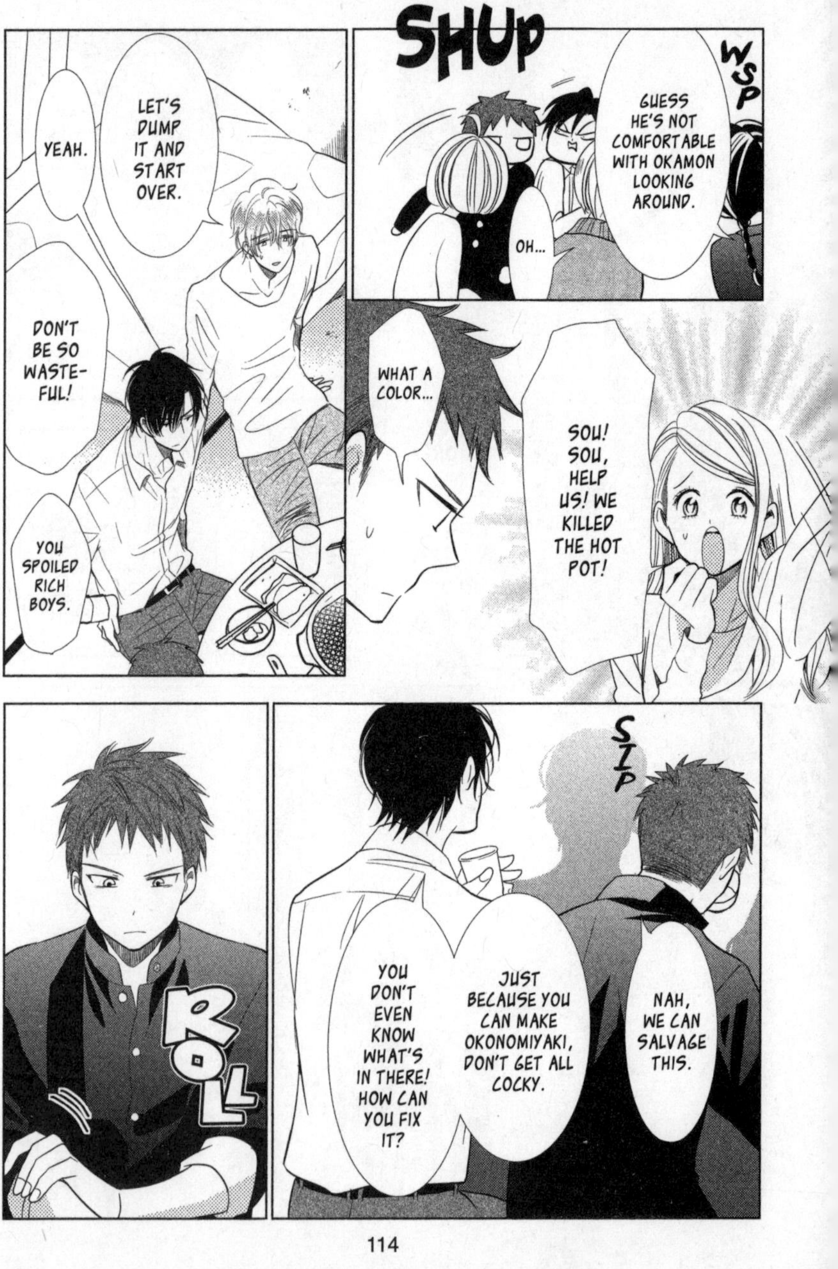
SHUP
WSP
GUESS HE'S NOT COMFORTABLE WITH OKAMON LOOKING AROUND.
OH...
SOU! SOU, HELP US! WE KILLED THE HOT POT!
WHAT A COLOR...
LET'S DUMP IT AND START OVER.
YEAH.
DON'T BE SO WASTE-FUL!
YOU SPOILED RICH BOYS.
SIP
NAH, WE CAN SALVAGE THIS.
JUST BECAUSE YOU CAN MAKE OKONOMIYAKI, DON'T GET ALL COCKY.
YOU DON'T EVEN KNOW WHAT'S IN THERE! HOW CAN YOU FIX IT?
ROLL

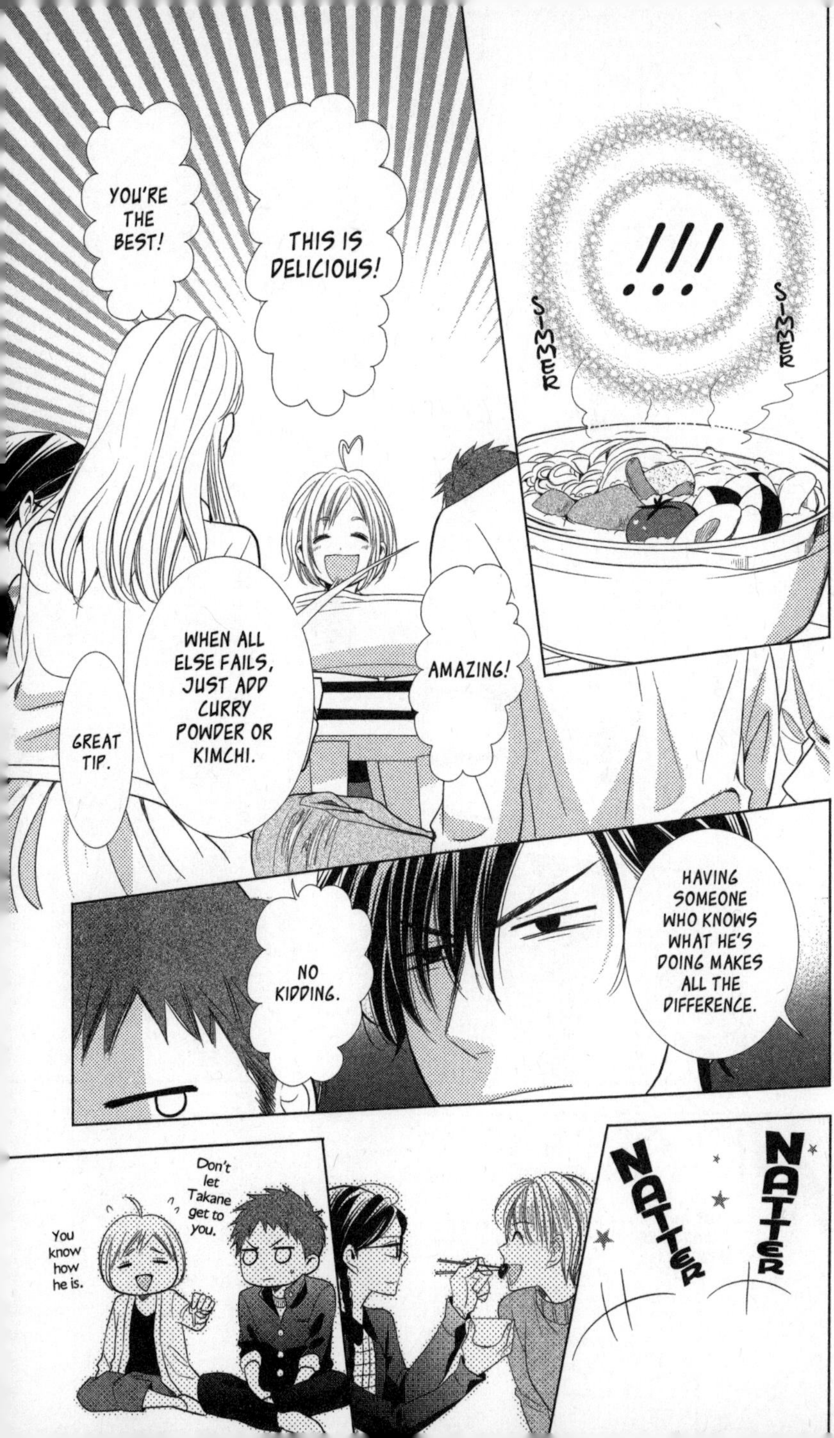
SIMMER
!!!
SIMMER
THIS IS DELICIOUS!
YOU'RE THE BEST!
AMAZING!
WHEN ALL ELSE FAILS, JUST ADD CURRY POWDER OR KIMCHI.
GREAT TIP.
HAVING SOMEONE WHO KNOWS WHAT HE'S DOING MAKES ALL THE DIFFERENCE.
NO KIDDING.
NATTER
NATTER
Don't let Takane get to you.
You know how he is.

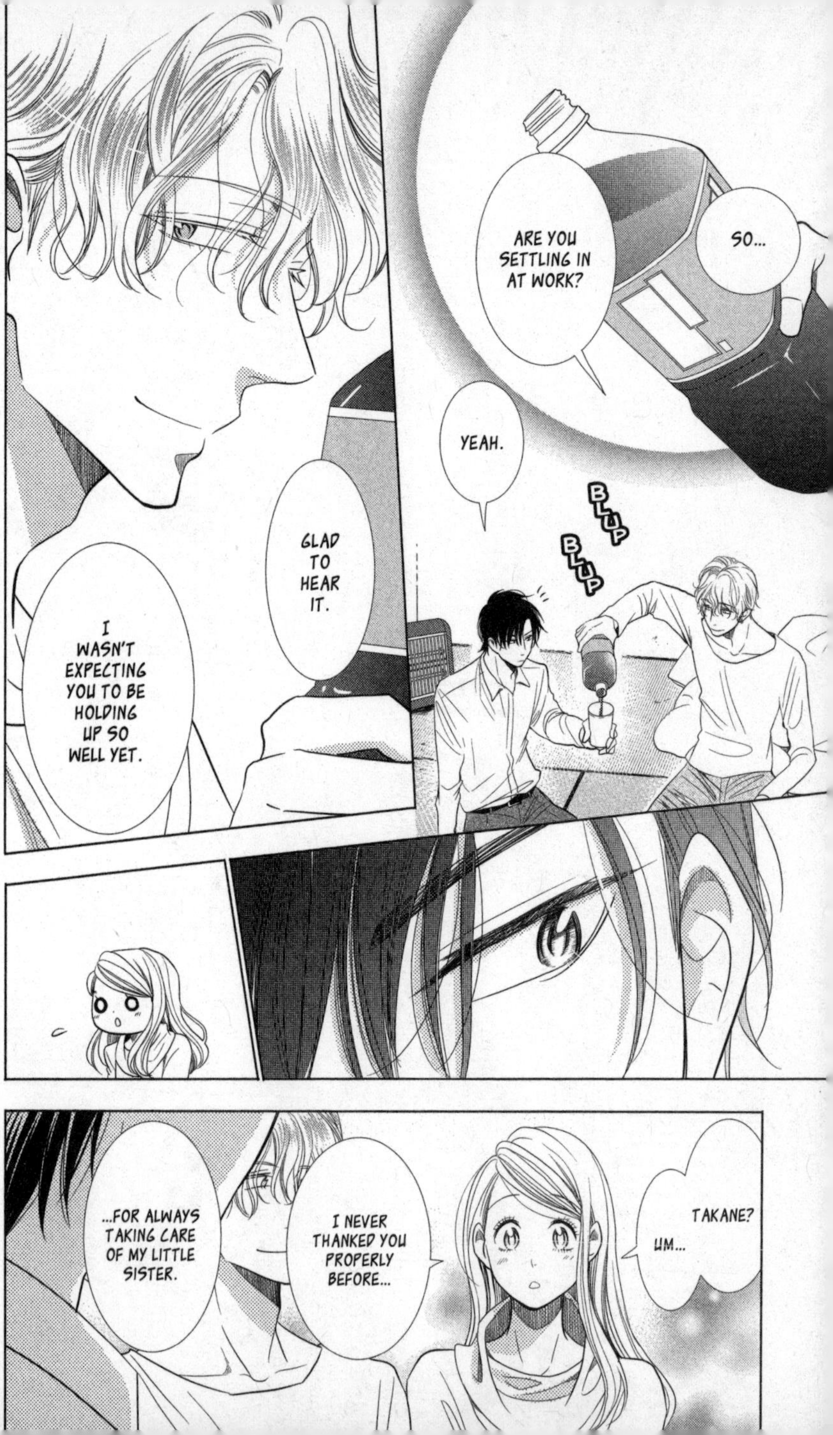
SO...
ARE YOU SETTLING IN AT WORK?
YEAH.
BLUP BLUP
GLAD TO HEAR IT.
I WASN'T EXPECTING YOU TO BE HOLDING UP SO WELL YET.
TAKANE? UM...
I NEVER THANKED YOU PROPERLY BEFORE...
...FOR ALWAYS TAKING CARE OF MY LITTLE SISTER.

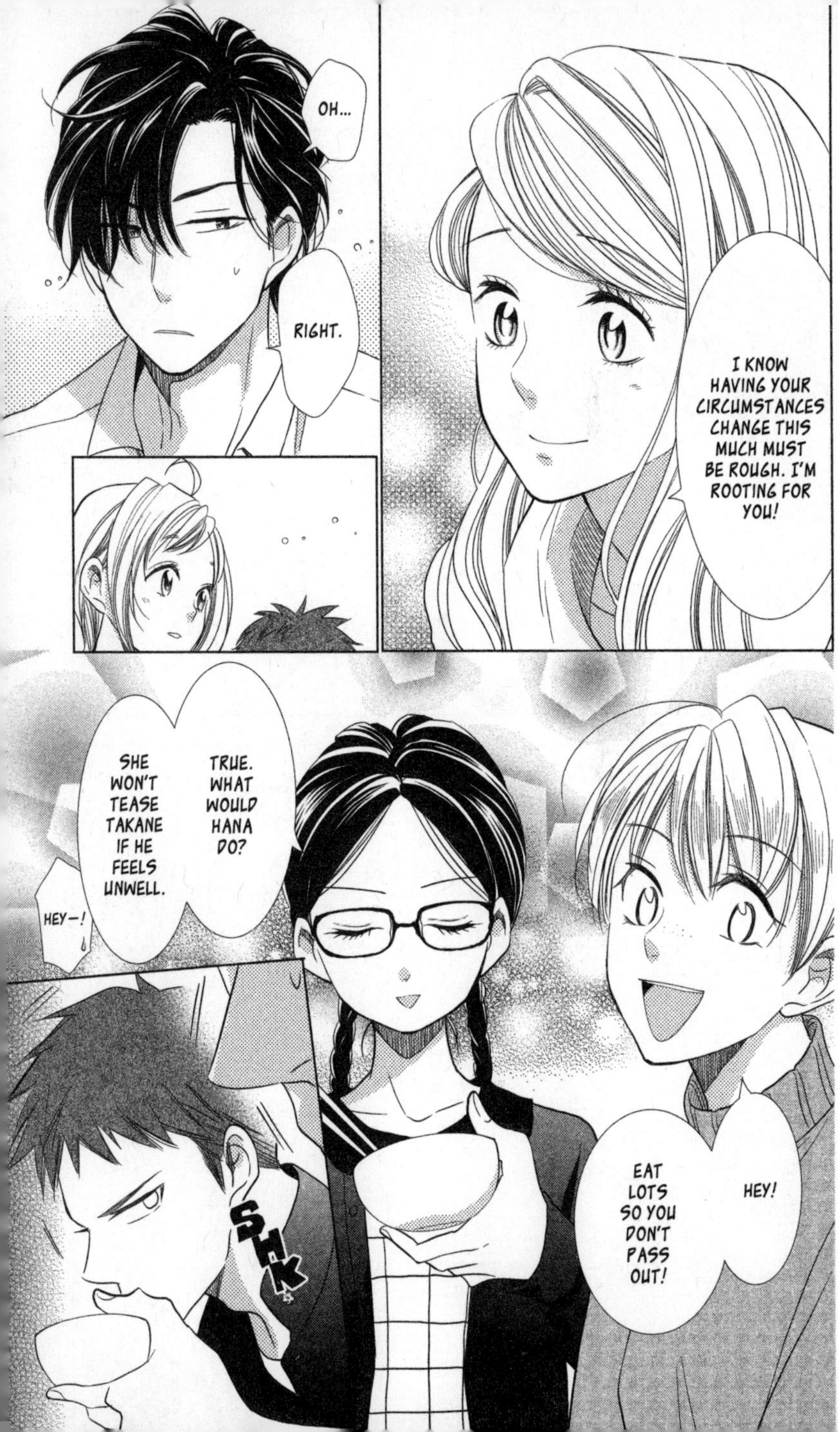
I KNOW HAVING YOUR CIRCUMSTANCES CHANGE THIS MUCH MUST BE ROUGH. I'M ROOTING FOR YOU!
OH...
RIGHT.
HEY!
EAT LOTS SO YOU DON'T PASS OUT!
TRUE. WHAT WOULD HANA DO?
SHE WON'T TEASE TAKANE IF HE FEELS UNWELL.
HEY—!
SHK

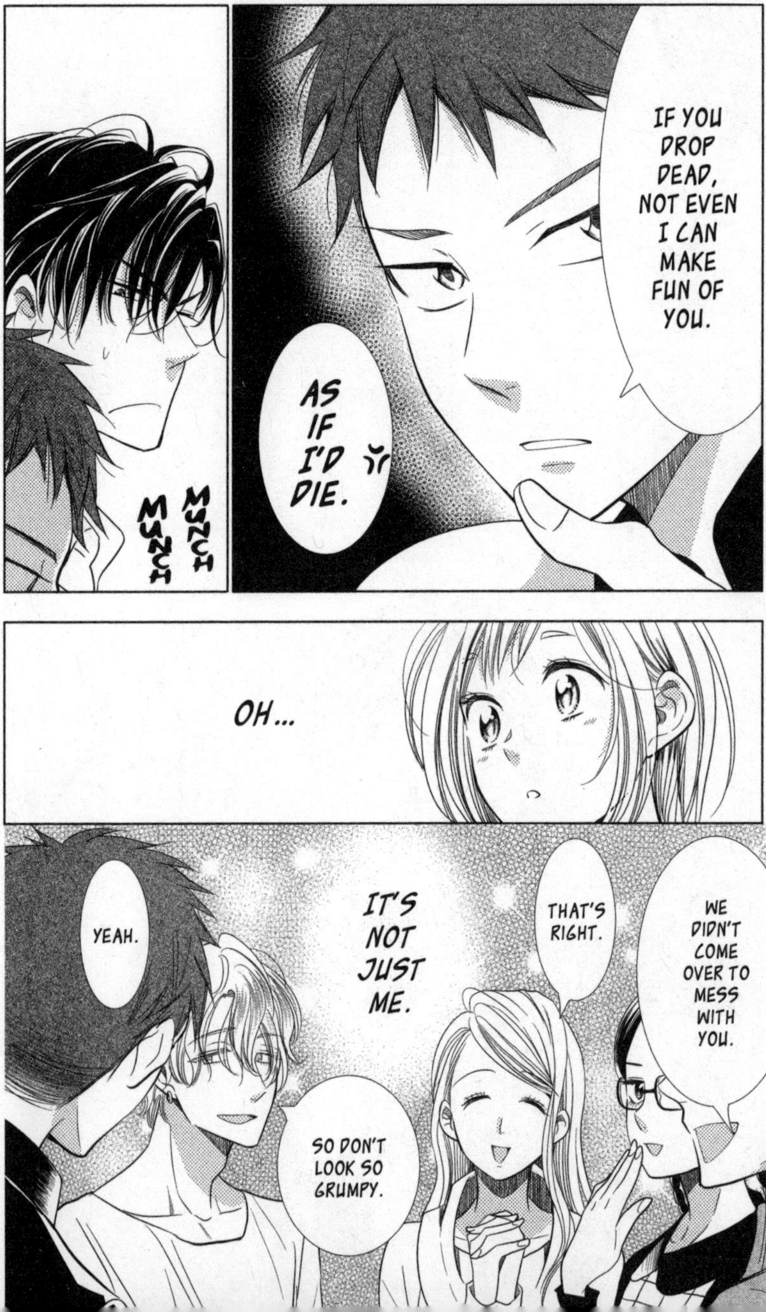
IF YOU DROP DEAD, NOT EVEN I CAN MAKE FUN OF YOU.
AS IF I'D DIE.
MUNCH MUNCH
OH...
WE DIDN'T COME OVER TO MESS WITH YOU.
THAT'S RIGHT.
IT'S NOT JUST ME.
YEAH.
SO DON'T LOOK SO GRUMPY.

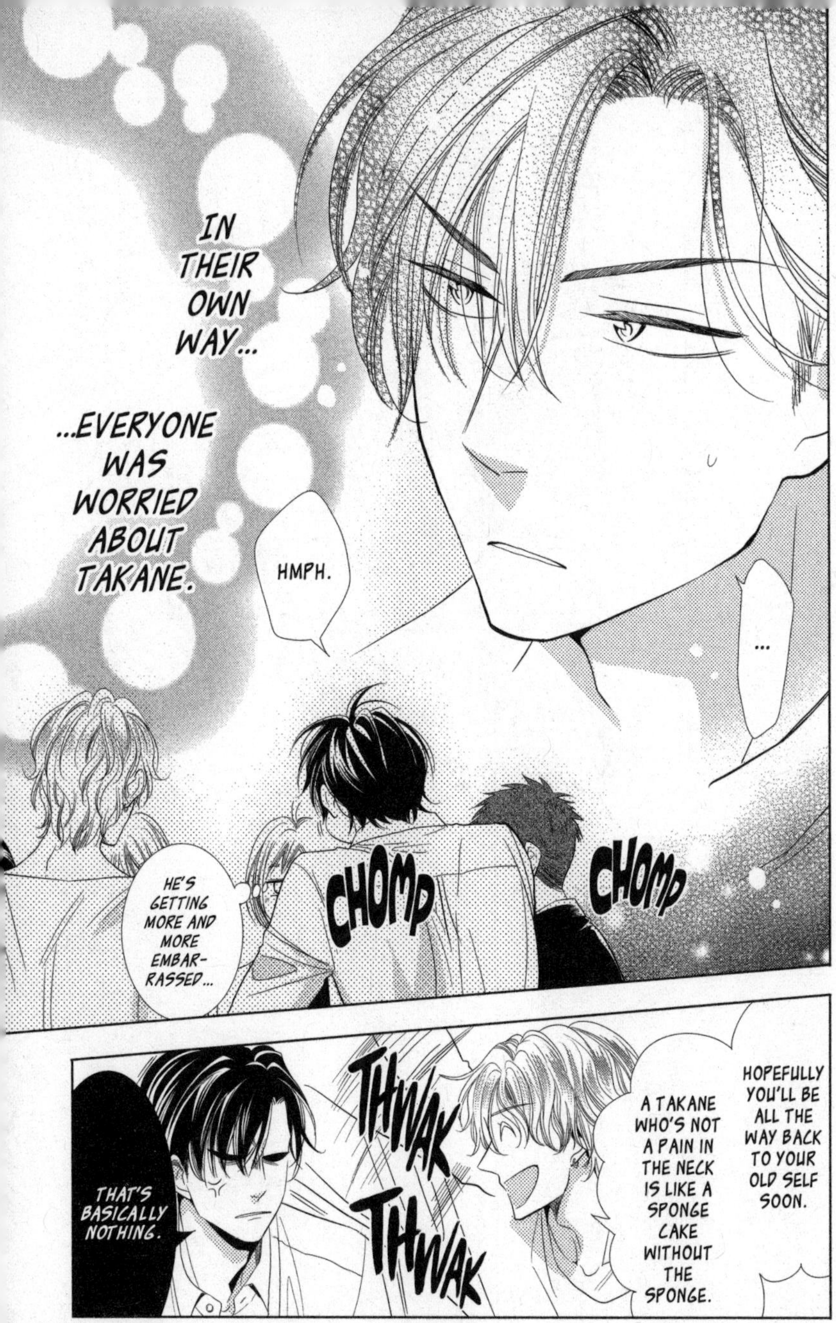
IN THEIR OWN WAY...
...EVERYONE WAS WORRIED ABOUT TAKANE.
HMPH.
...
CHOMP
CHOMP
HE'S GETTING MORE AND MORE EMBAR-RASSED...
HOPEFULLY YOU'LL BE ALL THE WAY BACK TO YOUR OLD SELF SOON.
A TAKANE WHO'S NOT A PAIN IN THE NECK IS LIKE A SPONGE CAKE WITHOUT THE SPONGE.
THWAK
THWAK
THAT'S BASICALLY NOTHING.

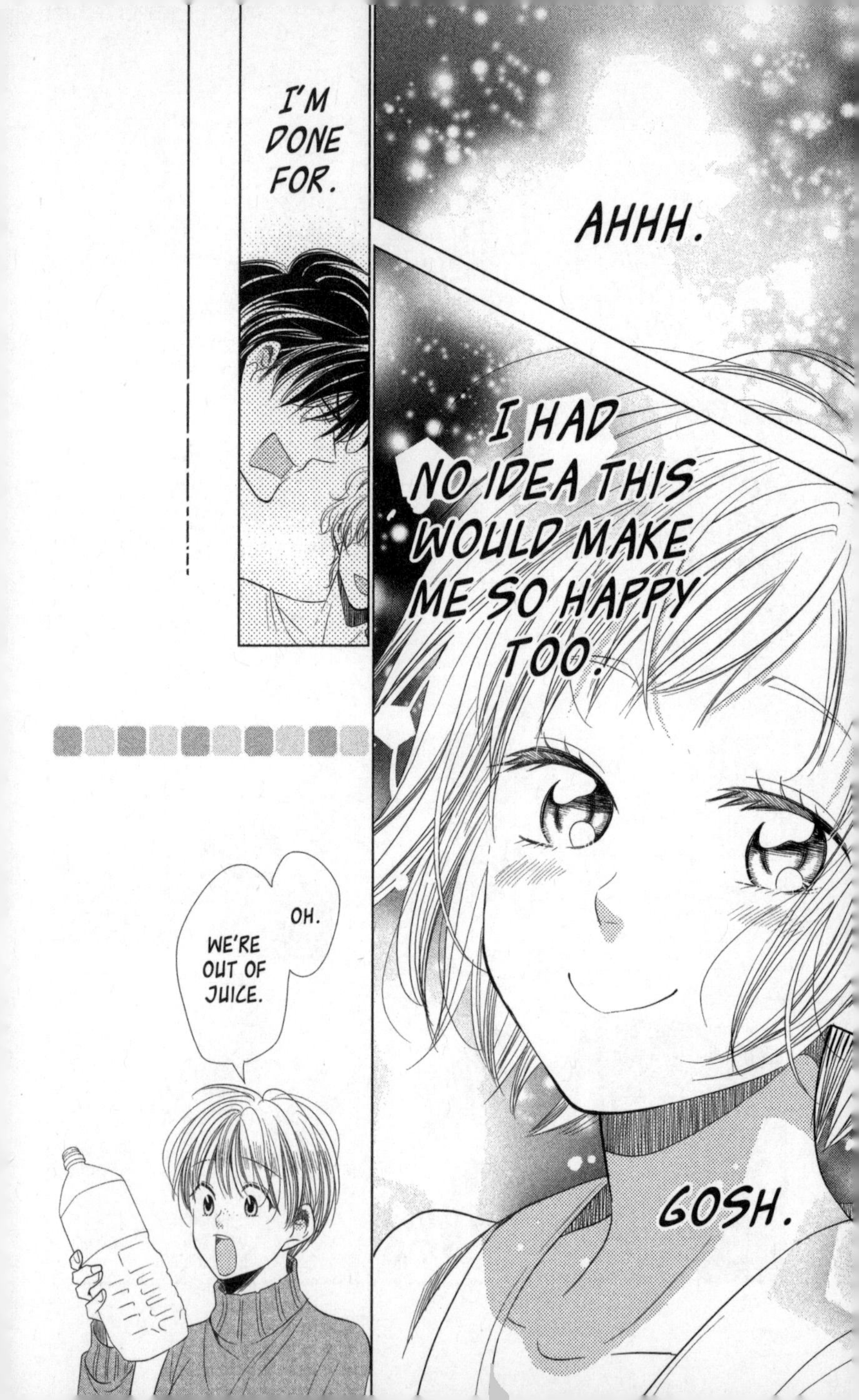
AHHH.
I HAD NO IDEA THIS WOULD MAKE ME SO HAPPY TOO.
GOSH.
I'M DONE FOR.
OH.
WE'RE OUT OF JUICE.

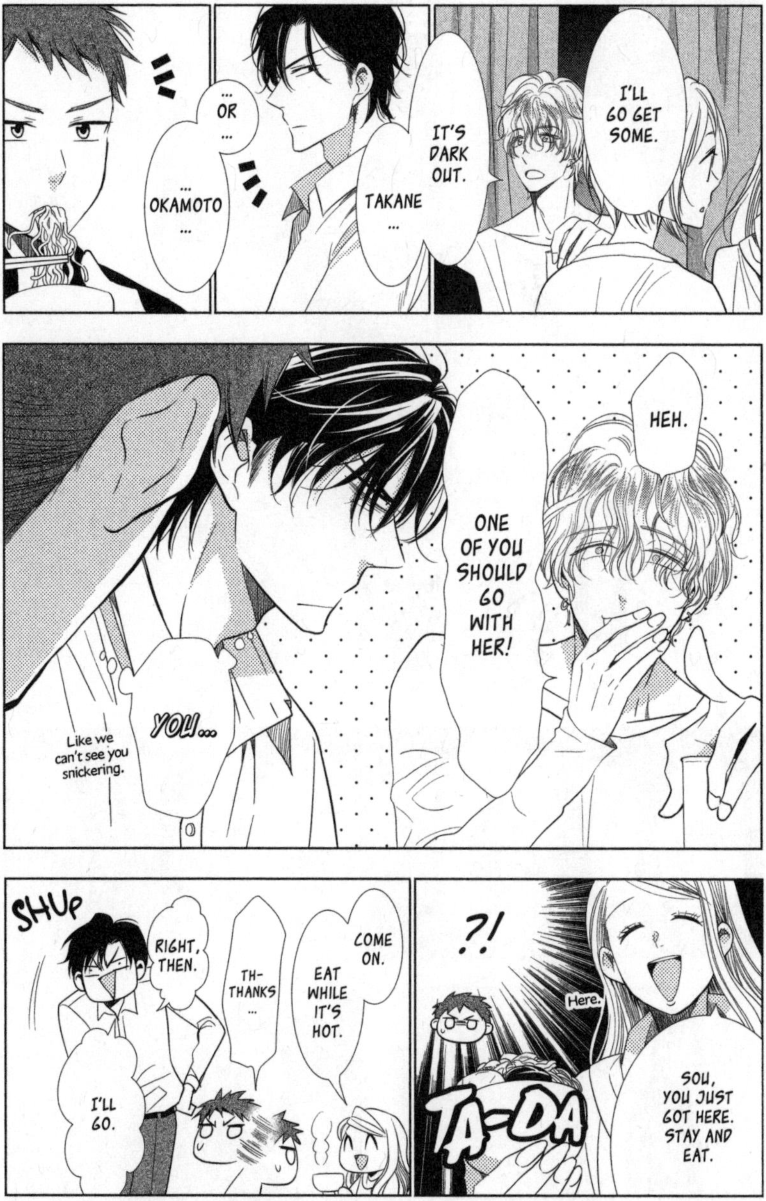
I'LL GO GET SOME.
IT'S DARK OUT.
TAKANE ...
... OR ...
... OKAMOTO ...
HEH.
ONE OF YOU SHOULD GO WITH HER!
YOU...
Like we can't see you snickering.
?!
Here.
TA-DA
SOU, YOU JUST GOT HERE. STAY AND EAT.
COME ON.
EAT WHILE IT'S HOT.
TH-THANKS ...
RIGHT, THEN.
SHUP
I'LL GO.

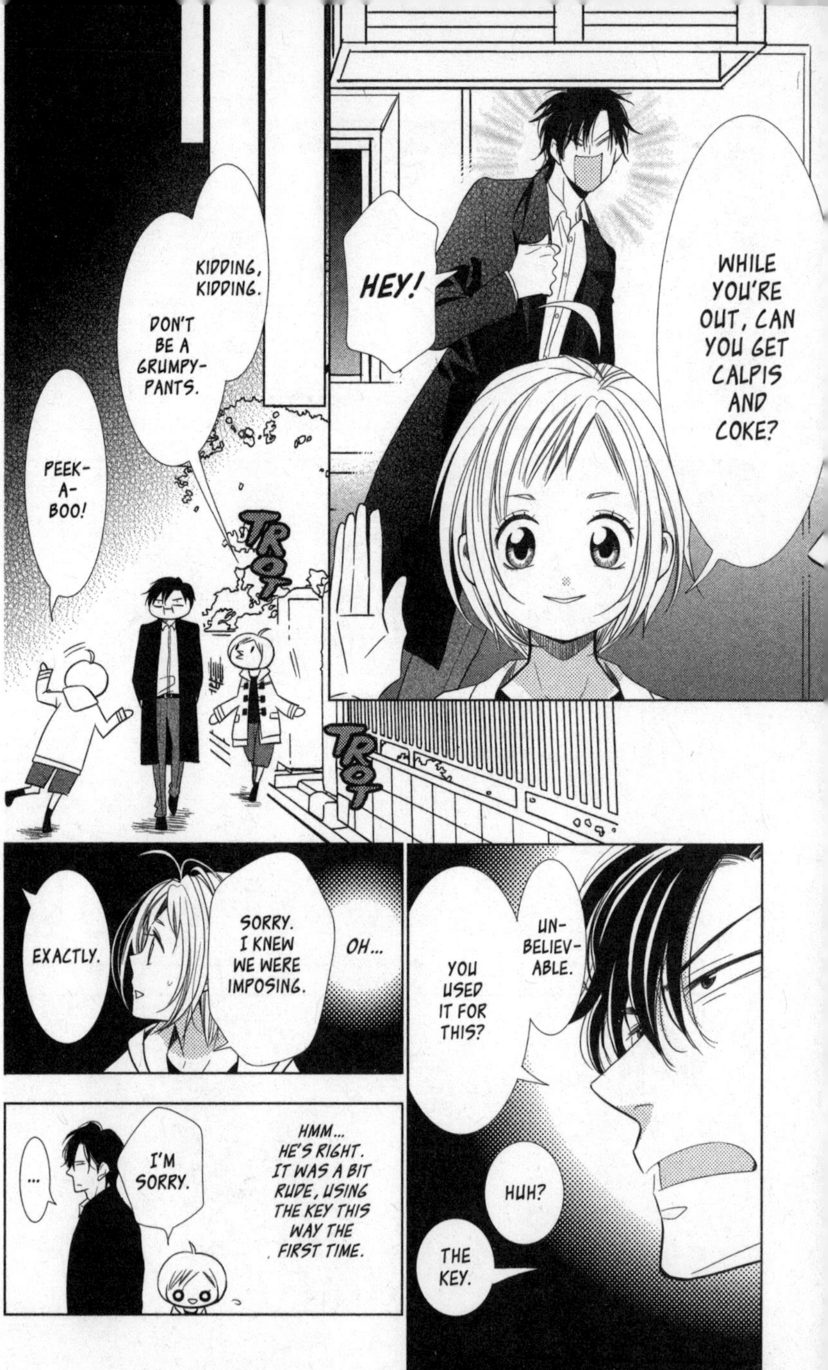
WHILE YOU'RE OUT, CAN YOU GET CALPIS AND COKE?
HEY!
KIDDING, KIDDING.
DON'T BE A GRUMPY-PANTS.
PEEK-A-BOO!
TROT
TROT
UN-BELIEV-ABLE.
YOU USED IT FOR THIS?
HUH?
THE KEY.
OH...
SORRY. I KNEW WE WERE IMPOSING.
EXACTLY.
HMM... HE'S RIGHT. IT WAS A BIT RUDE, USING THE KEY THIS WAY THE FIRST TIME.
I'M SORRY.
...

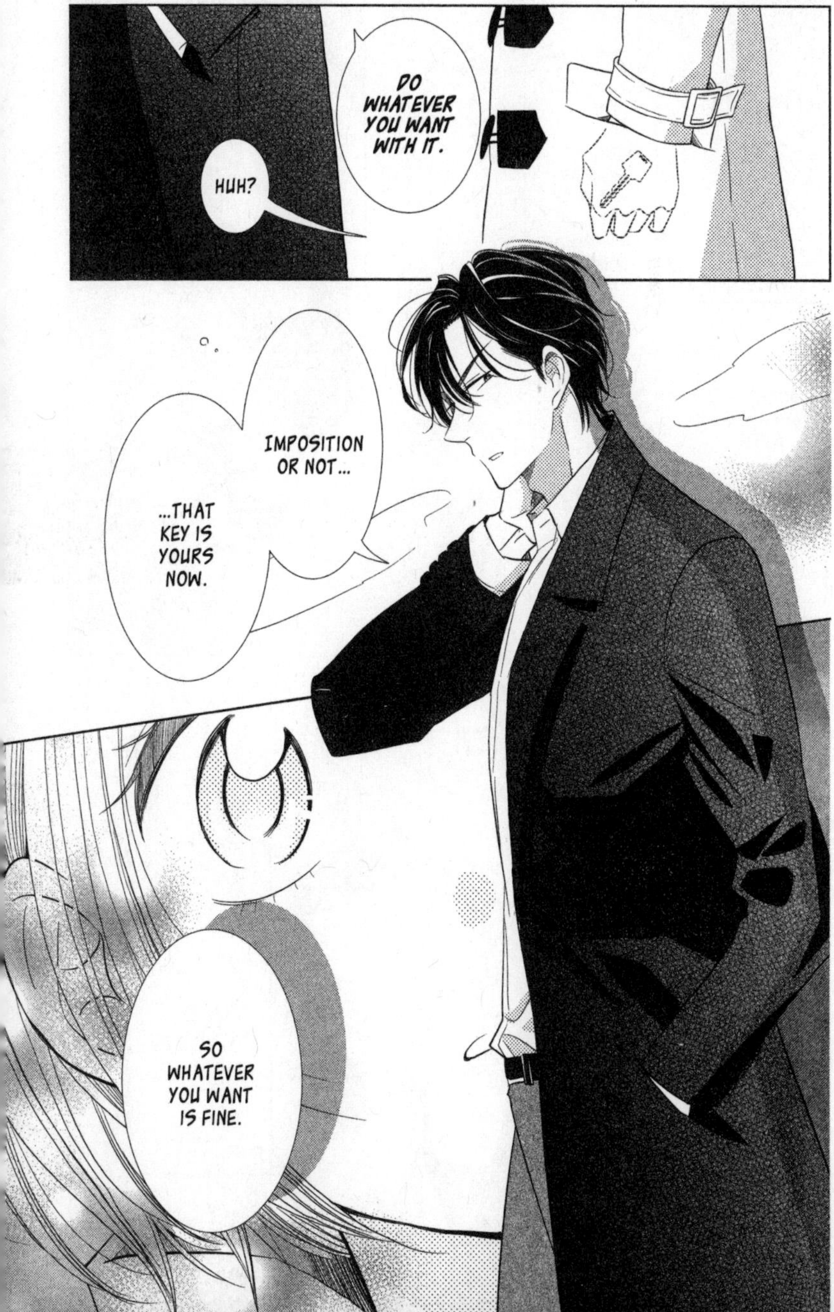
DO WHATEVER YOU WANT WITH IT.
HUH?
IMPOSITION OR NOT...
...THAT KEY IS YOURS NOW.
SO WHATEVER YOU WANT IS FINE.

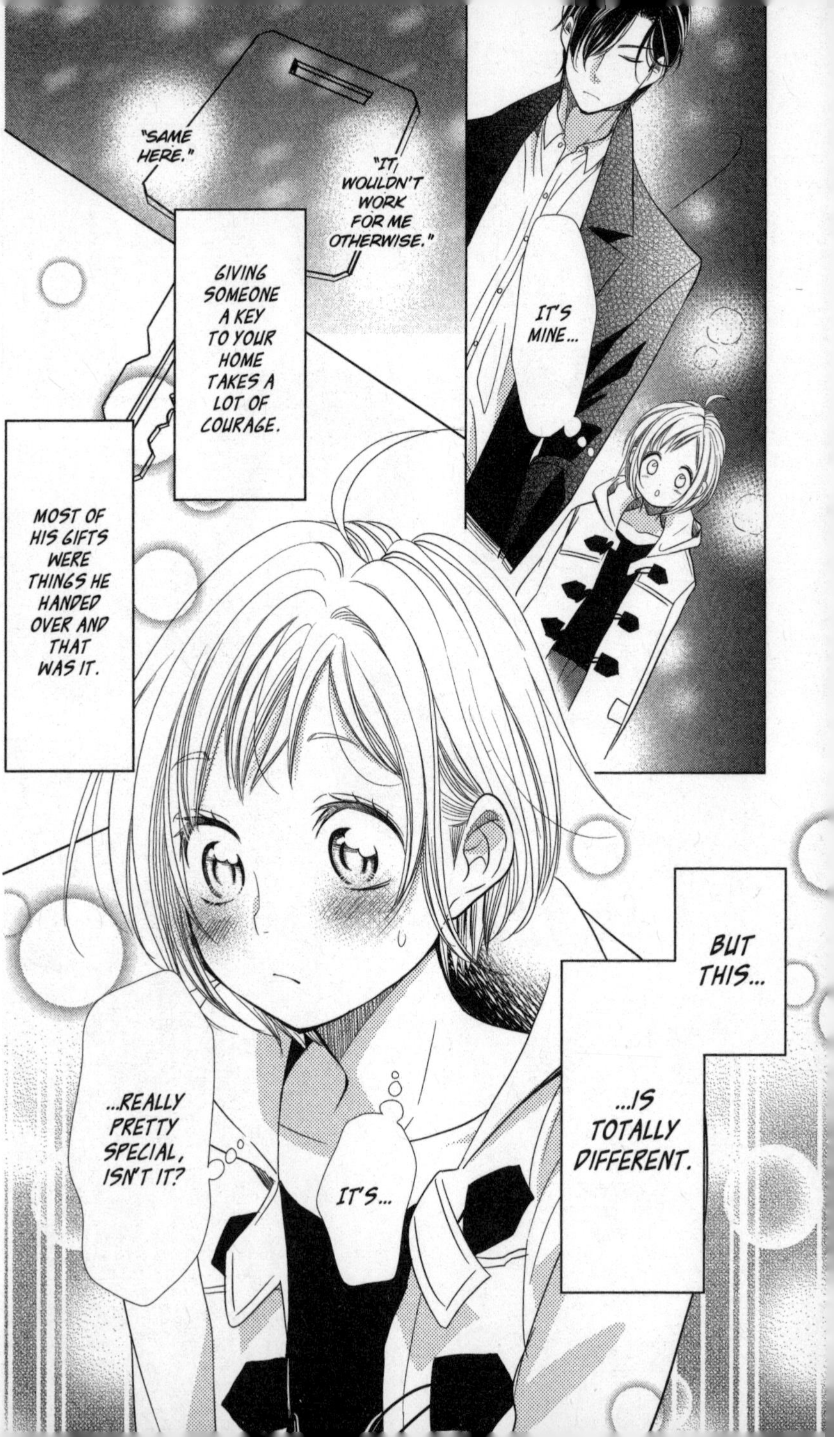
IT'S MINE...
"IT WOULDN'T WORK FOR ME OTHERWISE."
"SAME HERE."
GIVING SOMEONE A KEY TO YOUR HOME TAKES A LOT OF COURAGE.
MOST OF HIS GIFTS WERE THINGS HE HANDED OVER AND THAT WAS IT.
BUT THIS...
...IS TOTALLY DIFFERENT.
IT'S...
...REALLY PRETTY SPECIAL, ISN'T IT?

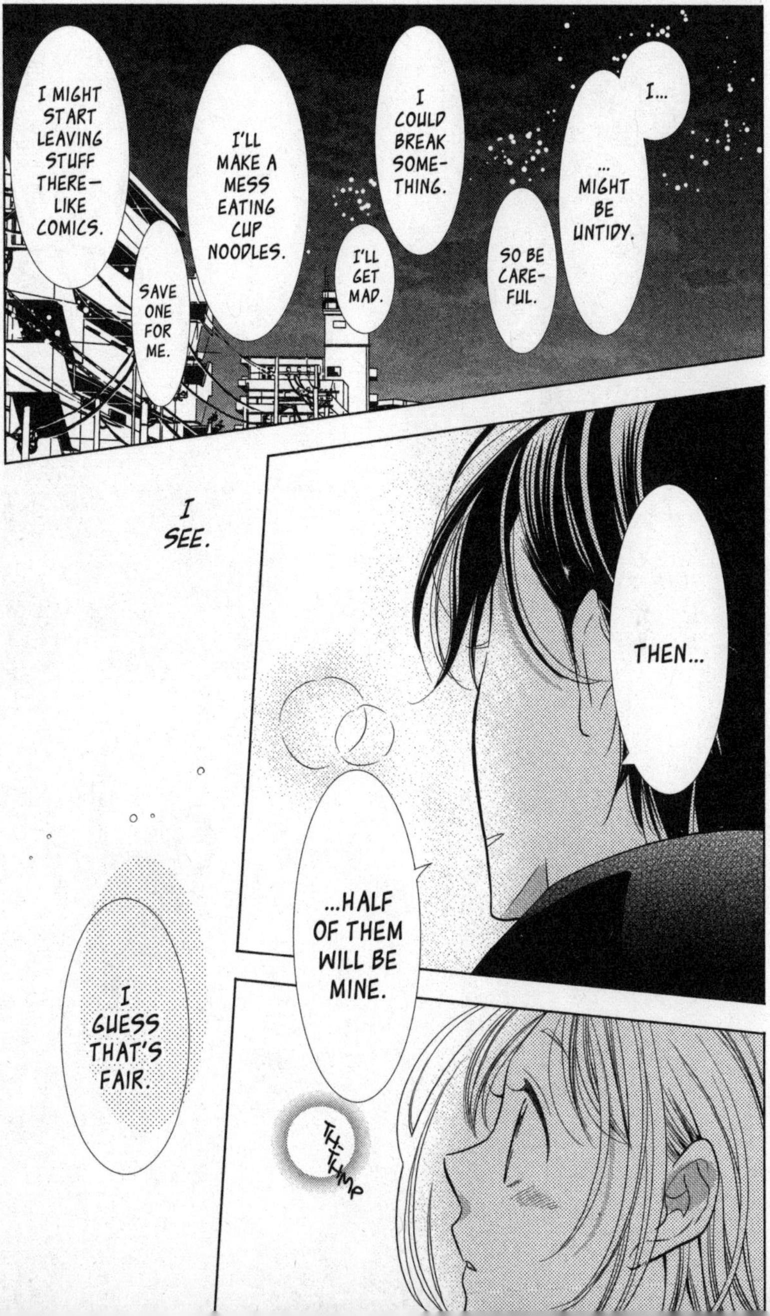
I...
...MIGHT BE UNTIDY.
SO BE CARE-FUL.
I COULD BREAK SOME-THING.
I'LL GET MAD.
I'LL MAKE A MESS EATING CUP NOODLES.
SAVE ONE FOR ME.
I MIGHT START LEAVING STUFF THERE—LIKE COMICS.
THEN...
...HALF OF THEM WILL BE MINE.
I SEE.
TH-THMP
I GUESS THAT'S FAIR.

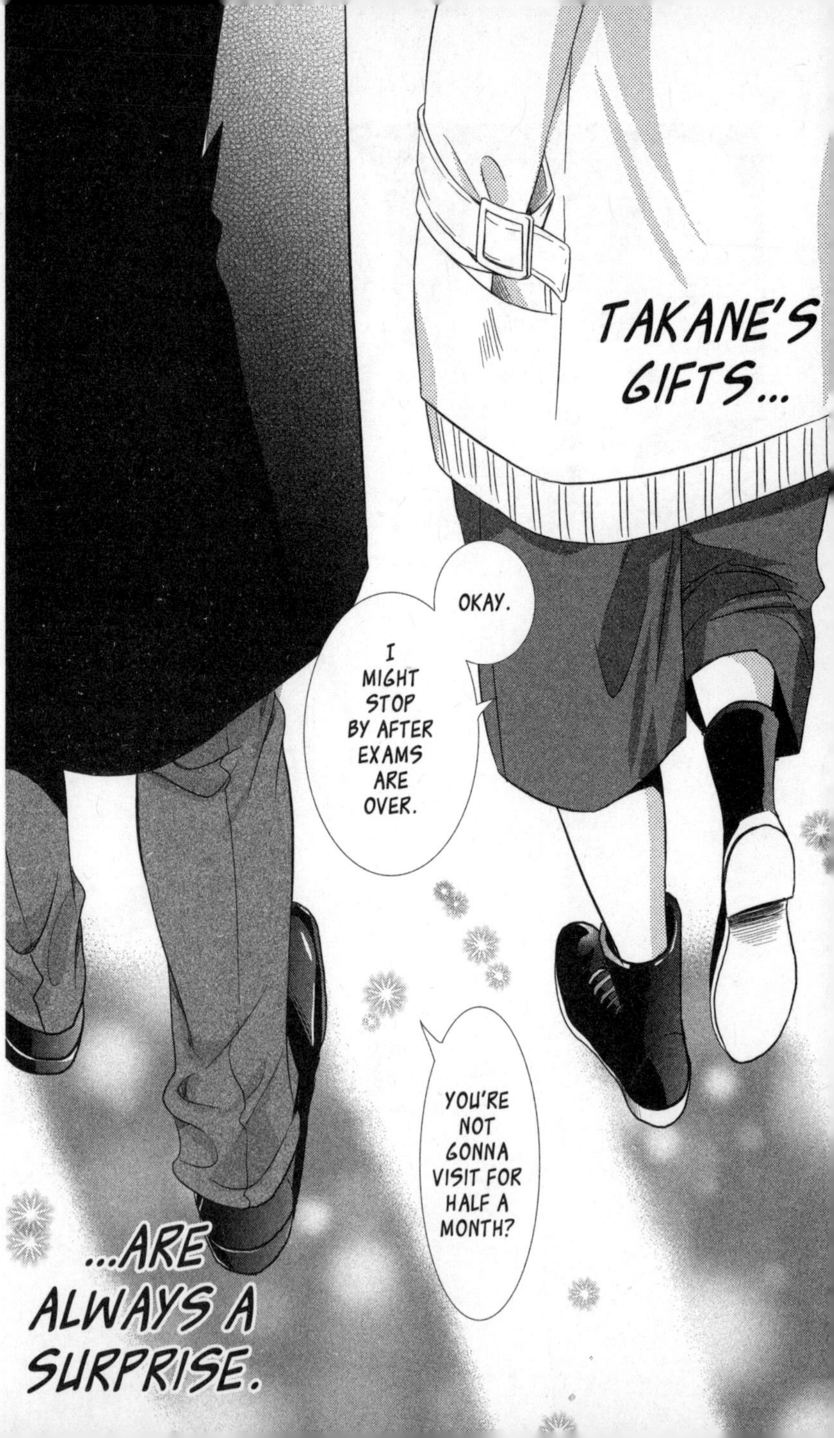
TAKANE'S GIFTS...
OKAY.
I MIGHT STOP BY AFTER EXAMS ARE OVER.
YOU'RE NOT GONNA VISIT FOR HALF A MONTH?
...ARE ALWAYS A SURPRISE.

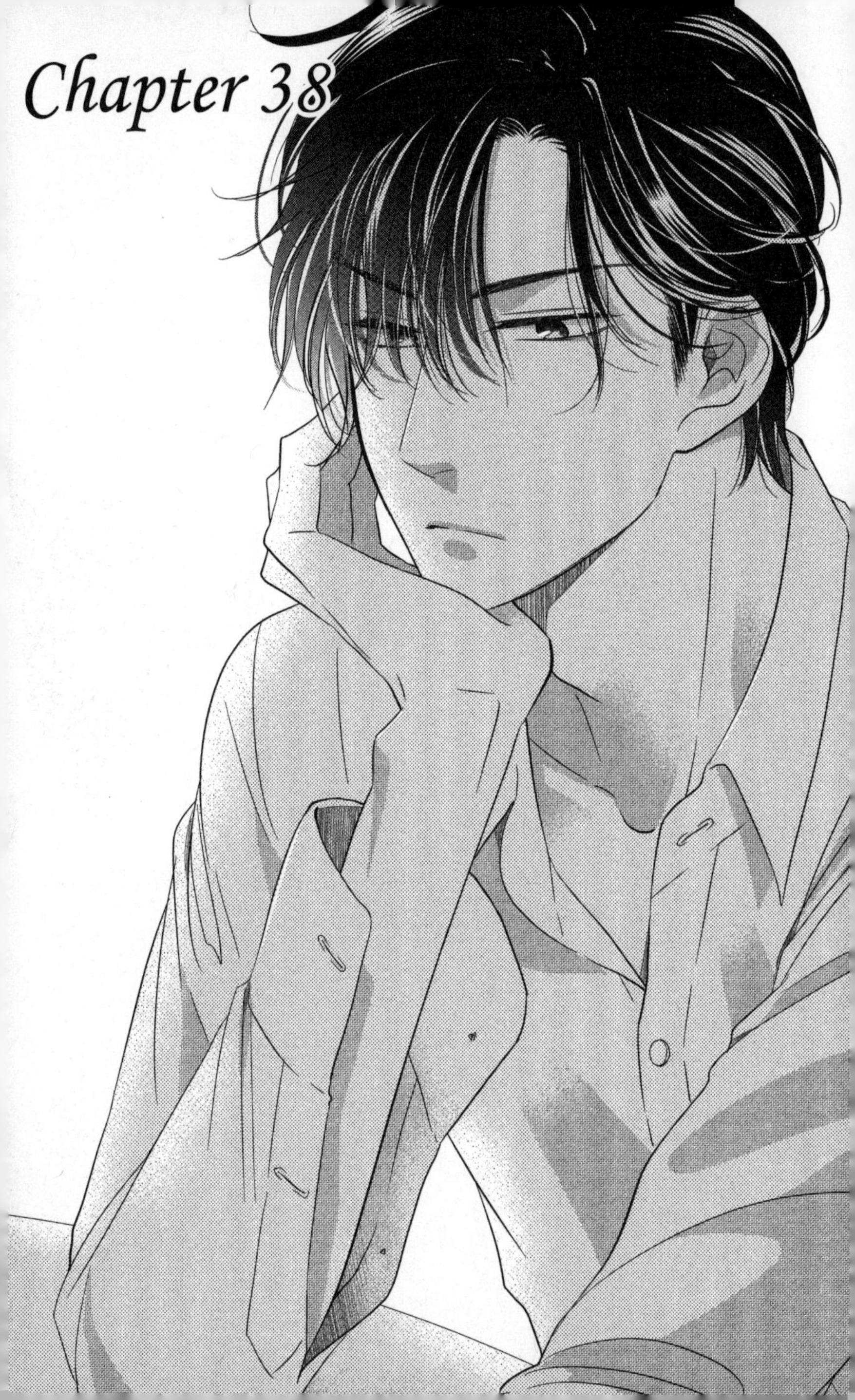
Chapter 38

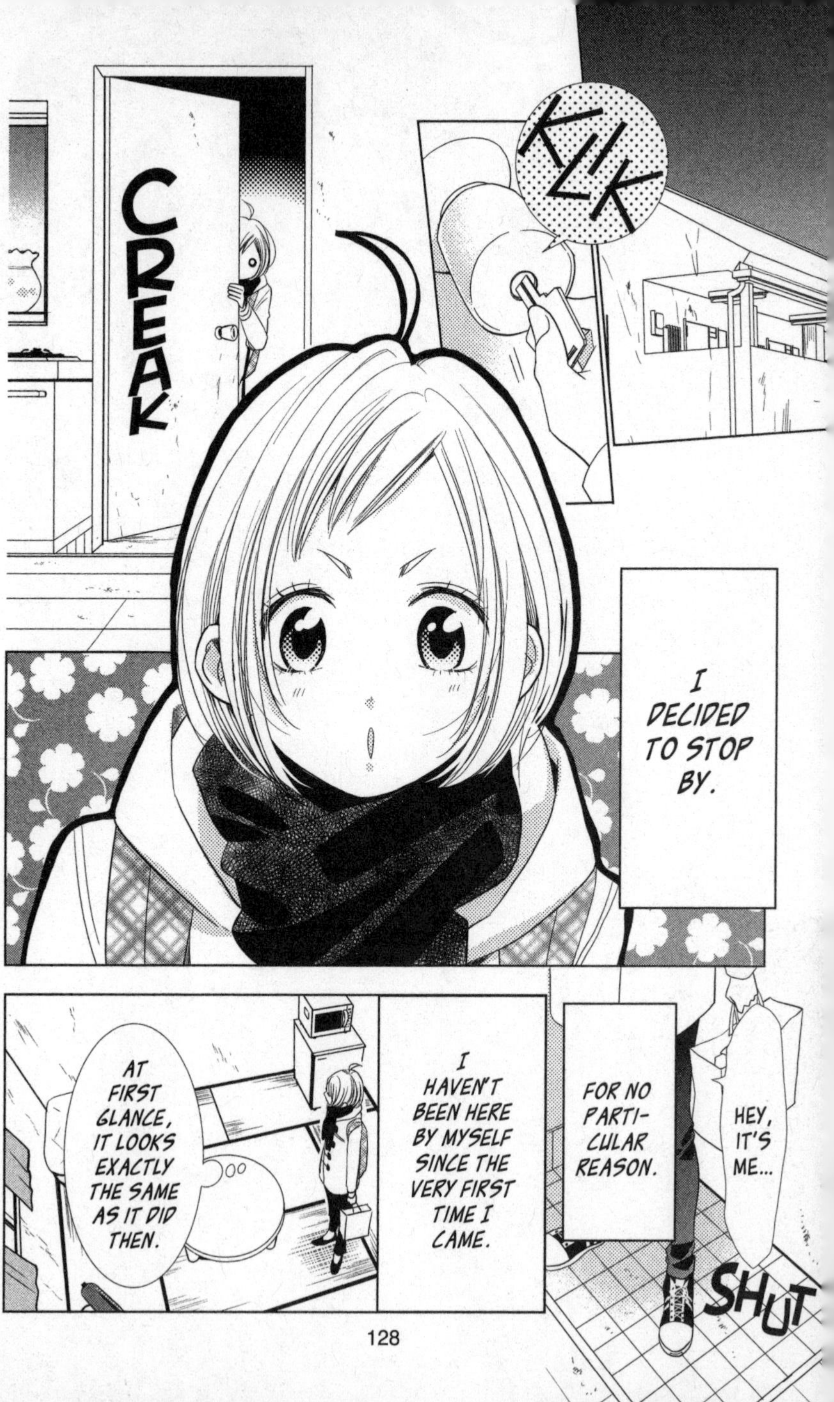
KLIK
CREAK
I DECIDED TO STOP BY.
HEY, IT'S ME...
SHUT
FOR NO PARTI-CULAR REASON.
I HAVEN'T BEEN HERE BY MYSELF SINCE THE VERY FIRST TIME I CAME.
AT FIRST GLANCE, IT LOOKS EXACTLY THE SAME AS IT DID THEN.

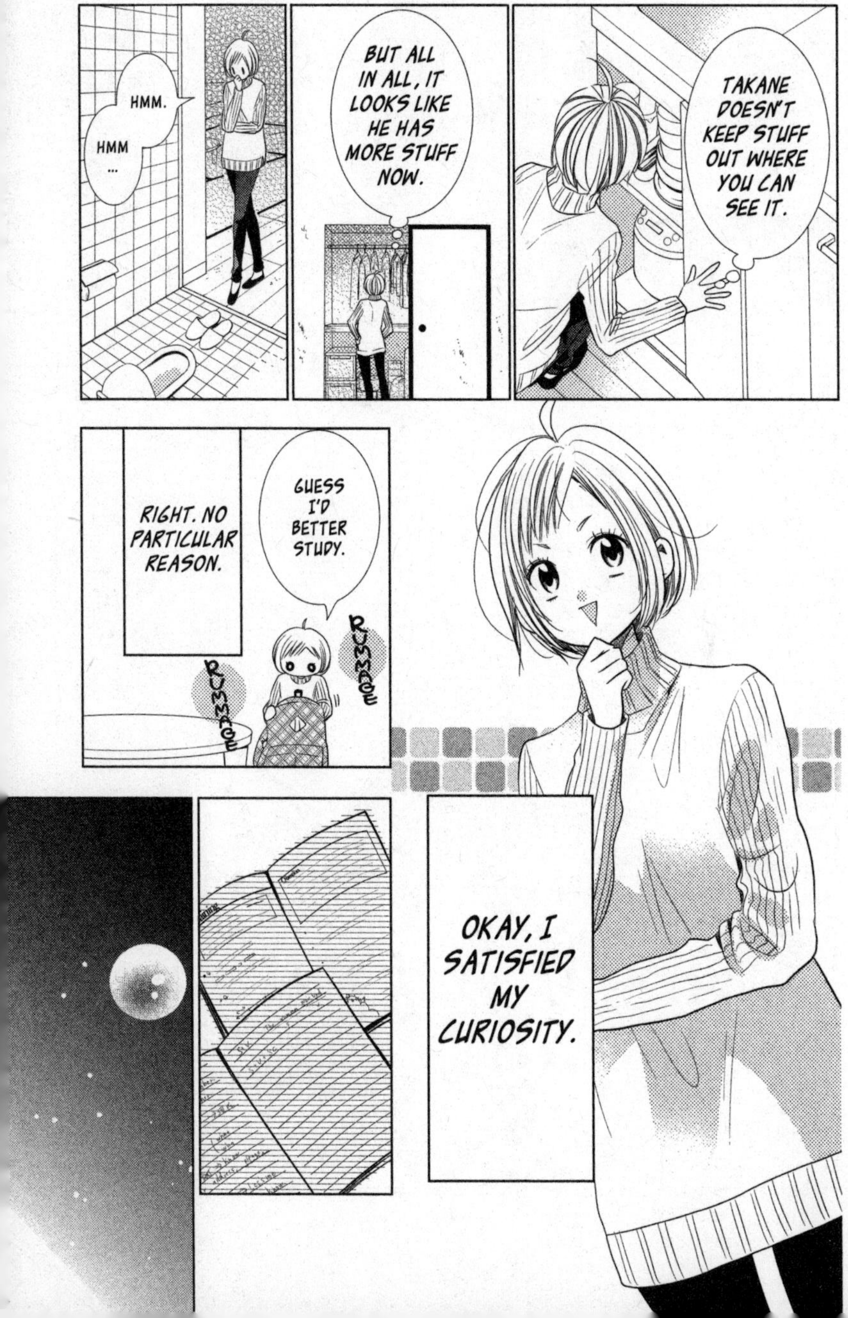
TAKANE DOESN'T KEEP STUFF OUT WHERE YOU CAN SEE IT.
BUT ALL IN ALL, IT LOOKS LIKE HE HAS MORE STUFF NOW.
HMM.
HMM ...
OKAY, I SATISFIED MY CURIOSITY.
RIGHT. NO PARTICULAR REASON.
GUESS I'D BETTER STUDY.
RUMMAGE
RUMMAGE

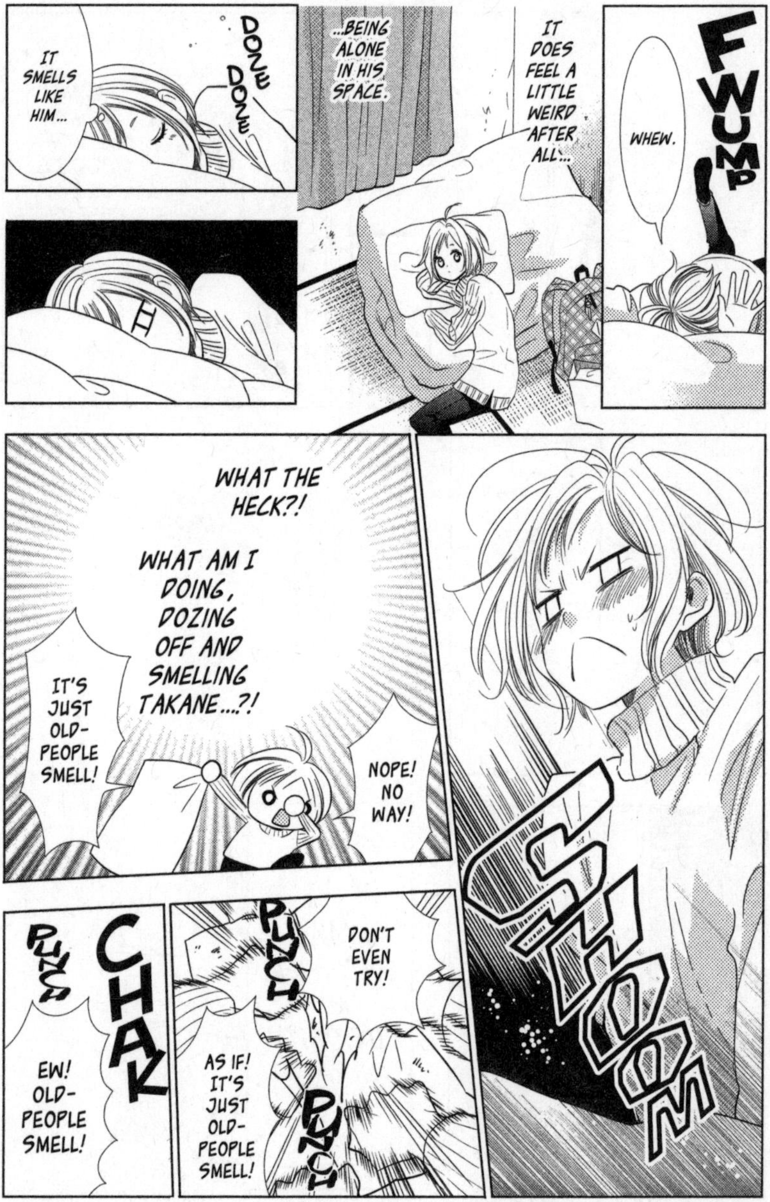
FWUMP
WHEW.
IT DOES FEEL A LITTLE WEIRD AFTER ALL...
...BEING ALONE IN HIS SPACE.
DOZE DOZE
IT SMELLS LIKE HIM...
WHOOM
WHAT THE HECK?!
WHAT AM I DOING, DOZING OFF AND SMELLING TAKANE...?!
NOPE! NO WAY!
IT'S JUST OLD-PEOPLE SMELL!
DON'T EVEN TRY!
PUNCH
AS IF! IT'S JUST OLD-PEOPLE SMELL!
PUNCH
CHAK
PUNCH
EW! OLD-PEOPLE SMELL!

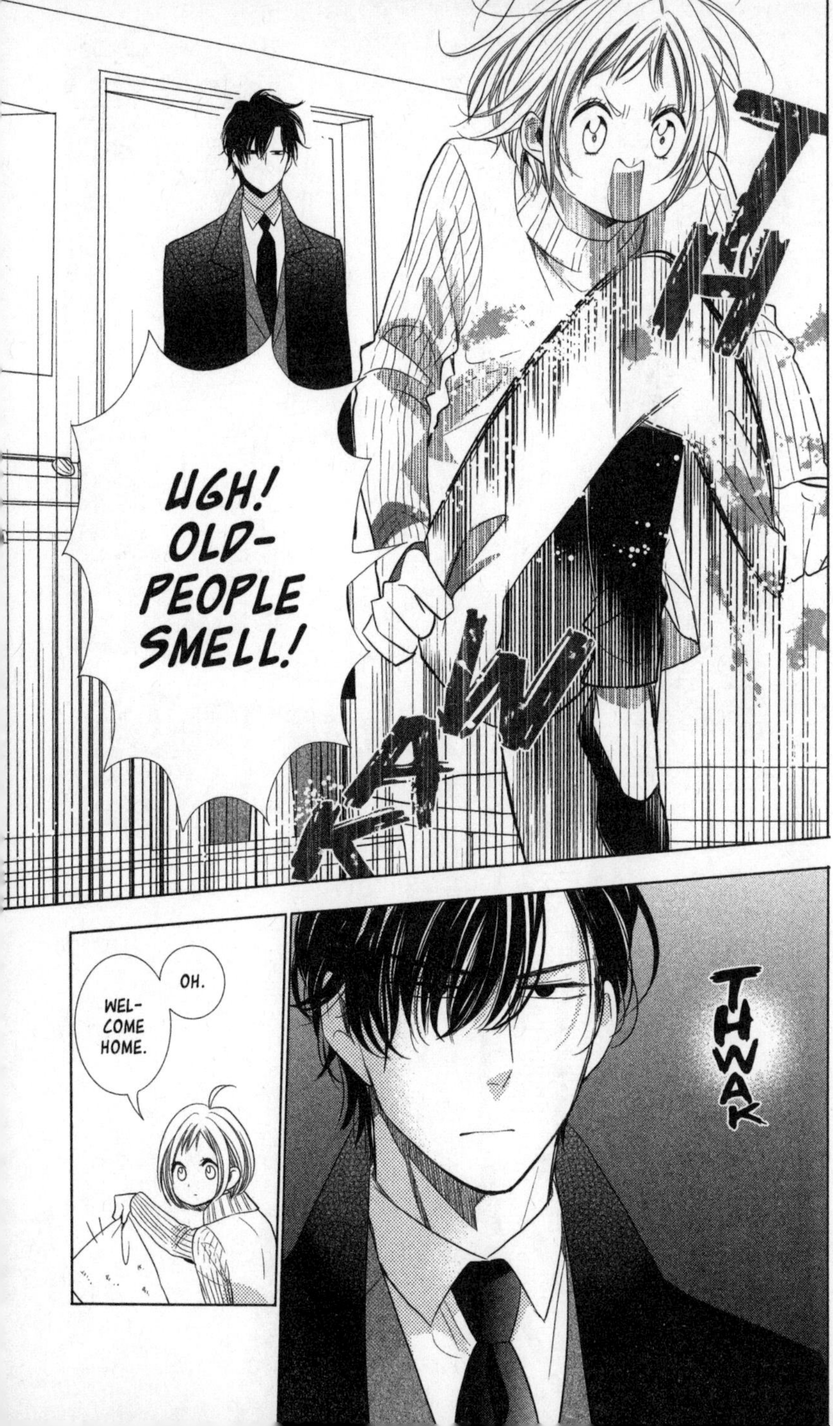
THWAK
UGH! OLD-PEOPLE SMELL!
THWAK
OH.
WEL-COME HOME.

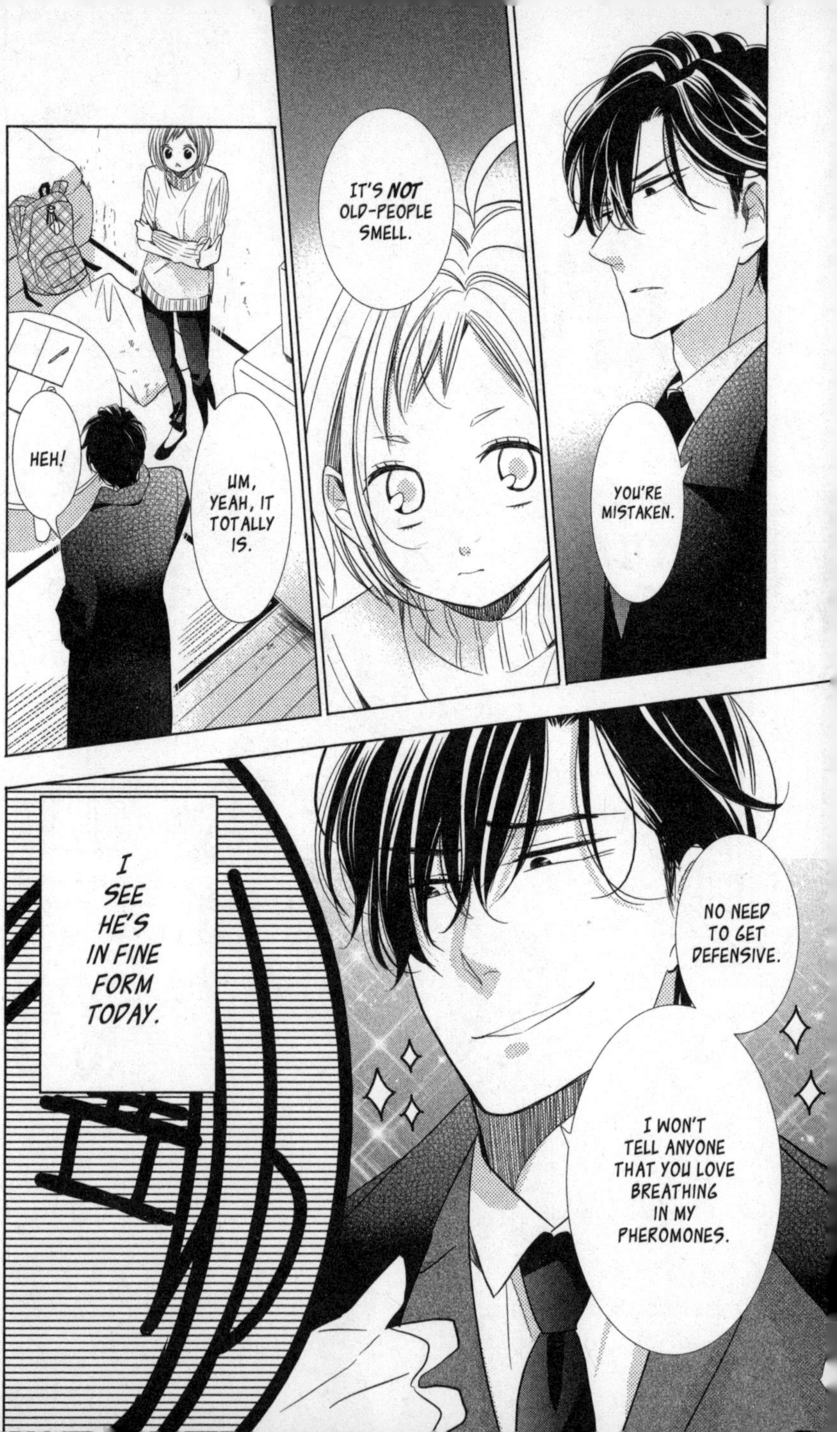
YOU'RE MISTAKEN.
IT'S NOT OLD-PEOPLE SMELL.
UM, YEAH, IT TOTALLY IS.
HEH!
NO NEED TO GET DEFENSIVE.
I WON'T TELL ANYONE THAT YOU LOVE BREATHING IN MY PHEROMONES.
I SEE HE'S IN FINE FORM TODAY.

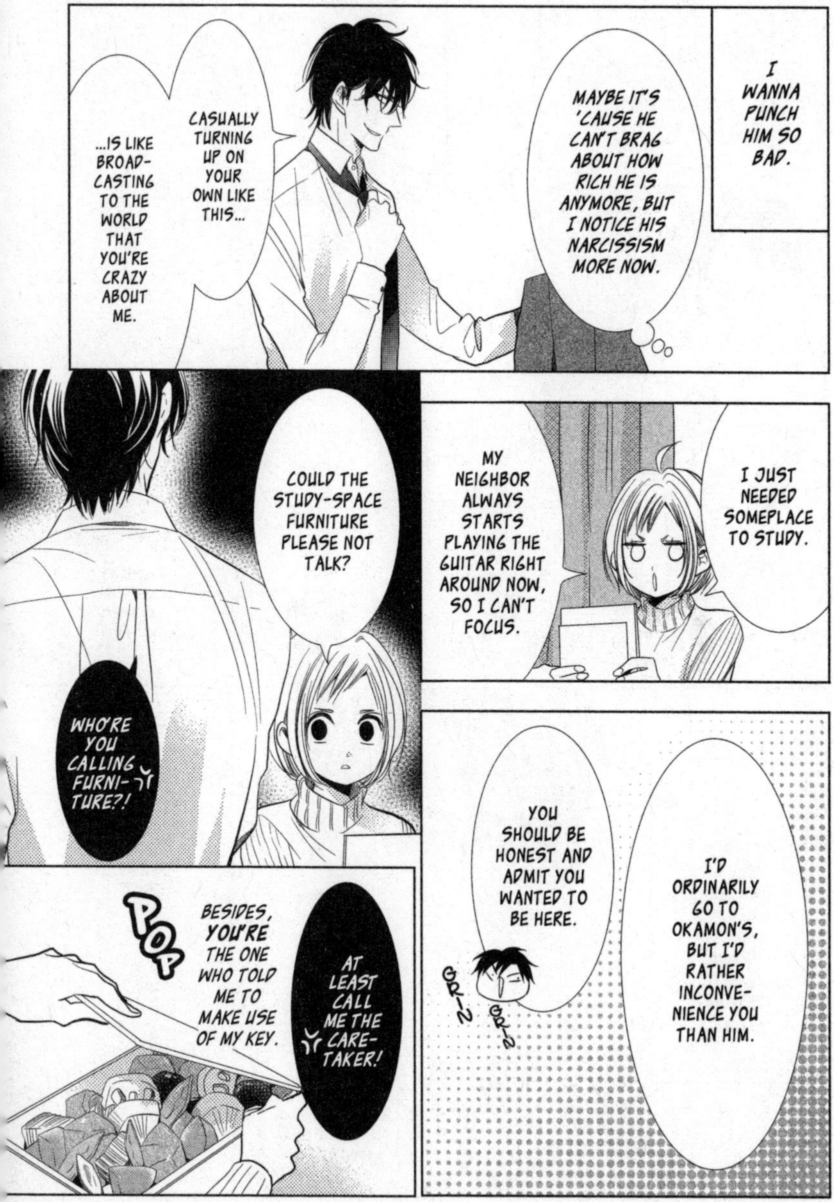
I WANNA PUNCH HIM SO BAD.
MAYBE IT'S 'CAUSE HE CAN'T BRAG ABOUT HOW RICH HE IS ANYMORE, BUT I NOTICE HIS NARCISSISM MORE NOW.
CASUALLY TURNING UP ON YOUR OWN LIKE THIS...
...IS LIKE BROADCASTING TO THE WORLD THAT YOU'RE CRAZY ABOUT ME.
I JUST NEEDED SOMEPLACE TO STUDY.
MY NEIGHBOR ALWAYS STARTS PLAYING THE GUITAR RIGHT AROUND NOW, SO I CAN'T FOCUS.
I'D ORDINARILY GO TO OKAMON'S, BUT I'D RATHER INCONVENIENCE YOU THAN HIM.
YOU SHOULD BE HONEST AND ADMIT YOU WANTED TO BE HERE.
GRIN GRIN
COULD THE STUDY-SPACE FURNITURE PLEASE NOT TALK?
WHO'RE YOU CALLING FURNITURE?!
AT LEAST CALL ME THE CARETAKER!
BESIDES, YOU'RE THE ONE WHO TOLD ME TO MAKE USE OF MY KEY.
POP

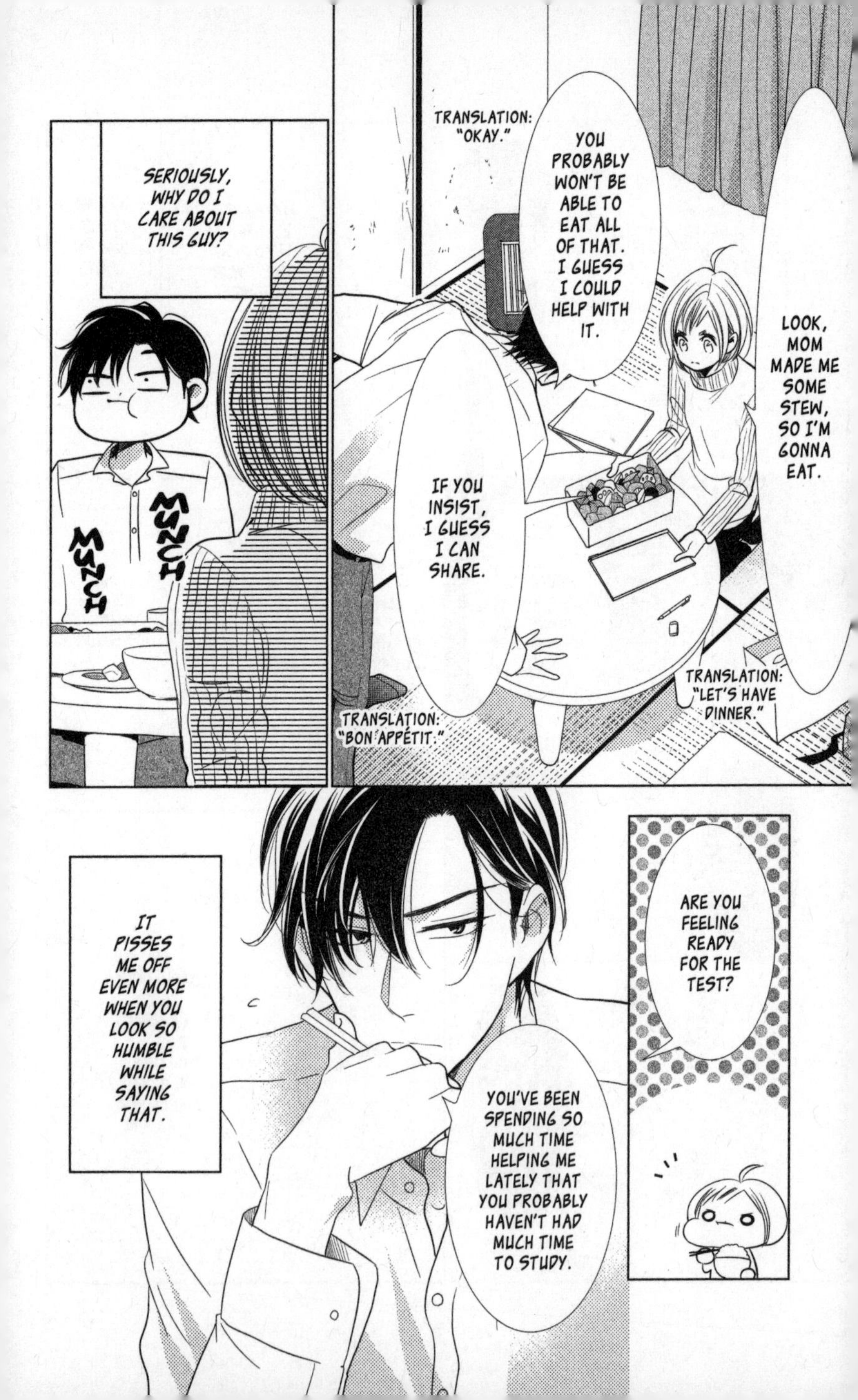
LOOK, MOM MADE ME SOME STEW, SO I'M GONNA EAT.
TRANSLATION: "LET'S HAVE DINNER."
YOU PROBABLY WON'T BE ABLE TO EAT ALL OF THAT. I GUESS I COULD HELP WITH IT.
TRANSLATION: "OKAY."
IF YOU INSIST, I GUESS I CAN SHARE.
TRANSLATION: "BON APPÉTIT."
SERIOUSLY, WHY DO I CARE ABOUT THIS GUY?
MUNCH
MUNCH
ARE YOU FEELING READY FOR THE TEST?
YOU'VE BEEN SPENDING SO MUCH TIME HELPING ME LATELY THAT YOU PROBABLY HAVEN'T HAD MUCH TIME TO STUDY.
IT PISSES ME OFF EVEN MORE WHEN YOU LOOK SO HUMBLE WHILE SAYING THAT.

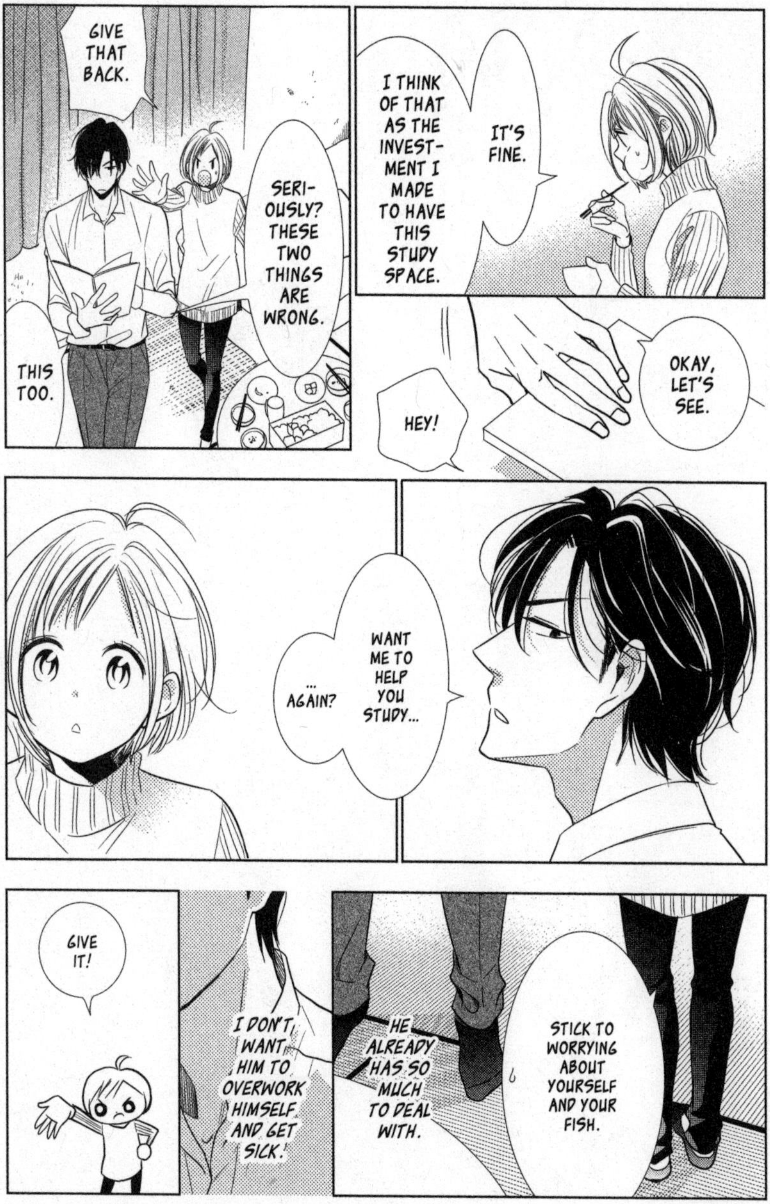
IT'S FINE.
I THINK OF THAT AS THE INVESTMENT I MADE TO HAVE THIS STUDY SPACE.
OKAY, LET'S SEE.
HEY!
GIVE THAT BACK.
SERIOUSLY? THESE TWO THINGS ARE WRONG.
THIS TOO.
WANT ME TO HELP YOU STUDY...
...AGAIN?
STICK TO WORRYING ABOUT YOURSELF AND YOUR FISH.
HE ALREADY HAS SO MUCH TO DEAL WITH.
I DON'T WANT HIM TO OVERWORK HIMSELF AND GET SICK.
GIVE IT!

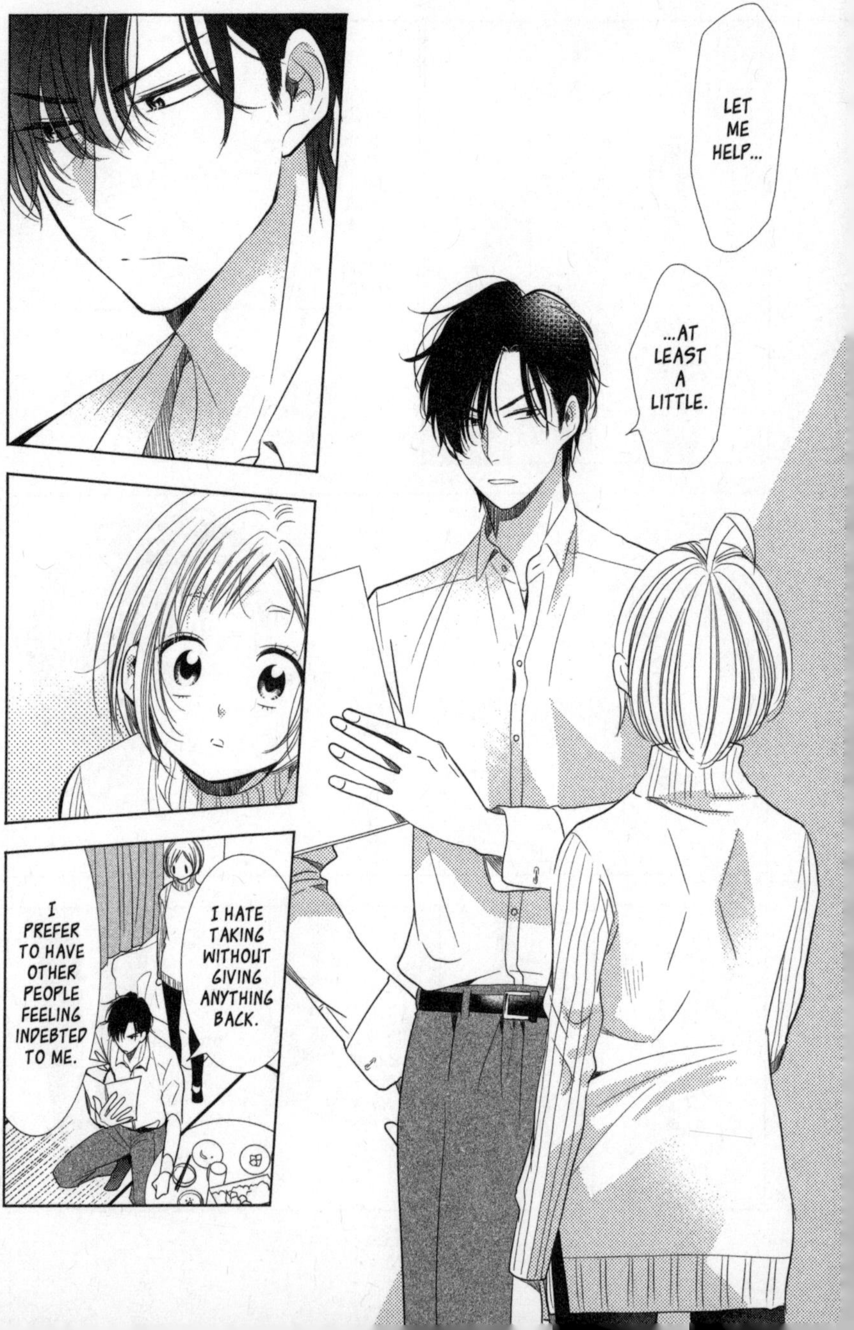
LET ME HELP...
...AT LEAST A LITTLE.
I HATE TAKING WITHOUT GIVING ANYTHING BACK.
I PREFER TO HAVE OTHER PEOPLE FEELING INDEBTED TO ME.

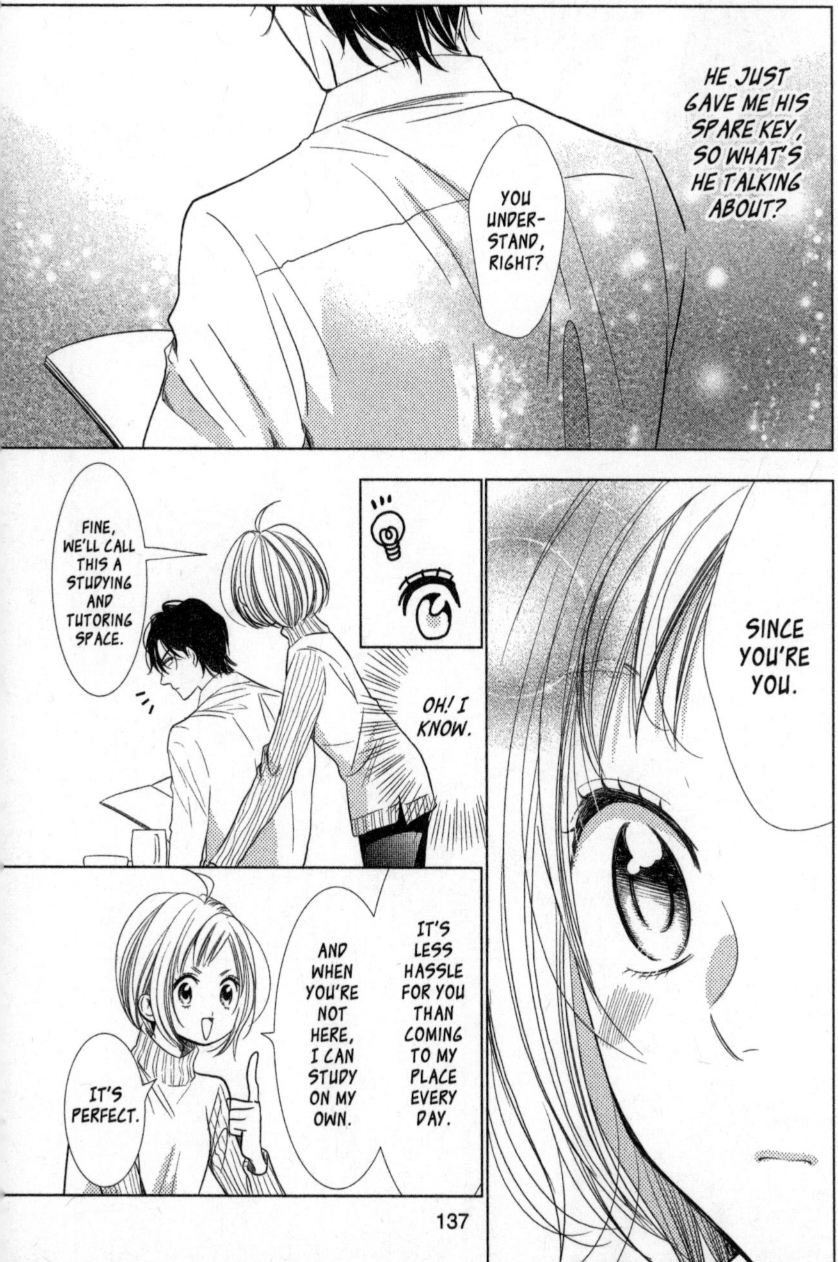
HE JUST GAVE ME HIS SPARE KEY, SO WHAT'S HE TALKING ABOUT?
YOU UNDER-STAND, RIGHT?
SINCE YOU'RE YOU.
OH! I KNOW.
FINE, WE'LL CALL THIS A STUDYING AND TUTORING SPACE.
IT'S LESS HASSLE FOR YOU THAN COMING TO MY PLACE EVERY DAY.
AND WHEN YOU'RE NOT HERE, I CAN STUDY ON MY OWN.
IT'S PERFECT.

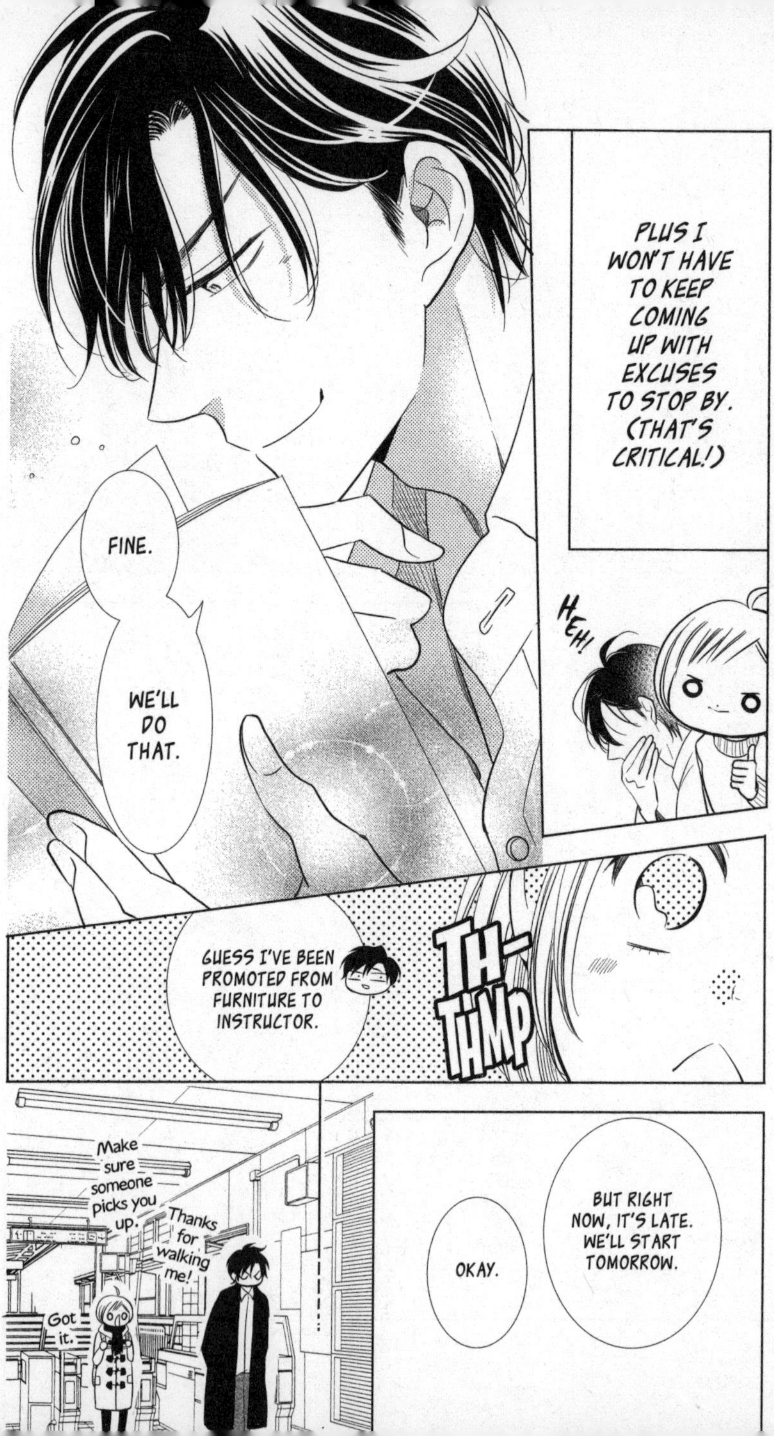
PLUS I WON'T HAVE TO KEEP COMING UP WITH EXCUSES TO STOP BY. (THAT'S CRITICAL!)
HEH!
FINE.
WE'LL DO THAT.
TH-THUMP
GUESS I'VE BEEN PROMOTED FROM FURNITURE TO INSTRUCTOR.
BUT RIGHT NOW, IT'S LATE. WE'LL START TOMORROW.
OKAY.
Make sure someone picks you up.
Thanks for walking me!
Got it.

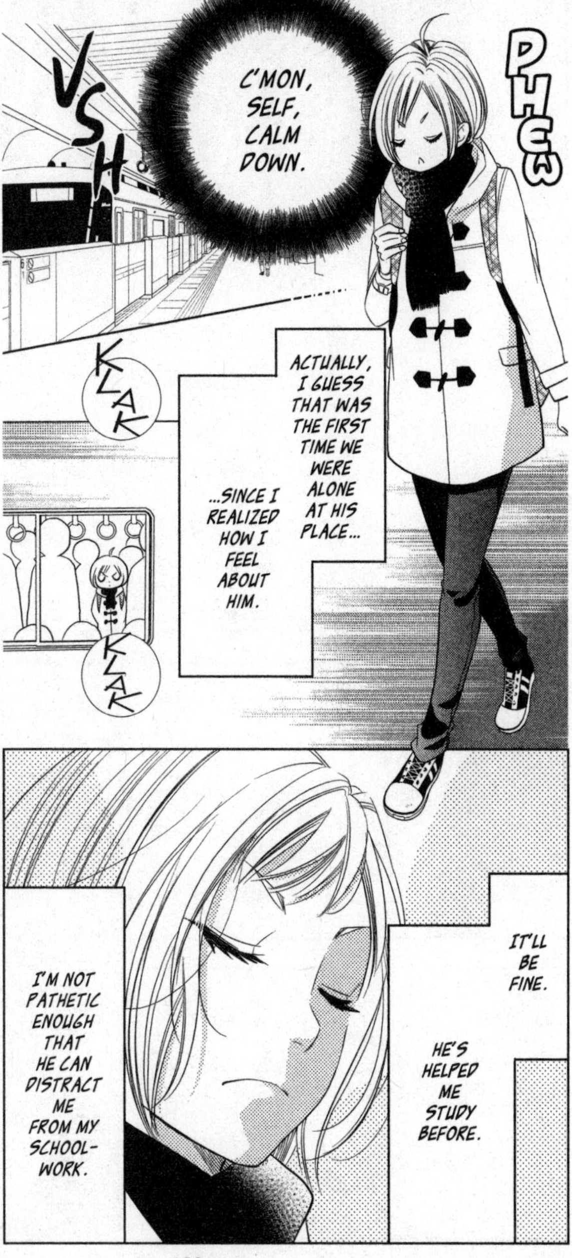
PHEW
C'MON, SELF, CALM DOWN.
VSH
ACTUALLY, I GUESS THAT WAS THE FIRST TIME WE WERE ALONE AT HIS PLACE...
...SINCE I REALIZED HOW I FEEL ABOUT HIM.
KLAK
KLAK
IT'LL BE FINE.
HE'S HELPED ME STUDY BEFORE.
I'M NOT PATHETIC ENOUGH THAT HE CAN DISTRACT ME FROM MY SCHOOL-WORK.

• Q & A •

I randomly chose some questions you've asked me in your letters.

Q. How many volumes will this series be?
A. That hasn't been decided yet.

Q. Do you prefer to study in the morning or at night?
A. At night.

Q. Have you had any jobs other than being a manga artist?
A. I worked part-time at an udon noodle shop. (During college.)
And I worked at a bank. (Only for a year.)

Q. Tell us about your childhood.
A. I was a shy, easily scared kid, but I was also curious about everything. I explored in the woods, I dug booby traps, I scaled the side of a mountain to look for a one-centimeter dog my friend swore she'd seen. I was always fascinated by imaginary or mythical things.

Q. How do people describe you?
A. I'd have to ask people to be certain, but I'm pretty sure there's no chance at all that they see me as personable and social.

• Special Thanks! •

All my readers
My main editor, S
Atsu-san, Emi-san
Naato-sama
The person who designed the cover
Everyone involved in this book!
Thank you very much!

I have an assistant who started helping me halfway through this book! I'm so grateful...!!! ✧✧

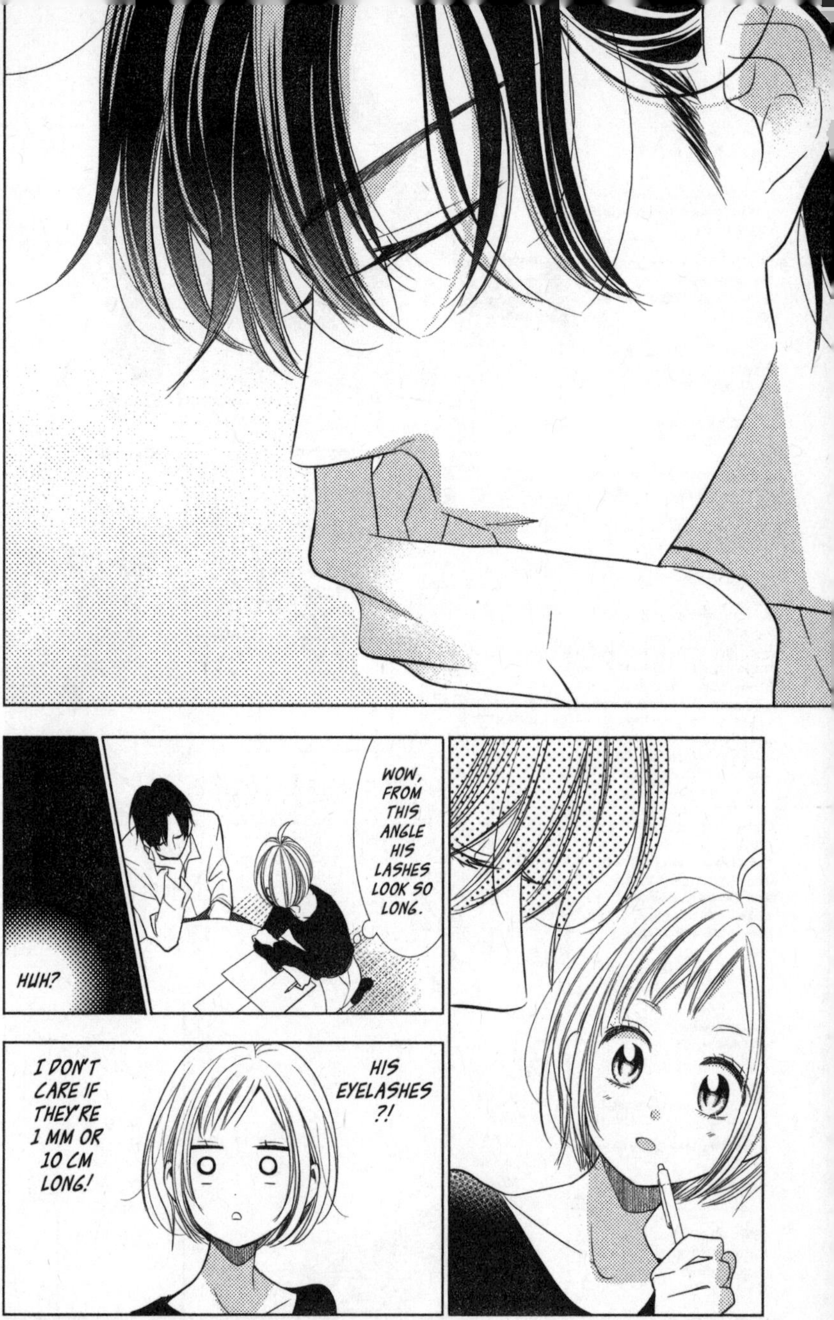
WOW, FROM THIS ANGLE HIS LASHES LOOK SO LONG.
HUH?
HIS EYELASHES ?!
I DON'T CARE IF THEY'RE 1 MM OR 10 CM LONG!

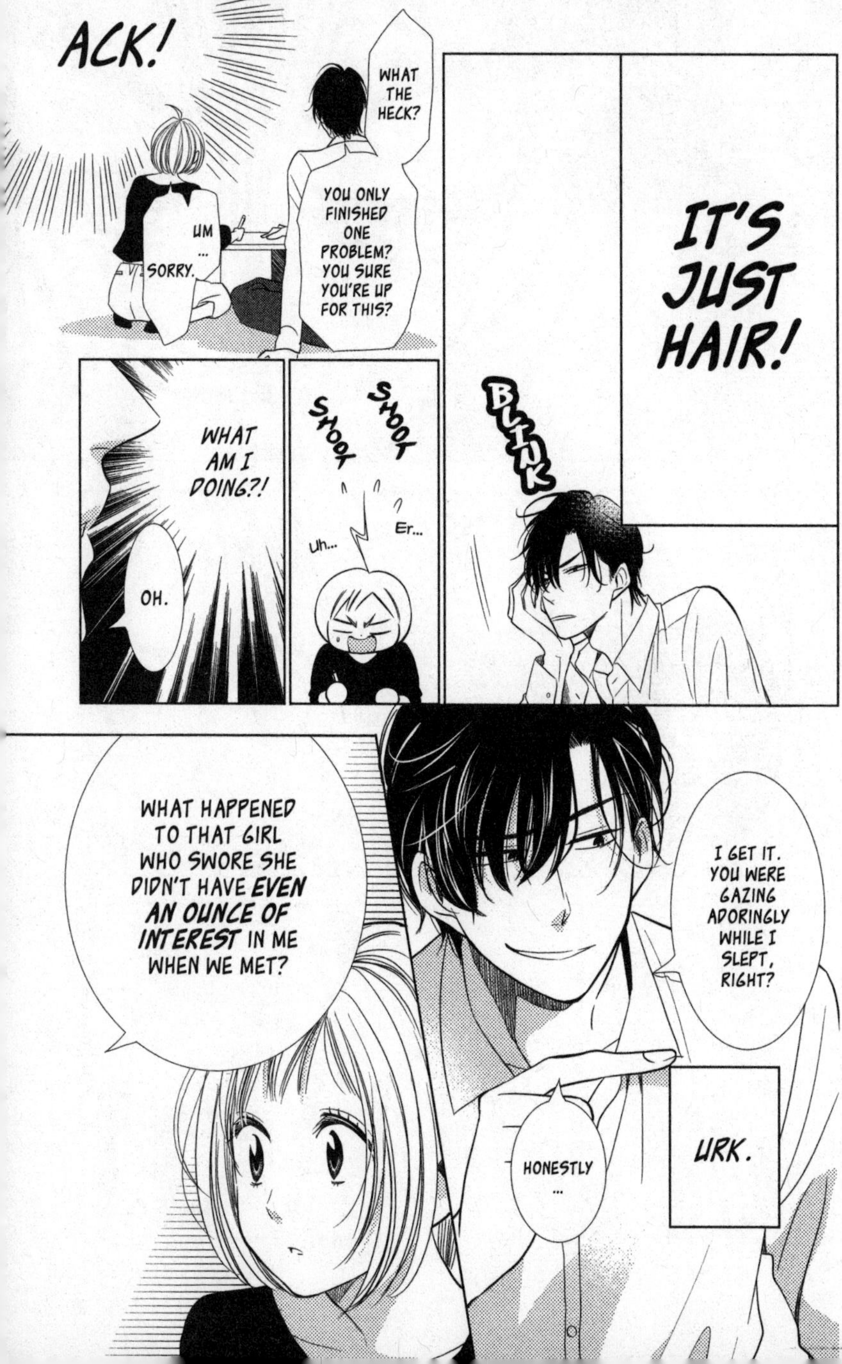
IT'S JUST HAIR!
BLINK
WHAT THE HECK?
YOU ONLY FINISHED ONE PROBLEM? YOU SURE YOU'RE UP FOR THIS?
ACK!
UM ... SORRY.
SHOOK SHOOK
Er...
Uh...
WHAT AM I DOING?!
OH.
I GET IT. YOU WERE GAZING ADORINGLY WHILE I SLEPT, RIGHT?
WHAT HAPPENED TO THAT GIRL WHO SWORE SHE DIDN'T HAVE EVEN AN OUNCE OF INTEREST IN ME WHEN WE MET?
URK.
HONESTLY ...

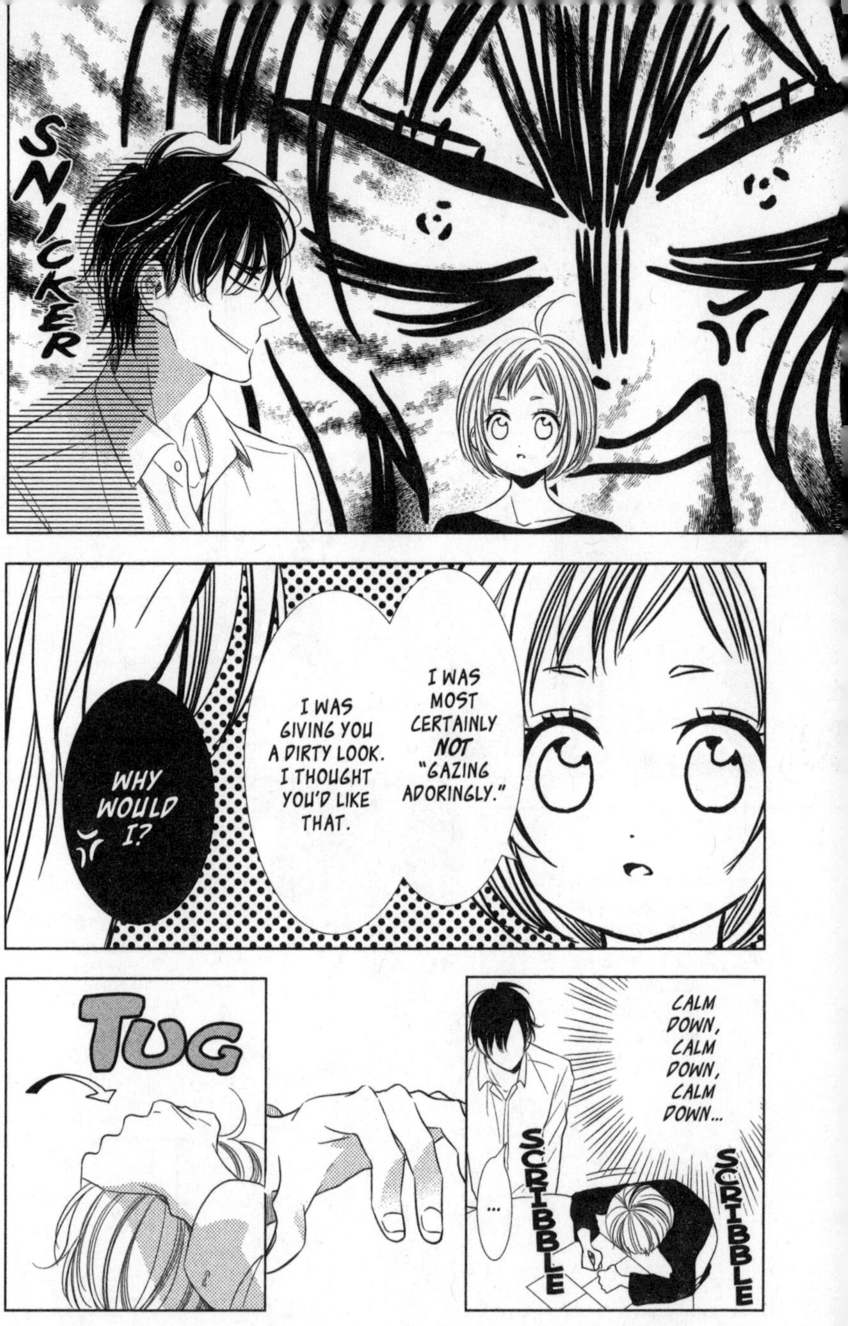
SNICKER
I WAS MOST CERTAINLY *NOT* "GAZING ADORINGLY."
I WAS GIVING YOU A DIRTY LOOK. I THOUGHT YOU'D LIKE THAT.
WHY WOULD I?
CALM DOWN, CALM DOWN, CALM DOWN...
SCRIBBLE
SCRIBBLE
...
TUG

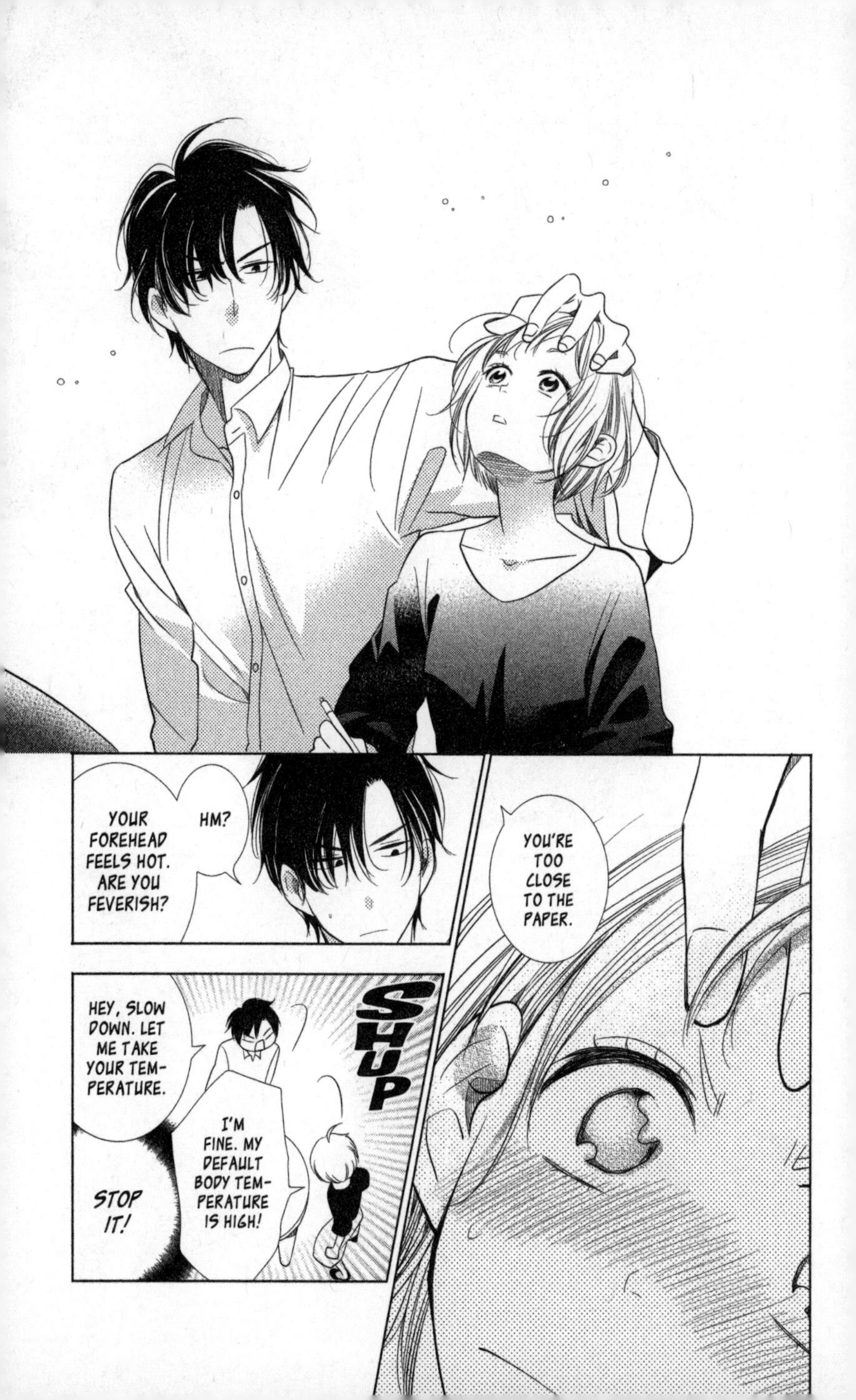
YOU'RE TOO CLOSE TO THE PAPER.
HM?
YOUR FOREHEAD FEELS HOT. ARE YOU FEVERISH?
SHUP
HEY, SLOW DOWN. LET ME TAKE YOUR TEMPERATURE.
I'M FINE. MY DEFAULT BODY TEMPERATURE IS HIGH!
STOP IT!

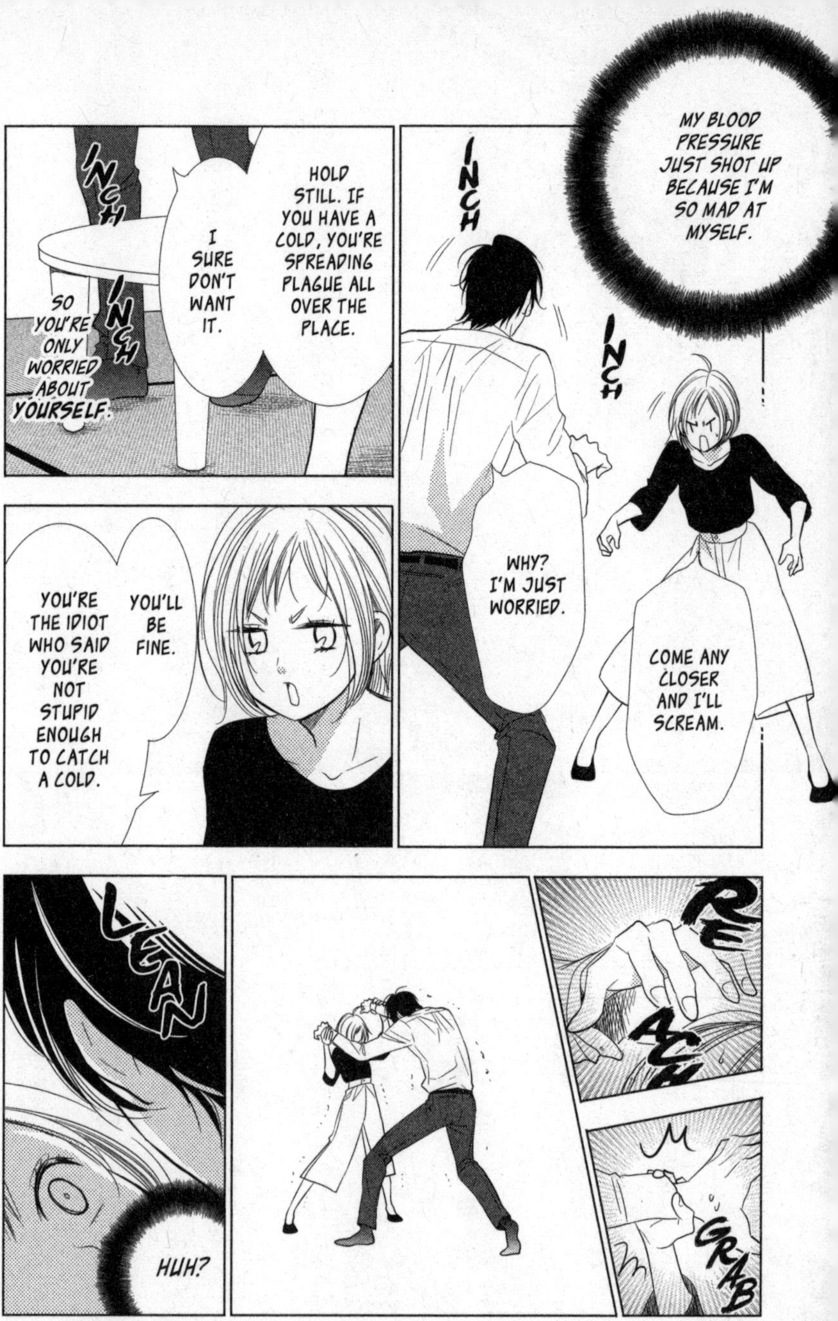
MY BLOOD PRESSURE JUST SHOT UP BECAUSE I'M SO MAD AT MYSELF.
INCH
INCH
COME ANY CLOSER AND I'LL SCREAM.
WHY? I'M JUST WORRIED.
HOLD STILL. IF YOU HAVE A COLD, YOU'RE SPREADING PLAGUE ALL OVER THE PLACE.
I SURE DON'T WANT IT.
INCH
INCH
SO YOU'RE ONLY WORRIED ABOUT YOURSELF.
YOU'LL BE FINE.
YOU'RE THE IDIOT WHO SAID YOU'RE NOT STUPID ENOUGH TO CATCH A COLD.
REACH
GRAB
LEAN
HUH?

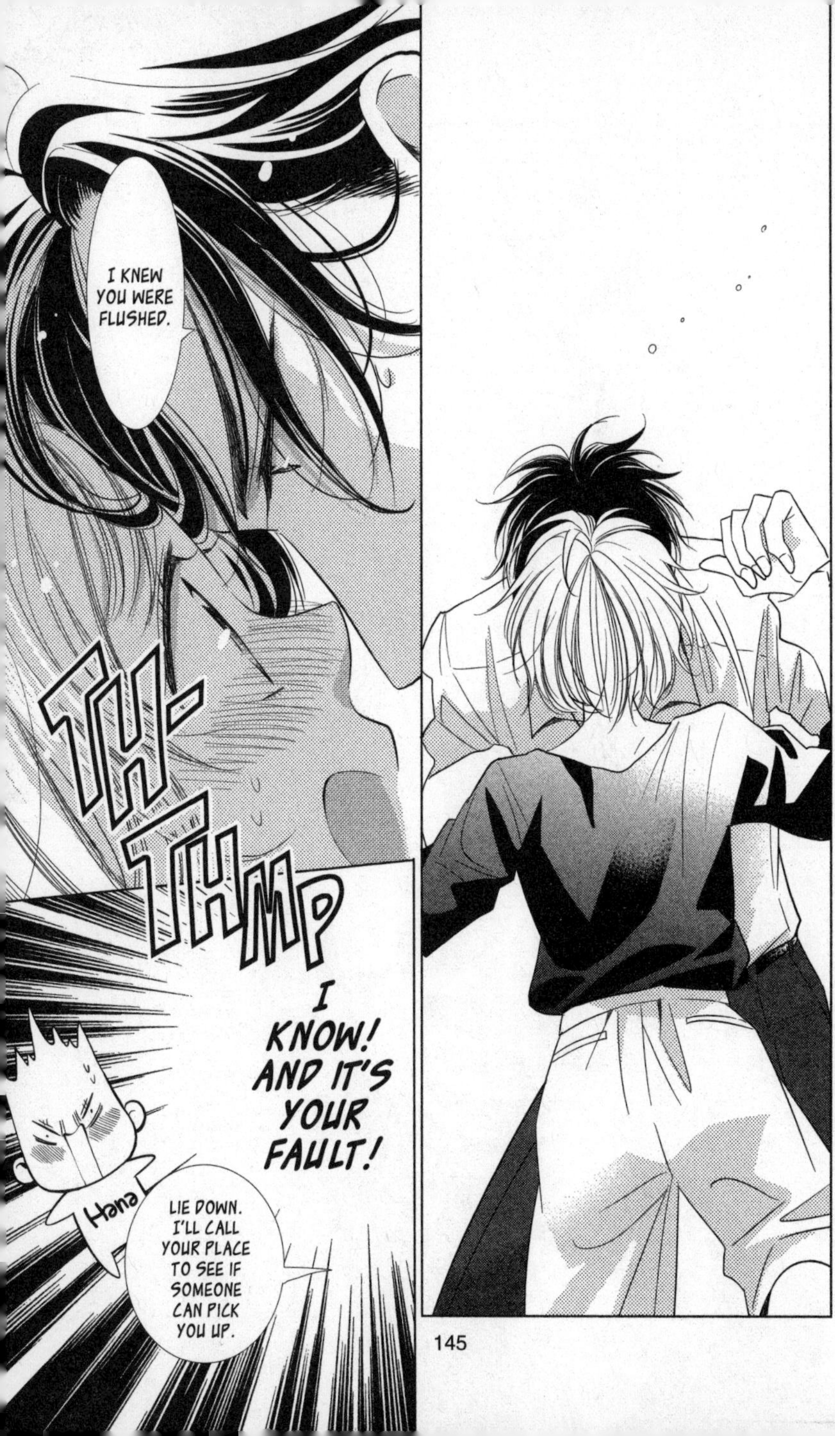
I KNEW YOU WERE FLUSHED.
TH-THMP
I KNOW! AND IT'S YOUR FAULT!
Hana
LIE DOWN. I'LL CALL YOUR PLACE TO SEE IF SOMEONE CAN PICK YOU UP.

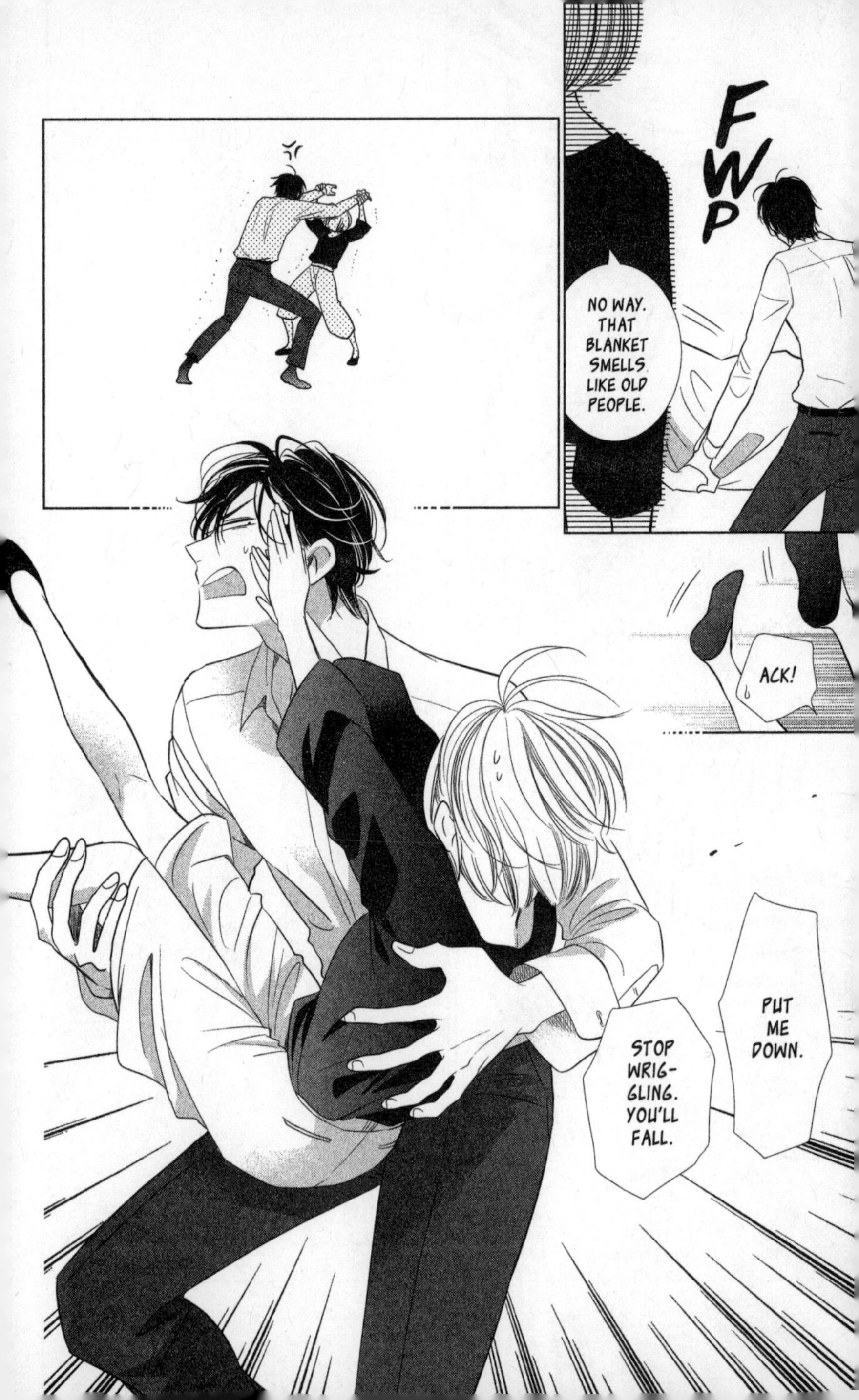
FWP
NO WAY. THAT BLANKET SMELLS LIKE OLD PEOPLE.
ACK!
PUT ME DOWN.
STOP WRIG-GLING. YOU'LL FALL.

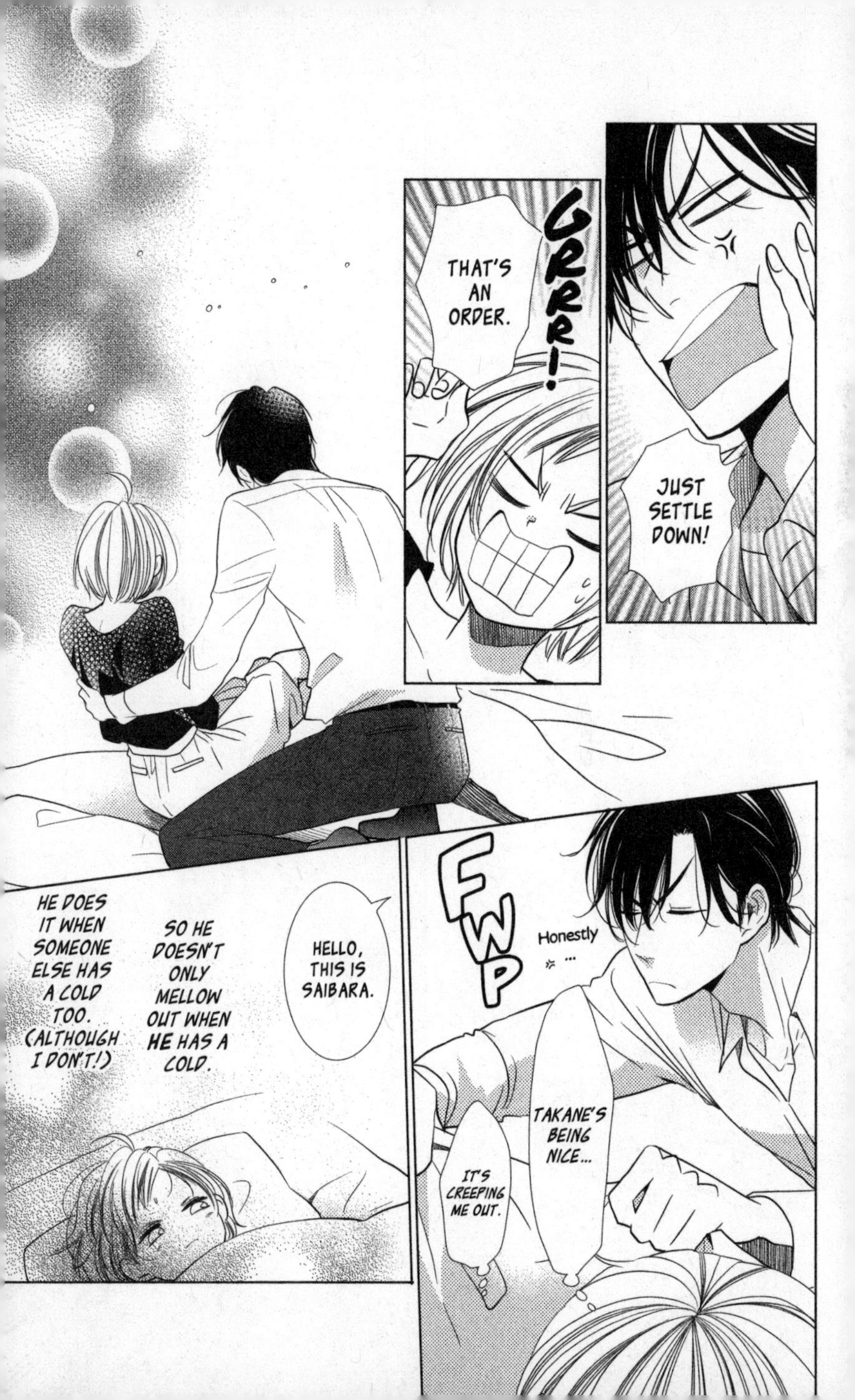
JUST SETTLE DOWN!
GRRR!
THAT'S AN ORDER.
FWP
Honestly...
TAKANE'S BEING NICE...
IT'S CREEPING ME OUT.
HELLO, THIS IS SAIBARA.
SO HE DOESN'T ONLY MELLOW OUT WHEN HE HAS A COLD.
HE DOES IT WHEN SOMEONE ELSE HAS A COLD TOO. (ALTHOUGH I DON'T!)

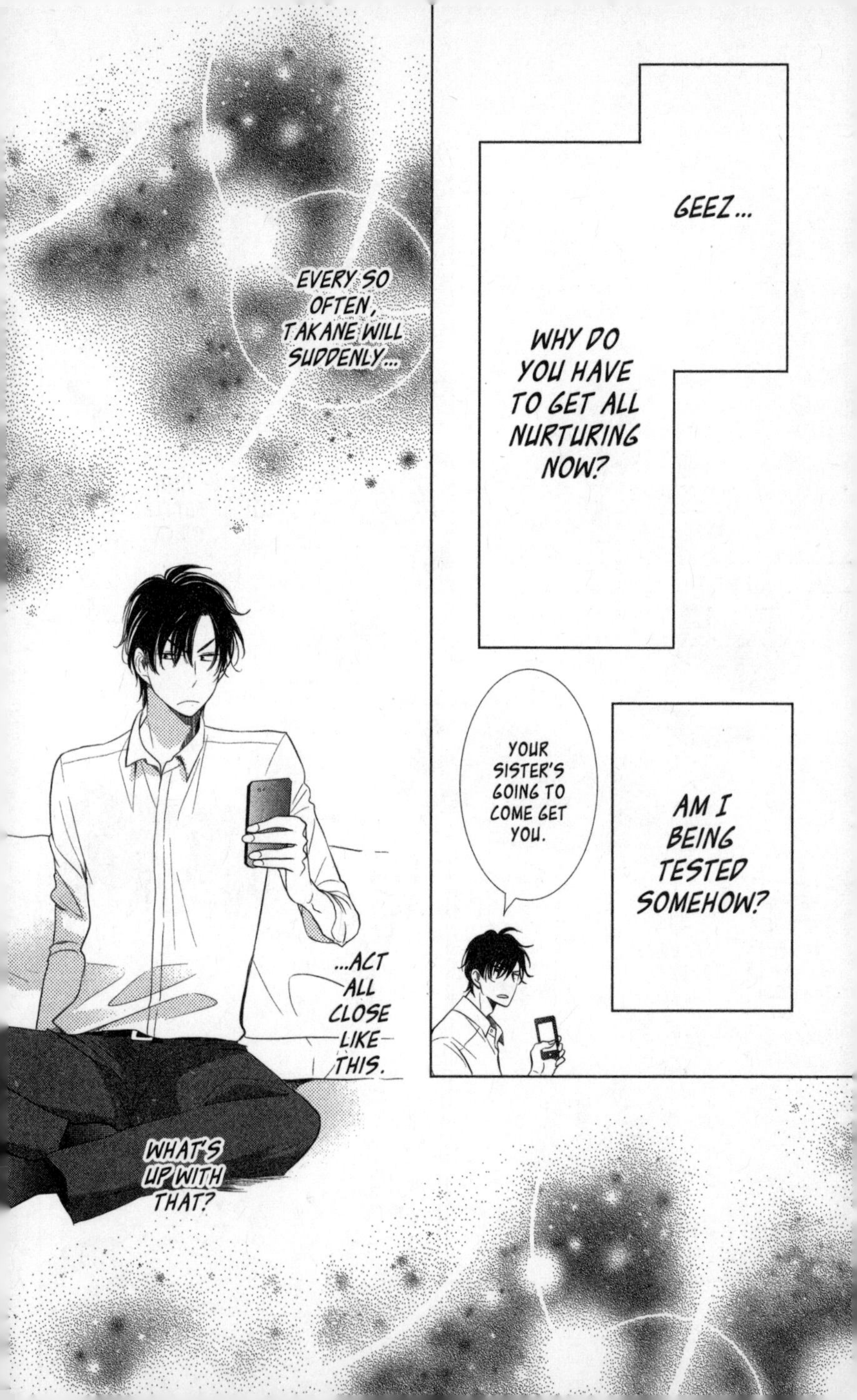
GEEZ...
WHY DO YOU HAVE TO GET ALL NURTURING NOW?
AM I BEING TESTED SOMEHOW?
YOUR SISTER'S GOING TO COME GET YOU.
EVERY SO OFTEN, TAKANE WILL SUDDENLY...
...ACT ALL CLOSE LIKE THIS.
WHAT'S UP WITH THAT?

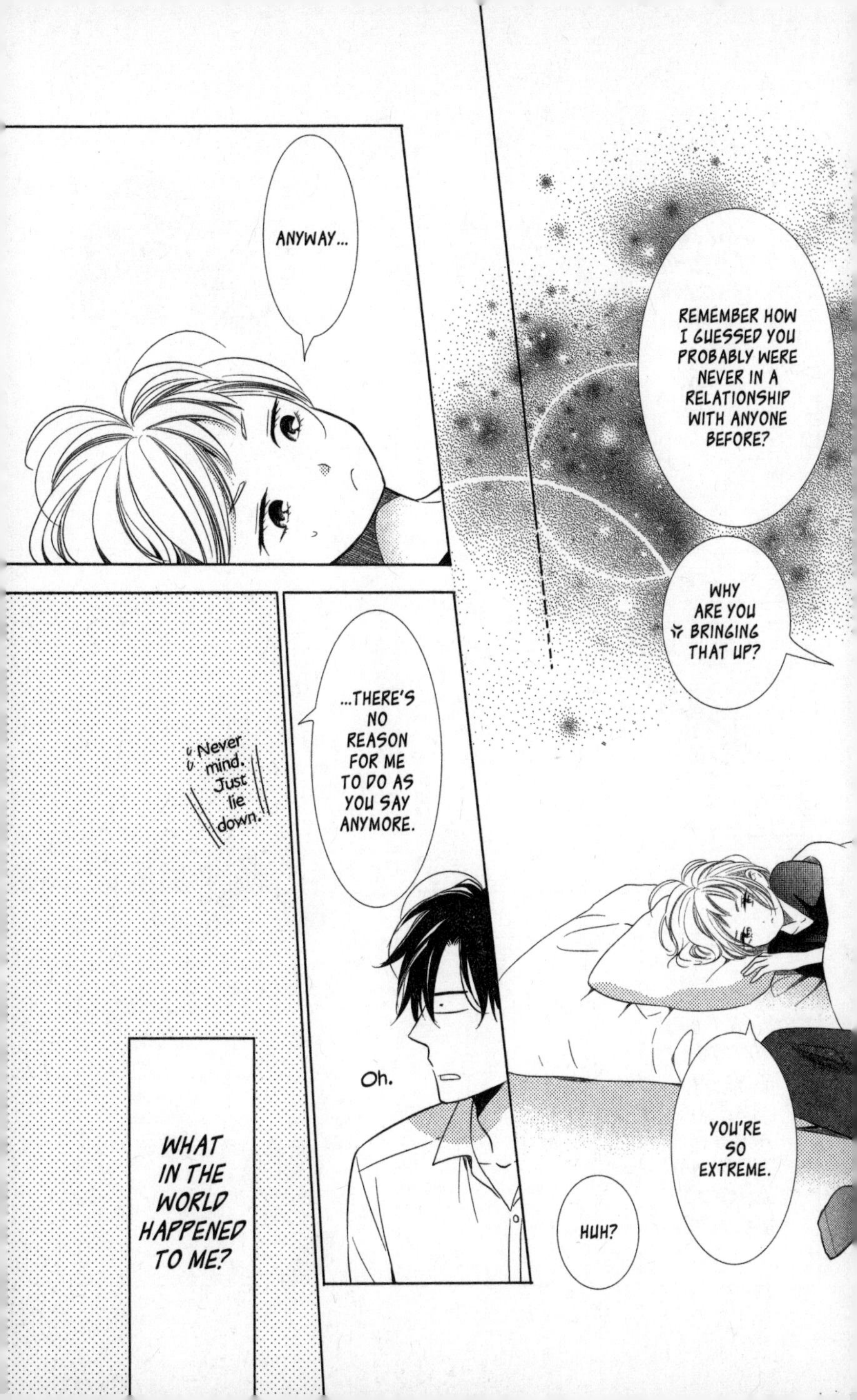
REMEMBER HOW I GUESSED YOU PROBABLY WERE NEVER IN A RELATIONSHIP WITH ANYONE BEFORE?
WHY ARE YOU BRINGING THAT UP?
YOU'RE SO EXTREME.
HUH?
ANYWAY...
...THERE'S NO REASON FOR ME TO DO AS YOU SAY ANYMORE.
Oh.
Never mind. Just lie down.
WHAT IN THE WORLD HAPPENED TO ME?

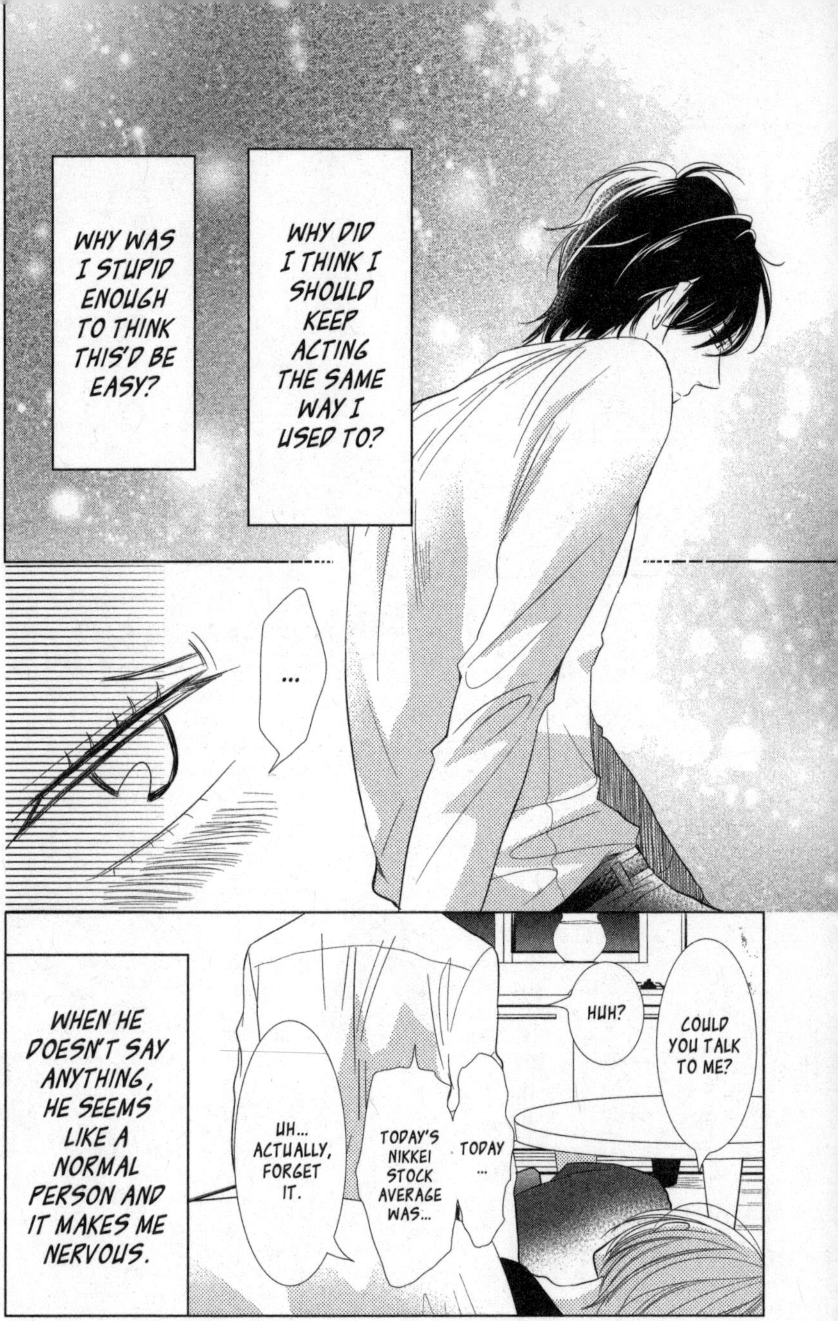
WHY DID I THINK I SHOULD KEEP ACTING THE SAME WAY I USED TO?
WHY WAS I STUPID ENOUGH TO THINK THIS'D BE EASY?
...
COULD YOU TALK TO ME?
HUH?
TODAY...
TODAY'S NIKKEI STOCK AVERAGE WAS...
UH... ACTUALLY, FORGET IT.
WHEN HE DOESN'T SAY ANYTHING, HE SEEMS LIKE A NORMAL PERSON AND IT MAKES ME NERVOUS.

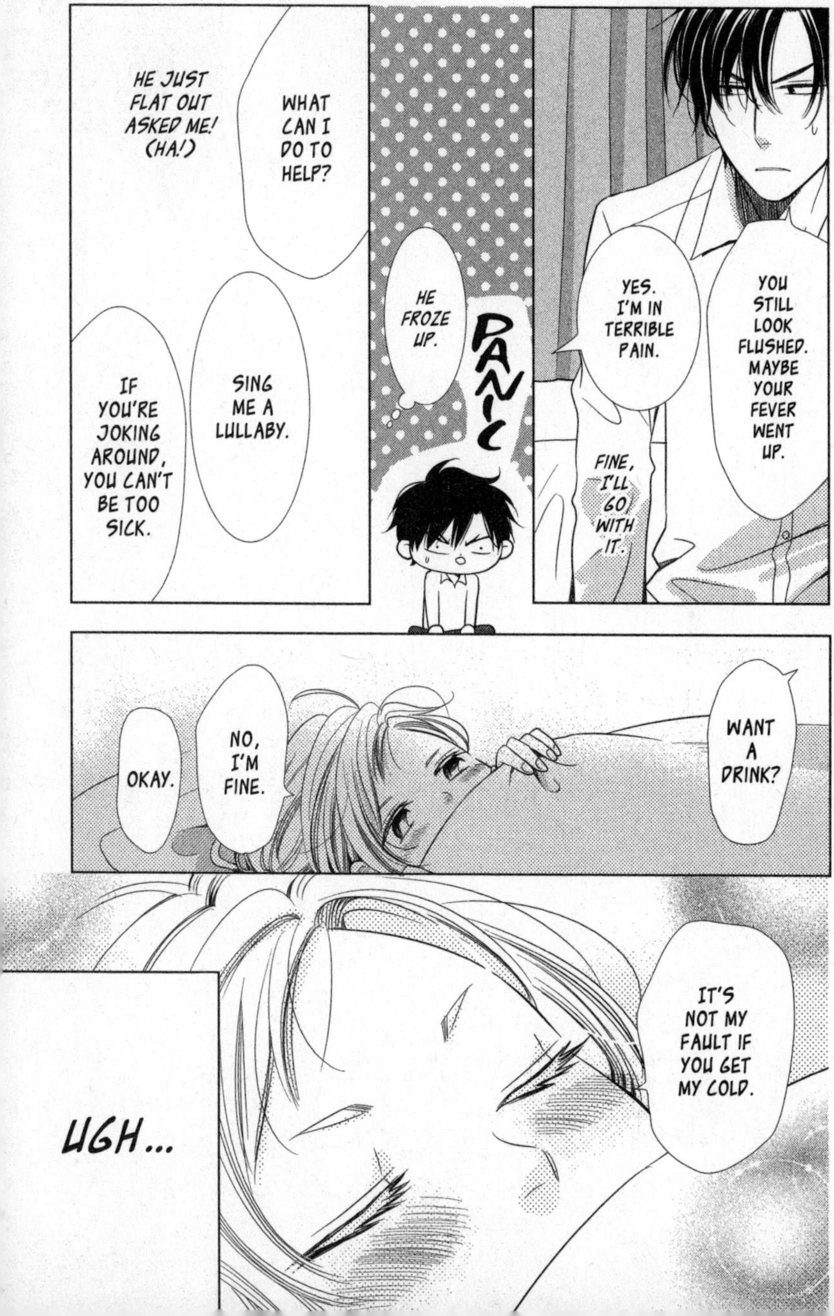
YOU STILL LOOK FLUSHED. MAYBE YOUR FEVER WENT UP.
YES. I'M IN TERRIBLE PAIN.
FINE, I'LL GO WITH IT.
PANIC
HE FROZE UP.
WHAT CAN I DO TO HELP?
HE JUST FLAT OUT ASKED ME! (HA!)
SING ME A LULLABY.
IF YOU'RE JOKING AROUND, YOU CAN'T BE TOO SICK.
WANT A DRINK?
NO, I'M FINE.
OKAY.
IT'S NOT MY FAULT IF YOU GET MY COLD.
UGH...

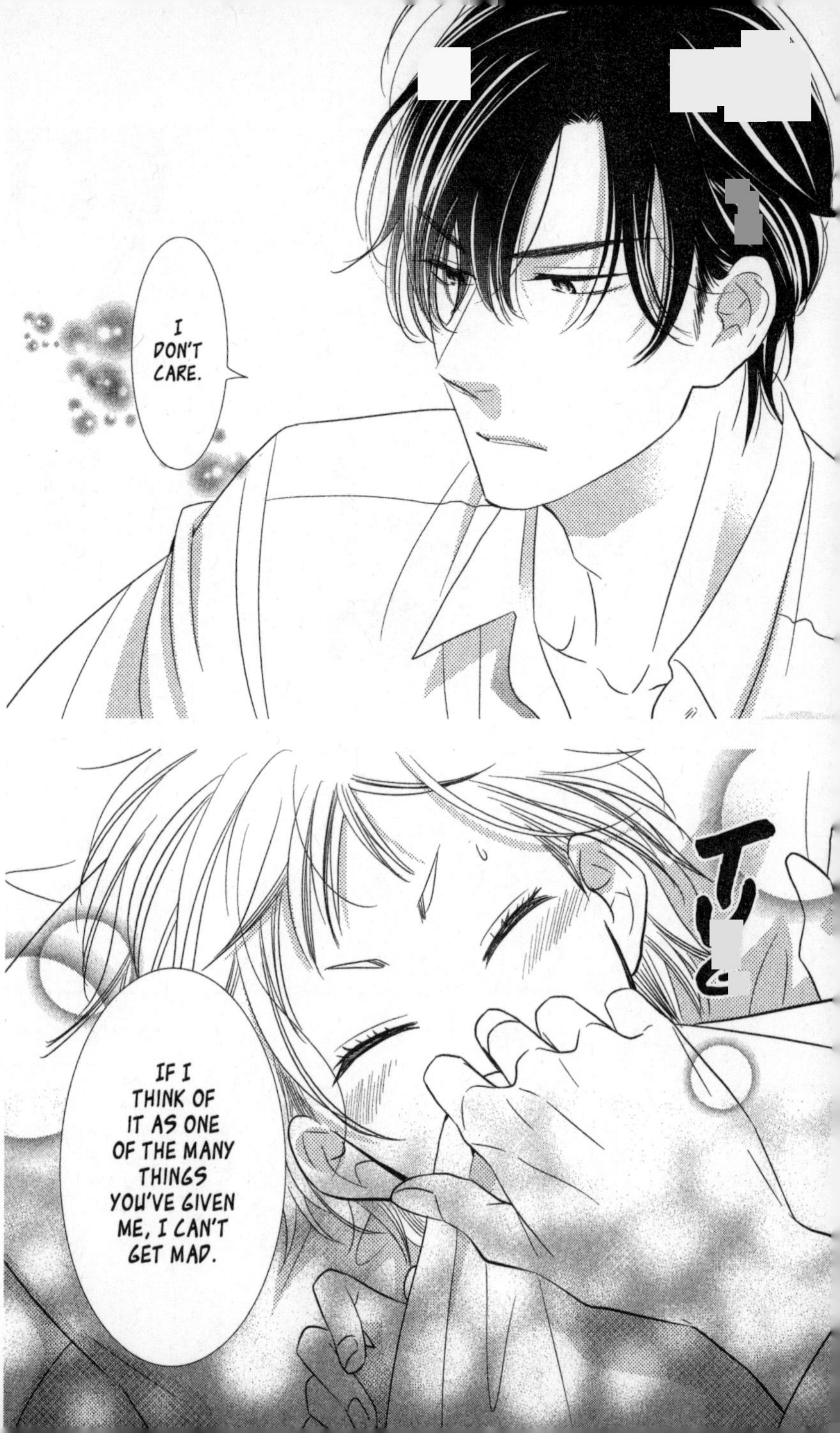
I DON'T CARE.
IF I THINK OF IT AS ONE OF THE MANY THINGS YOU'VE GIVEN ME, I CAN'T GET MAD.

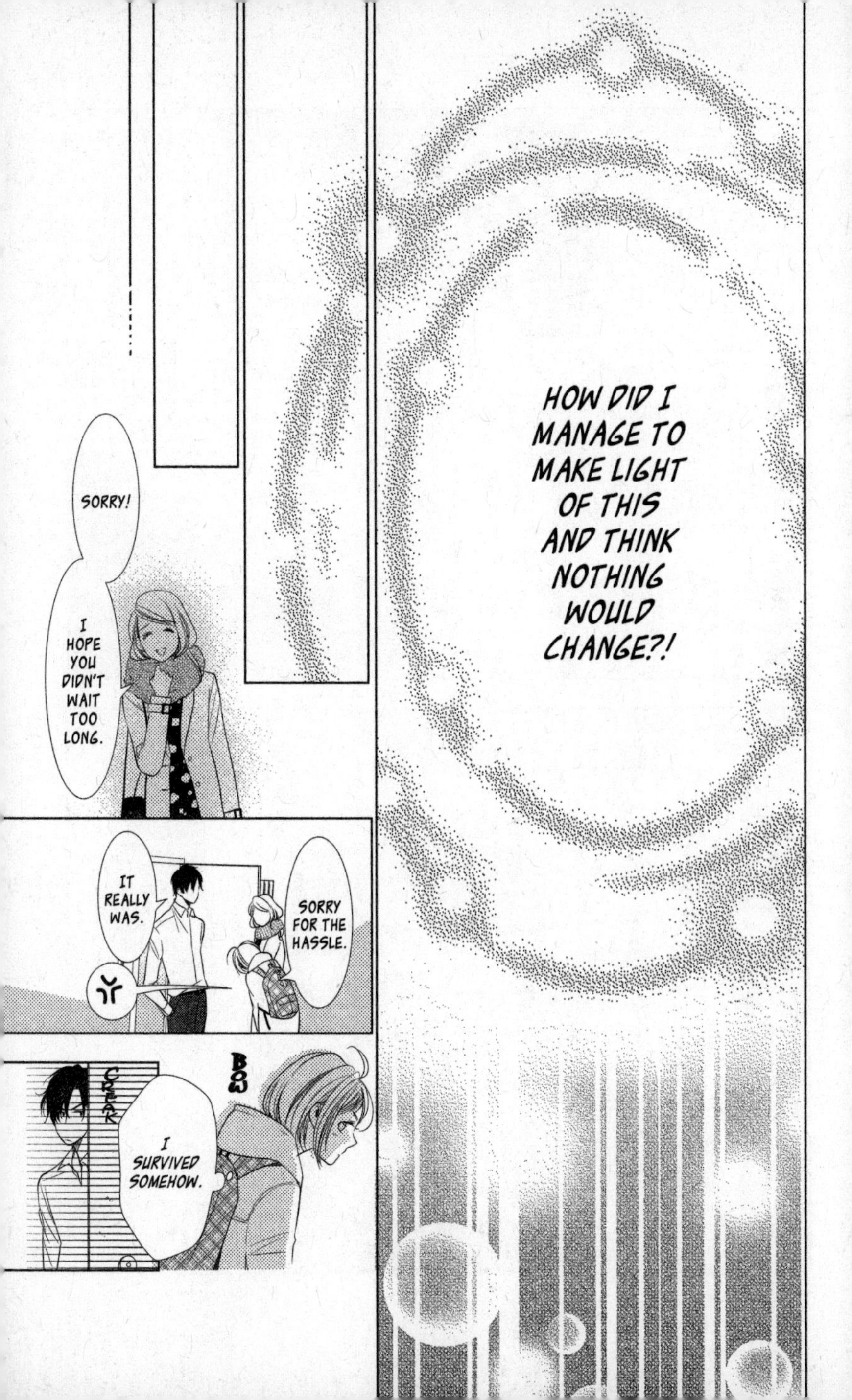
HOW DID I MANAGE TO MAKE LIGHT OF THIS AND THINK NOTHING WOULD CHANGE?!
SORRY!
I HOPE YOU DIDN'T WAIT TOO LONG.
SORRY FOR THE HASSLE.
IT REALLY WAS.
BOW
CREAK
I SURVIVED SOMEHOW.

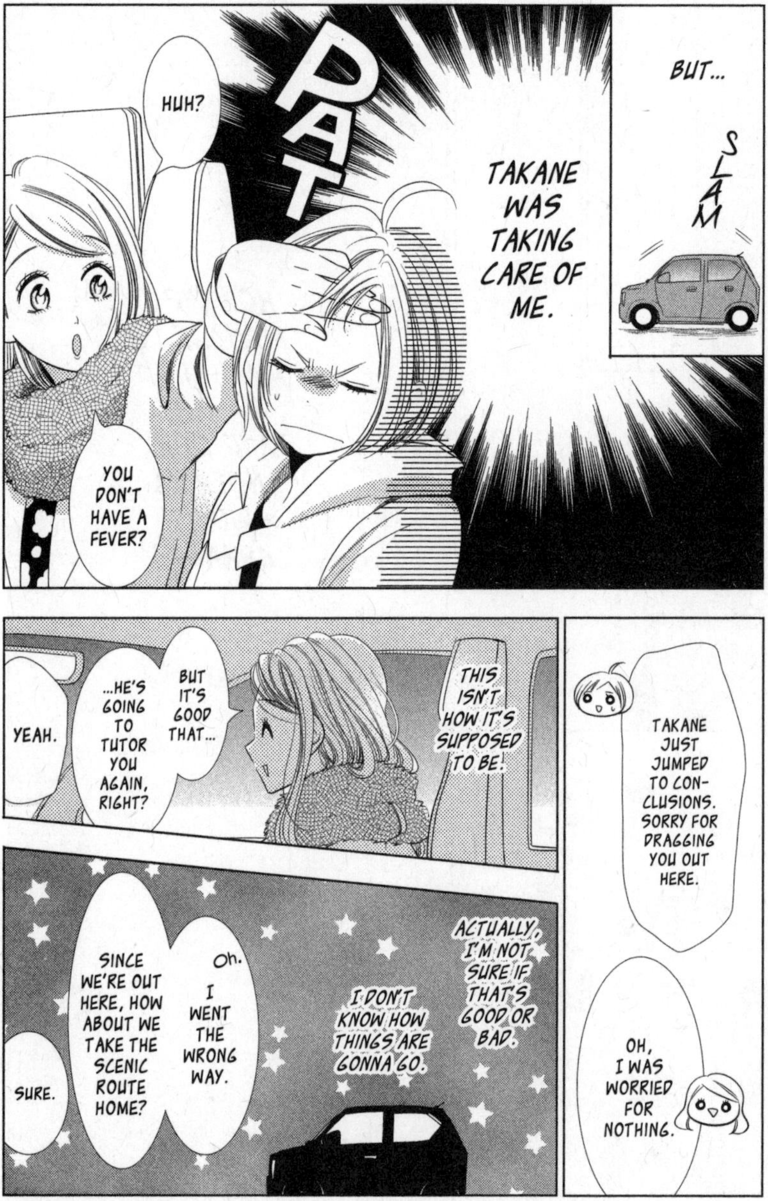
BUT...
SLAM
TAKANE WAS TAKING CARE OF ME.
PAT
HUH?
YOU DON'T HAVE A FEVER?
TAKANE JUST JUMPED TO CON-CLUSIONS. SORRY FOR DRAGGING YOU OUT HERE.
OH, I WAS WORRIED FOR NOTHING.
THIS ISN'T HOW IT'S SUPPOSED TO BE.
BUT IT'S GOOD THAT...
...HE'S GOING TO TUTOR YOU AGAIN, RIGHT?
YEAH.
ACTUALLY, I'M NOT SURE IF THAT'S GOOD OR BAD.
I DON'T KNOW HOW THINGS ARE GONNA GO.
Oh. I WENT THE WRONG WAY.
SINCE WE'RE OUT HERE, HOW ABOUT WE TAKE THE SCENIC ROUTE HOME?
SURE.

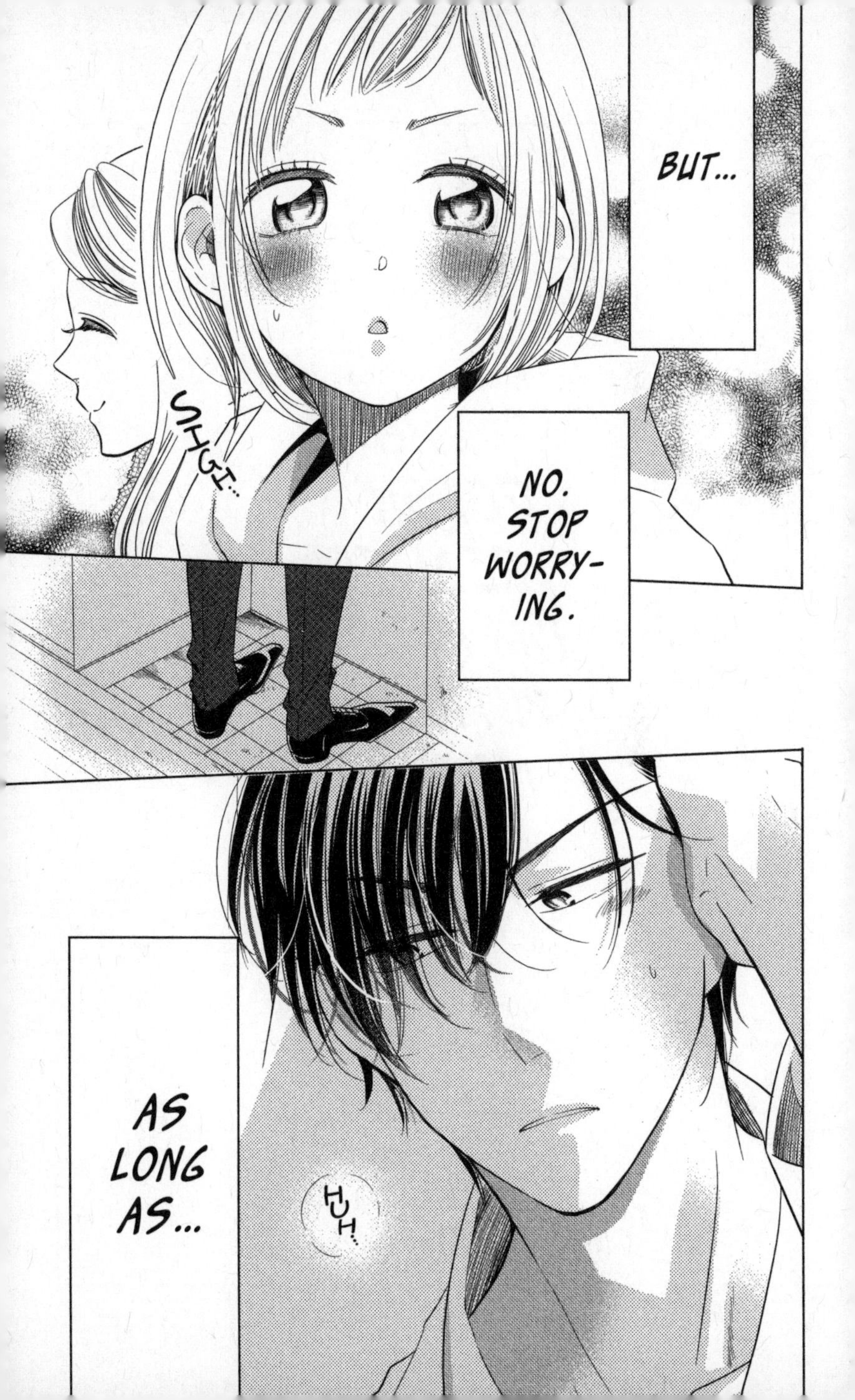
BUT...
NO. STOP WORRY-ING.
SHIGI...
AS LONG AS...
HUH...

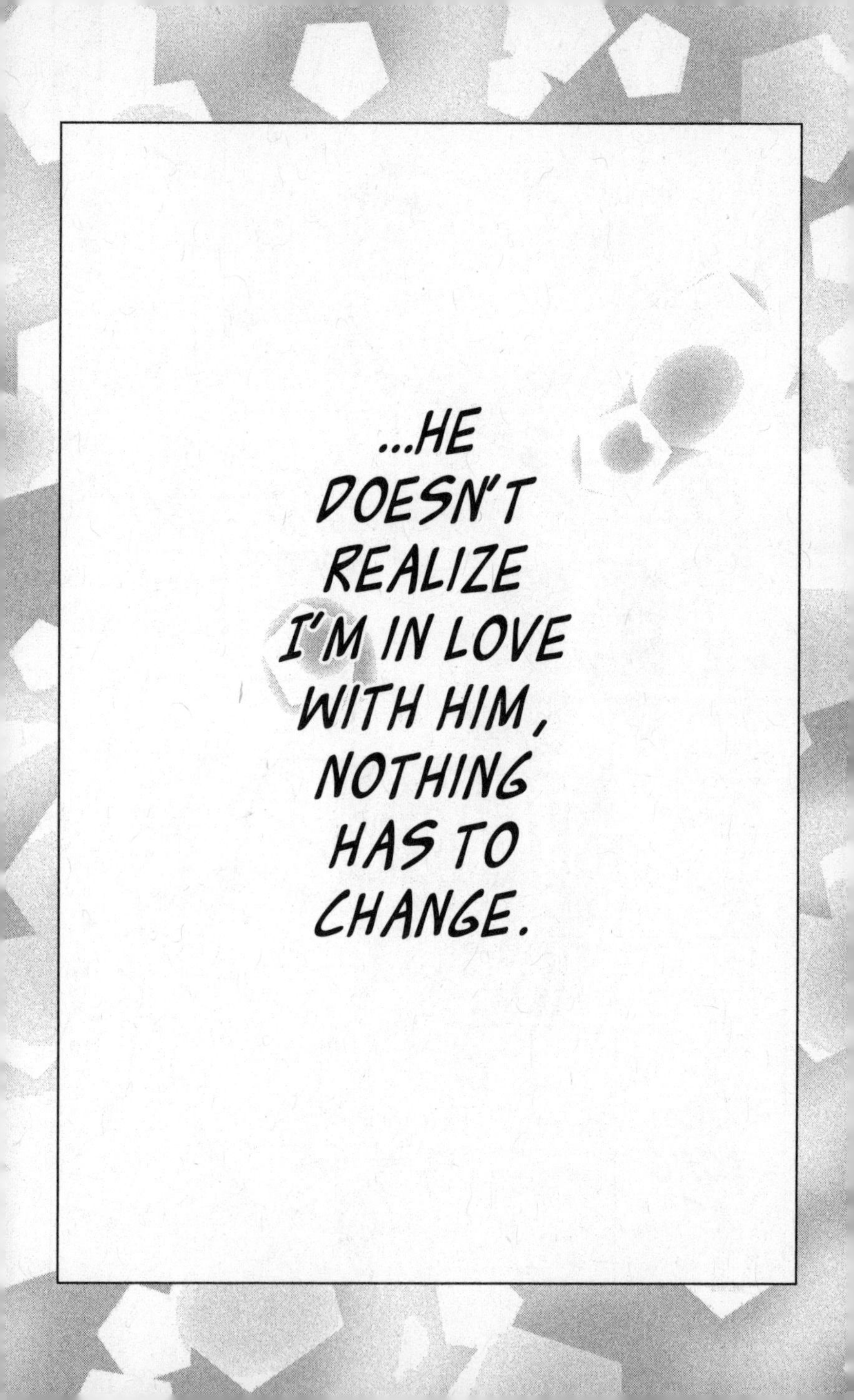
...HE DOESN'T REALIZE I'M IN LOVE WITH HIM, NOTHING HAS TO CHANGE.

Singing a Lullaby Is a Good Idea

GUESS I HAVE NO CHOICE.
WHAT?
ARE YOU GONNA SING?
HE STARTED SINGING SOME WESTERN LULLABY.
WOW, HE'S GOOD.
IMPROVISED
EYES CLOSED
RUNS
Oh
VOCAL HICCUPS
MELISMA
Baby
BUT HE JUST KEEPS GOING. I CAN'T LISTEN FOR THIS LONG!
mm
HEAD SHAKING
VIBRATO
IMPROVISED
MELISMA
Yeah
IMPROVISED

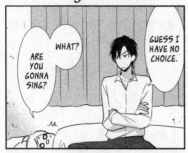

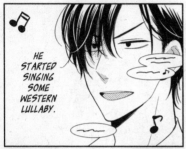

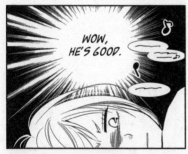

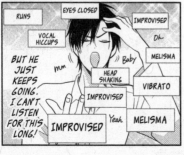

Old-People Smell

PABREZE
ANTI-BACTERIAL
¥280
Air Freshener ¥324
FTZ
IT BOTHERED HIM A LITTLE.
FTZ

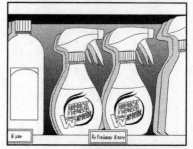

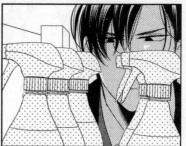

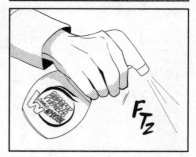

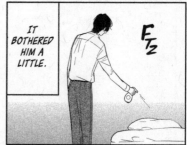

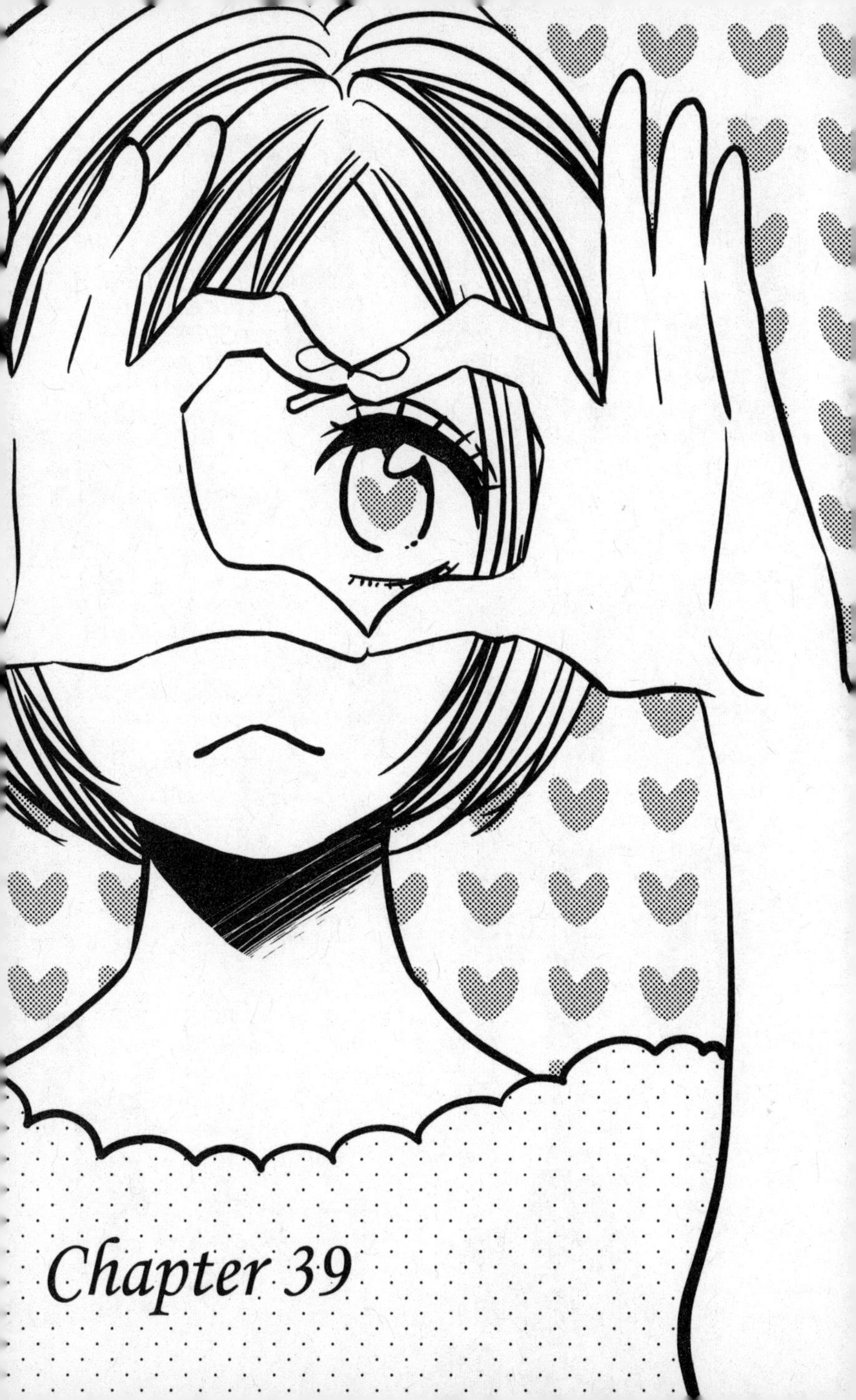
Chapter 39

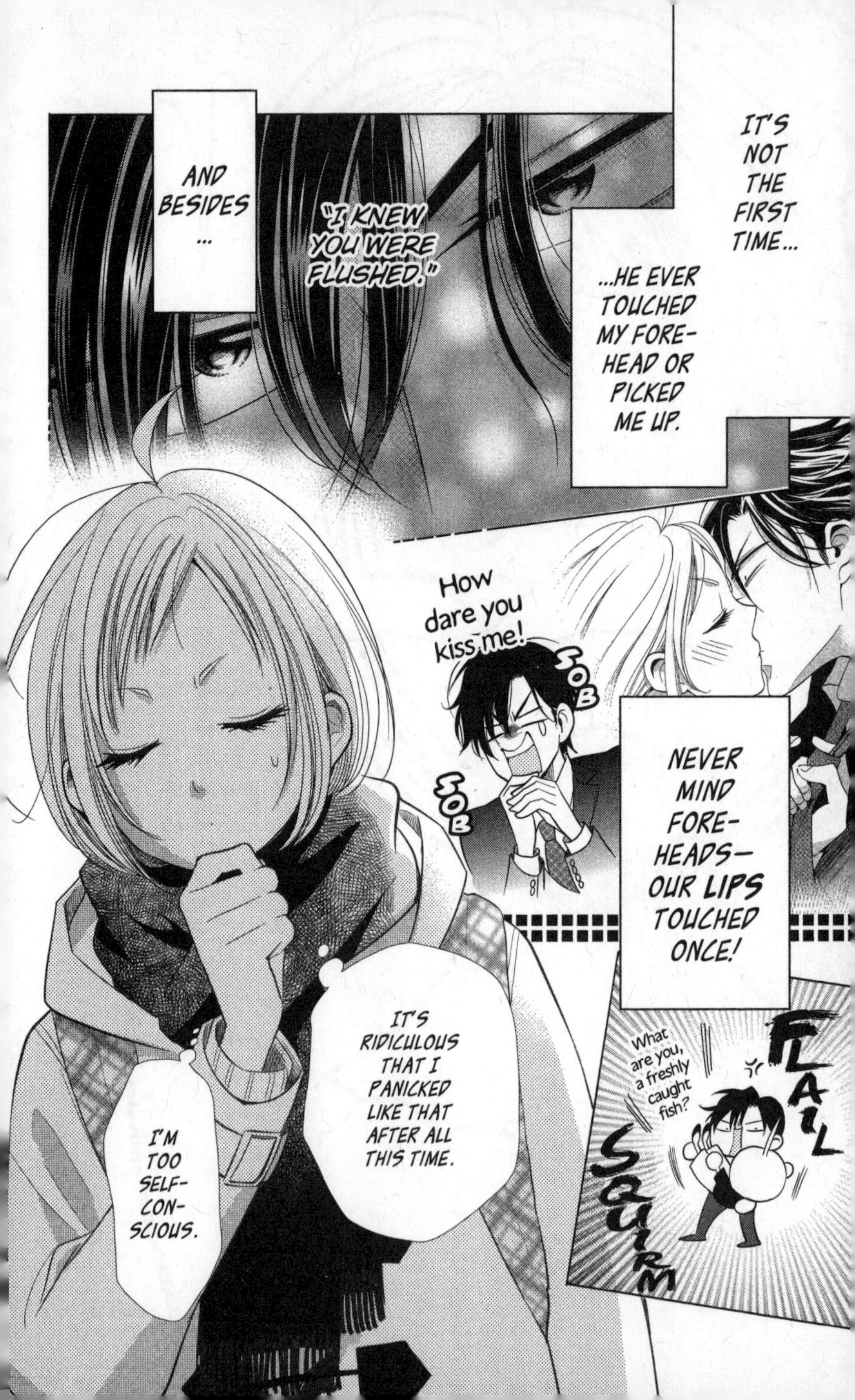
IT'S NOT THE FIRST TIME...
...HE EVER TOUCHED MY FORE-HEAD OR PICKED ME UP.
"I KNEW YOU WERE FLUSHED."
AND BESIDES ...
NEVER MIND FORE-HEADS— OUR LIPS TOUCHED ONCE!
How dare you kiss me!
SOB
SOB
What are you, a freshly caught fish?
FLAIL
SQUIRM
IT'S RIDICULOUS THAT I PANICKED LIKE THAT AFTER ALL THIS TIME.
I'M TOO SELF-CON-SCIOUS.

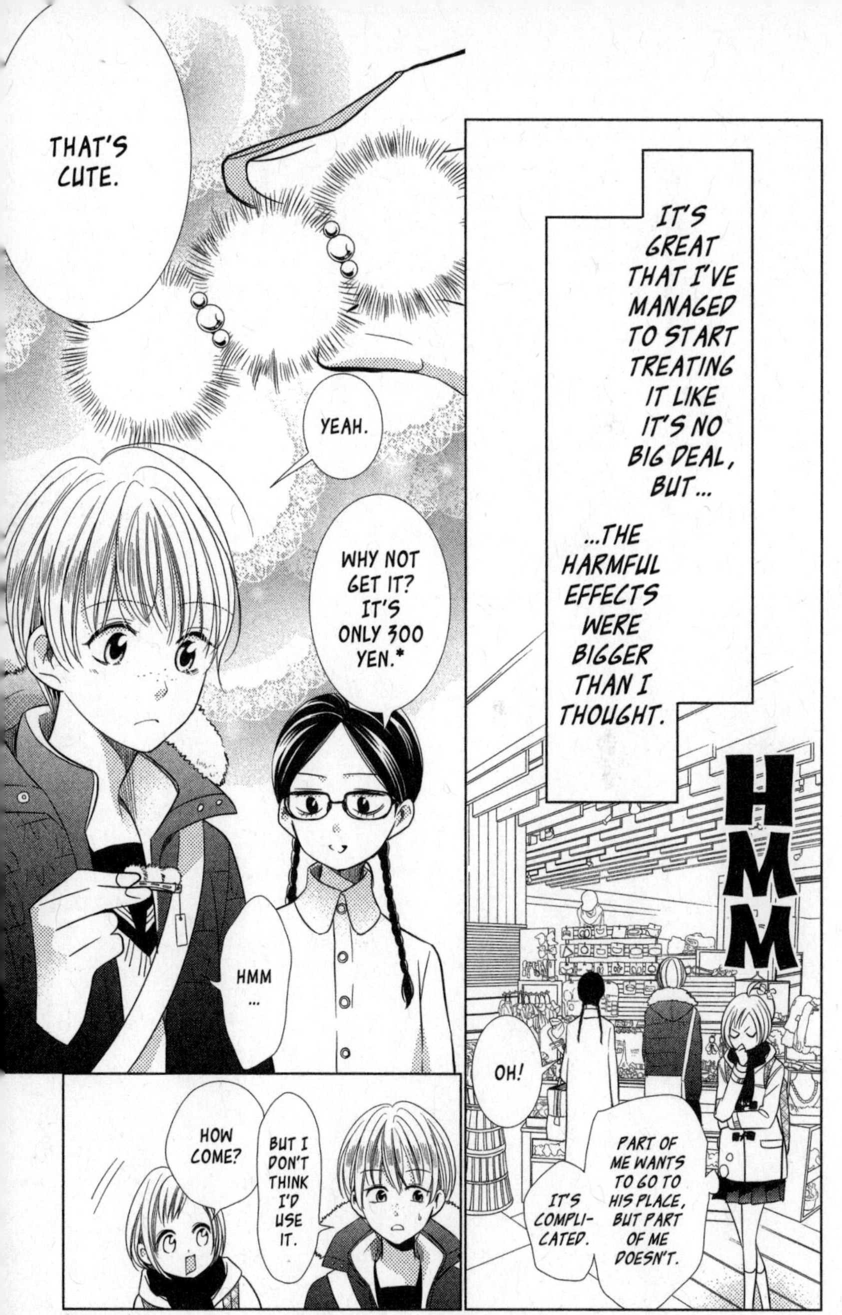
IT'S GREAT THAT I'VE MANAGED TO START TREATING IT LIKE IT'S NO BIG DEAL, BUT...
...THE HARMFUL EFFECTS WERE BIGGER THAN I THOUGHT.
HMM
OH!
PART OF ME WANTS TO GO TO HIS PLACE, BUT PART OF ME DOESN'T.
IT'S COMPLICATED.
THAT'S CUTE.
YEAH.
WHY NOT GET IT? IT'S ONLY 300 YEN.*
HMM...
HOW COME?
BUT I DON'T THINK I'D USE IT.

*ABOUT $3

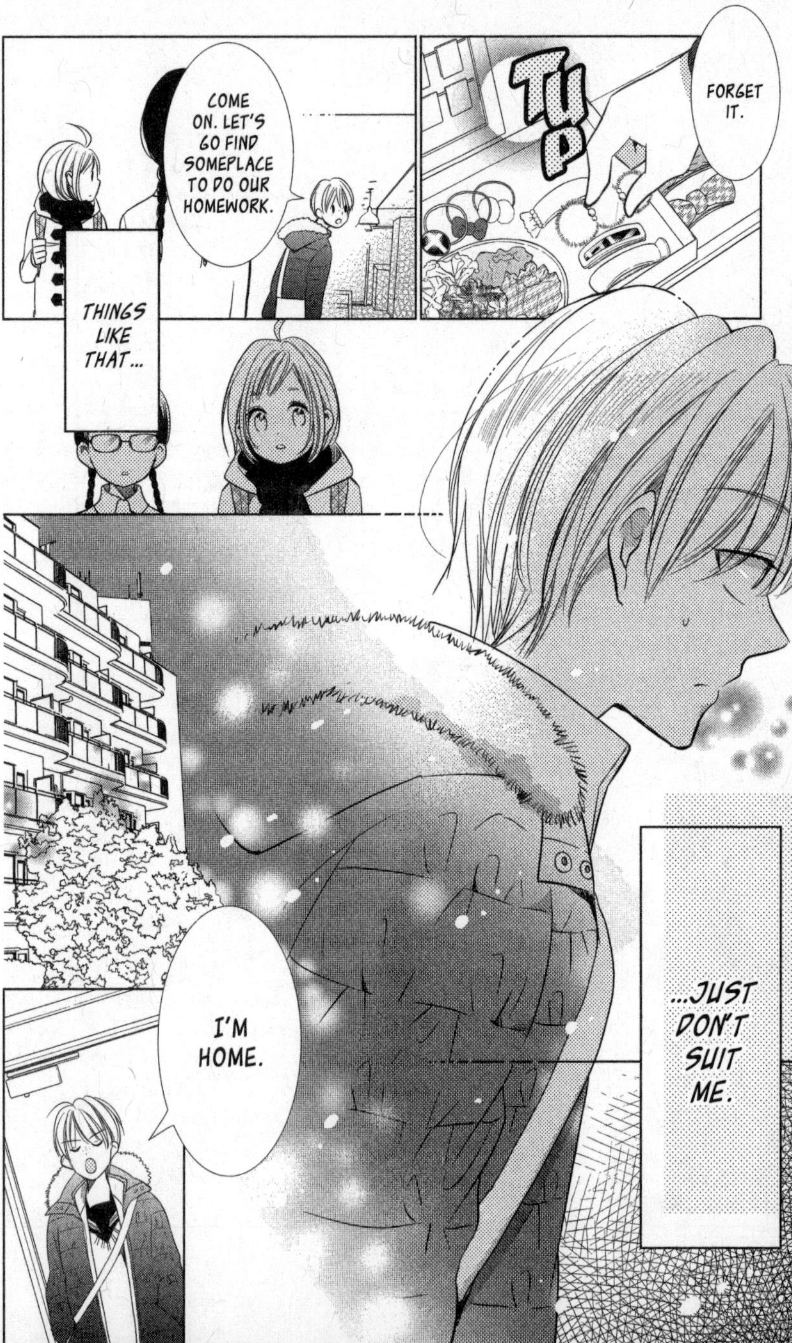
FORGET IT.
TUP
COME ON. LET'S GO FIND SOMEPLACE TO DO OUR HOMEWORK.
THINGS LIKE THAT...
...JUST DON'T SUIT ME.
I'M HOME.

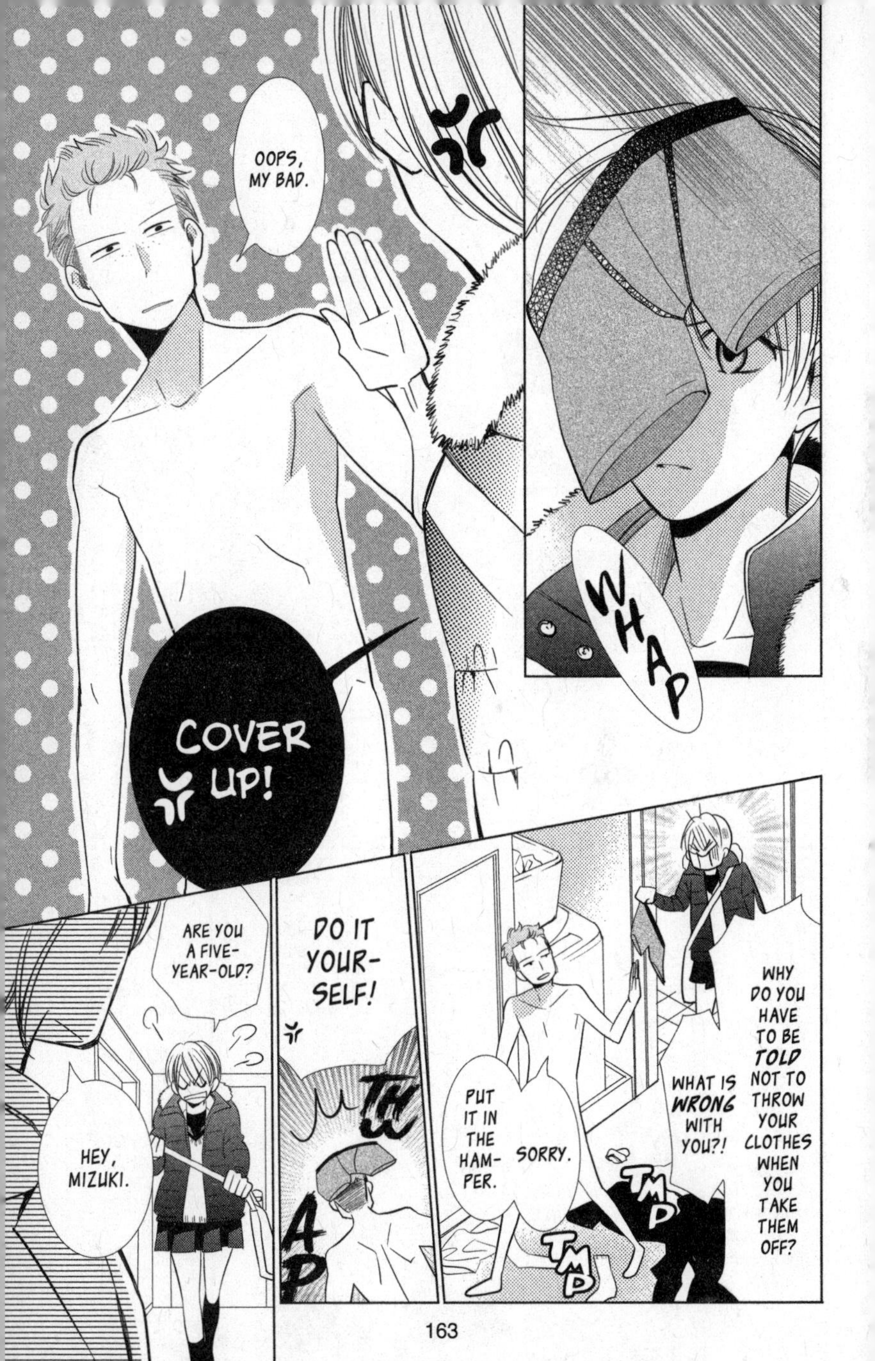
WHAP
OOPS, MY BAD.
COVER UP!
WHY DO YOU HAVE TO BE TOLD NOT TO THROW YOUR CLOTHES WHEN YOU TAKE THEM OFF?
WHAT IS WRONG WITH YOU?!
TMP
TMP
SORRY.
PUT IT IN THE HAMPER.
DO IT YOURSELF!
THWAP
ARE YOU A FIVE-YEAR-OLD?
HEY, MIZUKI.

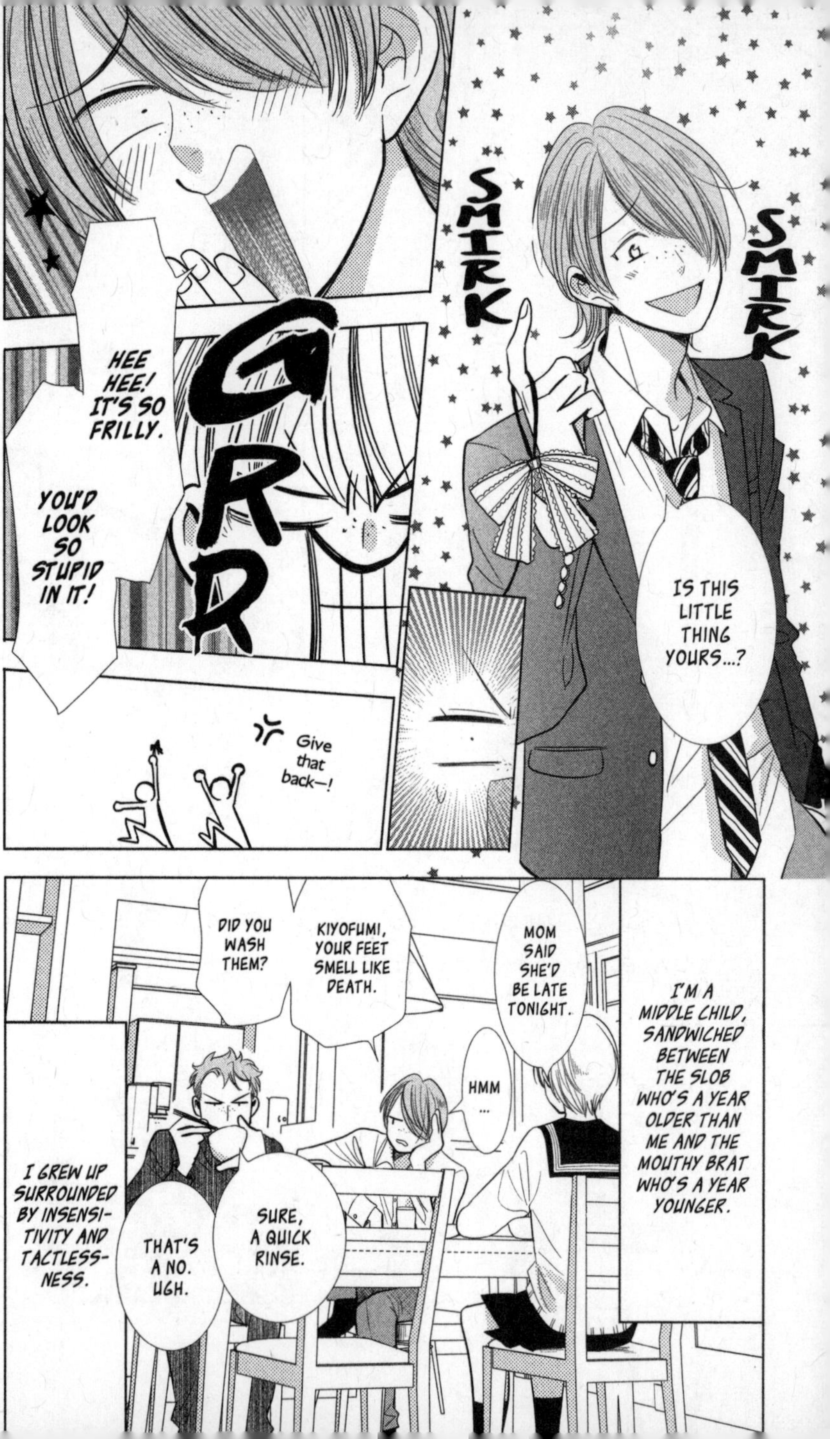
SMIRK SMIRK
IS THIS LITTLE THING YOURS...?
HEE HEE! IT'S SO FRILLY.
YOU'D LOOK SO STUPID IN IT!
GRR
Give that back—!
I'M A MIDDLE CHILD, SANDWICHED BETWEEN THE SLOB WHO'S A YEAR OLDER THAN ME AND THE MOUTHY BRAT WHO'S A YEAR YOUNGER.
MOM SAID SHE'D BE LATE TONIGHT.
HMM ...
KIYOFUMI, YOUR FEET SMELL LIKE DEATH.
DID YOU WASH THEM?
SURE, A QUICK RINSE.
THAT'S A NO. UGH.
I GREW UP SURROUNDED BY INSENSI-TIVITY AND TACTLESS-NESS.

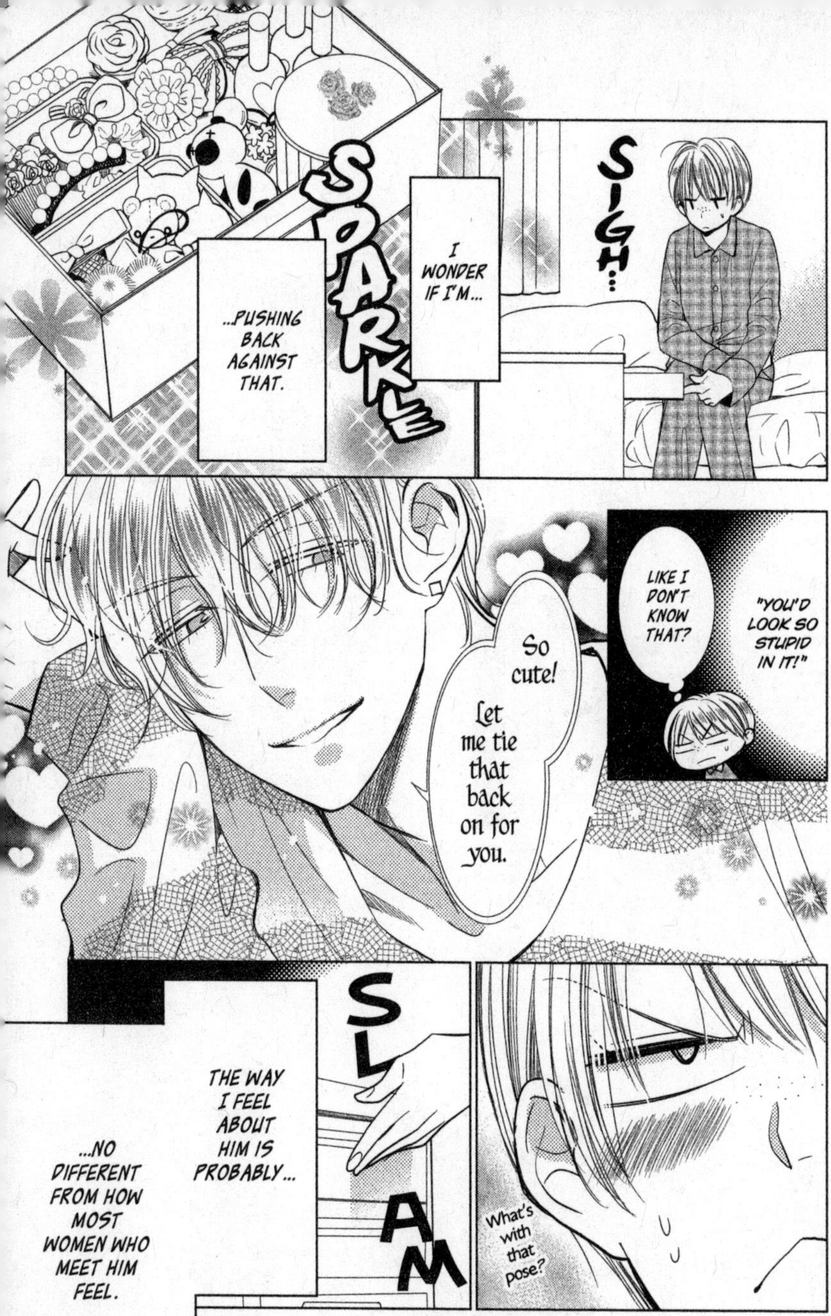
SIGH...
I WONDER IF I'M...
SPARKLE
...PUSHING BACK AGAINST THAT.
"YOU'D LOOK SO STUPID IN IT!"
LIKE I DON'T KNOW THAT?
So cute!
Let me tie that back on for you.
What's with that pose?
SLAM
THE WAY I FEEL ABOUT HIM IS PROBABLY...
...NO DIFFERENT FROM HOW MOST WOMEN WHO MEET HIM FEEL.

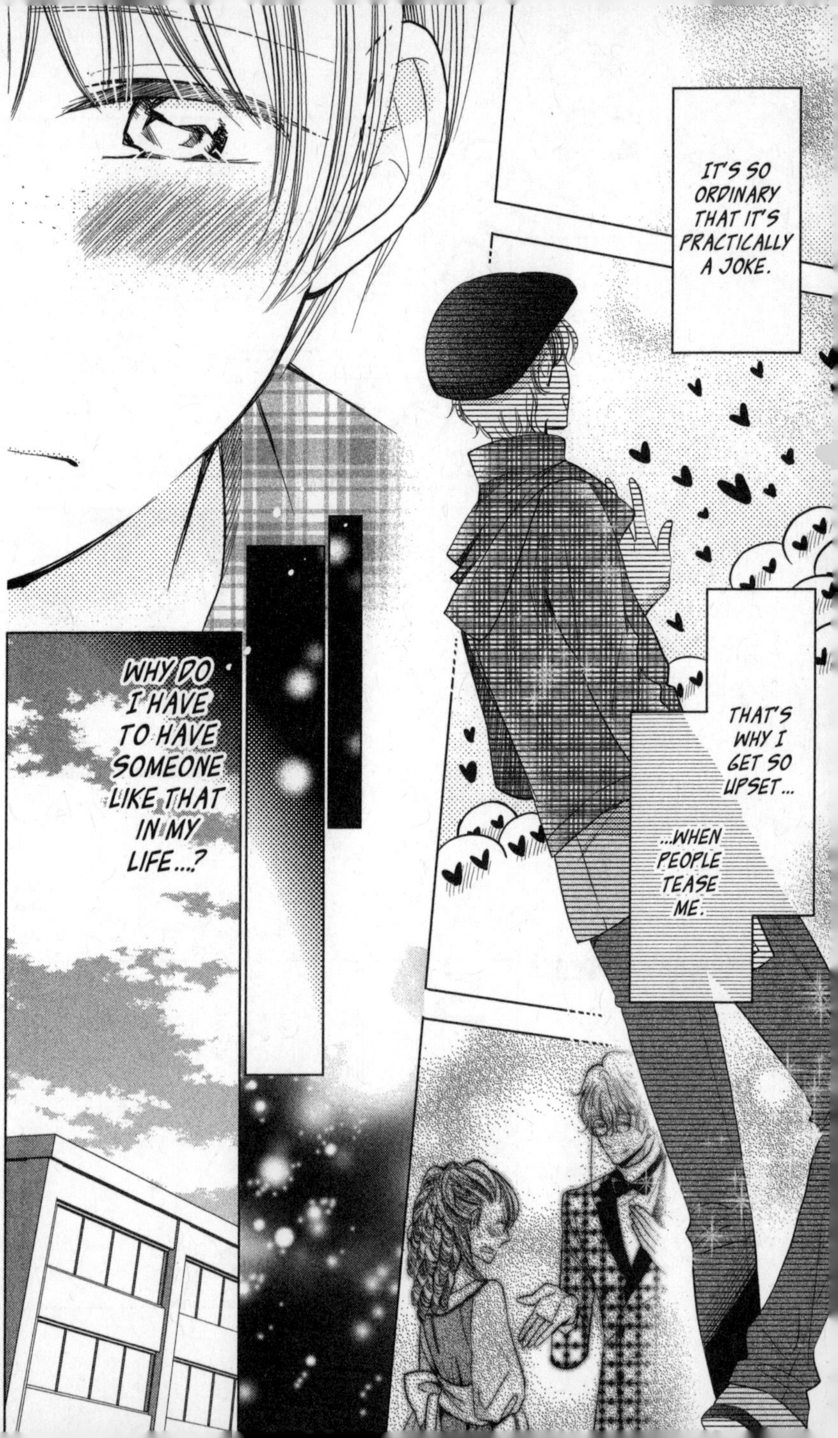
IT'S SO ORDINARY THAT IT'S PRACTICALLY A JOKE.
THAT'S WHY I GET SO UPSET...
...WHEN PEOPLE TEASE ME.
WHY DO I HAVE TO HAVE SOMEONE LIKE THAT IN MY LIFE...?

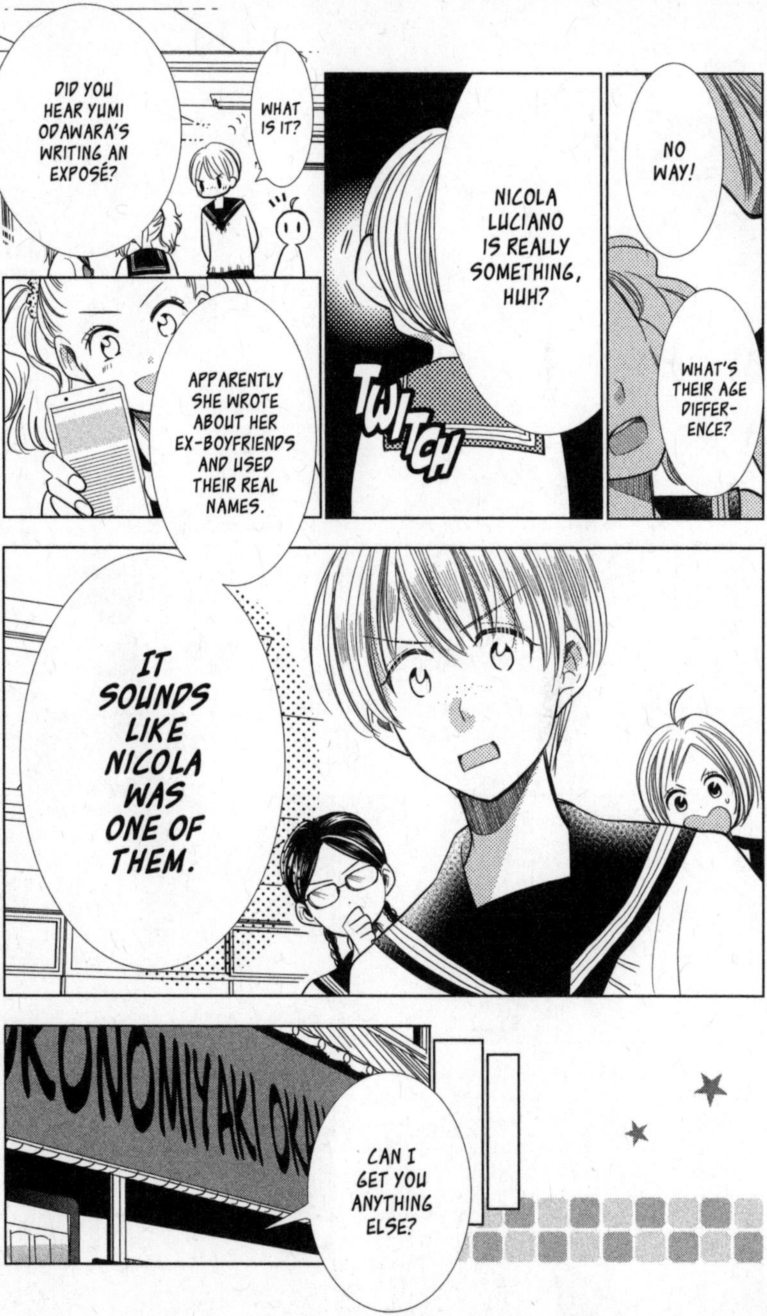
NO WAY!
WHAT'S THEIR AGE DIFFER-ENCE?
NICOLA LUCIANO IS REALLY SOMETHING, HUH?
TWITCH
DID YOU HEAR YUMI ODAWARA'S WRITING AN EXPOSÉ?
WHAT IS IT?
APPARENTLY SHE WROTE ABOUT HER EX-BOYFRIENDS AND USED THEIR REAL NAMES.
IT SOUNDS LIKE NICOLA WAS ONE OF THEM.
KONOMIYAKI OKA
CAN I GET YOU ANYTHING ELSE?

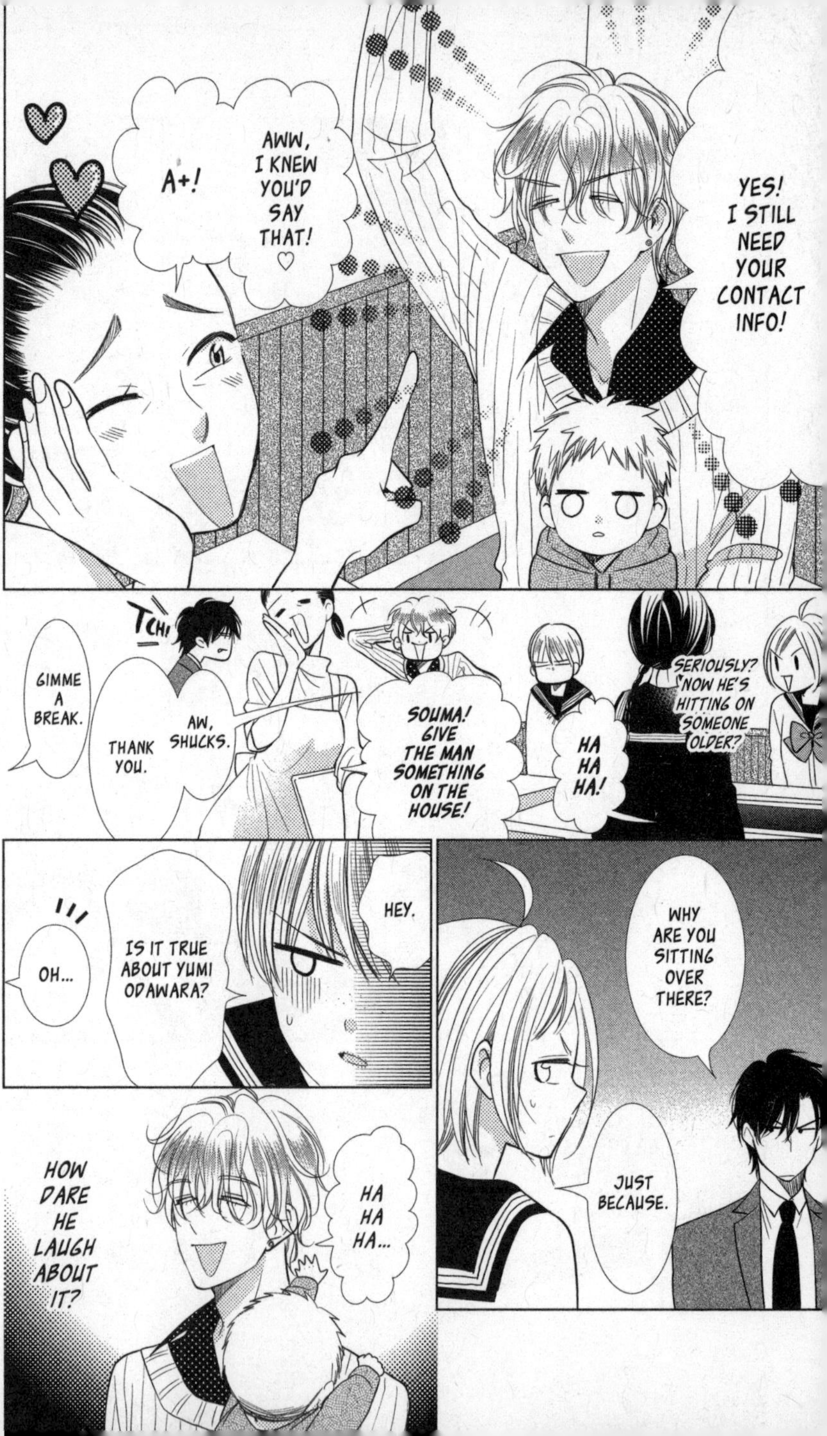
YES! I STILL NEED YOUR CONTACT INFO!
AWW, I KNEW YOU'D SAY THAT! ♡
A+!
SERIOUSLY? NOW HE'S HITTING ON SOMEONE OLDER?
HA HA HA!
SOUMA! GIVE THE MAN SOMETHING ON THE HOUSE!
AW, SHUCKS.
THANK YOU.
TCHI
GIMME A BREAK.
WHY ARE YOU SITTING OVER THERE?
JUST BECAUSE.
HEY.
IS IT TRUE ABOUT YUMI ODAWARA?
OH...
HA HA HA...
HOW DARE HE LAUGH ABOUT IT?

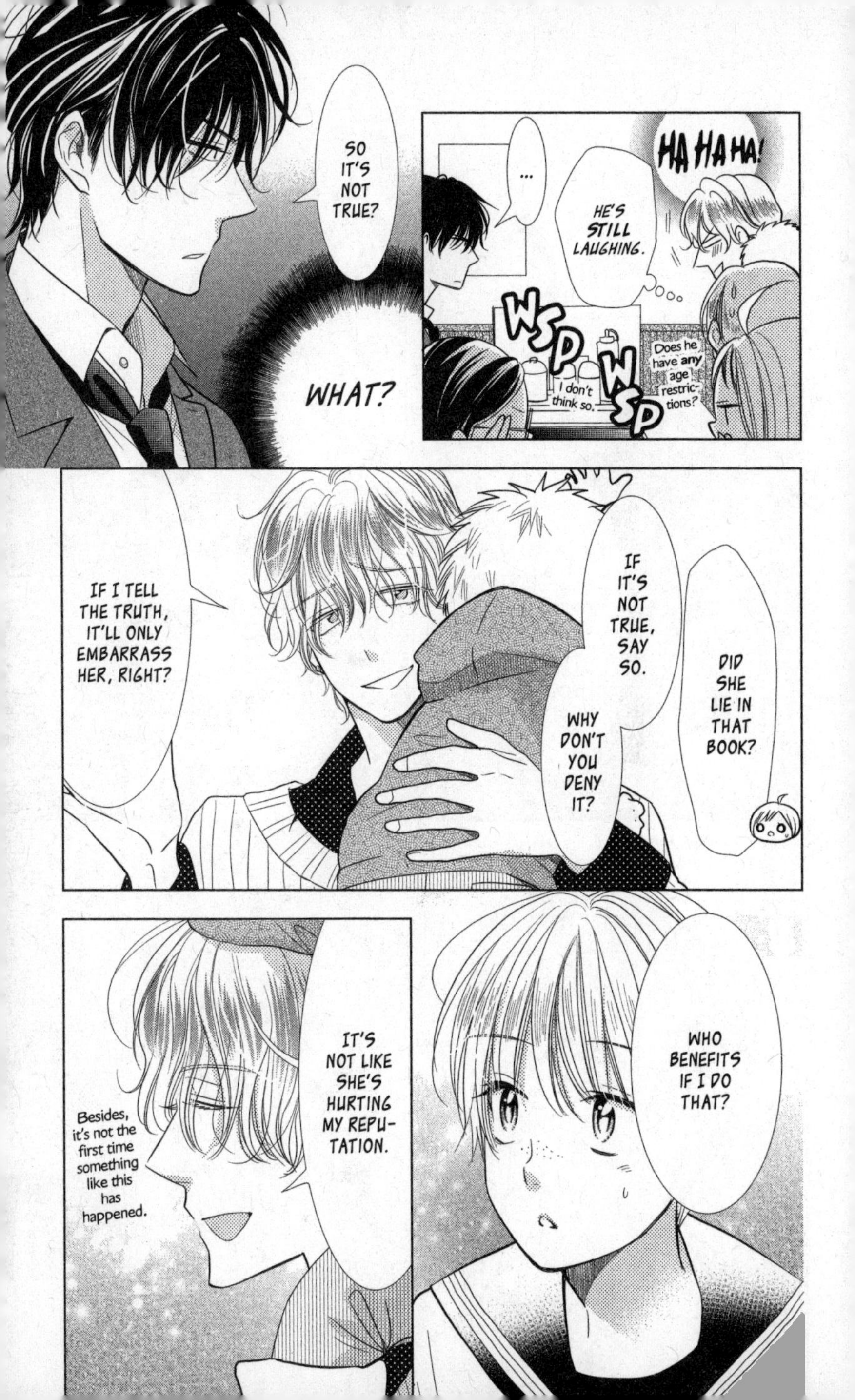
HA HA HA!
...
HE'S STILL LAUGHING.
WSP WSP
Does he have any age restrictions?
I don't think so.
SO IT'S NOT TRUE?
WHAT?
DID SHE LIE IN THAT BOOK?
IF IT'S NOT TRUE, SAY SO.
WHY DON'T YOU DENY IT?
IF I TELL THE TRUTH, IT'LL ONLY EMBARRASS HER, RIGHT?
WHO BENEFITS IF I DO THAT?
IT'S NOT LIKE SHE'S HURTING MY REPUTATION.
Besides, it's not the first time something like this has happened.

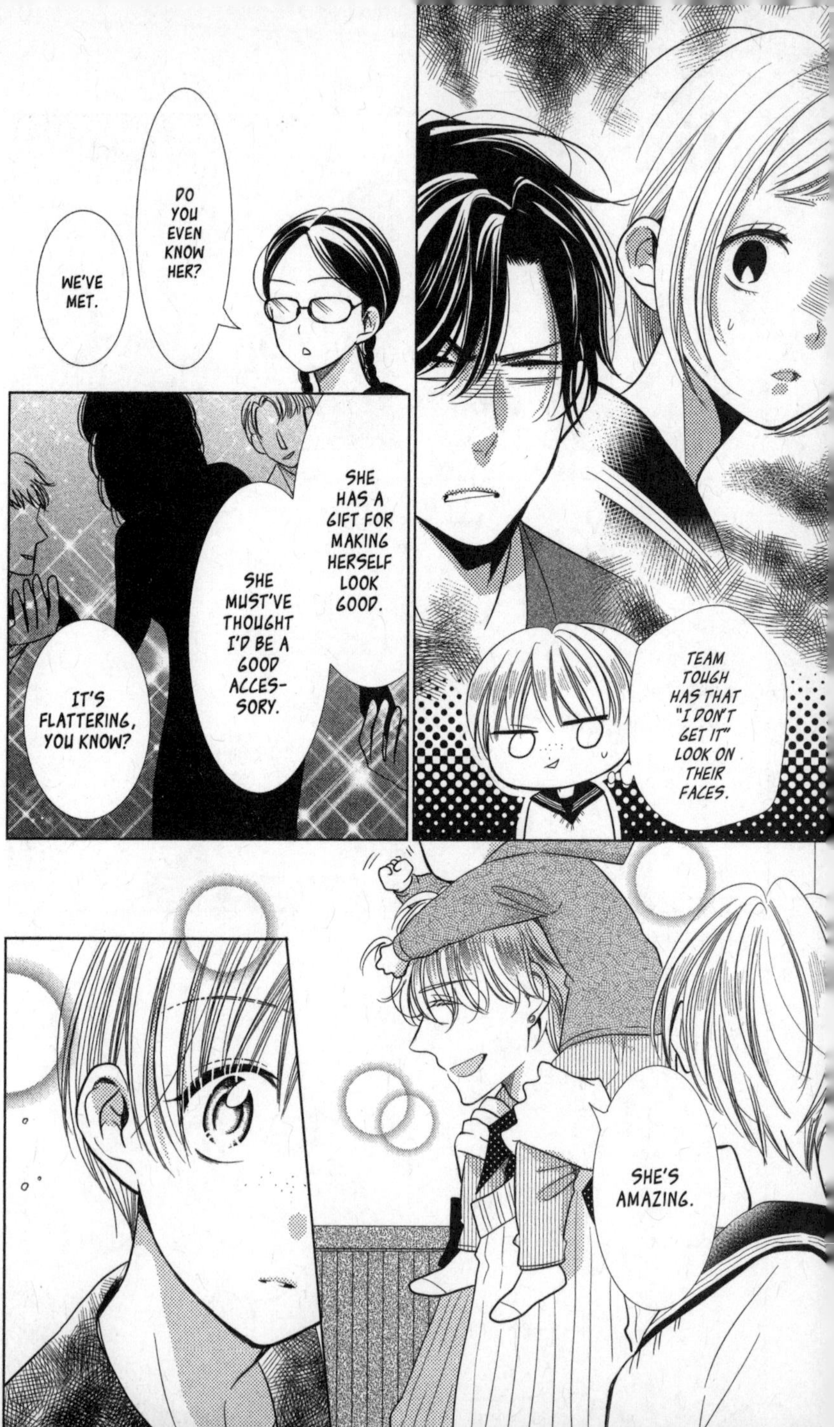
TEAM TOUGH HAS THAT "I DON'T GET IT" LOOK ON THEIR FACES.
DO YOU EVEN KNOW HER?
WE'VE MET.
SHE HAS A GIFT FOR MAKING HERSELF LOOK GOOD.
SHE MUST'VE THOUGHT I'D BE A GOOD ACCES-SORY.
IT'S FLATTERING, YOU KNOW?
SHE'S AMAZING.

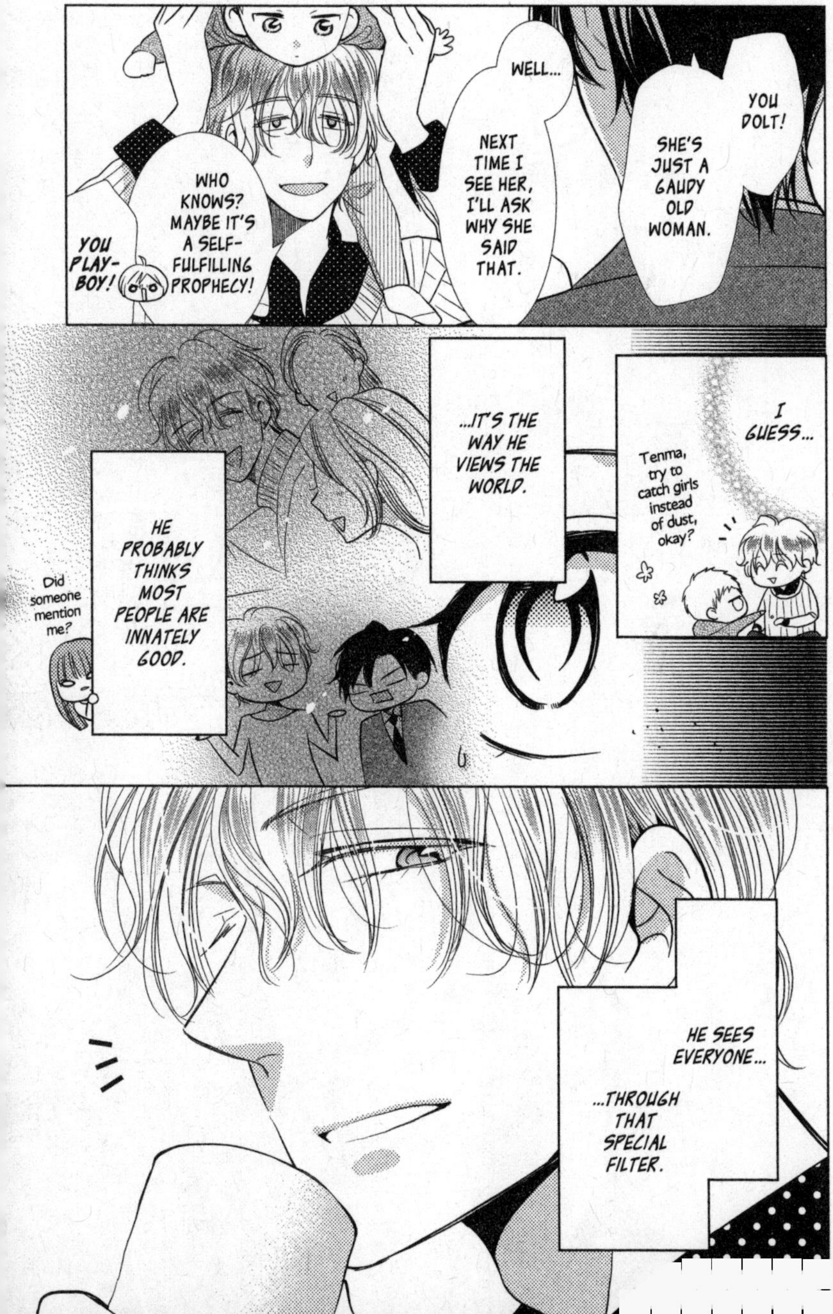
YOU DOLT!
SHE'S JUST A GAUDY OLD WOMAN.
WELL...
NEXT TIME I SEE HER, I'LL ASK WHY SHE SAID THAT.
WHO KNOWS? MAYBE IT'S A SELF-FULFILLING PROPHECY!
YOU PLAYBOY!
I GUESS...
Tenma, try to catch girls instead of dust, okay?
...IT'S THE WAY HE VIEWS THE WORLD.
HE PROBABLY THINKS MOST PEOPLE ARE INNATELY GOOD.
Did someone mention me?
HE SEES EVERYONE...
...THROUGH THAT SPECIAL FILTER.

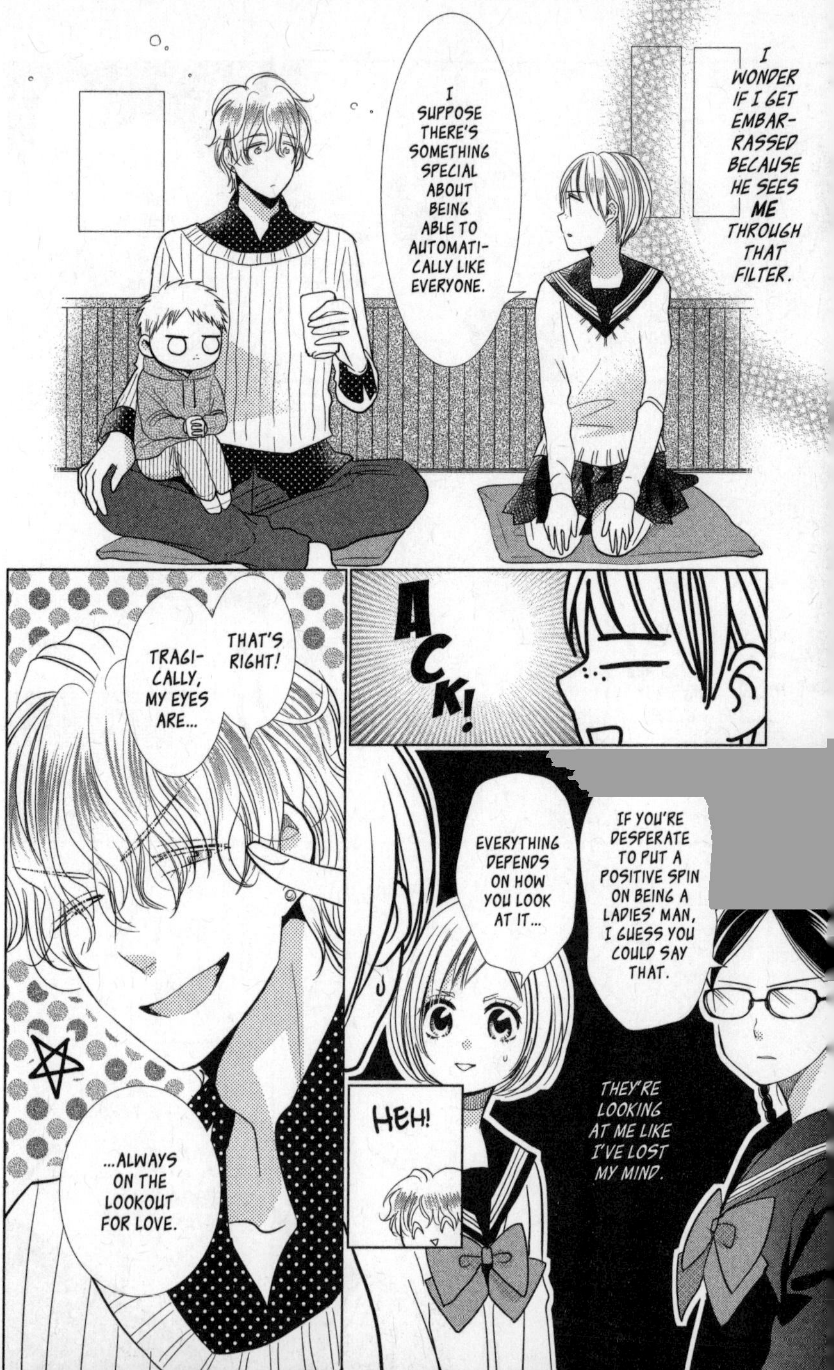
I WONDER IF I GET EMBARRASSED BECAUSE HE SEES ME THROUGH THAT FILTER.
I SUPPOSE THERE'S SOMETHING SPECIAL ABOUT BEING ABLE TO AUTOMATICALLY LIKE EVERYONE.
ACK!
IF YOU'RE DESPERATE TO PUT A POSITIVE SPIN ON BEING A LADIES' MAN, I GUESS YOU COULD SAY THAT.
EVERYTHING DEPENDS ON HOW YOU LOOK AT IT...
THEY'RE LOOKING AT ME LIKE I'VE LOST MY MIND.
HEH!
THAT'S RIGHT!
TRAGICALLY, MY EYES ARE...
...ALWAYS ON THE LOOKOUT FOR LOVE.

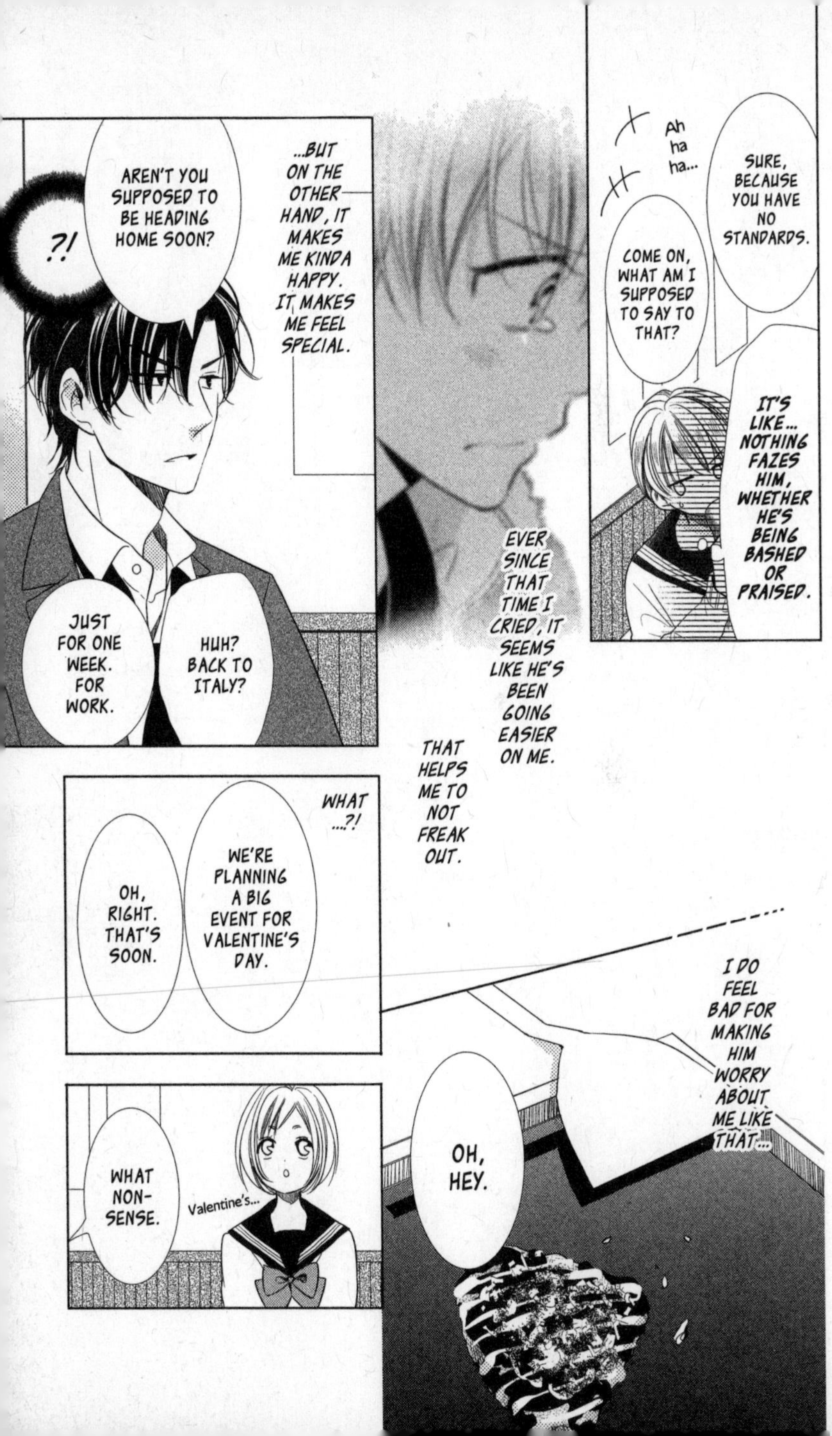
SURE, BECAUSE YOU HAVE NO STANDARDS.
Ah ha ha...
COME ON, WHAT AM I SUPPOSED TO SAY TO THAT?
IT'S LIKE... NOTHING FAZES HIM, WHETHER HE'S BEING BASHED OR PRAISED.
EVER SINCE THAT TIME I CRIED, IT SEEMS LIKE HE'S BEEN GOING EASIER ON ME.
THAT HELPS ME TO NOT FREAK OUT.
...BUT ON THE OTHER HAND, IT MAKES ME KINDA HAPPY. IT MAKES ME FEEL SPECIAL.
?!
AREN'T YOU SUPPOSED TO BE HEADING HOME SOON?
HUH? BACK TO ITALY?
JUST FOR ONE WEEK. FOR WORK.
I DO FEEL BAD FOR MAKING HIM WORRY ABOUT ME LIKE THAT...
OH, HEY.
WHAT ...?!
WE'RE PLANNING A BIG EVENT FOR VALENTINE'S DAY.
OH, RIGHT. THAT'S SOON.
Valentine's...
WHAT NON-SENSE.

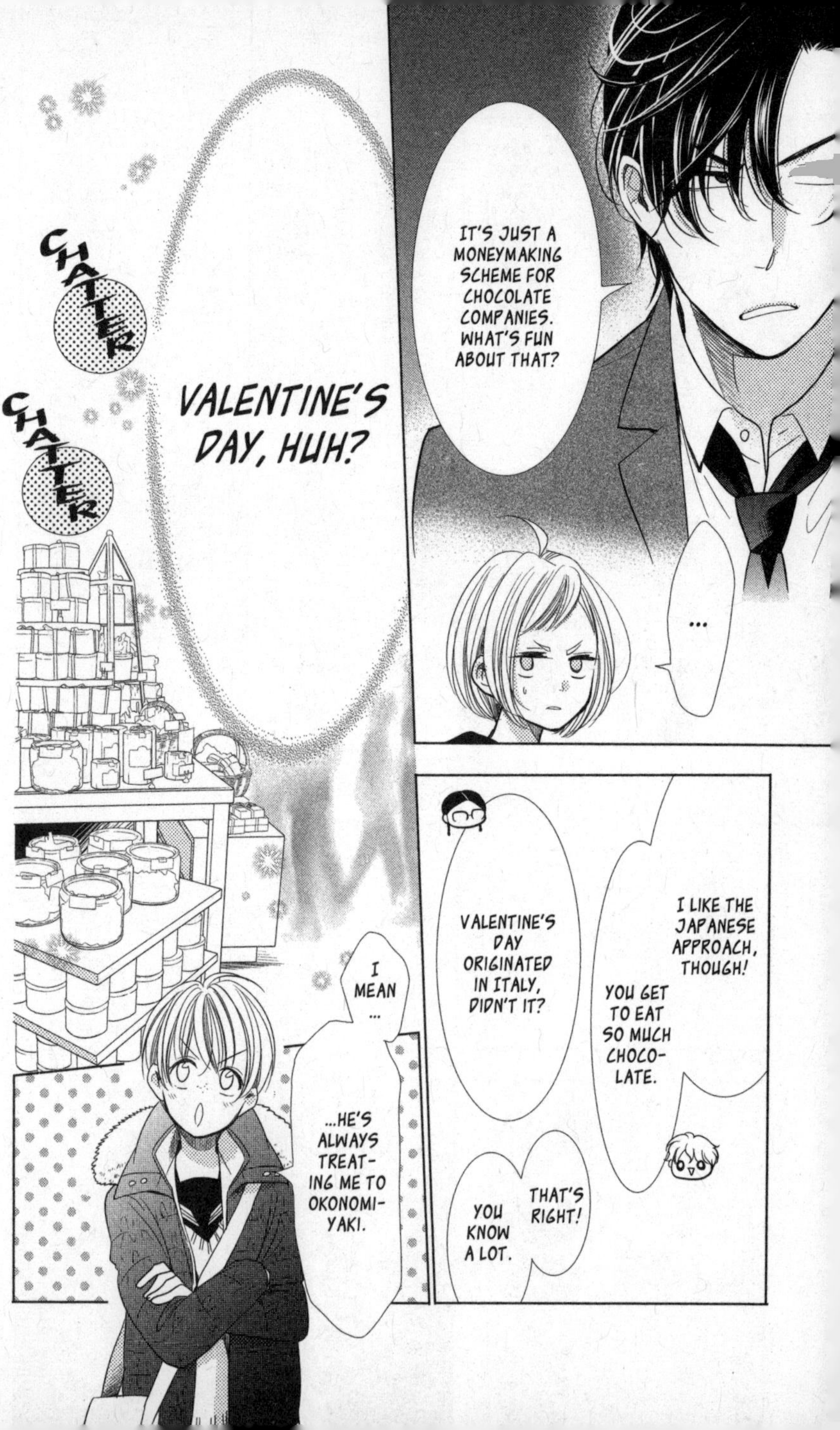

IT'S JUST A MONEYMAKING SCHEME FOR CHOCOLATE COMPANIES. WHAT'S FUN ABOUT THAT?
...
I LIKE THE JAPANESE APPROACH, THOUGH!
YOU GET TO EAT SO MUCH CHOCO-LATE.
VALENTINE'S DAY ORIGINATED IN ITALY, DIDN'T IT?
THAT'S RIGHT!
YOU KNOW A LOT.
VALENTINE'S DAY, HUH?
CHATTER
CHATTER
I MEAN ...
...HE'S ALWAYS TREAT-ING ME TO OKONOMI-YAKI.

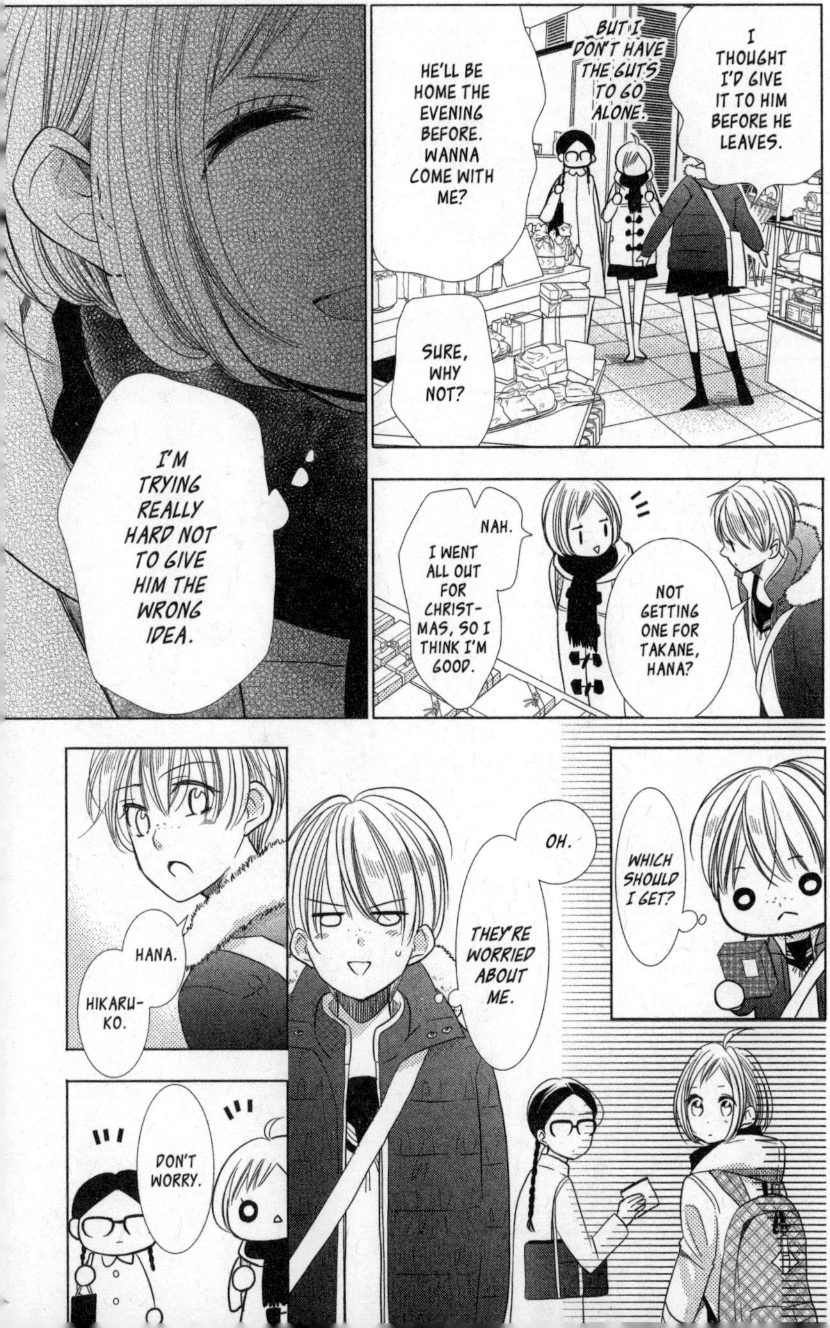
I THOUGHT I'D GIVE IT TO HIM BEFORE HE LEAVES.
BUT I DON'T HAVE THE GUTS TO GO ALONE.
HE'LL BE HOME THE EVENING BEFORE. WANNA COME WITH ME?
SURE, WHY NOT?
NOT GETTING ONE FOR TAKANE, HANA?
NAH.
I WENT ALL OUT FOR CHRIST-MAS, SO I THINK I'M GOOD.
I'M TRYING REALLY HARD NOT TO GIVE HIM THE WRONG IDEA.
WHICH SHOULD I GET?
OH.
THEY'RE WORRIED ABOUT ME.
HANA.
HIKARU-KO.
DON'T WORRY.

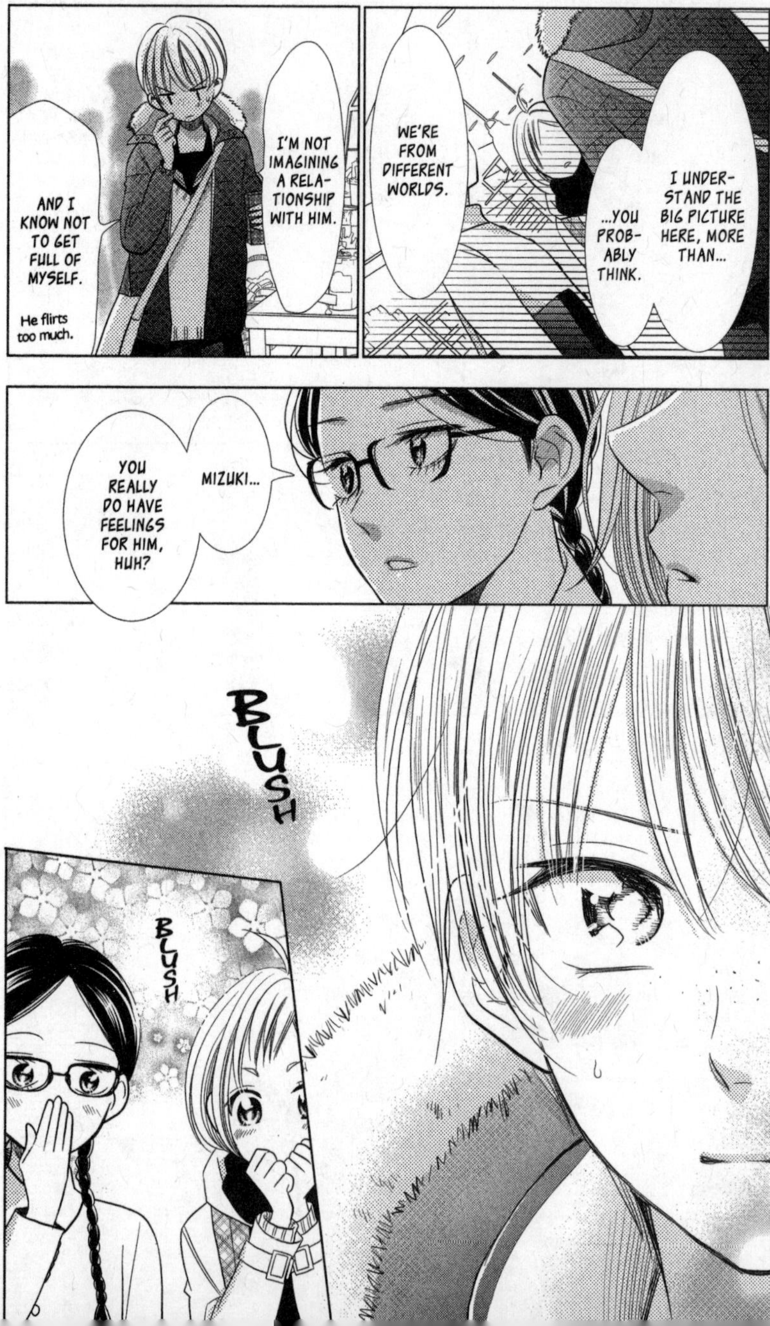
I UNDERSTAND THE BIG PICTURE HERE, MORE THAN...
...YOU PROBABLY THINK.
WE'RE FROM DIFFERENT WORLDS.
I'M NOT IMAGINING A RELATIONSHIP WITH HIM.
AND I KNOW NOT TO GET FULL OF MYSELF.
He flirts too much.
MIZUKI...
YOU REALLY DO HAVE FEELINGS FOR HIM, HUH?
BLUSH
BLUSH

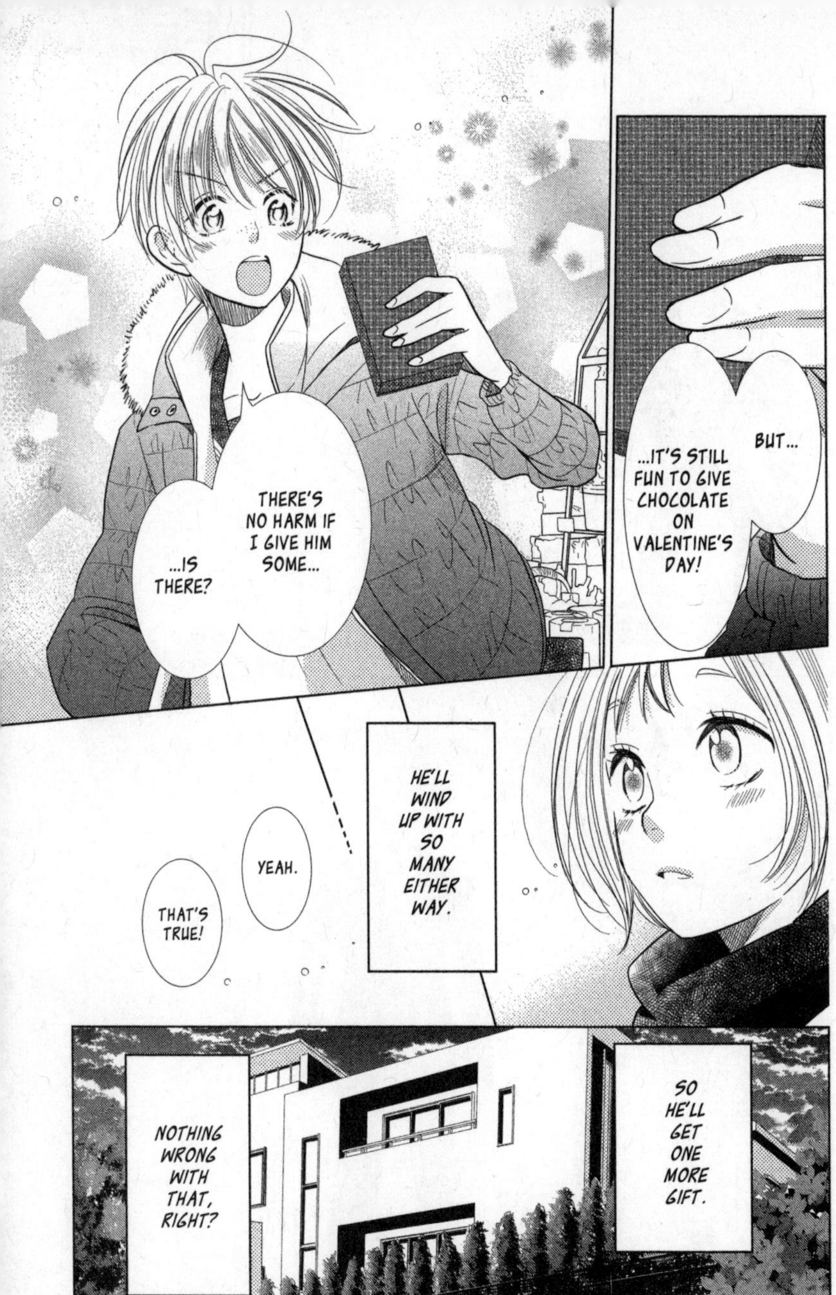
BUT...
...IT'S STILL FUN TO GIVE CHOCOLATE ON VALENTINE'S DAY!
THERE'S NO HARM IF I GIVE HIM SOME...
...IS THERE?
HE'LL WIND UP WITH SO MANY EITHER WAY.
YEAH.
THAT'S TRUE!
SO HE'LL GET ONE MORE GIFT.
NOTHING WRONG WITH THAT, RIGHT?

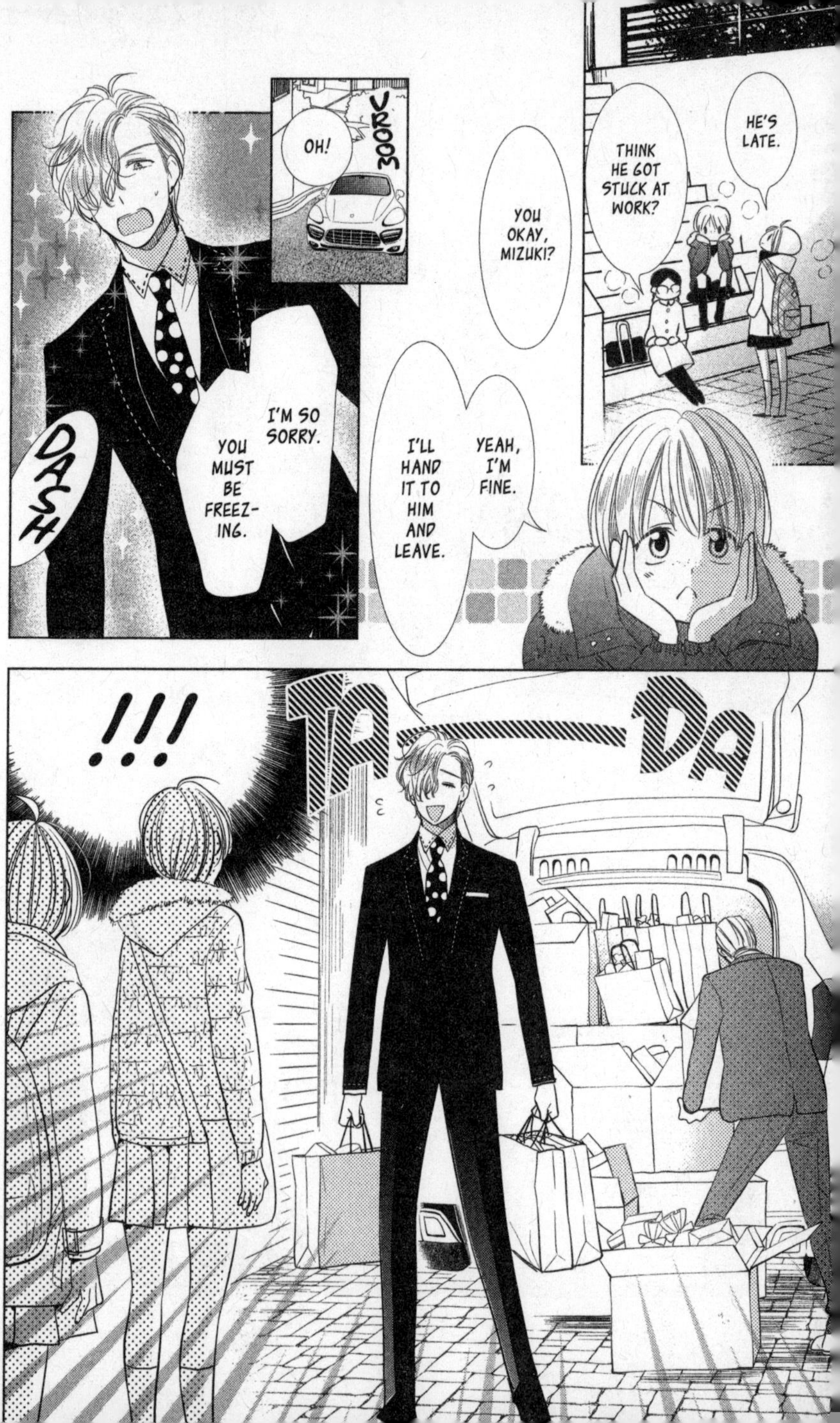
HE'S LATE.
THINK HE GOT STUCK AT WORK?
YOU OKAY, MIZUKI?
YEAH, I'M FINE.
I'LL HAND IT TO HIM AND LEAVE.
VROOM
OH!
I'M SO SORRY.
YOU MUST BE FREEZ-ING.
DASH
TA—DA
!!!

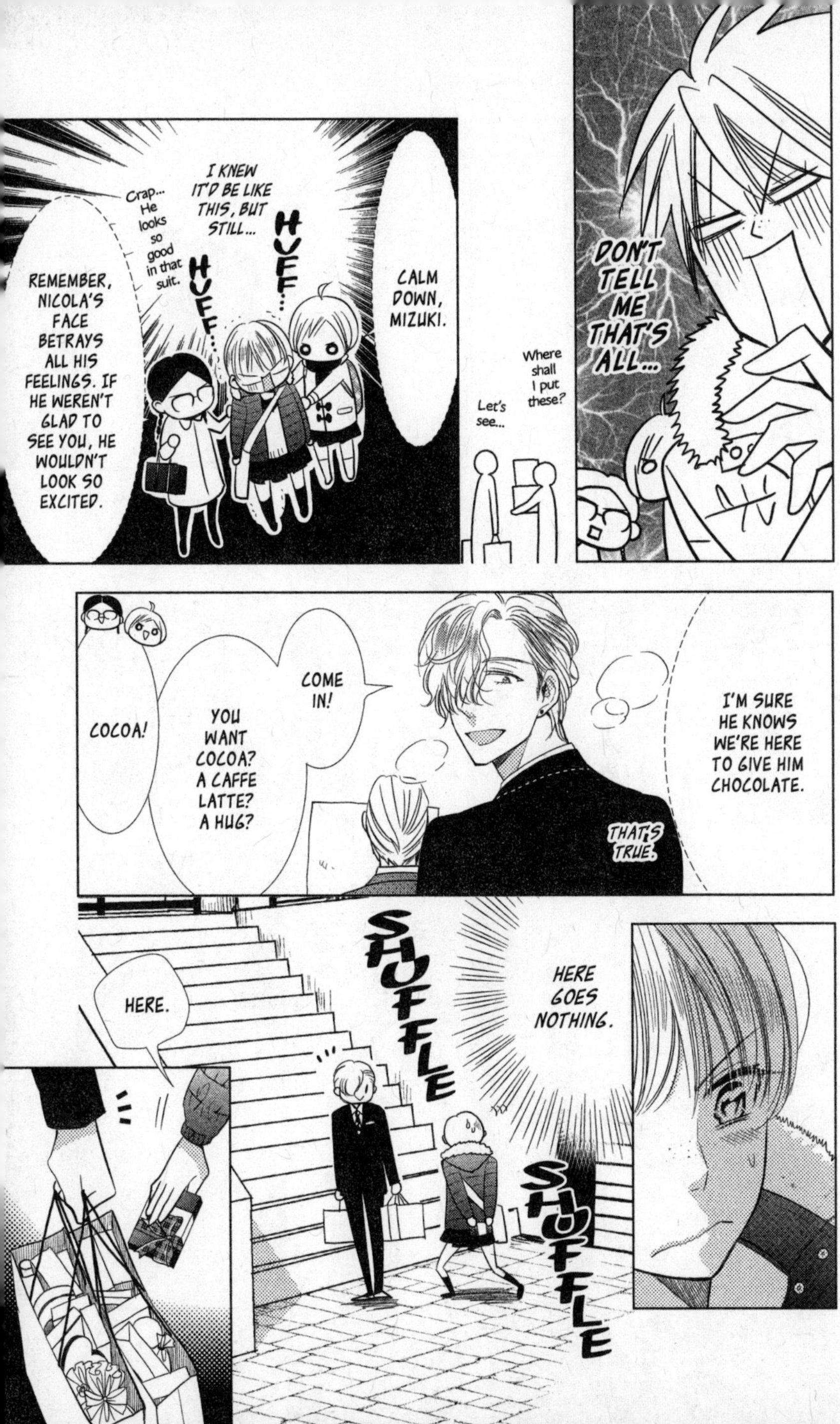
DON'T TELL ME THAT'S ALL...
Where shall I put these?
Let's see...
CALM DOWN, MIZUKI.
HUFF...
I KNEW IT'D BE LIKE THIS, BUT STILL...
HUFF...
Crap... He looks so good in that suit.
REMEMBER, NICOLA'S FACE BETRAYS ALL HIS FEELINGS. IF HE WEREN'T GLAD TO SEE YOU, HE WOULDN'T LOOK SO EXCITED.
I'M SURE HE KNOWS WE'RE HERE TO GIVE HIM CHOCOLATE.
THAT'S TRUE.
COME IN!
YOU WANT COCOA? A CAFFE LATTE? A HUG?
COCOA!
HERE GOES NOTHING.
SHUFFLE
SHUFFLE
HERE.

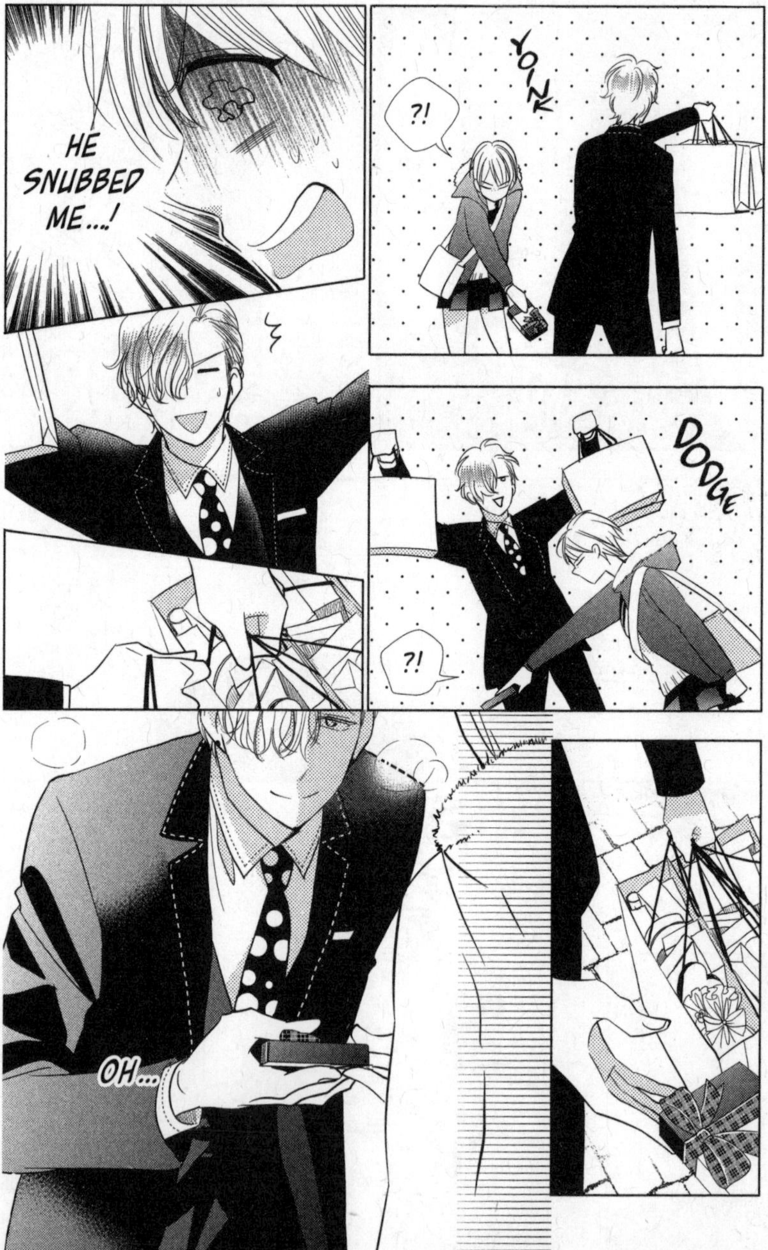
YOINK
?!
HE SNUBBED ME...!
DODGE
?!
OH...

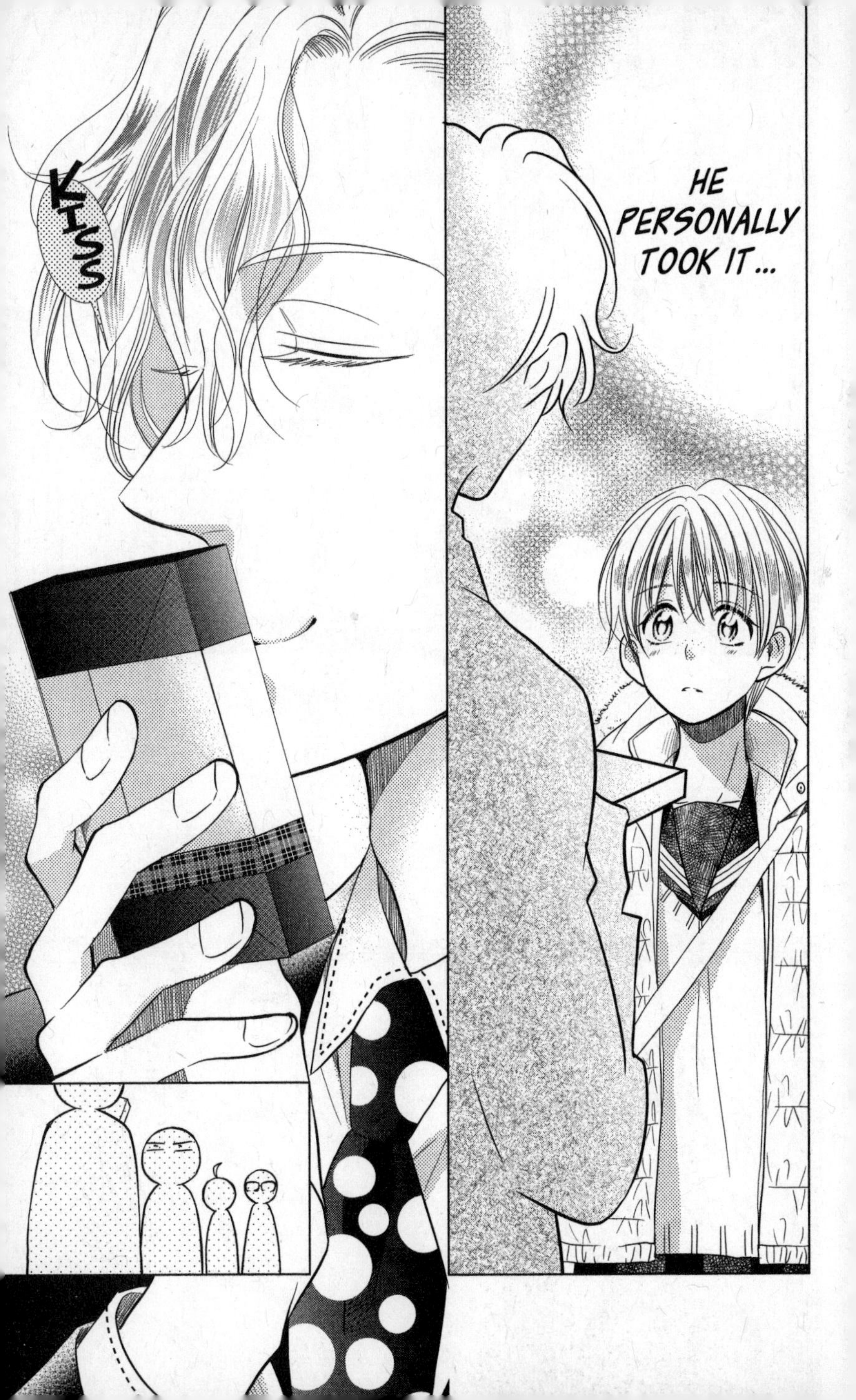
HE PERSONALLY TOOK IT...
KISS

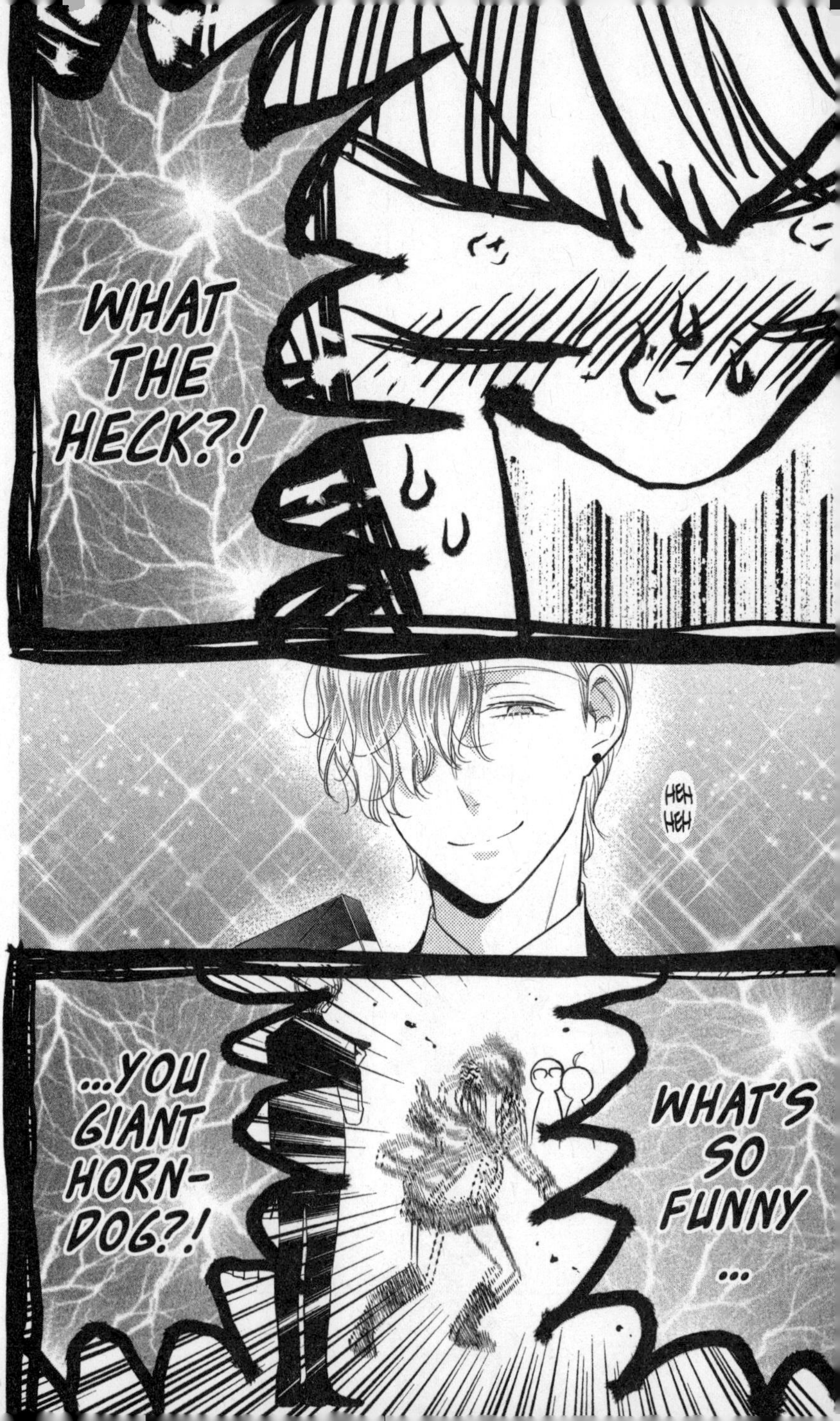
WHAT THE HECK?!
HEH HEH
WHAT'S SO FUNNY ...
...YOU GIANT HORN-DOG?!

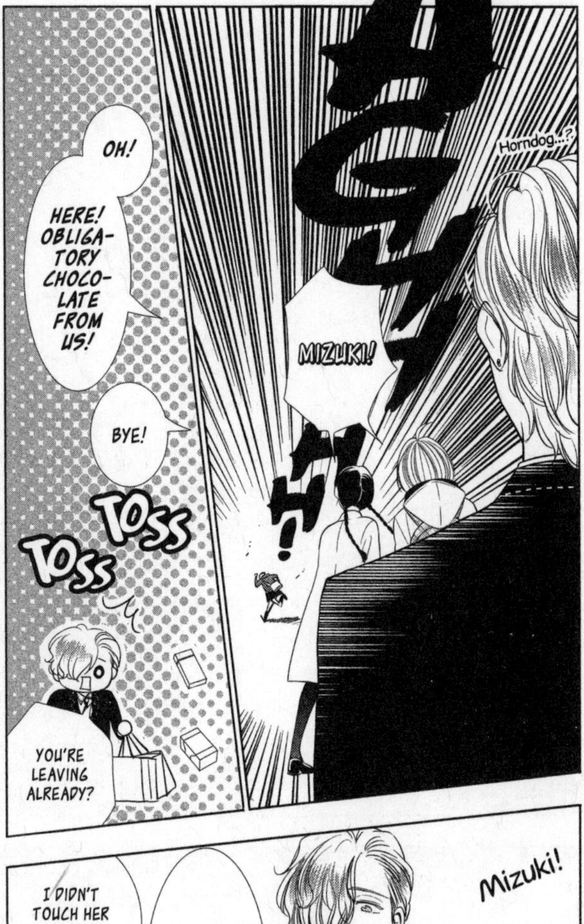
Horndog...?
MIZUKI!
OH!
HERE! OBLIGATORY CHOCOLATE FROM US!
BYE!
TOSS
TOSS
YOU'RE LEAVING ALREADY?
Mizuki!
AW... I DIDN'T GET A CHANCE TO THANK HER.
OBVIOUSLY, AFTER THAT PERFORMANCE.
I DIDN'T TOUCH HER OR SAY A WORD THOUGH.

The Ogawa
• Brothers •

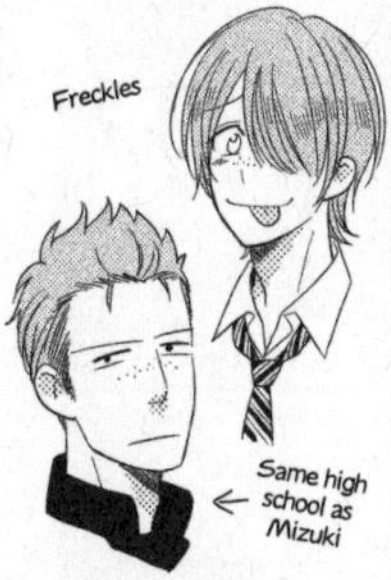
Freckles
Same high school as Mizuki

I'm not expecting them to reappear after this, but somehow I have lots of info about them.

Eldest son, Kiyofumi
(second-year in high school)

Eldest daughter, Mizuki
(first-year in high school)

Second-eldest son, Ryu
(third-year in junior high)

Their names all have to do with water. Mizuki's a supporting character, but her brothers completely overshadow her. Hang in there, Mizuki!

• Chapter 39 •
Illustration

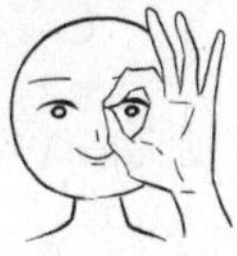

This is the pose I initially went for, but Hana's eyes are so big that when I made her do that, you could only see her pupil. The rest would be hidden by her hand.

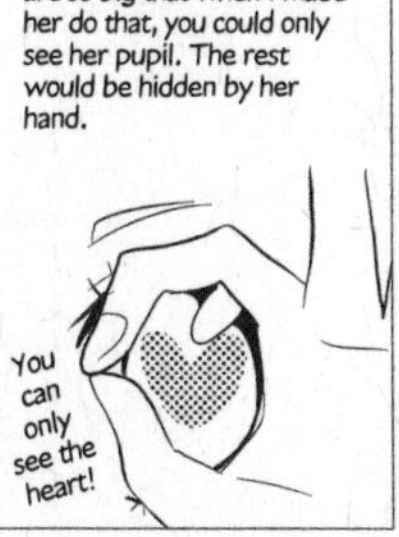
You can only see the heart!

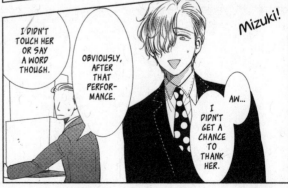

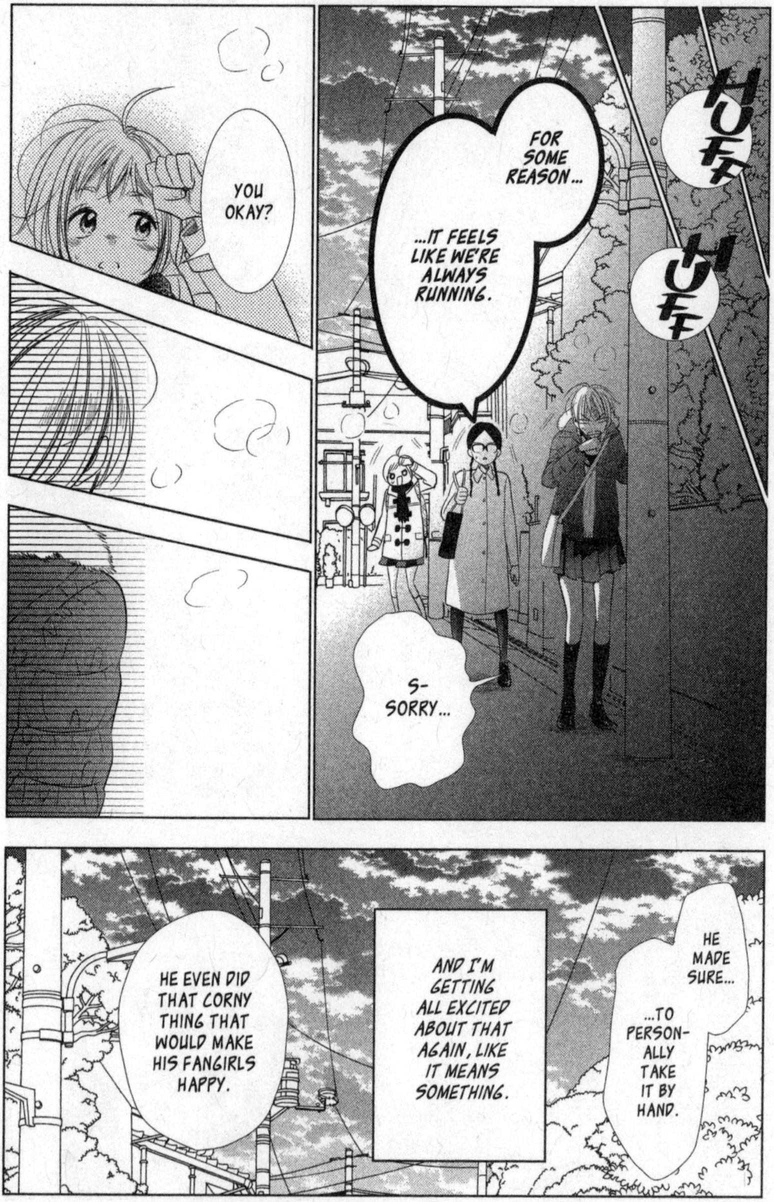
HUFF
HUFF
FOR SOME REASON...
...IT FEELS LIKE WE'RE ALWAYS RUNNING.
S-SORRY...
YOU OKAY?
HE MADE SURE...
...TO PERSON-ALLY TAKE IT BY HAND.
AND I'M GETTING ALL EXCITED ABOUT THAT AGAIN, LIKE IT MEANS SOMETHING.
HE EVEN DID THAT CORNY THING THAT WOULD MAKE HIS FANGIRLS HAPPY.

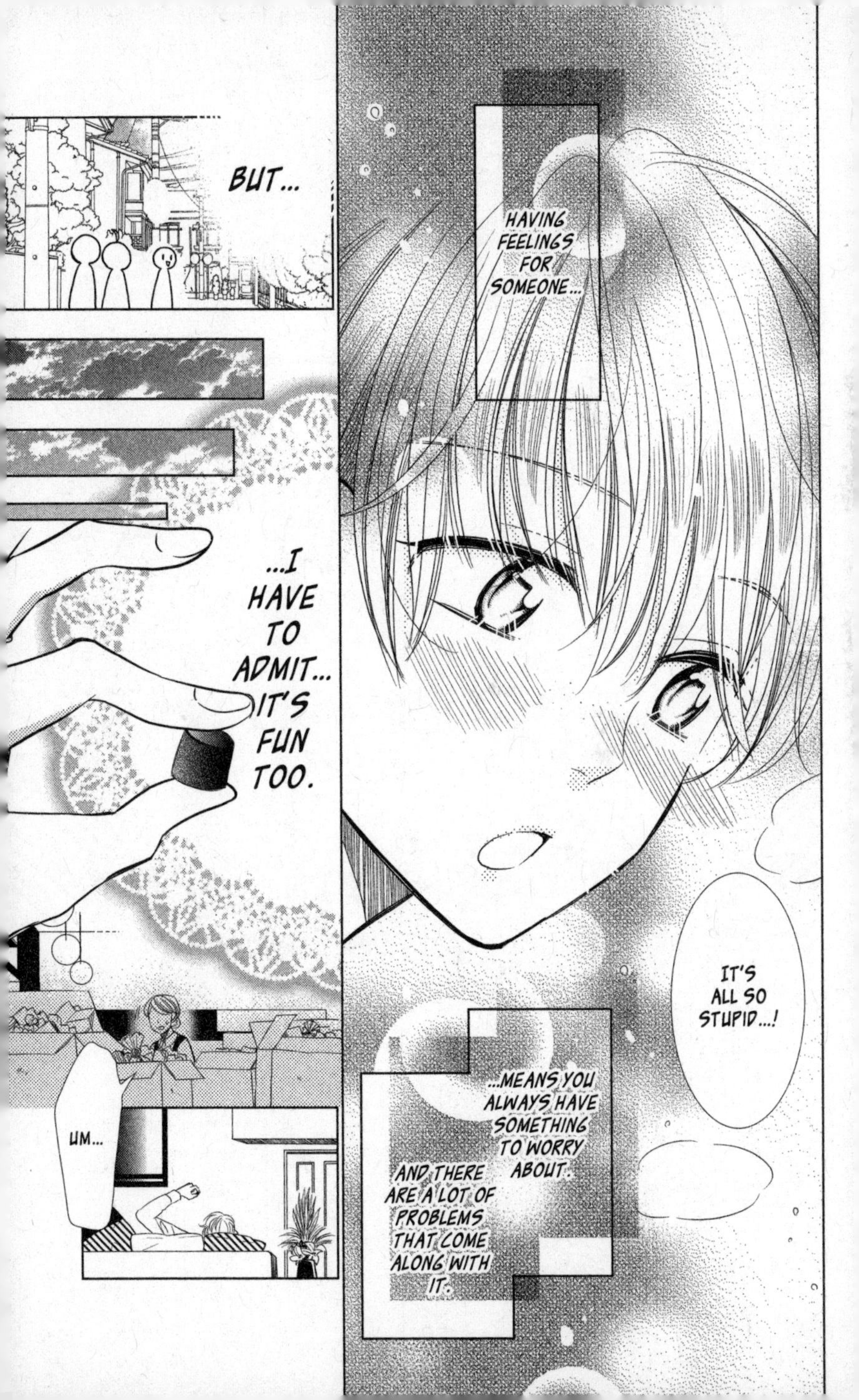
HAVING FEELINGS FOR SOMEONE...
IT'S ALL SO STUPID...!
...MEANS YOU ALWAYS HAVE SOMETHING TO WORRY ABOUT.
AND THERE ARE A LOT OF PROBLEMS THAT COME ALONG WITH IT.
BUT...
...I HAVE TO ADMIT... IT'S FUN TOO.
UM...

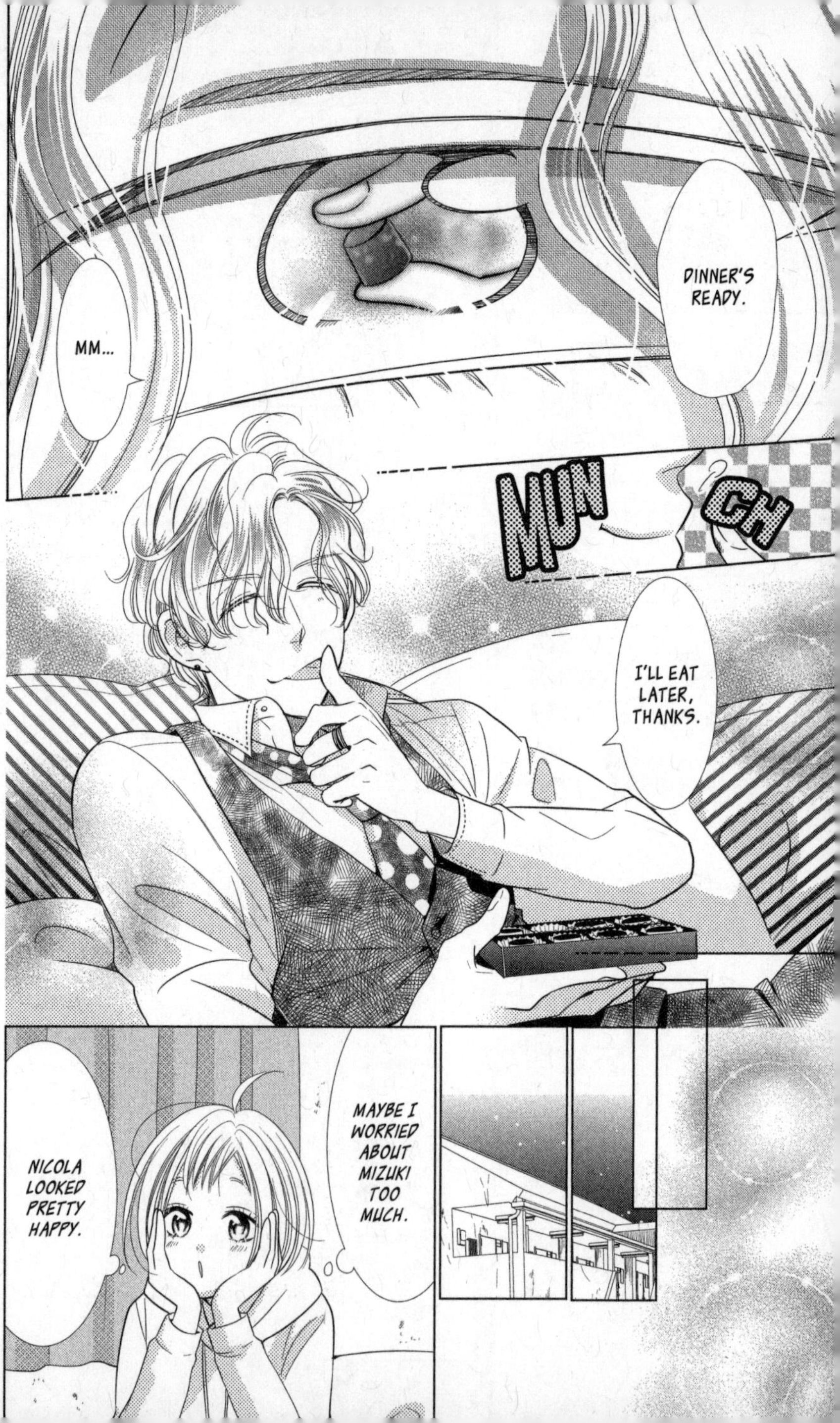
DINNER'S READY.
MM...
MUN CH
I'LL EAT LATER, THANKS.
MAYBE I WORRIED ABOUT MIZUKI TOO MUCH.
NICOLA LOOKED PRETTY HAPPY.

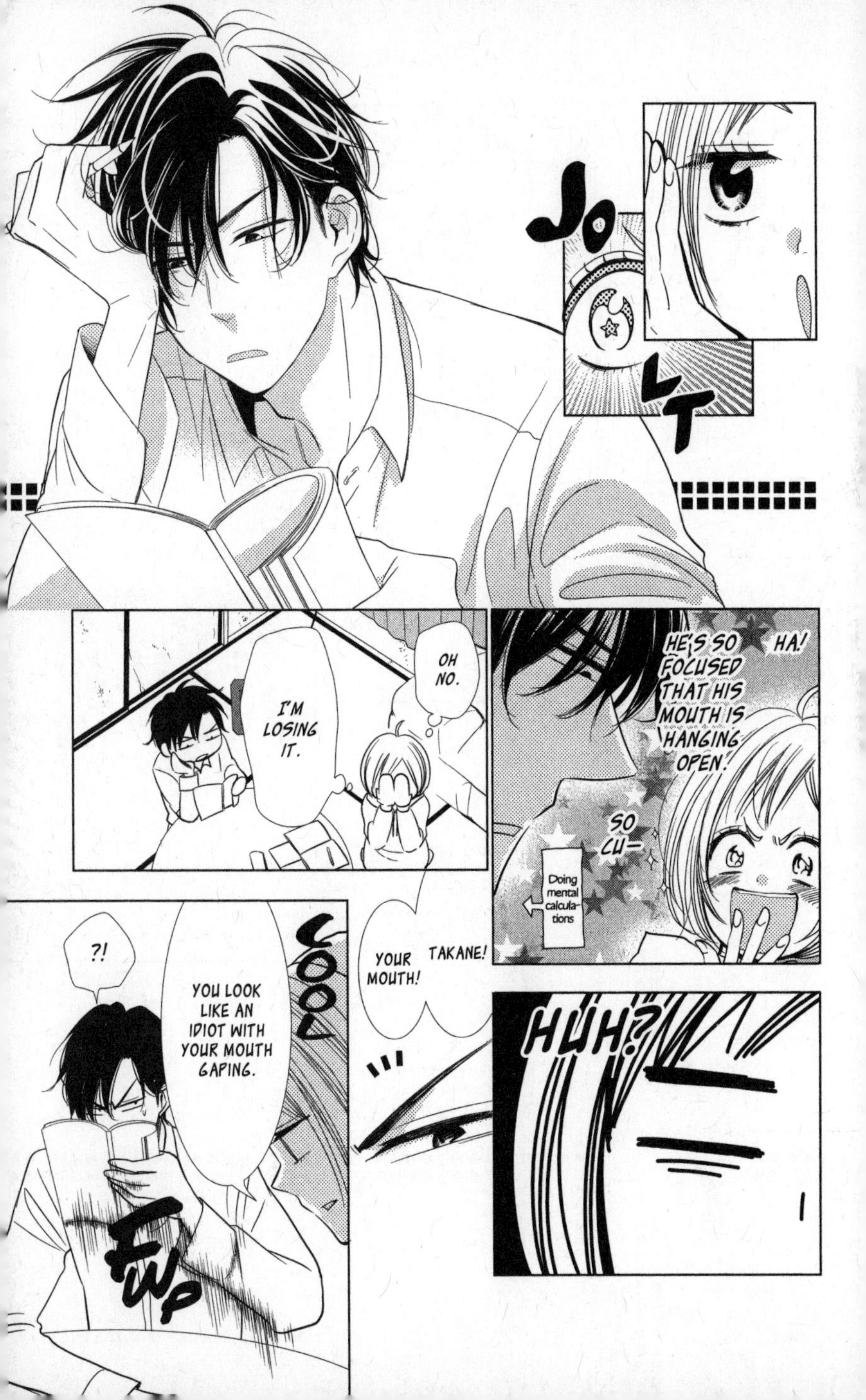
JOLT
HE'S SO FOCUSED THAT HIS MOUTH IS HANGING OPEN.
HA!
SO CU–
Doing mental calculations
OH NO.
I'M LOSING IT.
TAKANE! YOUR MOUTH!
HUH?!
...
COOL
?!
YOU LOOK LIKE AN IDIOT WITH YOUR MOUTH GAPING.
FWP

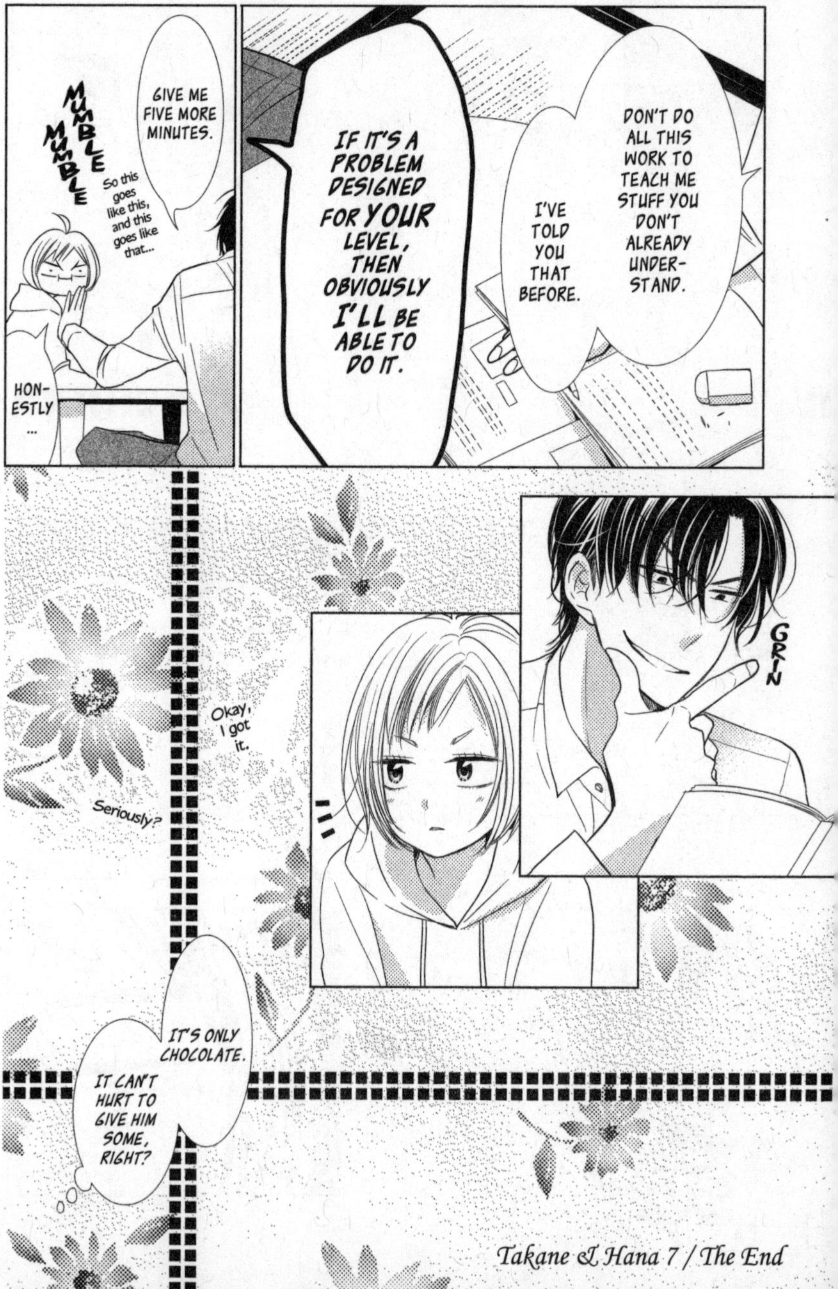
DON'T DO ALL THIS WORK TO TEACH ME STUFF YOU DON'T ALREADY UNDER-STAND.
I'VE TOLD YOU THAT BEFORE.
IF IT'S A PROBLEM DESIGNED FOR YOUR LEVEL, THEN OBVIOUSLY I'LL BE ABLE TO DO IT.
GIVE ME FIVE MORE MINUTES.
MUMBLE MUMBLE
So this goes like this, and this goes like that...
HON-ESTLY...
GRIN
Okay, I got it.
Seriously?
IT'S ONLY CHOCOLATE.
IT CAN'T HURT TO GIVE HIM SOME, RIGHT?
Takane & Hana 7 / The End

Smell

TAKANE STARTED NOTICING PEOPLE'S SCENTS.

HE HAS NO DISCERNABLE SMELL—NO PRESENCE AT ALL!

HERE YOU GO.

YOU TOO.

...

(No comment)

6—GOOD WORK TODAY.

NER- VOUS

CIAO! YOU ALIVE?

STAY AWAY!

YOU STINK THE MOST.

PERFUME PERFUME

HEAVY SCENT

MAKEUP

MAKEUP

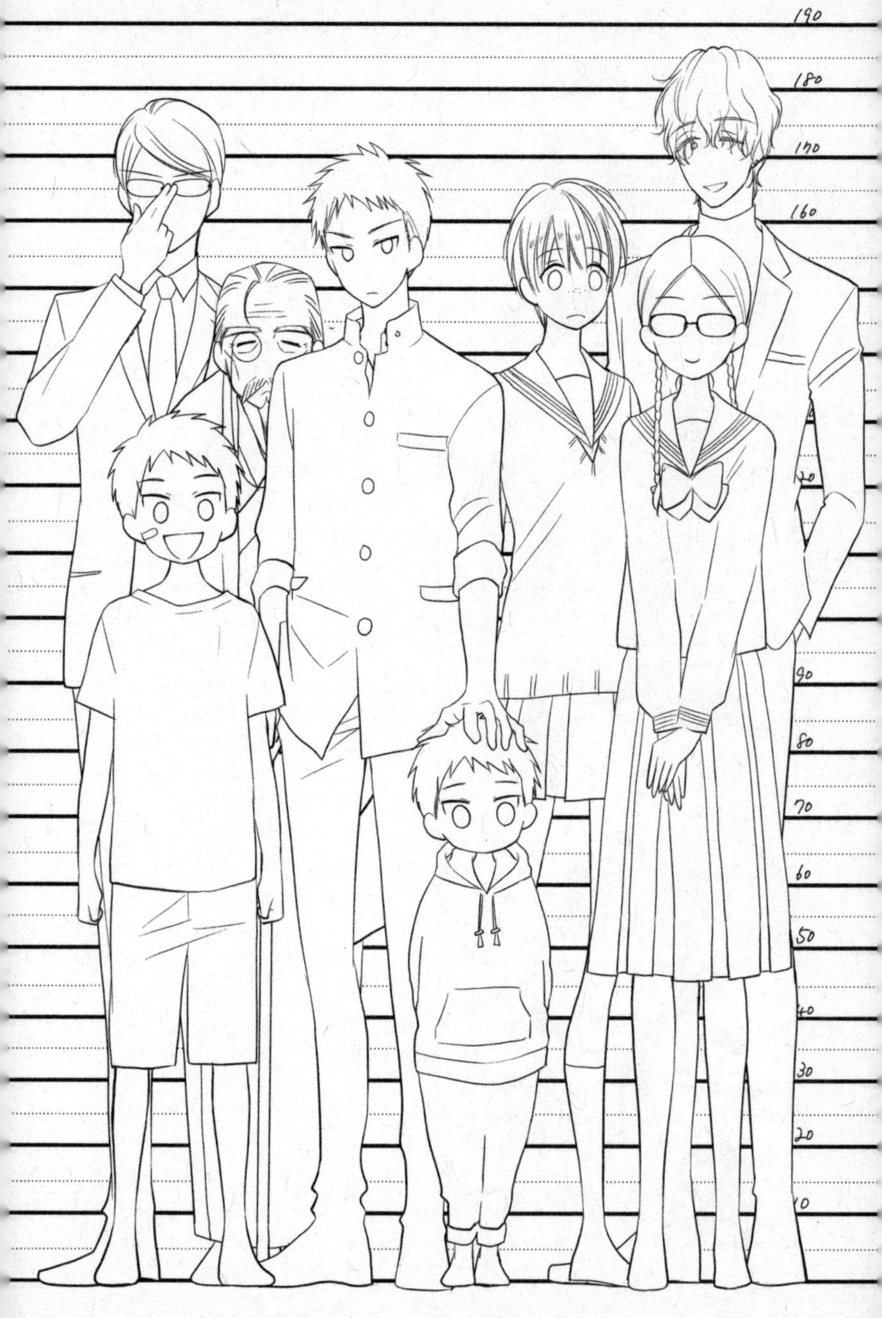
190
180
170
160
90
80
70
60
50
40
30
20
10

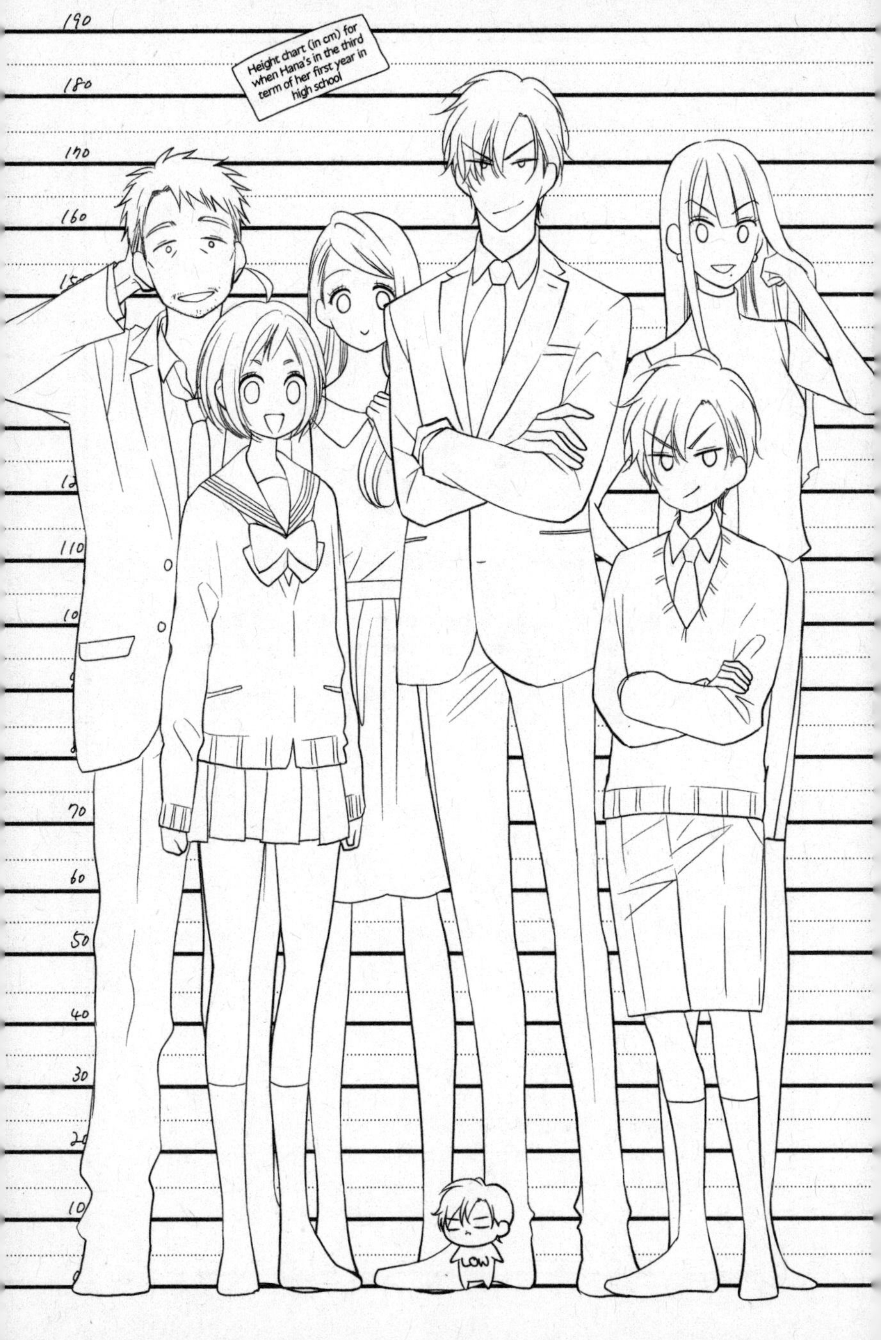
190
Height chart (in cm) for when Hana's in the third term of her first year in high school
180
170
160
110
70
60
50
40
30
10
LOW

This cover has a different vibe from the covers of volumes 5 and 6, so I'm worried about whether or not you'll be able to spot it at the bookstore!

—YUKI SHIWASU

Born on March 7 in Fukuoka Prefecture, Japan, Yuki Shiwasu began her career as a manga artist after winning the top prize in the Hakusensha Athena Newcomers' Awards from *Hana to Yume* magazine. She is also the author of *Furou Kyoudai* (Immortal Siblings), which was published by Hakusensha in Japan.

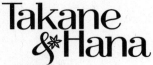

Takane & Hana

VOLUME 7
SHOJO BEAT EDITION

STORY & ART BY **YUKI SHIWASU**

ENGLISH ADAPTATION **Ysabet Reinhardt MacFarlane**
TRANSLATION **JN Productions**
TOUCH-UP ART & LETTERING **Annaliese Christman**
DESIGN **Shawn Carrico**
EDITOR **Amy Yu**

First published in Japan in 2017 by HAKUSENSHA, Inc., Tokyo.
English language translation rights arranged with HAKUSENSHA, Inc., Tokyo.

Printed in the U.S.A.

Published by VIZ Media, LLC
P.O. Box 77010
San Francisco, CA 94107

10 9 8 7 6 5 4 3 2 1
First printing, February 2019

ratings.viz.com RATED T TEEN

PARENTAL ADVISORY
TAKANE & HANA is rated T for Teen and is recommended for ages 13 and up. This volume contains suggestive themes.

VIZ MEDIA
viz.com

Shojo Beat
shojobeat.com

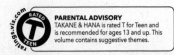

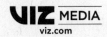

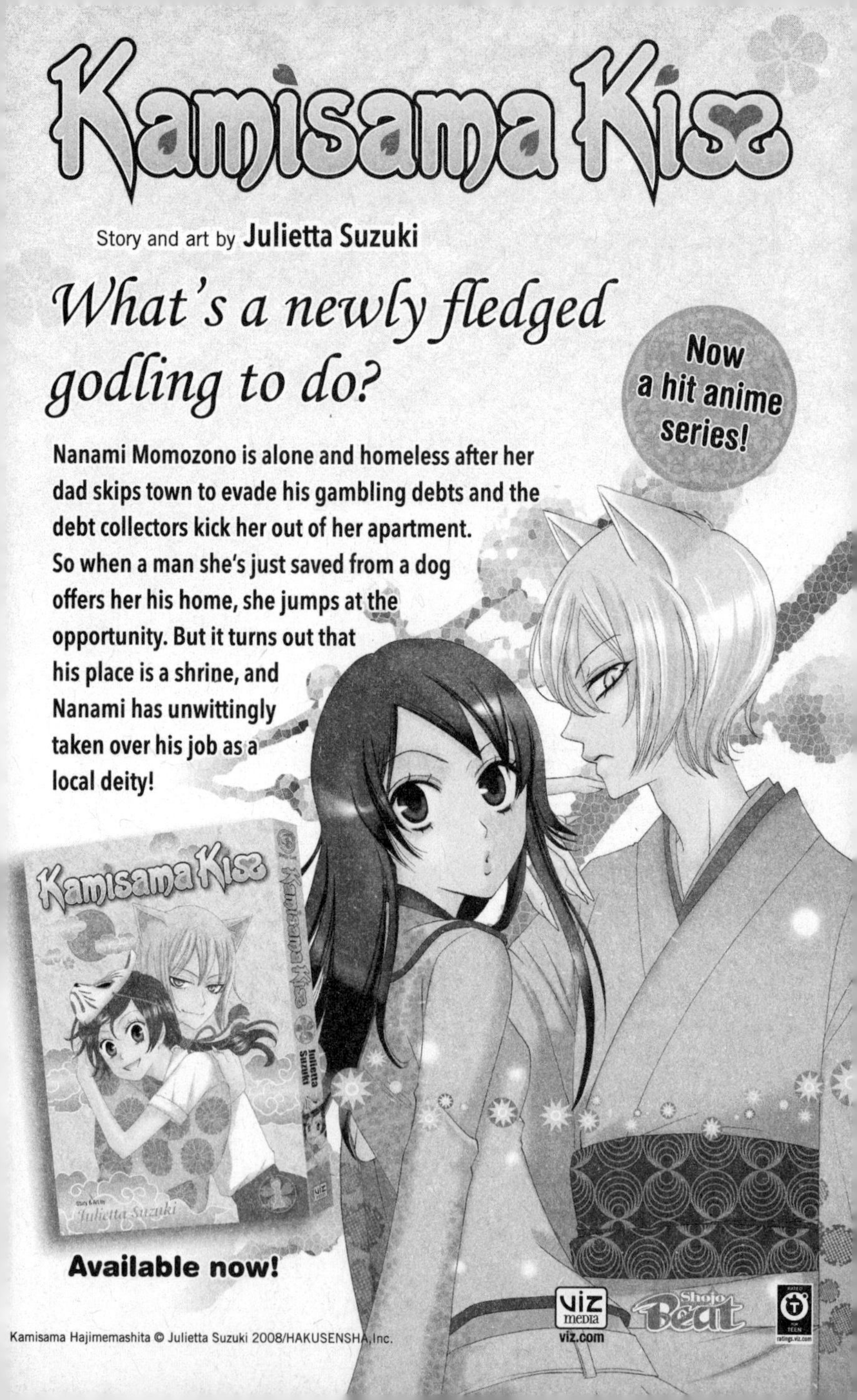
Kamisama Kiss
Story and art by Julietta Suzuki
What's a newly fledged godling to do?
Now a hit anime series!
Nanami Momozono is alone and homeless after her dad skips town to evade his gambling debts and the debt collectors kick her out of her apartment. So when a man she's just saved from a dog offers her his home, she jumps at the opportunity. But it turns out that his place is a shrine, and Nanami has unwittingly taken over his job as a local deity!
Kamisama Kiss
Julietta Suzuki
Available now!
Kamisama Hajimemashita © Julietta Suzuki 2008/HAKUSENSHA, Inc.
viz media
viz.com
Shojo Beat
RATED T FOR TEEN
ratings.viz.com

Ouran High School

Host Club

BOX SET

Story and Art by
Bisco Hatori

Escape to the world of the young, rich and sexy

All 18 volumes
in a collector's box
with an Ouran High
School stationery
notepad!

In this screwball romantic
comedy, Haruhi, a poor girl at
a rich kids' school, is forced to
repay an $80,000 debt by working
for the school's swankiest, all-
male club—as a boy! There she
discovers just how wealthy the six
members are and how different
the rich are from everybody else...

3-in-1 Vol. 1 ISBN: 978-1-4215-4224-9
3-in-1 Vol. 2 ISBN: 978-1-4215-4225-6
3-in-1 Vol. 3 ISBN: 978-1-4215-4229-4

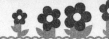

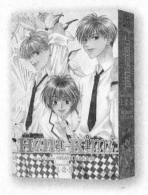

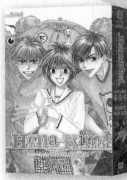

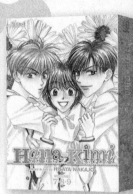

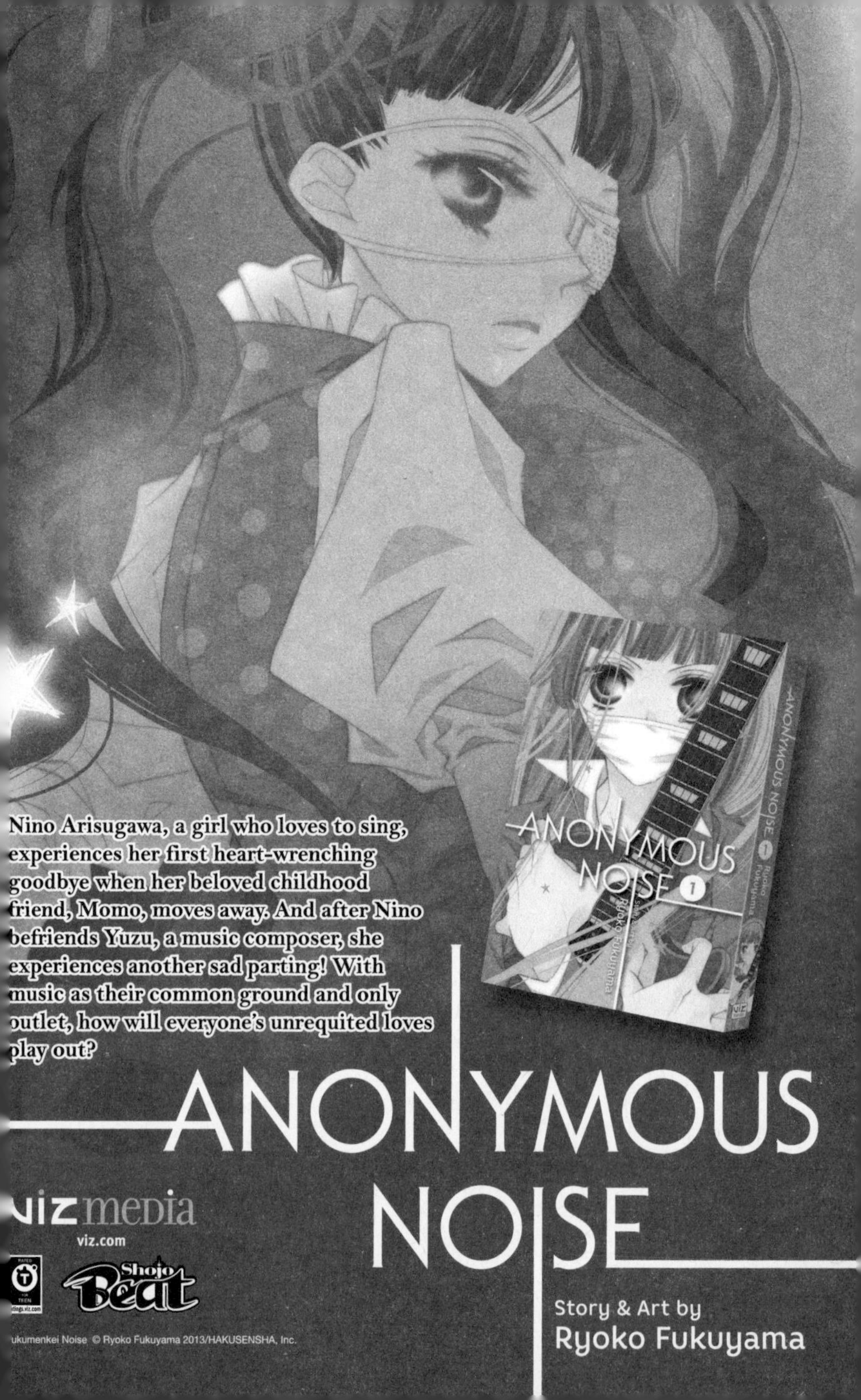
Nino Arisugawa, a girl who loves to sing, experiences her first heart-wrenching goodbye when her beloved childhood friend, Momo, moves away. And after Nino befriends Yuzu, a music composer, she experiences another sad parting! With music as their common ground and only outlet, how will everyone's unrequited loves play out?
ANONYMOUS NOISE 1
Ryoko Fukuyama
ANONYMOUS NOISE
Story & Art by
Ryoko Fukuyama
viz media
viz.com
Shojo Beat
ukumenkei Noise © Ryoko Fukuyama 2013/HAKUSENSHA, Inc.

Behind the Scenes!!

STORY AND ART BY BISCO HATORI

From the creator of Ouran High School Host Club

Ranmaru Kurisu comes from a family of hardy, rough-and-tumble fisherfolk and he sticks out at home like a delicate, artistic sore thumb. It's given him a raging inferiority complex and a permanently pessimistic outlook. Now that he's in college, he's hoping to find a sense of belonging. But after a whole life of being left out, does he even know how to fit in?!

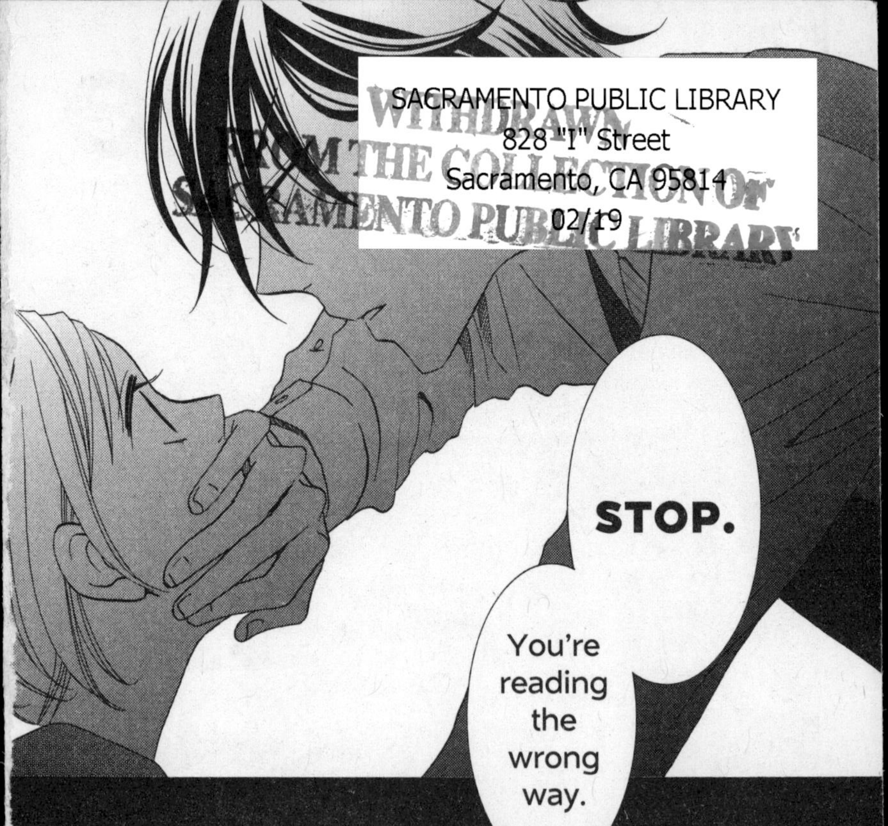
STOP.
You're reading the wrong way.

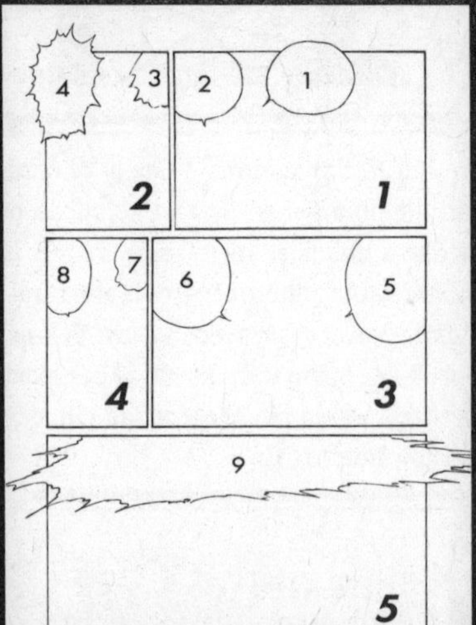

In keeping with the original Japanese comic format, this book reads from right to left—so action, sound effects and word balloons are completely reversed to preserve the orientation of the original artwork.

Check out the diagram shown here to get the hang of things, and then turn to the other side of the book to get started!